Ethics and Professional Responsibility for Legal Assistants

Ethics and Professional Responsibility for Legal Assistants

Third Edition

Therese A. Cannon
Educational Standards Consultant
Office of Admissions
The State Bar of California

Educational Consultant
ABA Standing Committee
on Legal Assistants

 ASPEN LAW & BUSINESS
A Division of Aspen Publishers, Inc.

Permissions
Aspen Law & Business
1185 Avenue of the Americas
New York, NY 10036

Printed in the United States of America

3 4 5 6

Library of Congress Cataloging-in-Publication Data

Cannon, Therese A.
    Ethics and professional responsibility for legal assistants /
Therese A. Cannon. — 3rd ed.
        p.   cm.
    Includes index.
    ISBN 0-7355-0233-1
    1. Legal assistants—United States.   2. Legal ethics—United
States.   I. Title.
KF320.L4C37   1999
174′.3′0973—dc21   98-35788
                                                                          CIP

About Aspen Law & Business Paralegal Textbook Division

In 1996, Aspen Law & Business welcomed the Paralegal Textbook Division of Little, Brown and Company into its growing business— already established as a leading provider of practical information to legal practitioners.

Acquiring much more than a prestigious collection of educational publications by the country's foremost authors, Aspen Law & Business inherited the long-standing Little, Brown tradition of excellence—born over 150 years ago. As one of America's oldest and most venerable publishing houses, Little, Brown and Company commenced in a world of change and challenge, innovation and growth. Sharing that same spirit, Aspen Law & Business has dedicated itself to continuing and strengthening the integrity begun so many years ago.

ASPEN LAW & BUSINESS
A Division of Aspen Publishers, Inc.
A Wolters Kluwer Company

This book is dedicated to my father

Summary of Contents

Contents

1. Regulation of Lawyers   1

2. Ethical Guidelines and Regulation of Legal Assistants

15

3. Unauthorized Practice of Law

43

4. Confidentiality   105

5. Conflicts of Interest   139

6. Advertising and Solicitation   195

7. Fees and Client Funds 235

10. Professionalism   363

Appendices

Preface

Approach

This book is written for paralegal students and working legal assistants, as well as the attorneys who employ them. It is intended for use primarily as a text but can be used by those in practice as a reference manual.

It has been more than 25 years since the advent of the paralegal profession. What started out as a modest proposal to improve the delivery of legal services has become a reality in law practice today. Legal assistants are now integral members of the legal services delivery team. Lawyers in all kinds and sizes of private law firms and those in corporate, government, and public sector settings rely heavily on legal assistants to accomplish their work. Legal assistants are highly educated and competent, engaging in ever-more sophisticated work in all areas of law practice.

The paralegal occupation has been one of the fastest growing in the country for at least a decade. It is estimated that there are more than 150,000 legal assistants employed across the country. The career is recognized by the general public, and young people learn of and aspire to it. The roles and functions of legal assistants continue to expand into new and exciting areas. The prestige of the occupation is also on the rise.

The past 30 years have also witnessed tremendous growth and change in the legal profession generally. The forces of change have been many, including the adoption of new technology, the use of marketing and advertising, greater competitiveness among firms for clients, the influx of new attorneys, increased attorney mobility, the development of mega-firms, the impact of a global economy, more complex laws, and legal specialization by firms. These changes have greatly affected legal ethics, in ways that probably no one anticipated.

The role of nonlawyers in providing legal services directly to the public has been the topic of intense debate as the public and the legal profession seek ways to improve access to legal services. New ethics rules continue to develop in response to this dynamic environment. It has become critically important for legal assistants to have a clear understanding of legal ethics—the concepts and rules that guide them in their work. This grounding is essential for legal assistants to function effectively and with integrity in modern law practice, to be alert to ethical delimmas that occur in their daily work lives, to develop a framework for ethical decision making, and to keep abreast of changes in ethical rules as they develop.

Organization and Coverage of the Third Edition

The book is comprehensive and covers all the major areas of legal ethics, placing special emphasis on how the rules affect legal assistants. The book begins with a chapter on the regulation of attorneys because legal assistants must understand how the legal profession is regulated generally to understand their place in it and the impact that their conduct has on the attorneys who employ them. Chapter 2 contains a brief history of the paralegal career and the efforts made to guide and regulate it. This chapter also examines ethical guidelines developed by both bar and paralegal associations, including one of the most important areas of concern for legal assistants, the unauthorized practice of law. Chapter 3 covers this topic, from an introduction to the concept of unauthorized practice to the specific functions that either are prohibited outright to nonlawyers or are on the borderline. Chapters 2 and 3 both include material on the provision of legal services directly to clients by nonlawyers, an area of growing interest and intense controversy. Confidentiality is covered in Chapter 4. In discussing the attorney-client privilege, the work product rule, and the ethics rules regarding confidentiality, the chapter outlines the most common ways that confidentiality is violated and the ways to avoid violating it. Special emphasis was added in this edition to the new issues that have arisen out of technological changes.

Chapter 5 covers conflicts of interest, a critical concern of legal assistants right now because of the changing nature of law practice and paralegals' role in it. This chapter includes an in-depth discussion of how conflicts rules apply to legal assistants, including the use of screens and conflicts checks. Rules regarding legal advertising and solicitation, with a discussion of current Supreme Court cases and information on marketing of legal services, are covered in Chapter 6. Chapter 7 is is devoted to financial matters, often the source of ethical problems for legal assistants and lawyers. It offers a thorough discussion of billing, fees, statutory fee awards that include compensation for paralegal work, fee-splitting, referral fees, partnerships between attorneys and nonlawyers, and handling client funds. Chapter 8 on competence defines the concept of competence specifically in relation to legal assistants and includes a discussion of malpractice. Special issues confronted by litigation paralegals are covered in Chapter 9. Finally, Chapter 10 examines professionalism, issues facing legal assistants in today's law firm environment, and pro bono work.

Key Features

Each chapter begins with an overview that describes in a few words the main topics of the chapter. The text body of each chapter is divided topically. Key terms are spelled out in italics when first introduced. At the end of each chapter are review questions that test each student's memory and understanding of the material. The discussion questions that follow the review questions may be assigned to students or used for in-class discussion. Some questions are designed to challenge students to apply the concepts and rules to hypothetical fact situations: some call for additional legal research or factual investigation. Cases at the end of the chapters demonstrate how the rules introduced in the chapters are applied, specifically to legal assistants whenever possible. Other cases present key principles in professional responsibility that all legal assistants should be familiar with. Several new cases are included in the third edition, reflecting the rapid changes taking place in unauthorized practice, confidentiality, conflicts of interest, and other areas, as courts address the application of ethics rules to legal assistants.

Recognizing that all paralegal programs teach ethics, but each in its own way, I have chosen a comprehensive approach so that professors may use the entire book in full courses on legal ethics or use only selected parts in programs that teach ethics in several courses or across the curriculum. The accompanying Teacher's Manual should help teachers to incorporate ethics material into their substantive courses.

Acknowledgments

Finally, I have many people to thank for their support and assistance. The American Association for Paralegal Education, National Association of Legal Assistants, National Federation of Paralegal Associations, Legal Assistant Management Association, and my colleagues with the American Bar Association Standing Committee on Legal Assistants and Approval Commission. Many thanks go to Carole L. Mostow of the ABA Center for Professional Responsibility for sharing her vast knowledge. Special thanks go to the many students I have had the pleasure of teaching in the past few years. Their inquisitiveness and desire to look at difficult and complex issues made our discussions spirited and productive and enriched this edition of the book. And, finally, my heartfelt appreciation to the wonderful people at Aspen, especially Carol McGeehan and Betsy Kenny, whose patience, warmth, intelligence, and talents made this book possible.

I would like to thank the following copyright holders who kindly granted their permission to reprint from the following materials.

American Bar Association. Model Guidelines for the Utilization of Legal Assistant Services. Copyright © 1991 by the American Bar Association. All rights reserved. Reprinted by permission of the American Bar Association.

National Association of Legal Assistants, Code of Ethics and Professional Responsibility. Copyright © 1975, Revised 1979, 1988, 1995. Reprinted by permission of the National Association of Legal Assistants, 1516 S. Boston #200, Tulsa, OK 74119.

————. Model Standards and Guidelines for Utilization of Legal Assistants. Annotated. Copyright © 1984. Revised 1991, 1997. Reprinted with permission of the National Association of Legal Assistants, 1516 S. Boston #200, Tulsa, OK 74119.

National Federation of Paralegal Associations, Model Code of Ethics and Professional Responsibility. Copyright © 1993 by the National Federation of Paralegal Associations, Inc. All rights reserved. Reprinted by permission of the National Federation of Paralegal Associations, Inc.

Regulation of Lawyers

This chapter provides basic background on the regulation of lawyers because legal assistants, who work under the supervision of lawyers, need to understand the rules governing lawyer conduct and how those rules affect them. Chapter 1 covers:

- the inherent power of the courts over the practice of law
- the organized bar's participation in lawyer regulation
- the role of the legislature and state statutes in governing the conduct of lawyers
- the American Bar Association and its influence on legal ethics
- sanctions for lawyer misconduct

A. State Courts and Bar Associations

Like other professions that affect the public interest, the legal profession is subject to regulation by the states. Unlike these other regulated professions, however, the regulation of the legal profession falls mainly to the judiciary rather than the legislature. Because of the function of lawyers in the court system and the separation of powers, the judiciary has historically asserted inherent authority over lawyers.

The highest court in each state and in the District of Columbia is responsible for making rules related to law practice admission and to lawyers' ethical conduct. The codes of ethical conduct promulgated by the states' highest courts include mechanisms for disciplining lawyers who violate the codes. Most state legislatures have also passed statutes that supplement the ethical rules adopted by the court. Some states consider legislative authority over the practice of law to be concurrent with the judicial authority; others consider legislative action to be only in aid of judicial action. A few state supreme courts have delegated substantial authority over the practice of law to the legislature. The New York state legislature has the power to regulate the legal profession and has vested the power to impose sanctions on lawyers with the intermediate courts (which are called supreme courts in New York although they are not the highest state courts). Sometimes the judiciary and the legislature have conflicting ideas about matters affecting the practice of law, and a court will be called on to strike down legislation. Several state supreme courts (for instance, Arizona, Colorado, Idaho, and Washington) have held unconstitutional legislation that would have authorized non-lawyers to engage in conduct that the court considered to be the practice of law. (See the *Bennion* and *UPL Committee* cases at the end of this chapter for examples.) Local court rules also govern attorneys' conduct in matters before the courts.

In practice, many state supreme courts rely heavily on state bar associations to carry out their responsibilities for regulating the practice of law. These courts have delegated authority to the bar as a way to relieve the ever-growing burden that handling these matters in addition to their caseload represents.

Some state bar associations are *integrated,* which means that membership is compulsory. In a state with an integrated bar, annual dues to renew the practitioner's law license carry automatic membership in the state bar. Some states have purely voluntary state bar associations; funds to operate the admissions and disciplinary functions in the state are derived from annual licensing or registration fees. Integrated bars generally play a more active role in the admissions and disciplinary functions of the court as well as in all matters relating to the legal profession.

The disciplinary system has come under attack in recent years as consumers' distrust of lawyers has grown and complaints about lawyers to courts and bar associations have increased. Both state bar committees and the ABA's McKay Commission have called for reform of the disciplinary system, recommending quick public resolution of complaints. Most jurisdictions have responded, adopting a wide array of changes in their systems, including the use of mediation and arbitration, ethics training for lawyers, random audits of client trust accounts, provision for firm-wide responsibility for ethical breaches and making disciplinary proceedings and records open to the public from their initiation. Such reform is considered essential both to lawyers' retaining control over the profession through self-regulation and to restoring public confidence in the profession.

B. American Bar Association

Most states have patterned their codes of ethics on the models of the American Bar Association (ABA). The ABA is a national voluntary professional association of lawyers currently with over 385,000 members, about half of the lawyers in the country. Over 100 years old, the ABA is the chief national professional association for lawyers, carrying a strong voice in matters affecting substantive law, the judiciary, and the administration of justice. Among its many contributions to the profession is the promulgation of model codes of ethics.

The ABA first published the Canons of Professional Ethics in 1908. These Canons were patterned after the first code of ethics for lawyers adopted in 1887 by the Alabama State Bar Association. Prior to the adoption of state codes, lawyer conduct was governed largely by common law and some statutes. The 1908 Canons consisted of 32 statements of very general principles about attorney conduct, mainly conduct in the courtroom. Many states adopted these ABA Canons through court rule or statute.

In 1964, the ABA began work on a new set of ethical guidelines at the request of its then-president, Lewis F. Powell, who later served on the U.S. Supreme Court. This new code, called the Model Code of Professional Responsibility, was published in 1969. It was designed as a prototype for states to use in developing their own codes. The Model Code, which was adopted at least in part by every state, contains

- *Canons,* or statements of general concepts;
- *Disciplinary Rules,* or mandatory rule statements; and
- *Ethical Considerations,* or interpretive comments that are aspirational or advisory.

While the Model Code was quite well received, other events in the legal field led to a call for a revised code within a very short time. Watergate was one of the most pivotal of these events. The misconduct of so many lawyers in this tremendous scandal seriously damaged the public image of lawyers and focused attention on the potential for harm from such misconduct. Also during this period the U.S. Supreme Court decided several cases relating to the legal profession that struck down rules prohibiting lawyer advertising. Finally, changes in law practice brought about by certain economic developments and the proliferation of new laws resulted in more and different kinds of ethical problems that were not addressed effectively in the Model Code.

In 1977, the ABA established a new body to revisit the Model Code. It was called the Commission on the Evaluation of Professional Standards and came to be known as the Kutak Commission, after its chair. After six years of study, debate, drafting, and redrafting, the new Model Rules of Professional Conduct were adopted by the ABA in 1983. The Model Rules are formatted differently than the Model Code; the difference between mandatory and aspirational language has been eliminated. Each of the rules is written in a directive style and is followed by interpretive comments. As of this writing, 40 states plus the District of Columbia and the Virgin Islands have adopted some version of the new Model Rules; nine jurisdictions still have codes based on the Model Code. California has its own code that is not based on either the Model Code or Model Rules.

In August 1997, the American Bar Association launched a new review of the Model Rules, designated Ethics 2000. The ABA's 13-member Commission on the Evaluation of the Rules of Professional Conduct will evaluate the Model Rules and make recommendations in the year 2000. It is uncertain whether this review will lead to a complete revision of the Model Rules. Thirty amendments have been made to the Model Rules since their adoption and more are bound to follow as the bar attempts to keep pace with the rapidly changing legal practice environment.

C. State Statutes and Other Forms of Regulation

While the state codes of ethics contain most of the rules with which we are concerned in this text, attorney conduct is also governed by statutes. For example, some states have statutes that prohibit attorneys from engaging in certain conduct in their professional capacity as lawyers and provide for criminal and civil penalties. As we will see in Chapter 3, several states have laws that make the unauthorized practice of law a crime, usually a misdemeanor.

Usually not binding on attorneys but often consulted when ethical issues arise are ethics opinions of state and local bar associations and the ABA. Bar associations have ethics committees that consider ethical dilemmas posed to them by attorney-members. The committees write opinions that are published in bar journals or manuals to give additional guidance to other attorneys facing similar dilemmas. Some state and ABA advisory opinions will be cited in this text.

D. Sanctions and Remedies

Four main formal sanctions imposed on lawyers for ethical misconduct are available to the state's highest court or other disciplinary body. The most severe sanction is *disbarment,* in which a lawyer's license to practice law is revoked. Disbarment is only imposed for the most egregious violations or when there is a long-term pattern of serious unethical conduct. While disbarment is in theory "permanent," most admitting authorities do occasionally re-admit a disbarred lawyer after some period of time if the lawyer can demonstrate complete rehabilitation.

The second most severe sanction is *suspension,* in which the attorney is deprived of the right to practice law for a specified period of time. Some disciplinary authorities also have the option of imposing *probation,* under which the disciplined attorney may continue to practice on the condition that certain requirements are met, such as restitution to injured clients, passing an ethics examination, attending ethics "school" or participating in counseling. Sometimes a suspension is stayed but the attorney remains on probation for some period during which the disciplinary body may reinstitute the suspension if further ethical violations come to light. The mildest sanction is a *reprimand,* sometimes called a *reproval.* This represents a slap on the hand, a warning that the conduct will not be tolerated. Reprimands may be public—placed in the public record and published in a bar journal—or private—confidentially communicated in writing to the attorney. In either case, the reprimand becomes part of the attorney's record at the court or the state bar. It is considered further in determining the appropriate sanction if other violations occur.

In deciding the appropriate sanction, the disciplinary body considers the nature and severity of the offense and whether the attorney has a record of prior misconduct. Other aggravating and mitigating factors may be taken into account, such as the extent to which the attorney cooperated in the investigation and appreciates the seriousness of the matter, the attorney's reputation and contributions to the community through public service and professional activities, the circumstances surrounding the offense and the extent to which these make the attorney more or less culpable for the conduct, and whether the offense was a one-time incident because of those circumstances or is likely to be repeated. The attorney's remorse and willingness to remedy the problems that may have led to the discipline are critical in determining the sanction.

In addition to direct discipline by the court or state bar, an attorney may be prosecuted criminally for violations of statutes governing attorney conduct or conduct that may relate to an attorney's practice, such as laws prohibiting solicitation of clients in hospitals and jails and laws limiting the methods that can be used to collect debts. Civil *legal malpractice* lawsuits brought by former clients also constitute a major incentive for conforming to ethical requirements and standards of practice. (See Chapter 8 for more on legal malpractice.) The courts exercise contempt power to sanction lawyers appearing before them who engage in improper conduct that affects the administration of justice and the smooth functioning of the courts. (See Chapter 9 on Special Issues in Advocacy.) And the courts also play a major role in deciding on matters in the growing ethical area of conflicts of interest because they rule on motions to disqualify counsel, usually brought by the opposing counsel, who claims that a lawyer or law firm has a conflict of interest that jeopardizes client confidentiality.

REVIEW QUESTIONS

1. What branch of government is primarily responsible for regulating attorney conduct?
2. What role do state bar associations play in governing lawyer conduct?
3. What is an integrated bar? How does it differ from a voluntary bar?

4. What is the American Bar Association? What role, if any, does it play in overseeing attorney conduct?
5. When did the states first begin to adopt ethics codes?
6. Name and describe the three versions of model ethical rules that have been adopted by the ABA.
7. Why did the ABA decide so soon after the Model Code was adopted to undertake a major revision of it?
8. What are ethics opinions? Who writes them? Are they binding on attorneys?
9. Name and describe the three main direct sanctions for attorney misconduct that are enforced by the highest state court or state bar.
10. Name some other sanctions or remedies for attorney misconduct besides those named in question 9.

DISCUSSION QUESTIONS

1. Is your state's bar integrated?
2. Does your state have any laws that govern attorney conduct? If so, where do you find these in the state statutes?
3. When were the current rules of ethics in your state adopted? Do they follow the ABA Model Code or the Model Rules?
4. Does your state or local bar association publish ethics opinions? If so, where do you find these?
5. Look at the ABA Model Code and Model Rules and compare the format. Which do you find easier to work with?
6. Has your state's highest court decided any cases in which the authority of the legislature to regulate attorneys was an issue?

CASES FOR ANALYSIS

The Washington Supreme Court case that follows demonstrates how the courts assert their inherent authority over the practice of law. In this case, state legislation that authorized escrow agents and officers to perform duties found by the court to constitute the practice of law was struck down as violating the court's constitutional authority to regulate the practice of law. Later, the Washington Supreme Court adopted the Limited Practice Rules for Closing Officers, which authorize much of the activity described in this statute.

Bennion, Van Camp, Hagen & Ruhl
v. Kassler Escrow, Inc.
96 Wash. 2d 443, 635 P.2d 730 (1981)

Defendant petitioner is a registered escrow agent under the Escrow Agent Registration Act. . . . and employs licensed escrow officers for closing real estate transactions. Petitioner closed several real estate transactions and in the process prepared documents and performed other services. Two of these transactions involved earnest money agreements specifying that the place of closing was to be the office of the plaintiff respondent, a law firm. Respondent brought suit alleging that the escrow company had engaged in the unauthorized practice of law. . . . Respondent sought a permanent injunction enjoining petitioner from performing any acts constituting the practice of law.

Subsequent to the filing of the action, the legislature enacted RCW 19.62 authorizing certain lay persons to perform tasks relating to real estate transactions. Specifically, the act allows escrow agents and officer to

> select, prepare, and complete documents and instruments relating to such loan, forbearance, or extension of credit, sale, or other transfer of real or personal property, limited to deeds, promissory notes, deeds of trusts, mortgages, security agreements, assignments, releases, satisfactions, reconveyances, contracts for sale or purchase of real or personal property, and bills of sale . . .

RCW 19.62.010(2).

Petitioner, in reliance upon the statute, moved to dismiss the action for injunctive relief, which motion was denied by the trial court. Respondent moved for, and the trial court granted, a partial summary judgment declaring RCW 19.62 unconstitutional.

The line between those activities included within the definition of the practice of law and those that are not is oftentimes difficult to define. Recently, in *Washington State Bar Ass'n v. Great W. Union Fed. Sav. & Loan Ass'n,* 91 Wash. 2d 48, 586 P.2d 870 (1978), we concluded that preparation of legal instruments and contracts that create legal rights is the practice of law. . . .

The statute in question is a direct response to our holding. We reaffirm that definition. RCW 19.62 authorizes a lay person involved with real estate transactions to "select, prepare, and complete documents and instruments" that affect legal rights. As such the statute allows the practice of law by lay persons. Petitioner requests this court to redefine the practice of law so that the conduct allowed by the statute does not

●

constitute the practice of law. Petitioner asserts that there is a trend allowing lay persons to perform certain services such as those authorized by RCW 19.62 and our holding RCW 19.62 unconstitutional would not protect the public in any way. We disagree. . . .

Petitioner's activities and those activities authorized by RCW 19.62 constitute the practice of law and do not come within any exception. Inasmuch as RCW 19.62 authorizes lay persons to perform services we have defined as the practice of law, it must fall. The statutory attempt to authorize the practice of law by lay persons is an unconstitutional exercise of legislative power in violation of the separation of powers doctrine.

Const. art. 4. §1 provides in pertinent part: "judicial power of the state shall be vested in a supreme court. . . ." An essential concomitant to express grants of power is the inherent powers of each branch. See generally *In re Juvenile Director,* 87 Wash. 2d 232, 552 P.2d 163 (1976). Inherent power is that

> authority not expressly provided for in the constitution but which is derived from the creation of a separate branch of government and which may be exercised by the branch to protect itself in the performance of its constitutional duties.

In re Juvenile Director, at 245, 552, P.2d 163.

It is a well established principle that one of the inherent powers of the judiciary is the power to regulate the practice of law. The court's powers include the power to admit one to the practice of law and this necessarily encompasses the power to determine qualifications and standards.

The court, in *Graham* [citation omitted], citing to *Sharood v. Hatfield,* 296 Minn. 416, 210 N.W.2d 275 (1973), held that the

> regulation of the practice of law and " 'the power to make the necessary rules and regulations governing the bar was intended to be vested exclusively in the supreme court, free from the dangers of encroachment either by the legislative or executive branches.' "

86 Wash. 2d at 633, 548 P.2d 310. "The unlawful practice of law by laymen is a judicial matter addressed solely to the courts." *Washington Ass'n of Realtors,* 41 Wash. 2d at 707, 251 P.2d 619.

Since the regulation of the practice of law is within the sole province of the judiciary, encroachment by the legislature may be held by this court to violate the separation of powers doctrine. The separation of powers doctrine is a fundamental principle of the American political system. For a historical discussion of the doctrine and its importance, see *In re Juvenile Director,* 87 Wash. 2d at 238-43, 552 P.2d 163. We have previously held:

> The legislative, executive, and judicial functions have been carefully separated and, notwithstanding the opinions of a certain class of our society to the contrary, the courts have ever been alert and resolute to keep these functions properly separated. To this is assuredly due the steady equilibrium of our triune governmental system. The courts are jealous of their own prerogatives and, at the same time, studiously careful and sedulously determined that neither the executive nor legislative department shall usurp the powers of the other, or of the courts.

In re Bruen, 102 Wash. at 478, 172 P. 1152.

Thus, the power to regulate the practice of law is solely within the province of the judiciary and this court will protect against any improper encroachment on such power by the legislative or executive branches. In passing RCW 19.62, allowing lay persons to practice law, the legislature impermissibly usurped the court's power. Accordingly, RCW 19.62 is unconstitutional as a violation of the separation of powers doctrine.

We affirm the trial court's summary judgment on the constitutional issue as well as that court's refusal to dismiss the request for injunctive relief. The cause is hereby remanded for trial.

Questions about the Case

1. In your jurisdiction, who handles escrows and real estate closing on residential property—lawyers or licensed agents or brokers?
2. If nonlawyers handle these functions, how are they regulated?
3. Do you think the functions that agents were licensed to perform under the Washington statute are rightfully classified by the court as the practice of law?
4. What is the basis of the court's authority for striking down the statute?
5. Are you convinced by the court's reasoning that it should have exclusive authority over the practice of law?
6. How should proponents of measures that affect the practice of law proceed to avoid having their rules or statutes held unconstitutional?
7. Do you think it is best for the court to have sole authority over the practice of law? Why or why not? What role, if any, should be played by the legislative and executive branches?

In this case, the state's highest court exercised its exclusive authority over the practice of law to endorse legislation that authorized nonlawyers to assist persons in ways that are typically categorized as the practice of law.

Unauthorized Practice of Law Committee v. State Department of Workers' Compensation
543 A.2d 662 (Rhode Island 1988)

This case comes before us on appeal by the defendants from a judgment entered in the Superior Court declaring portions of two statutes enacted by the General Assembly (citations omitted), unconstitutional as violative of this court's exclusive power to regulate the practice of law. We reverse. . . .

At its 1985 session the General Assembly enacted a set of comprehensive statutory provisions that created a Department of Workers' Compensation. . . .

The General Assembly, in attempting to implement the scheme of establishing informal hearings within the department as an initial procedure to supplement the formal hearings before the Workers' Compensation Commission, created an office of employee assistants. The function and purpose of these employee assistants are set forth in §42-94-5 as follows:

> The director of the department of workers' compensation shall provide adequate funding for an office of employee assistants and shall, subject to the personnel law, appoint the assistants to the staff of the department. Assistants should, at a minimum, demonstrate a level of expertise roughly equivalent to that of insurance claims' analysts or adjusters. The purpose of employee assistants shall be to provide advice and assistance to employees under the workers' compensation act and particularly to assist employees in preparing for and assisting at informal conferences under §28-33-1.1. . . .

In the course of proceedings in the Superior Court, evidence was adduced concerning regulations of the Department of Workers' Compensation and also a position description filed in the department of personnel which defined the duties of employee assistants as follows:

> To provide technical advice and assistance to various parties involving their rights and obligations under the Workers' Compensation Act.

> To assist the injured employee in preparation for and at informal Workers' Compensation hearings, and to help in providing the necessary documentation at said hearings.
>
> To provide both routine and technical advice and/or information to the general public regarding rights and responsibilities under the Workers' Compensation Act.
>
> To attempt to settle disputes between injured workers, insurance companies, employers, purveyors of services, and any other interested parties prior to an informal hearing.
>
> To conduct in person interviews; both in office and field.
>
> To gather and prepare information necessary for use at informal hearings.
>
> To do related work as required.

At the conclusion of the presentation of evidence and argument in the Superior Court, the trial justice held that the duties of the employee assistants constituted the practice of law under definitions recognized by this court. . . .

It has long been the law of this state that the definition of the practice of law and the determination concerning who may practice law is exclusively within the province of this court and, further, that the Legislature may act in aid of this power but may not grant the right to anyone to practice law save in accordance with standards enunciated by this court. (Citations omitted.)

However, it should be noted that since 1935 the General Assembly has without interference by this court permitted a great many services that would have come within the definition of the practice of law to be performed by insurance adjusters, town clerks, bank employees, certified public accountants, interstate commerce practitioners, public accountants (other than certified public accountants), as well as employee assistants. The plain fact of the matter is that each of these exceptions enacted by the Legislature constituted a response to a public need. In each instance the Legislature determined that the persons authorized to carry out the permitted activities were qualified to do so. . . .

We must remember that the practice of law at a given time cannot be easily defined. Nor should it be subject to such rigid and traditional definition as to ignore the public interest. . . .

We are of the opinion that the informal hearings, together with lay representation, may well serve the public interest. We concluded from the evidence introduced that the employee assistants will be adequately trained to carry out the relatively simple and repetitive functions which they will be called upon to perform. We do require, however, that in the event an employee is denied compensation at such a hearing the employee be given an opportunity to consult with an attorney of his choice in order to determine whether he or she will appeal to the Workers' Compensation Commission. This consultation should be paid for at state expense at a reasonable fee to be determined by the director. In the event that an attorney chooses to represent the employee before the commission, such attorney would be paid by the employer if the employee prevails as presently provided by law. *See* G.L. 1956 (1986 Reenactment) §28-35-32.

In authorizing the employee assistants to carry out the functions authorized by §42-94-5, we are dealing with a question of first impression and are relying to a great extent upon the legislative findings that declare the necessity for an informal prompt hearing in the event of controversy. Therefore, this grant of authorization is made upon a somewhat experimental basis. Consequently we shall leave the matter open for the Unauthorized Practice of Law Committee to come again before the court in the event that the public, and particularly employees, are not adequately protected by the services of the employee assistants. Meanwhile the act may be implemented in the form in which it is presently cast, with the single modification set forth in this opinion.

For the reasons stated, the defendants' appeal is sustained. The judgment of the Superior Court is reversed. The papers in the case may be remanded to the Superior Court with directions to enter judgment for the defendants but without prejudice to the plaintiff to bring a new complaint in the event that the public interest shall so warrant in the future, as indicated heretofore in this opinion.

MURRAY, Justice, dissenting.

I respectfully disagree with the majority. I would affirm the trial justice's decision on the basis that the language in G.L. 1956 (1984 Reenactment) §42-94-5, as amended by P.L. 1986, ch. 1, §3, allows a group of nonlicensed employees to perform duties which are equivalent to those reserved for qualified, licensed attorneys. Employee assistants who engage in the unauthorized practice of law serve to the detriment of the public, and this court, by permitting such conduct, compromises established professional standards requisite for the proper administration of justice. . . .

Questions about the Case

1. How did the Rhode Island Supreme Court come to hear this case? What was the lower court's ruling?
2. What system did the Workers' Compensation statute establish that was objectionable to the lower court?
3. Examine the definitions of the practice of law in Chapter 3 and

evaluate whether employee assistants functioning under the authority of this statute would be engaging in the "practice of law."

4. What are the reasons that this court decided to endorse the legislation? Are these good reasons?
5. What does the court say about other inroads into the practice of law by nonlawyers? Is this important to the court's ruling?
6. Does the court abdicate its exclusive authority over the practice of law?

Ethical Guidelines and Regulation of Legal Assistants

This chapter begins by tracing the history of the paralegal profession. It moves on to examine the attempts made to regulate the profession during its brief history and the ways in which legal assistants' conduct is regulated or guided directly. Chapter 2 covers:

- the evolution and rapid growth of the paralegal profession since its inception in the late 1960s
- the American Bar Association's involvement in the field
- the development of professional associations for legal assistants
- past and present efforts to regulate legal assistants
- the distinctions between certification, licensing, and limited licensing
- the liability of legal assistants as agents of attorneys
- state and American Bar Association guidelines on the utilization of paralegal services
- ethics guidelines promulgated by paralegal associations

A. A Brief History of the Paralegal Profession

1. The Beginnings

The use of specifically educated nonlawyers to assist lawyers in the delivery of legal services is a relatively new phenomenon in the history of American law: The concept is barely 30 years old.

The paralegal field's beginnings can be traced directly back to the 1960s when the rapidly rising cost of legal services, combined with the lack of access to legal services for low- and middle-income Americans, caused government, consumer groups, and the organized bar to take a close look at the way legal services were being delivered.

In response, the federal government established the Legal Services Corporation to provide funding for legal services to the indigent, low-cost legal clinics started to appear, and pre-paid legal plans were developed. Practitioners and the organized bar also began to look inward, examining the way in which the practice of law was conducted in order to determine what could be done to keep costs under control without sacrificing quality. The answers they came up with included better management, increased automation, and the use of legal assistants. In 1967, the American Bar Association (ABA) endorsed the concept of the paralegal and, in 1968, established its first committee on legal assistants, which has since become the Standing Committee on Legal Assistants.

During the late 1960s and early 1970s, the ABA and several state and local bar associations conducted studies on the use of legal assistants. While many studies showed initial attorney resistance to legal assistants, actual use was on the rise.

2. Growth through the 1970s

The first formal paralegal training programs were established in the early 1970s. In 1971, there were only 11 programs scattered across the country. In 1974, the ABA adopted guidelines for the paralegal curriculum and, in 1975, began to approve paralegal programs under those guidelines. There were nine paralegal programs approved that year.

In the mid-1970s, the first professional paralegal associations were formed. Dozens of groups cropped up locally. The National Federation of Paralegal Associations (NFPA) and National Association of Legal Assistants (NALA) were established. Paralegal educators formed their own organization, the American Association for Paralegal Education (AAfPE). In the 1980s, a group of paralegal supervisors and managers started the Legal Assistant Management Association (LAMA). In 1976, the NALA established its Certified Legal Assistant program, a voluntary certification program consisting of two days of examinations covering judgment and communications, ethics, human relations, legal terminology and research, and analysis, and four substantive areas of law practice selected by the candidate from a list of eight.

In 1978, the U.S. Bureau of Labor Statistics predicted that the paralegal career would be one of the fastest growing occupations in the 1980s, with a growth rate of 132 percent by 1990. Continued growth was predicted through the year 2000.

3.   New Directions in the 1980s

Job opportunities expanded and changed dramatically during the 1970s and 1980s. While the first paralegals were employed primarily in small law firms and legal aid organizations, large private law firms soon became a major employer of paralegals. In 1975, the federal government recognized the existence of this new occupation by creating a new job classification for legal assistants. States, counties, and cities soon followed suit.

In the late 1970s and early 1980s, many legal assistants began free-lancing, handling specialized matters for attorneys on an as-needed, independent-contractor basis. This practice has evolved into full-service paralegal support companies. These companies employ a permanent full-time staff of legal assistants and offer long- and short-term services in virtually all areas of law practice.

The 1980s were an era of tremendous growth for the paralegal profession. Job opportunities expanded in all sectors of employment. Legal assistants were granted new recognition by the organized bar and practitioners. Clients came to accept paralegals, and even to demand that they be included on the legal services delivery team. Legal assistants, like attorneys, also became more specialized during this period, in particular in large law firms, corporate law departments, and government agencies, where legal assistants tend to work in only one area of law practice.

4.   From the 1990s into the New Millennium

Estimates vary on the number of legal assistants employed in the United States. Most sources indicate that there are well over 150,000.

Five or six hundred paralegal educational programs are operating, more than 200 of which are approved by the American Bar Association and nearly 300 of which are members of the American Association for Paralegal Education. Most surveys show that well over half of legal assistants hold a baccalaureate degree and even more have formal paralegal education.

During 1995 and '96, the National Federation of Paralegal Associations (NFPA) developed a new certification examination called the Paralegal Advanced Competency Examination (PACE). This test is designed to measure the competency of experienced legal assistants with a Bachelor's Degree and at least two years of documented work in the field. NFPA plans to develop state-specific examinations in the next phase of its certification program. NFPA's current membership is about 17,000 with 55 affiliated local associations. NALA now has more than 18,000 members and 90 affiliates. Nine thousand legal assistants have been certified by NALA and another 750 have gone on to become certified in specialty areas. The Legal Assistant Management Association, representing supervisors of legal assistants mainly in large law firms and corporate law departments, has about 500 members and local chapters in major cities across the country.

The early to mid-1990s saw a tight job market for legal assistants because of the general economic downturn; however, since the economy has recovered and is booming, the job market for legal assistants has exploded, with firms competing for the best graduates of paralegal programs and offering incentives for experienced legal assistants to change positions. Within the paralegal field, emphasis continues to increase on ever-higher levels of education and skills, a push for voluntary certification, opportunities for growth into new areas of employment and law practice, and a undiminished debate over the role of nonlawyer legal service providers.

B. Direct Regulation of Legal Assistants: Certification and Licensing

1. Definitions

Certification of an occupation is a form of voluntary recognition of an individual who has met specifications of the granting agency or organization. Both NALA's Certified Legal Assistant program and the NFPA's PACE are forms of certification. *Licensing* is a mandatory form of regulation in which a government agency grants permission to an individual to engage in an occupation and/or use a particular title. Only a person who is so licensed may engage in this occupation. There is no licensing of paralegals at the present time in the United States. Attorneys are "licensed" by the state in which they practice. Typically, both licensing and certification require applicants to meet specified requirements regarding education and moral character and to pass an examination.

2. Regulation of Attorney-Supervised Legal Assistants

Periodically throughout the history of the paralegal profession, the need for certification or licensing has been raised and debated. In the last decade, this debate has become intense and heated, in large part because of the impetus provided by the discussions about nonlawyer legal service providers.

Early in the profession's evolution, Oregon adopted a voluntary certification program for legal assistants. It was abolished after a few years because of low participation. This experience is unlikely to be repeated in Texas, which adopted a voluntary certification program for paralegals in 1994. The only state to have such a program at present. Texas administers its program through its Board of Legal Specialization. Certification examinations are given in a number of areas, including family law, civil trial practice, criminal law, and personal injury practice.

Certification, valid for five years, is renewable upon demonstrated participation in continuing education, employment by a Texas attorney, and substantial involvement in the specialty area. Nearly 300 legal assistants have been certified since the program began in 1994.

Whether other jurisdictions will follow suit remains to be seen. Several other states are studying certification and licensing.

The national paralegal associations continue to promote voluntary certification, NALA through its Certified Legal Assistant program and NFPA through its new Paralegal Advanced Proficiency Examination. On a national level, these organizations want to be poised for regulation when it comes by having proven examinations in place that can be adopted by states. At the state level, three statewide organizations have joined with NALA to develop state-specific certification examinations that can be taken by CLAs. These three organizations are the California Alliance of Paralegal Associations, Florida Legal Assistants, Inc., which has had an examination since the early 1980s, and the Louisiana State Paralegal Association. It should be noted that both national organizations have moved their positions slightly and seem more amenable to the idea

19

of licensing of attorney-supervised paralegals so long as that licensing expands rather than restricts the work that legal assistants can do.

The ABA Standing Committee on Legal Assistants has issued two policy statements on certification and licensing, in 1975 and in 1986. In both instances, the Standing Committee rejected the notion that legal assistants needed to be licensed, relying on the extensive ethical and disciplinary requirements to which lawyers are subject as the appropriate means to protect consumers. In 1997, the Legal Assistant Management Association issued a statement in which it took the position that licensing of legal assistants who work under lawyer supervision was unnecessary for the protection of the public and would unduly interfere with lawyers' prerogative to hire the best qualified persons for the job.

In connection with its work on licensing and certification in 1986, the ABA Standing Committee on Legal Assistants developed a definition of legal assistant/paralegal, which was later adopted by the House of Delegates in conjunction with the establishment of associate membership for legal assistants. This definition was revised by the Standing Committee in 1997 and was adopted by the House of Delegates at its annual meeting in August 1997. It reads as follows:

> A legal assistant or paralegal is a person, qualified by education, training or work experience, who is employed or retained by a lawyer, law office, corporation, governmental agency or other entity and who performs specifically delegated substantive legal work for which a lawyer is responsible.

This new definition was written in recognition of the progress that the paralegal occupation has made in the last decade and differs from the previous one in several respects, the most important of which is to move away from the strict language of "attorney direction and supervision" over legal assistants to an expanded notion of "lawyer responsibility" for the work product.

In the early 1990s, the ABA embarked on a major study of the role of paralegals and nonlawyer legal service providers through its Commission on Nonlawyer Practice. This commission, composed of 16 persons, leaders from the paralegal associations as well as interested ABA entities such as the Standing Committee, was charged with the task of "conduct[ing] research, hearings and deliberations to determine the implications of nonlawyer practice for society, the client and the legal profession." After three years, during which time it heard testimony of more than 400 witnesses and examined more than 2000 documents, it issued its eagerly awaited report and recommendations. The report did not take a position on regulation of supervised legal assistants, but cited the previous ABA position against mandatory licensing. However, the report in one of its major recommendations did call for the expansion of the range of activities in which traditional paralegals may engage with continued accountability in the lawyer. Other recommendations concerning direct providers of legal services are discussed in section 4, below.

3.   The Arguments about Regulation of Attorney-Supervised Paralegals

The issues relating to regulation of legal assistants who work under the supervision of attorneys are significantly different from those who call themselves independent paralegals who seek to provide legal services directly to the public.

The primary arguments against licensing of traditional legal assistants are that it would:

- not benefit the public because attorney-employers are already fully accountable to clients;
- increase the cost of legal services;
- stifle the developments of the profession;
- inappropriately limit entry into the profession;
- unnecessarily standardize paralegal education; and
- limit legal assistants from moving into new areas of practice or duties.

In addition, opponents cite the practical difficulty of determining exactly what legal tasks and functions could be assigned exclusively to legal assistants through this regulatory process.

Arguments favoring the licensing of traditional paralegals center mainly on the benefits to the profession, in terms of establishing it as a separate and autonomous but allied legal career, one with its own identity and a concomitant increase in societal status and rewards.

Proponents believe regulation would:

- provide appropriate public recognition for legal assistants as important members of the legal services delivery team;
- ensure high standards and quality of work by legal assistants;
- expand the use of legal assistants, thereby expanding access to legal services and lowering costs;
- provide guidance to clients and employers of legal assistants regarding the paralegal role and qualifications;

- encourage needed standardization in paralegal education; and
- possibly permit legal assistants to engage in some work they are not currently permitted to do under state statutes and case law.

With or without certification or licensing, the remarkable growth of the paralegal field will undoubtedly continue. At the grassroots level, practitioners in all areas of practice and in all kinds of organizations and firms have accepted that the use of legal assistants is the most effective way to deliver quality legal services at a reasonable cost. These attorneys and the paralegals they employ continue to find new and better ways to get the job done.

4. Nonlawyer Legal Service Providers

The 1980s and '90s witnessed a resurgence of interest in reforming the legal services delivery system as the lack of access to legal services by low- and middle-income Americans again became increasingly apparent. Study after study has indicated that the vast majority of Americans do not have access to legal services, cannot afford an attorney when they need one, and do not know how to go about finding an attorney. Low-income persons in particular are seeking other ways to access the legal system, and are more frequently than ever representing themselves with or without the assistance of self-help manuals and nonlawyers. The ABA Commission on Nonlawyer Practice found that some form of nonlawyer practice exists in virtually every jurisdiction and that more than half the states had considered proposals related to the regulation of nonlawyer practice.

Some consumer groups as well as nonlawyer practitioners them-selves are actively advocating legislation that would authorize nonlawyers to engage in some tasks otherwise considered the practice of law and therefore within the exclusive domain of licensed attorneys. While there is substantial resistance to this concept from many practicing attorneys, there has also been support for it going back to an earlier ABA commission report that favored the idea of "limited licensing." The report also recommended that the bar "[e]ncourage innovative methods which simplify and make less expensive the rendering of legal services" and went on to discuss nonlawyer practice as follows:

> In addition, the limited licensing of paralegals to perform certain functions seems to be a desirable step. Possible areas for the provision of such limited services include certain real estate closings, the drafting of simple wills, and selected tax services now being performed by lawyers

(footnote omitted). That is not to say that lawyers should not perform these services in the future. But, they should have to compete with properly licensed paraprofessionals. The continuing high cost of legal services requires that such approaches be considered if clients of ordinary means are to be served at all.

Care must be exercised in having paraprofessionals enter these areas and in making sure that the training, supervision and testing required is comprehensive. No doubt, many wills and real estate closings require the services of a lawyer. However, it can no longer be claimed that lawyers have the exclusive possession of the esoteric knowledge required and are, therefore, the only ones able to advise clients on any matter concerning the law. Inroads on lawyer exclusivity have been made and will continue to be made. Lawyer resistance to such inroads for selfish reasons only brings discredit on the profession. . . .

A few years later, the ABA National Conference on Access to Justice in the early 1990s again endorsed the expanded role of nonlawyers in the delivery of legal services, including pilot programs of lay advocacy. However, the conference participants could not agree about regulation of nonlawyers playing such a role or about the value and effectiveness of establishing a second tier of legal service providers, who many believed could not perform quality services at substantially lower costs than attorneys can under the present system.

The proponents of limited licensure disagree on the appropriate level of regulation. Some favor a simple registration procedure under which practitioners would simply register their names and addresses with an agency or the courts. Others want to create higher standards for consumer protection and generally favor educational requirements, a licensing examination, bonding or insurance requirements, and continuing education.

The ABA Commission on Nonlawyer Practice issued its report, *Nonlawyer Activity in Law-Related Situations,* in August 1995. The report contained several important findings, including the following:

- the last 20 years have seen a decline in the enforcement of laws prohibiting the unauthorized practice of law;
- self-representation is common and those representing themselves gather information on how to proceed from a variety of sources;
- many organizations that might not consider themselves to be legal service providers do in fact offer legal advice, e.g., unions, banks, title companies;
- the number of nonlawyer legal service providers (called legal technicians in the report) is growing and the quality of their services varies;
- the paralegal profession has expanded, the level of education possessed

23

by legal assistants has increased and nature of work performed by paralegals has evolved since the inception of the occupation;
- the liability of nonlawyer legal service providers varies from situation to situation and place to place.

The summary of recommendations issued in the commission's report reads as follows:

> Whereas, Increasing the Public's Access to the Justice System and to Affordable Assistance With Its Legal and Law-Related Needs Is an Urgent Goal of the Legal Profession and the States; and
> Whereas, The Protection of the Public from Harm Arising From Incompetent and Unethical Conduct By Persons Providing Legal or Law-Related Services Is an Urgent Goal of Both the Legal Profession and the States; and
> Whereas, When Adequate Protections for the Public Are in Place, Nonlawyers Have Important Roles to Perform in Providing the Public With Access to Justice;
> THEREFORE, The American Bar Association Commission on Nonlawyer Practice Recommends:

1. The American Bar Association, State, Local and Specialty Bar Associations, the Practicing Bar, Courts, Law Schools, and the Federal and State Governments Should Continue to Develop and Finance New and Improved Ways to Provide Access to Justice to Help the Public Meet Its Legal and Law-Related Needs.
2. The Range of Activities of Traditional Paralegals Should Be Expanded With Lawyers Remaining Accountable for their Activities.
3. States Should Consider Allowing Nonlawyer Representation of Individuals In State Administrative Agency Proceedings. Nonlawyer Representers Should Be Subject To the Agencies' Standards of Practice and Discipline.
4. The American Bar Association Should Examine Its Ethical Rules, Policies and Standards to Ensure that they Promote the Delivery of Affordable Competent Services and Access to Justice.
5. The Activities of Nonlawyers Who Provide Assistance, Advice and Representation Authorized by Statute, Court Rule or Agency Regulation Should Be Continued, Subject to Review By the Entity Under Whose Authority the Services Are Performed.
6. With Regard to the Activities of All Other Nonlawyers, States Should Adopt an Analytical Approach in Assessing Whether and How To Regulate Varied Forms of Nonlawyer Activity that Exist or Are Emerging in Their Respective Jurisdictions. Criteria for this Analysis Should Include the Risk of Harm These Activities Present, Whether Consumers Can Evaluate Providers' Qualifications, and Whether the Net Effect of Regulating the Activities Will Be a Benefit to the Public.

State Supreme Courts Should Take the Lead in Examining Specific Nonlawyer Activities Within Their Jurisdictions With the Active Support and Participation of the Bar and Public.

The ABA printed and distributed copies of the report to all entities within the ABA and to state and local bar associations and other interested persons and groups. Neither the House of Delegates nor the Board of Governors adopted the commission's recommendations as policy, but rather asked all ABA entities to study the report and to address the recommendations as they relate to each entity's mission and goals. While some commentators would have preferred a stronger endorsement of the commission's recommendations, the long process of education and consensus building is continuing both within the ABA and at the state level. This result seems appropriate in view of the commission's third and sixth recommendations, which call on states to consider the development of a greater role for nonlawyer legal service providers as a means to increase access to legal services.

C. State Guidelines for the Utilization of Legal Assistants

In an effort to promote the effective and ethical use of legal assistants, some states have adopted guidelines to assist attorneys in working with legal assistants. At the time of this writing, the following 25 states have some kind of guidelines: Colorado, Connecticut, Georgia, Idaho, Illinois, Indiana, Iowa, Kansas, Kentucky, Michigan, Missouri, Nebraska, New Hampshire, New Mexico, New York, North Carolina, North Dakota, Rhode Island, South Carolina, South Dakota, Texas, Utah, Virginia, Washington, and West Virginia.

In Indiana, Kentucky, New Mexico, North Dakota, Rhode Island, and South Dakota, the guidelines have been adopted by the highest court of the state. In other states, the guidelines have been approved by the state bar association, a state bar committee on legal assistants, or both. Connecticut and New York both revised their guidelines in the last few years.

Some of the states that have adopted guidelines have also prepared accompanying statements on the effective use of legal assistants. Detailed listings of paralegal job functions accompany the Colorado, Georgia, and New York guidelines.

All the state guidelines cover several critical areas of ethics and come into play when nonlawyers, not bound to state ethics codes as lawyers are, perform professional-level work and are interacting with clients and the public. These key areas, covered in later chapters of this text, are

- unauthorized practice of law;
- disclosure of status as legal assistant;
- confidentiality;
- conflicts of interest; and
- supervision and delegation.

In addition, some guidelines cover financial arrangements between lawyers and paralegals.

In 1991 the ABA adopted Model Guidelines for the Utilization of Legal Assistant Services, included in the Appendix at page 379. These guidelines were written to provide a model for states that may wish to adopt such guidelines and to encourage attorneys to use legal assistants effectively and appropriately. Fourteen of the jurisdictions with guidelines have either adopted the ABA guidelines or amended existing guidelines in response to the ABA model.

D. Paralegal Associations' Codes of Ethics and Guidelines

The two major national paralegal professional associations both have codes of ethics to guide the conduct of their members. The NALA first adopted its Code of Ethics and Professional Responsibility in 1975; it made minor revisions in 1979 and 1988 and completed a major revision in 1995. The NFPA first adopted its Affirmation of Responsibility in 1977 and made minor revisions in 1981. It adopted a completely new code in 1993. The current codes of both organizations are included in the Appendix beginning at pages 407 and 411. NFPA, an umbrella organization, encourages its local member organizations to adopt its new Model Code. Since its creation in 1993, the new code has been adopted by several local associations.

In 1997, NFPA adopted Model Disciplinary Rules to establish mechanisms for the enforcement of the ethics rules. The Model Disciplinary Rules set forth procedures for the investigation and prosecution of ethics code violations and for hearings and appeals and institute a system of sanctions.

The NALA has both individual members and affiliated local chapters. All members sign a statement of commitment to NALA's code on their membership application. A mechanism is in place at the national level to investigate allegations of code violations and to remove from membership or to remove the CLA designation from any member who has violated the code. Since there is no active policing, the NALA relies on complaints from its members or the public to bring violations to its attention. As of this date, only one person has been removed from membership through this process. In addition to signing the statement of commitment on the membership application, legal assistants who are certified by NALA must reaffirm their commitment to the NALA code every five years when they submit verification that they have completed their continuing education hours, a requirement for continued status as a Certified Legal Assistant.

In 1984 the NALA also adopted Model Standards and Guidelines for the Utilization of Legal Assistants. The dual purposes of these guidelines are to serve as an educational and informational tool for individual attorneys and state bars. and to provide a model for states seeking to develop their own guidelines. The NALA primarily considers the guidelines to be an educational tool and therefore not binding on its members. The guidelines periodically are updated to include new annotations to cases, and so forth.

The National Federation of Paralegal Associations issues ethics opinions on current concerns of interest to practicing legal assistants. These opinions have addressed such matters as communications over the Internet and the role of paralegals who work in the corporate setting.

Both organizations make literature on ethics available. Their addresses, phone numbers, and websites are as follows:

The National Association of Legal Assistants
1516 S. Boston, Suite 200
Tulsa, Oklahoma 74119
918-587-6828
http://www.nala.org

The National Federation of Paralegal Associations
P.O. Box 33108
Kansas City, Missouri 64114-0108
816-941-4000
http://www.paralegals.org

In addition to the two national organizations, some local and regional associations have created and adopted their own ethics rules, borrowing from NALA, NFPA, and the ABA. Examples of two excellent local codes are those of the California Alliance of Paralegal Associations and the Virginia Alliance of Legal Assistant Associations, whose guidelines also include educational standards for legal assistants.

E. Liability of Paralegals as Agents of Attorneys

Because legal assistants are not attorneys, they are neither bound by state codes of ethics for attorneys nor subject to sanctions for breaches of those codes. Without certification, licensing, or some other form of direct regulation of the paralegal occupation, a legal assistant is bound to comply with high standards of professional behavior primarily because the attorney for whom the legal assistant works is responsible for any lapses in the legal assistant's behavior. Attorneys therefore have a strong incentive to ensure that the legal assistants they employ are familiar with the state's ethics code and comply with it. Some states specifically require that attorneys take affirmative steps to educate legal assistants about the attorney's ethical obligations and to ensure their compliance.

The ABA Model Rules of Professional Conduct contain an important section on supervision that has no counterpart in the older Model Code. Rule 5.3 provides as follows:

With respect to a nonlawyer employed or retained by or associated with a lawyer:

(a) a partner in a law firm shall make reasonable efforts to ensure that the firm has in effect measures giving reasonable assurance that the person's conduct is compatible with the professional obligations of the lawyer;

(b) a lawyer having direct supervisory authority over the nonlawyer shall make reasonable efforts to ensure that the person's conduct is compatible with the professional obligations of the lawyer; and

(c) a lawyer shall be responsible for conduct of such a person that would be a violation of the Rules of Professional Conduct if engaged in by a lawyer if:

(1) the lawyer orders or, with the knowledge of the specific conduct, ratifies the conduct involved; or

(2) the lawyer is a partner in the law firm in which the person is employed, or has direct supervisory authority over the person, and knows of the conduct at a time when its consequences can be avoided or mitigated but fails to take reasonable remedial action.

While this rule applies to all nonlawyers in the lawyer's office, it has special application for paralegals who often work closely with clients and have ready access to sensitive and confidential information. The comments to this rule in the annotated version of the Model Rules refer to lawyer's obligations to ensure that paralegals are not engaging in unauthorized practice of law, are not mishandling client trust funds, and are not acting negligently.

Legal assistants have one other very meaningful incentive for complying with high standards of conduct—they are potential defendants in civil legal malpractice suits brought by clients who believe their attorneys have acted negligently. Paralegals are subject to the same general tort principles that apply to lawyers and other professionals. They are liable for negligent or intentional misconduct that injures a client.

The lawyers for whom they work are also liable under the doctrine of respondeat superior, or vicarious liability. Under this principle of agency law, employers are responsible for the acts of their employees carried out in the course and scope of their employment.

Since clients always name their attorneys and rarely name their attorneys' paralegals as defendants in malpractice cases, there is little case law available defining the standards of conduct to which paralegals are held. As a general rule, legal assistants would be held to the same standard of care, skill, and knowledge common to other legal assistants so long as they do not hold themselves out as attorneys and perform typical paralegal tasks. For a recent analysis of paralegal's tort liability, see Honchar, Evolving Standards of Nonlawyer Liability, *The Professional Lawyer*, Vol. 6, No. 3 (May 1995).

Two cases at the end of the chapter provide examples of attorneys being held responsible for the actions of their nonlawyer staff. The *Musselman* case at page 31 involves a malpractice action in which a legal assistant played a part. In the *Lawless* case beginning at page 34, a lawyer is disciplined as a result of the actions of a paralegal.

REVIEW QUESTIONS

1. When and why did the paralegal profession begin?
2. What are the two main professional associations for legal assistants?
3. What is certification? What is licensing?
4. What states have some form of voluntary certification of legal assistants? Who is responsible for these programs in these states?
5. What are the two national associations' programs for paralegal certification called? How do they differ?
6. What is limited licensure? How do nonlawyer legal service providers

differ from traditional legal assistants who work under the supervision of attorneys? How do they differ from freelance or independent contractor paralegals?

7. What are the arguments in favor of the licensing of traditional paralegals? The arguments against?

8. How does the ABA stand on the issue of paralegal certification and licensing? What about its position on regulation of nonlawyer legal service providers?

9. How many states have guidelines for the utilization of legal assistants? What is their purpose?

10. What are the ABA Model Guidelines for the Utilization of Legal Assistant Services?

11. Do NALA and NFPA have rules on the conduct of legal assistants? If so, how are these rules enforced?

12. What are the NALA Model Standards and Guidelines for the Utilization of Legal Assistants? What do they contain? What is their purpose?

13. Can a legal assistant who is negligent while working on a client's case be sued by the client for malpractice? Can this legal assistant's attorney-employer be sued? If so, on what grounds?

14. Is an attorney responsible for a legal assistant's breaches of conduct such that the appropriate state body may discipline the attorney? Can the same state body discipline the legal assistant?

15. What does ABA Model Rule 5.3 say about attorney responsibility for paralegals?

DISCUSSION QUESTIONS

1. Is there a local paralegal association in your area? Is it affiliated with the NALA or NFPA?

2. Do you think that legal assistants working under the supervision of attorneys should be licensed? Why, or why not?

3. Do you think that nonlawyer legal service providers should be licensed? Prosecuted for unauthorized practice of law?

4. If you were creating a licensing scheme for nonlawyer legal service providers, what would it include?

5. If nonlawyer legal service providers were licensed in your state, would you be interested in becoming licensed? Why, or why not?

6. Does your state or local bar have a committee that concerns itself with legal assistants? Does your state or local bar have guidelines for attorneys who work with paralegals? Has it considered licensing of traditional paralegals or independent paralegals who provide services directly to the public?

7. Who is covered or not covered by the ABA definition of a legal assistant? Do you like this definition? Why, or why not? How would you change it?
8. What methods can you suggest to improve access to legal services for low- and middle-income persons?
9. Can you find any legal malpractice cases in your state in which a legal assistant was implicated?
10. What do you think of the ABA Commission on Nonlawyer Practice recommendations? Do they go far enough? Have they been addressed in your state?
11. Is voluntary certification through NALA or NFPA popular in your state or local area? Why, or why not?
12. Has your jurisdiction adopted Model Rule 5.3 or some version of it? Are there any disciplinary cases or ethics opinions interpreting this rule?

CASES FOR ANALYSIS

The *Musselman* case below demonstrates how a legal assistant might become involved in a transaction that results in harm to a client, thus becoming the subject of a malpractice suit.

Musselman v. Willoughby Corp.
230 Va. 337, 337 S.E.2d 724 (1985)

This is an attorney malpractice case arising from a real estate transaction. The lawyer represented a corporate client and employed an untrained paralegal who played a significant role in the closing of the transaction.

The relevant facts mainly are undisputed. Appellee Willoughby Corporation, the plaintiff below, was formed in September 1974 by a large number of holders of O'Neill Enterprises, Inc. real estate bonds which had been secured by undeveloped land known as the "Willoughby Tract," lying in the City of Charlottesville and Albemarle County. When O'Neill Enterprises defaulted and went into bankruptcy, the bondholders formed Willoughby Corporation (hereinafter, the Corporation) in order to sell or develop the property to recoup their investments.

Appellant Robert M. Musselman, a defendant below, represented the bondholders in formation of the Corporation. He became attorney for the Corporation and also served as its Secretary. He was not a member of the Board of Directors. The daily operations of the Corporation were handled from defendant's law office by defendant's employees. One director testified that Musselman took "a very dominant role in the affairs of the corporation" and that the Board looked to defendant for "guidance and leadership."

Upon formation of the Corporation, several tracts of land, residential and commercial, were combined. One of the parcels, an 11.5-acre commercial piece known as Parcel 9, is the subject of this controversy.

In 1976, aware that the Board of Directors wished to sell a portion of the Willoughby Tract, defendant contracted Thomas J. Chandler, Jr., a local real estate broker, who obtained an offer to purchase Parcel 9. The offer was made by Charles W. Hurt, a medical doctor who had been a real estate developer in the Charlottesville and Albemarle County area for a number of years. . . .

Subsequently, another standard form purchase contract for $215,000 was completed dated May 6, 1976. The purchaser was shown to be "Charles Wm. Hurt or Assigns." . . . The contract was executed by Hurt, by Musselman on behalf of the Corporation as corporate Secretary, and by the realtor. . . .

[Stanley K. Joynes, III,] had been employed by Musselman in June 1977. Joynes had just graduated from college but had no formal training either as a lawyer or a paralegal. His main responsibility, under Musselman's direction, was to "shepherd the Willoughby Project along." Joynes attended his first Board meeting in July 1977 and was chosen Assistant Secretary of the Corporation.

In the course of the September 1977 Board meeting, defendant was directed to close the Hurt transaction "as soon as possible." Three weeks later, Stuart F. Carwile, Hurt's attorney, notified Musselman by letter dated September 22, 1977 that his client desired to take title to Parcel 9 as follows:

> Stuart F. Carwile and David W. Kudravetz, as trustees for the Fifth Street Land Trust, pursuant to the terms of a certain land trust agreement dated 22 September 1977.

Carwile advised that after Musselman submitted a draft of the deed, Carwile would forward the proposed deed of trust and note for defendant's approval.

The paralegal then prepared the deed, with "some assistance" from other employees of defendant, in accordance with Carwile's request showing the Land Trust as grantee. Joynes arranged for Frankel to execute the deed, dated October 5, 1977, and on that day participated with Carwile in the closing of the transaction. Musselman was out of town on business on both October 4th and 5th. In the course of the closing on October 5th, the paralegal accepted the deed of trust, and other closing documents prepared by Carwile, which specifically exculpated Hurt from personal liability in the transaction as beneficiary under the land trust.

At this point, we note several important undisputed facts. First, the Board of Directors, upon being advised that Hurt, a man of substantial wealth, was to be the purchaser of Parcel 9, intended to rely on Hurt's potential personal liability as a part of the security for payment of the deferred purchase price. Second, Musselman maintained in his trial testimony that he was authorized by the Board to execute the contract of the sale on behalf of the Corporation, and this was not contradicted by any witnesses. In addition, Musselman testified that Joynes, the paralegal, represented the Corporation at the closing, acting within his authority as an employee of defendant. Also, none of the Board members, prior to closing, ever examined either the proposed contract of March 26 or the final contract dated May 6, Moreover, no member of the Board knew before closing that the contract showed the purchaser to be "Hurt or Assigns." In addition, Musselman always was of the opinion that the foregoing language in the contract authorized Hurt to escape personal liability under the contract by assigning his rights in the contract to whomever he chose. Also, Musselman never called the language to the Board's attention or explained its meaning to the Board. Finally, the fact that the closing documents exculpated Hurt from personal liability as beneficiary under the land trust was never revealed or explained to the Board of Directors prior to closing. . . .

The Land Trust defaulted under the terms of the $170,000 note in respect to an interest payment due on April 1, 1978. Subsequently, this action to recover the principal sum. plus interest, due under the real estate transaction was filed in September 1978 in numerous counts against Hurt and Musselman. The proceeding against Hurt was severed and he was eventually dismissed by the trial court as a party defendant.

The Corporation's action against Musselman was based on alternative theories. The plaintiff charged that defendant breached certain fiduciary duties in his capacity as an officer of the Corporation. In addition, the Corporation alleged that Musselman, in his capacity as attorney for the Corporation, was negligent and breached his fiduciary duty as counsel to the Corporation.

At the March 1982 trial, the jury was permitted, under the instructions, to find against defendant in his capacity either as attorney, or as an officer of the Corporation, or as both attorney and officer. The jury found against defendant in his capacity as attorney only and fixed the damages, which were not in dispute, at $243,722.99. This sum represented the principal amount due on the obligation, plus interest through the last day of trial. The trial court entered judgment on the verdict in June 1982, and we awarded defendant this appeal in July 1983. . . .

Inexplicably, defendant's main contentions on appeal are based on the faulty premise that he lacked corporate authority to act in executing the contract containing the "or Assigns" language and in completing the conveyance to a land trust, while, in the process, exculpating Hurt from personal liability. This argument is totally inconsistent with defendant's trial testimony that he did, in fact, have authority to execute the contract. It is also at odds with the uncontroverted evidence about defendant's "dominant roll" in acting for the Corporation. . . .

There is no merit to this argument. Musselman, being authorized to execute the contract and to close the transaction, had the responsibility as counsel to advise his client, immediately upon discovery of the "problem," that it should attempt to rescind the transaction, if we assume an attempt at rescission would have been successful. Instead, defendant at no time advised the Board of Directors that it should pursue rescission. . . .

For these reasons, the judgment of the trial court will be affirmed.

Questions about the Case

1. What functions did the legal assistant Joynes perform in this transaction? Do you think any of these were inappropriate functions? Were they carried out competently?
2. What were the mistakes made by the attorney Musselman in this case? How should he have acted so as not to be negligent?
3. Do you think that Musselman adequately supervised Joynes?
4. Why was Joynes not named as a defendant in this action? Was he not in error, or did the court hold Musselman liable for Joynes's mistakes?
5. Did he fact that Joynes was "untrained" affect the court's thinking?

Attorneys are responsible for the actions of their employees, including legal assistants who are independent contractors, and may be disciplined when their inaction or neglect results in harm to a client.

Florida Bar v. Lawless
640 So. 2d 1098 (Fla. 1994)

A Canadian couple, Michael and Barbara Seguin, hired Lawless in 1987 to help them acquire permanent residency status in the United

States. Lawless initially contracted to acquire residency status for Michael Seguin for a flat fee of $5,000 plus expenses. The Seguins later met with Lawless and paralegal Charles Aboudraah. Although Aboudraah did not work in Lawless's office, Lawless had worked with the paralegal and said he was experienced in immigration cases. Lawless said he would supervise the case, but the Seguins were to contact Aboudraah if they had questions.

From March 19, 1987, through February 11, 1988, the Seguins paid $12,546 to Aboudraah, including $725 to pursue a visa for Barbara Seguin. They thought these payments included the remaining $2,500 of Lawless's flat fee and that Aboudraah gave Lawless a share of these payments. Aboudraah told the Seguins their paperwork had been filed with the Immigration and Naturalization Service and that they were waiting for the INS to send visa cards.

In January 1990 the Seguins received a letter from the INS seeking information about their residency status and indicating that they had not responded to other letters about the matter. When the Seguins asked Lawless and Aboudraah about the letter, they were assured Aboudraah was handling their case.

Soon, however, the Seguins learned that the INS was investigating Aboudraah. Aboudraah became less available to them and he ultimately closed his office. The Seguins contacted Lawless, who discovered that there was no application on file for either Barbara or Michael Seguin. Thus, the Seguins had been living illegally in the United States since 1986.

In April 1990 Lawless told the Seguins he had not received any money from their payments to Aboudraah. He also said he had not been associated with Aboudraah in more than two years. Although Lawless submitted visa applications for the Seguins, they eventually consulted another attorney because they did not think Lawless understood the immigration procedures needed to conclude their case. The Seguins ultimately obtained visas that allowed them to live legally in the United States and operate their business.

The Bar filed a formal complaint against Lawless in 1992. . . .

The Bar argues that given Lawless's disciplinary history, nothing less than a ninety-one-day suspension is an adequate sanction. Lawless contends that a public reprimand is sufficient because this Court has imposed public reprimands in other cases involving a lawyer's failure to supervise nonlawyer employees. . . .

First, we uphold the referee's recommendation that Lawless pay restitution to the Seguins during his probation. We agree with the referee that "had it not been for [Lawless], the Seguins would not have been subjected to Charles Aboudraah's misconduct." Lawless's initial contract with the Seguins called for a $5,000 flat fee plus expenses. After Lawless introduced the Seguins to Aboudraah and assured them he was supervising the case, the Seguins paid $12,546 to Aboudraah. Whether Lawless ever received that money is not the issue: He was responsible for the conduct of his nonlawyer employee and thus must reimburse the Seguins.

Second, we find that the referee's recommendations about supervising paralegals and removing Lawless's name from lawyer referral lists are appropriate in this case. These sanctions will apply during Lawless's suspension and probation. . . .

Accordingly, we suspend Lawless from the practice of law for ninety days, followed by a three-year probationary period. We also impose the other penalties the referee recommended. See supra note 1. . . .

Questions about the Case

1. Was the paralegal Aboudraah an employee or an independent contractor? What facts support your conclusion? Does it make any difference in this case?
2. Did the attorney Lawless supervise the paralegal adequately?
3. Did the attorneys maintain a direct relationship with the clients?
4. Do you believe the sanctions were appropriate? Discuss both the suspension and the penalties listed in footnote 1.
5. What do you think would have happened if the clients had filed a malpractice suit?

In this interesting case, a paralegal who is the recipient of a gift from an elderly client is held not to be a fiduciary to the client by virtue of her status as a paralegal. This case demonstrates the lack of clear and consistent case law about the liability of legal assistants in their professional capacity.

In Re Estate of Divine
635 N.E.2d 581 (Ill. App. 1 Dist. 1994)

Beginning in approximately 1979, Giancola was employed in Chicago by attorney Samuel Poznanovich as a part-time secretary in his law office. Eventually, she became his full-time secretary. Giancola received

1. The referee recommended that Lawless be required to remove "Immigration Law" from his letterhead unless he is certified by the Florida Bar; to refrain from supervising paralegals; to refrain from splitting fees with nonlawyers; to complete a legal ethics course; to remove his name from lists of lawyer referral service; and to reimburse clients Michael and Barbara Seguin for $12,546 they paid paralegal Charles Aboudraah.

a paralegal certificate from Roosevelt University in 1980, and took an H & R Block tax course in 1970. Poznanovich employed one other secretary in addition to Giancola.

In 1981, Richard and his wife, Lila, came to Poznanovich's office for income tax services. The Divines did not have any children and both were retired. Giancola estimated that they were in their "early seventies" in 1981. Giancola interviewed the Divines, took tax information from them such as W-2 forms and copies of their previous tax returns, and introduced them to Poznanovich. After this initial meeting, Poznanovich prepared the Divines' tax returns every year until 1986. Each year, Giancola would interview the Divines and gather their tax information. She never prepared their taxes, but simply gathered information for Poznanovich's use. In 1985, Poznanovich also represented Richard in a personal injury case. Giancola was not involved in that case. Additionally, Richard called Poznanovich occasionally for legal advice on other matters. Before 1986, Giancola and Poznanovich saw the Divines only at the law office, although, according to Poznanovich, the relationship became "more and more friendly" each year.

In December 1986, Lila died. Richard called Giancola at the office to tell her about Lila's death. Giancola stated that Richard had "depended on Lila for just about everything" and was very lonely without Lila. Also, he was "unable to do for himself." Giancola went to visit Richard in his apartment on Coles Avenue "within a day or two" of Lila's death. Richard was afraid to leave the apartment alone and could not walk long distances because "his legs were bad." Richard's relatives and Poznanovich also testified that Richard had physical problems with his legs. Giancola stated that for "the most part," Richard was confined to his apartment. After Giancola's first visit, Richard frequently called her and she visited his apartment once or twice a week. Richard asked her to assist him in getting his groceries and other necessities. Richard gave Giancola money for the groceries and supplies. She testified that he did not give her a "fee" for her services, but admitted that sometimes he gave her "something for [her]self." He did his own cooking while living in the Coles Avenue apartment.

Giancola believed that the neighborhood around Coles Avenue was too dangerous for Richard, and she did not like going there to visit him. She suggested that he move to a safer area; she also mentioned to Poznanovich that Richard's neighborhood was unsafe. Poznanovich's office is located in a building he and his sister own. There are four residential apartments in that building which are rented by Poznanovich and his sister. Giancola occasionally takes the rent checks from tenants for Poznanovich. When an apartment became vacant in Poznanovich's building, Giancola told Richard it "would be easier" if he moved into

37

that apartment. She did not know that Richard's relatives wanted him to move to Michigan City, Indiana. . . .

In addition to getting his supplies and cooking his meals, Giancola cashed checks for Richard and made bank deposits for him. She wrote out the checks for all his bills. She explained that she would write the checks, he would sign them, and she would mail them. All these transactions involved only Richard's personal checking account. Richard would discuss "personal problems" with Giancola, but did not talk to her about legal matters. . . .

In November, 1987, Richard called Poznanovich and asked him to come to his apartment. In the apartment, Richard told Poznanovich that he wanted to "put his affairs in order." First, he handed two bank account passbooks to Poznanovich and said "I want this for my sweetheart." Richard told Poznanovich that his "sweetheart" was Giancola, and that he wanted her to have the two accounts. These two accounts were separate from Richard's personal checking account which Giancola used for his finances. Richard told Poznanovich he did not want to leave the accounts to Giancola in his will because he wanted her "to have them now." Richard explained: "As far as I'm concerned, if it were not for her, I would be dead now." Poznanovich suggested that the accounts be made joint accounts, like the accounts Richard had shared with Lila. When Poznanovich assured Richard that a joint tenancy would allow Giancola to have the money immediately, Richard told Poznanovich to change the two accounts to joint accounts. Giancola was not present during this discussion. Poznanovich testified that he did not receive any direct or indirect financial benefit from this transaction.

Next, Richard asked Poznanovich to draft a will for him. The will made Poznanovich executor of the estate and gave $3000 each to Giancola and Poznanovich. Poznanovich testified: "I had a problem with [Richard] inserting me as a beneficiary under the will, . . . [and] we agreed that if I were to remain in the will as a beneficiary, I would waive my executor's fee, which I did." The will made one other specific bequest of $2000, then left one half of the residuary estate to the petitioners and one half to four other family members. After his death, the value of Richard's estate, in addition to the joint accounts, was approximately $150,000.

Poznanovich obtained two signature cards from the bank and had the accounts changed to joint accounts. On November 14, 1987, he asked Giancola to sign these signature cards. Neither Richard nor Poznanovich ever discussed the accounts with Giancola before presenting her with the cards. They also did not discuss the transactions with any members of Richard's family. . . .

At the hearing in the trial court and in this court the petitioners argued that the actions of Poznanovich and Giancola are inextricably intertwined and that because Giancola was a paralegal and an employee of the lawyer, Poznanovich, who was a fiduciary as a matter of law, so also is Giancola a fiduciary as a matter of law. They also repeatedly assert that Poznanovich gained financially from the transactions which benefitted Giancola. Nonetheless, they never requested that Poznanovich or Giancola return the $3000 bequests and they do not challenge the validity of the will. Additionally, they have never made Poznanovich a party to these proceedings. Essentially, the petitioners argue that Poznanovich's questionable action of drafting a will which gave him a gift and his status as an attorney should be imputed to Giancola and that she should be liable because of his actions.

Under certain circumstances, one person will be charged with liability for the actions of or knowledge given to another person. For example, actions by one partner will be imputed to another partner. (Citation omitted.) Also, an employer will be held liable for certain actions of his employee. (Citation omitted.) There is no case law holding an employee liable for the acts of his employer, however, and the petitioners cite no law to support their position that Giancola should be accountable for Poznanovich's actions. Unfortunately, there also is no case law in Illinois involving the narrower question of a paralegal's fiduciary duty to his employer's client, making this a case of first impression. In fact, we have found no reported case in the United States involving a paralegal's fiduciary responsibility, as a paralegal, to his attorney's client.

Moreover, there is very little case law from Illinois or any jurisdiction generally discussing paralegals. Two cases address the somewhat analogous issue of a paralegal's possible liability for legal malpractice. A divided Nevada Supreme Court, in *Busch v. Flangas* (1992), 108 Nev. 821, 837 P.2d 438, held that an attorney's law clerk or paralegal who attempts to provide legal services can be liable for malpractice to the client. On the other hand, the *Busch* dissent argued that a law clerk or paralegal, as an employee of an attorney, owes no duty to the attorney's client, but is liable only to the attorney. (*Busch*, 837 P.2d at 441 (Springer, J., dissenting).) The Court of Appeals of Ohio, without extensive discussion, determined that a paralegal could not be sued for legal malpractice because she was not an attorney. *Palmer v. Westmeyer* (1988), 48 Ohio App.3d 296, 549 N.E.2d 1202, 1209.

On the other hand, the idea that an attorney is liable, in malpractice or as an ethical violation, for his paralegal's acts is well-supported in Illinois. . . .

Several Illinois cases support the idea that paralegals are an extension of their employing attorney. For example, the presence of an attorney's employee, such as a secretary or law clerk, does not destroy the attorney-client privilege for material disclosed to the attorney in the employee's presence. (Citations omitted.) Also, in the majority of Illinois cases discussing paralegals, which involve disputed attorney fee petitions, the courts have held that an attorney may recover reasonable fees for time properly spent by his paralegal. . . .

Based on these cases, we refuse to treat Poznanovich and Giancola as a unit for purposes of Giancola's liability. It is clear that Poznanovich, as a licensed attorney and as an employer, could be held liable for Giancola's actions. Nonetheless, holding Giancola liable as if she were an attorney is not consistent with general *respondeat superior* law or with the decisions discussed above treating paralegals as subordinate employees of attorneys. The theme running through all these cases is that paralegals do not independently practice law, but simply serve as assistants to lawyers. They are not equal or autonomous partners. Thus, while supervisors properly are held liable for paralegals' actions, the subordinate paralegals should not be liable for the actions of these supervisors. Therefore, we refuse to find that Giancola owed Richard a fiduciary duty simply because she worked for Richard's attorney, and we refuse to hold that paralegals are fiduciaries to their employers' clients as a matter of law. . . .

The trial judge correctly found that there was no evidence Giancola participated in the transfer of the funds from Richard's private accounts into the joint accounts. The petitioners have presented no evidence that Giancola was present when Richard and Poznanovich established the joint accounts or that she knew about the transfer before it occurred. They do not even argue that Giancola somehow participated in the transfer.

We also agree with the judge's determination that there was no showing that Richard was incompetent at the time the transfer was made and there was no showing of undue influence on the part of Giancola that caused Richard to make the transfer.

We also wish to make it clear that we are not saying that the evidence shows that Poznanovich did anything improper. We have discussed his "actions" only in the general sense to illustrate that, while he was a fiduciary to Richard as a matter of law and if he had been the recipient of the joint account funds, the burden of proof would have been on him to show that the transaction was proper, his fiduciary obligations may not be imposed upon Giancola. Nor are we saying that an improper transfer may never be shown under circumstances like those present in this case. If the petitioners had offered evidence from which it could be inferred that collusion existed between Poznanovich and Giancola or that Poznanovich gained financially in any way from the transfer, our holding would be different. But neither the trial judge nor this court may decide a case on speculation, guess, conjecture or suspicion.

For these reasons, the judgment of the circuit court is affirmed.

Questions about the Case

1. What was the paralegal's relationship with the client and how did it evolve over time?
2. Was there any evidence that the paralegal took advantage of the client?
3. Did the petitioners sue the lawyer? On what grounds did they sue the paralegal?
4. Under this case, can a paralegal be held liable for the actions of his/her employing lawyer? Could the lawyer be held liable for the actions of the paralegal?
5. Does a paralegal have a fiduciary duty directly to a client in Illinois?
6. Review the rules in Chapter 5 about accepting gifts from clients and determine if either the lawyer or the paralegal in this case violated those rules. What should they have done to protect against a lawsuit like this one?

Unauthorized Practice of Law

This chapter outlines the limitations on who can practice law, especially those limitations that most affect legal assistants. Chapter 3 covers:

- the history of the unauthorized practice of law from the colonial era to present
- definitions of the practice of law
- the attorney's ethical responsibility to prevent the unauthorized practice of law and to supervise legal assistants
- key areas of concern to legal assistants in the unauthorized practice of law area, including:
  - court appearances, depositions, pleadings, and giving legal advice
  - job functions that may constitute the unauthorized practice of law
  - nonlawyer practice before administrative agencies
  - the disclosure of the legal assistant's status
  - legal assistants working as independent contractors

A. A Brief History

Limitations on who can practice law in the United States can be traced back to the colonial era. At that time a proliferation of untrained practitioners caused local courts to adopt rules requiring attorneys who appeared before them to have a license granted by the court. Additional rules adopted during this period limited the amount of fees that could be charged and dictated that attorneys could not refuse to take a case. The stated purposes of these rules were to prevent stirring up of litigation by unscrupulous "pettifoggers" and "mercenary" attorneys, to stop incompetence that harmed not only the clients but the administration of justice and dignity of the courts, and to prevent exploitive, excessive fees.

These early limitations on the practice of law hardly evolved to their present state smoothly. Many of these rules. along with later rules that governed the training of lawyers and their admission to the bar, were eliminated during an era of deprofessionalization in the early nineteenth century, only to reemerge in the late nineteenth century. State and local bar associations began to gain strength during this period, in part because of concern over the large numbers of lawyers competing for legal work with one another and with newly developing businesses, such as collection agencies, banks and trust companies, accountants, and administrative agencies that permitted lay appearances. The first unauthorized practice statutes were passed in several states during the 1850s, prohibiting court appearances by anyone not licensed as an attorney and prohibiting the practice of law by court personnel such as bailiffs. The first unauthorized practice cases were also brought during this period. These cases held it improper for an unlicensed person to hold himself or herself out as an attorney and for a nonlawyer to form a partnership with a lawyer.

The definition of the practice of law being formulated in these cases was gradually broadened to cover activities beyond court appearances. Most early cases defined the practice of law as the preparation of documents by which legal rights are secured. New justifications for restricting the right to practice law to licensed attorneys emerged, including the lawyer's professional independence, moral character, and special training as well as the fact that lawyers are subject to sanctions for breaches of duty or competence, unlike unlicensed practitioners.

Some legal historians and commentators believe that the height of unauthorized practice restrictions came during the Depression when lawyers needed most to protect their economic interests from competition. Bar associations became especially powerful trade organizations during this era. Unauthorized practice statutes were passed in virtually all states, making it a crime to practice law without a license. The definition of the practice of law was further expanded to include "all services customarily rendered by lawyers," a not-very-helpful tautology to practitioners trying to determine if their behavior was illegal.

In 1930, the American Bar Association (ABA) created its powerful Special Committee on the Unauthorized Practice of Law, which by the late 1950s had agreements called Statements of Principles with accountants, collection agencies, insurance adjusters, life insurance underwriters, publishers, and realtors, to name a few. These agreements, later rescinded when it became apparent that they would be found illegal under the Sherman Antitrust Act, delineated which activities of a legal nature these other nonattorney professionals could engage in without stepping into the forbidden realm of the practice of law. Most state and local bar associations also had committees monitoring the activities of these competitor organizations, and many also entered into Statements of Principle with nonlawyer legal service providers. The California State Bar, for example, had 20 such agreements, which were rescinded in 1979.

Criminal prosecutions and civil suits to restrain unauthorized practice slowed during the 1960s and 1970s. It was during this period that the sale of legal self-help kits and books were determined by the courts not to constitute the unauthorized practice of law and that the movement to expand access to legal services by alternative means started to take hold.

The 1980s experienced a resurgence of unauthorized practice prosecutions because of the increased number of independent paralegals providing low-cost legal services directly to the public. Many factors together have created the need for such legal services providers: the decrease in funding for the Legal Services Corporation that formerly supplied legal services to persons of low and moderate incomes; the increase in the need for legal services because of the proliferation and complexity of laws; and the rising cost of legal services provided by lawyers, making it difficult and sometimes impossible for even middle-income Americans to employ a lawyer when they need one.

Most nonlawyer legal service providers work in the areas of practice in which low- and moderate-income people need assistance, such as landlord/tenant matters, divorce, child support, bankruptcy, and immigration. Some run "typing services" that assist persons only by typing documents, usually to be filed with the court, after the "customer" fills in the blanks. Others provide more complete information and assistance, helping the customer to decide what forms to use, what information to include on the forms, and where to file them. Nonlawyer legal service providers call themselves "independent paralegals," "legal technicians," or "document preparers."

45

Although by no means certain, it is estimated that there are about 10,000 nonlawyers providing legal help directly to the public. Most of these service providers handle some combination of family law and bankruptcy matters. According to the National Association of Independent Paralegals, a professional association for nonlawyer practitioners, about half of these "independent paralegals" attended college, and over one-fourth attended a paralegal educational program. About a quarter have law office experience.

While the unmet need for legal services is well documented, lawyers are largely opposed to giving up any of their traditional functions to nonlawyers. Clearly, lawyers have both monopolistic, economic reasons for this stance and legitimate professional and societal concerns about the quality of legal services that someone not trained as a lawyer can provide. The debate has taken on national proportions and undoubtedly will continue throughout the 1990s.

While the debate rages on, prosecutions against nonlawyer legal service providers are on the rise. No formal studies document the exact increase in prosecutions; however, during the early 1990s most states reported criminal prosecutions for unauthorized practice of law and for injunctive relief against nonlawyer legal service providers after decades of virtually no such cases. (Forty jurisdictions reported active or moderately active UPL enforcement in the 1990s according to a study conducted by the ABA Standing Committee on Lawyers' Responsibility for Client Protection, *1994 Survey on the Unauthorized Practice of Law/Nonlawyer Practice.*) Most cases have been against bankruptcy, landlord-tenant, and family law practitioners where there has been egregious or incompetent conduct that harmed consumers. But some recent prosecutions have resulted from lawyer complaints rather than from disgruntled consumers.

Defendants in widely publicized prosecutions in several states have argued unsuccessfully that they are not giving legal advice but are simply assisting lay persons in the preparation of legal documents. Some defendants in unauthorized practice prosecutions have argued that a statutory power of attorney from a client gives a nonlawyer the authority to represent the client in litigation. In one case that has addressed this issue, the California Court of Appeal concluded that the power of attorney did not extend the privilege of practicing law to its holder. *Drake v. Superior Court of San Diego County,* 21 Cal. App. 4th 1826, 26 Cal. Rptr. 2d 829 (1994). Other defendants have claimed, to no avail, a public necessity defense based on the lack of availability of legal services for their clients.

Meanwhile, several states have seen proposed legislation that would define the practice of law more expansively or would institute harsher penalties for the unauthorized practice of law, or have stepped up their efforts to prosecute unauthorized practice cases. For example, in one such state, Pennsylvania, the unauthorized practice statute was amended to increase penalties and to include specific references to "legal assistant" and "paralegal" to make certain that persons who call themselves paralegals know that they can be prosecuted criminally for violations of the statute (see Pennsylvania Consolidated Statutes, §2524(a), amended 1996). North Carolina has recently started to crack down on unlicensed independent paralegals who are performing title searches without attorney supervision. And in 1996, after developing a ten-point plan to step up prosecutions of unauthorized practice, a plan that included legislative proposals to make unauthorized practice a felony, the California State Bar abandoned its get-tough position in the face of vehement opposition from consumer groups and independent paralegals. In another interesting move in an area that most experts considered settled, in 1997 the Unauthorized Practice of Law Committee of the State Bar of Texas began investigating the publication of self-help books and software by Nolo Press.

Bankruptcy reform legislation adopted in the 1990s contains provisions that limit the role of nonlawyer practitioners in Chapter 7 filings, including barring the use of the terms "legal" or "paralegal" in business names. Bankruptcy judges and practitioners are among the most vocal opponents of nonlawyer legal services providers.

Several states have taken action to regulate nonlawyers who assist persons with immigration matters, including Arizona, Illinois, and Oregon. While federal statutes establish nationwide standards for accredited visa consultants, some immigration "consultants" do not fall within the reach of these federal laws and widespread abuses of clients have been documented in the immigrant community.

Several states have determined that the preparation of living trust documents constitutes the practice of law, paving the way for the prosecution of many companies that market living trust plans. Most decisions hold that the client's decision on whether a living trust is appropriate, the attendant preparation and execution of documents, and the funding of the trust are functions that require an attorney's judgment and involvement (see, for example, Florida Bar re: Advisory Opinion on Nonlawyer Preparation of Living Trusts, 613 So. 2d 426 (Fla. 1992), California State Bar Ethics Opinion 97-148, South Dakota Bar Ethics Opinion 91-14, Colorado 90-87, and Pennsylvania 90-65). Lawyers in several jurisdictions have been disciplined for participating in businesses that promoted and sold living trusts for aiding in the unauthorized practice of law. Most courts find that these lawyers have abdicated their responsibility to advise clients about the ramifications of such an important legal decision as making a living trust. The lawyers in these cases either failed to supervise the work of their employees in counseling clients and preparing the documents for them, or were asked to review documents by the nonlawyer operators who had already advised the clients and prepared documents for them with no attorney involvement whatsoever. For one example, see *In re Morin* at the end of this chapter.

Finally, there is a growing trend toward the discipline of lawyers who are running large volume practices and inadequately supervising their paralegals and other employees. In most of these cases, the paralegals are accepting clients, having them sign retainer agreements, preparing legal documents for them, and counseling them about their legal rights with little or no lawyer involvement and no direct relationship between the lawyer and the client. In some cases, there has also been unlawful solicitation of clients by the nonlawyers coupled with compensation arrangements that violate rules against fee splitting and/or lawyers and nonlawyers entering into a partnership for the practice of law. These fee-related and solicitation issues are covered in Chapters 6 and 7.

B. Practice of Law Defined

No one definitive list of activities constitutes the practice of law. As you can see from the foregoing history, the concept is actually a somewhat flexible one that has changed over time by the push and pull of economics, political and professional activity, public pressure and consumerism, and the complexity of laws. The oft-quoted ABA Model Code of Professional Responsibility (ABA Model Code) EC 3-5 states: "It is neither necessary nor desirable to attempt the formulation of a single, specific definition of what constitutes the practice of law."

Court decisions throughout the country have come up with a wide variety of tests for determining what defines the practice of law. A few unauthorized practice statutes attempt to define the practice of law; most do not. It is generally agreed that these tests fall into three or four categories. One excellent statement of these tests is found in Charles W. Wolfram's treatise Modern Legal Ethics (1986). Wolfram divides the cases defining the practice of law into three categories:

1. *The professional judgment test.* Using this test, the court will ask whether the activity at issue is one which requires the lawyer's special training and skills. Wolfram suggests that a better version of this test would be "whether the matter handled was of such complexity that only a person trained as a lawyer should be permitted to deal with it." Id. at 836.

2. *The traditional areas of practice test.* This test asks whether the function in question is one that would traditionally be performed by an attorney or is commonly understood to be the practice of law. This is probably the least useful or meaningful test as it is self-defining and overbroad, and encompasses all common lawyer activities whether or not they relate to the law, require a lawyer's expertise, and so forth. Id.
3. *The incidental legal services test.* This test draws a line around the practice of law based on whether the activity is essentially legal in nature or is a law-related adjunct to some business routine. Filling out a simple legal document incidental to a banking or real estate transaction, for which no separate fee is charged, would not constitute the practice of law under this definition. Id.

Some scholars would add other tests, such as whether the activity in question is characterized by a personal relationship between lawyer and client or whether the activity is one for which the public interest would best be served by limiting it to licensed attorneys.

These general tests have been translated into some more specific rules in cases throughout the country. Cases have been brought as criminal prosecutions for unauthorized practice—a misdemeanor in more than 30 states—and in civil contempt proceedings (a remedy in more than 25 states) or actions for injunctive relief, usually brought by bar associations or courts to stop someone from engaging in activities believed to be the practice of law (available as a remedy in at least 40 jurisdictions). Additional deterrents to unauthorized practice include: liability for negligent performance, unenforceability of the contract for legal services, court dismissal of an action, and a court's voiding of a judgment in which a nonlawyer represented the prevailing party.

A few examples of definitions of the practice of law may be instructive.

According to the generally understood definition of the practice of law, it embraces the preparation of pleadings and other papers incident to actions of special proceedings, and the management of such actions and proceedings on behalf of clients before judges in courts. However, the practice of law is not confined to cases conducted in court. In fact, the major portion of the practice of any capable lawyer consists of work done outside of the courts. The practice of law involves not only appearance in court in connection with litigation, but also services rendered out of court, and includes the giving of advice or the rendering of any service requiring the use of legal skill or knowledge, such as preparing a will, contract, or other instrument, the legal effect of which under the facts and conclusions involved must be carefully determined.

Davies v. Unauthorized Practice Committee of State Bar of Texas, 431 S.W.2d 590, at 593 (Tex. Civ. App., 1968).

> In general, one is deemed to be practicing law whenever he furnishes to another advice or service under circumstances which imply the possession and use of legal knowledge and skill. The practice of law includes "all advice to clients, and all actions taken for them in matters connected with the law.". . . Practice of law includes the giving of legal advice and counsel, and the preparation of legal instruments and contracts of which legal rights are secured. . . . Where the rendering of services for another involves the use of legal knowledge or skill on his behalf—where legal advice is required and is availed of or rendered in connection with such services—these services necessarily constitute or include the practice of law.

In re Welch, 185 A.2d 458, 459 (Vt. 1962). Also see the definitions offered by other courts in each of the cases at the end of this chapter.

A growing number of states are attempting to define the practice of law in statutes that set penalties for unauthorized practice. A few examples of these statutes follow.

> The "practice of the law" is hereby defined to be and is the appearance as an advocate in a representative capacity or the drawing of papers, pleadings or documents or the performance of any act in such capacity in connection with proceedings pending or prospective before any court of record, commissioner, referee or any body, board, committee or commission constituted by law or having authority to settle controversies.

Missouri Revised Statutes, §484.010.

> (1) "Practice law" means to engage in any of the following activities:
> (i) giving legal advice;
> (ii) representing another person before a unit of the State government or of a political subdivision; or
> (iii) performing any other service that the Court of Appeals defines as practicing law.
> (2) "Practice law" includes:
> (i) advising in the administration of probate of estate of decedents in an orphans' court of the State;
> (ii) preparing an instrument that affects title to real estate;
> (iii) preparing or helping in the preparation of any form or document that is filed in a court or affects a case that is or may be filed in a court; or
> (iv) giving advice about a case that is or may be filed in a court.

Maryland Business Occupations and Professions Code, §10-101(h).

Finally, some jurisdictions define the practice of law in a court rule.

> "Practice of Law" means the provision of professional legal advice or services where there is a client relationship of trust or reliance. One is presumed to be practicing law when engaging in any of the following conduct on behalf of another:
>
> (A) Preparing any legal document, including any deeds, mortgages, assignments, discharges, leases, trust instruments or any other instruments affecting interests in real or personal property, wills, codicils, instruments affecting the disposition of property of decedents' estates, other instruments intended to affect or secure legal rights, and contracts except routine agreements incidental to a regular course of business;
> (B) Preparing or expressing legal opinions;
> (C) Appearing or acting as an attorney in any tribunal;
> (D) Preparing any claims, demands or pleadings of any kind, or any written documents containing legal arguments or interpretation of law, for filing in any court or administrative tribunal;
> (E) Providing advice or counsel as to how any of the activities described in subparagraph (A) through (D) might be done, or whether they were done, in accordance with applicable law;
> (F) Furnishing an attorney or attorneys, or other persons, to render the services described in subparagraphs (a) through (c) above.

Rules of the District of Columbia Court of Appeals, Rule 49(b)(2).

C. Attorney's Responsibility to Prevent the Unauthorized Practice of Law

Rules that prohibit the unauthorized practice of law do not affect only nonlawyer legal service providers who deal directly with the public. Ample opportunity exists in a traditional legal setting for a nonlawyer—especially a paralegal—employed by a lawyer to overstep the accepted boundaries into the practice of law. See the *Morin* case at the end of this chapter for an example.

Lawyers are obligated by various rules not to aid the unauthorized practice of law. In many states, a statute prohibits a lawyer from aiding unauthorized practice. In others, the ethical codes contain such a restriction. See ABA Model Rules of Professional Conduct (ABA Model Rules) 5.5(b); ABA Model Code DR 3-101(A).

This prohibition makes attorneys responsible for the training of, supervision of, and delegation of legal work to the nonlawyers whom they employ. The obligation of adequate supervision applies to all areas of ethics—such as confidentiality, conflicts, and competence—but carries special force in the area of unauthorized practice. Cases interpreting Rule 5.5 and comparable provisions make clear that lawyers are responsible for the actions of their nonlawyer assistants, including actions that constitute UPL. Forming a partnership with a nonlawyer and dividing legal fees with a nonlawyer are also forbidden under this restriction. Chapter 7 discusses these topics further.

Rule 5.3 of the ABA Model Rules entitled Responsibilities Regarding Nonlawyer Assistants had no predecessor in the ABA Model Code. It presumably was included in the newer Model Rules in recognition of the increased use of nonlawyer assistants in the law firm. It states that a lawyer is responsible for making "reasonable efforts to ensure that the [nonlawyer assistant's] conduct is compatible with the professional obligations of the lawyer." The comment to Rule 5.3 speaks to the lawyer's duty to instruct and supervise assistants, especially with regard to confidentiality, responsibility for work product, and the nondelegable fiduciary responsibility for client trust accounts.

Guideline 1 of the ABA Model Guidelines for the Utilization of Legal Assistant Services (ABA Model Guidelines) phrases this responsibility a bit differently, stating that a lawyer is "responsible for all of the professional actions of a legal assistant performing . . . services at the lawyer's direction. . . ." The comment to Guideline 1 notes the attorney's duty to employ and delegate work to legal assistants who are competent for the task. Most state guidelines refer to the lawyer's responsibility for legal assistants' conduct; the comment to Guideline 1 cites several of these states' guidelines.

Guideline 2 provides an expansive definition of the permissible functions of a legal assistant by prohibiting lawyers from delegating to legal assistants only "those tasks proscribed to one not licensed as a lawyer by statute, administrative rule or regulation, controlling authority, the ABA Model Rules of Professional Conduct, or these Guidelines."

See also Guidelines 2, 4, and 5 of the NALA Model Standards and Guidelines for the Utilization of Legal Assistants, Canons 1 through 5 of the NALA Code of Ethics and Professional Responsibility, and Canon 7 of the NFPA Model Code of Ethics and Professional Responsibility, all found in this book's Appendix.

The following sections of Chapter 3 cover the areas in which unauthorized practice most directly affects legal assistants.

D. What Constitutes the Unauthorized Practice of Law

1. Court Appearances

The one lawyering function that universally has been considered exclusive to licensed attorneys is the representation of a client in court proceedings. You will recall from the brief history of unauthorized practice at the beginning of this chapter that this was the first kind of restriction placed on nonlawyer practitioners in the early days of the United States.

The rationale for this rule is strongly supported by the avowed purposes of unauthorized practice rules generally. Presumably, a court appearance, especially an adversarial one such as a pre-trial motion or a trial, requires knowledge and skills that only a lawyer possesses by virtue of long and specialized education, training, and experience. Many would say that appearing in court on behalf of a client represents the highest use of an attorney's professional judgment and skills. In addition to benefiting from an attorney's special competence, the client is protected by ethical rules to which only an attorney is bound on matters relating to attorney-client privilege, conflicts of interest, and confidentiality. A court appearance is the legal event that decides a client's rights and responsibilities; he or she deserves the best protection and most highly qualified representation at this critical moment. Further, incompetent representation in court damages not only the client, but the administration of justice as well.

Despite the clear rules and strong rationale for these prohibitions on the nonlawyer's role in court-related matters, a few notable exceptions do exist. Perhaps most important is the general rule of self-representation. The right of self-representation in federal courts is guaranteed by statute. 28 U.S.C. § 1654 (1948). Any doubt about the constitutional right to represent oneself in state court was resolved in *Faretta v. California,* 422 U.S. 806 (1975). However, cases in federal and several state courts have determined that the right to self-representation does not encompass a right to be represented by a nonlawyer.

Some states have carved out narrow exceptions for the marital relationship. A California statute, for instance, permits one nonlawyer spouse to represent the other if both are joined as defendants in the same case and are appearing pro se. Cal. Code of Civ. Proc. §371. However, parents cannot generally represent their children in actions before the courts nor can a nonlawyer plaintiff represent other nonlawyer co-plaintiffs.

All jurisdictions have rules permitting law students to engage in limited practice under lawyer supervision, and nearly all allow law students to represent clients in court. This exception has been created for the dual purposes of providing practical training for law students and increasing the availability of legal services. Rules governing law student practice vary from jurisdiction to jurisdiction. Most states' rules identify specific qualifications that the law student must meet, require certification of the student by the law school dean and attorney-sponsor, and impose strict limitations on the kind of court appearances that the law student may make without being accompanied by the supervising attorney.

In some local jurisdictions, legal assistants are allowed to make appearances for their attorney-employers in uncontested matters. A growing number of enlightened state courts permit such appearances under local court rules, including courts in the states of Indiana and Washington. For example, Seattle-King County, Washington, Court Rule 54(f)(4) permits legal assistants who are registered with the local bar association to present stipulated, ex parte and uncontested orders in court when such orders are based solely on the documents in the record. Legal assistants must have six months of work experience with an attorney, must devote at least half their work time to paralegal tasks, and must have a certificate from an ABA-approved program or the equivalent.

2.   Depositions

The rationale for prohibiting nonlawyer representation in court appearances extends to another aspect of the litigation process: the taking of depositions. In a *deposition,* one of the key discovery tools, the attorney asks questions in person of an opposing or a third party. The responses are given orally under oath and are recorded by a court reporter/stenographer, who then produces a transcript of the questions and answers.

A deposition may be introduced in court. It carries the same weight as testimony given under oath in court. This testimony may be used as trial to impeach the credibility of a witness or party, or in lieu of direct testimony if the deponent is no longer available.

The attorney's role in representing a client being deposed includes making objections to questions on evidentiary grounds and preserving these objections for the record. Typically, objections are based on relevancy or privilege. The attorney who is deposing a party or witness is performing a task similar to that of direct examination in a trial and therefore must be familiar with the complex rules of evidence.

During a deposition, the attorney wants to learn as much as possible about the facts of the case from the opposition's or witness's perspective, especially if there is information that weakens the opponent's case. This requires not only a full understanding of the factual and legal issues, but highly developed skills in phrasing questions so as to elicit candid and thorough responses, perhaps beyond those the party intends to reveal.

It is a well-accepted principle that legal assistants may not conduct a deposition. Although rarely challenged, one state has issued an ethics opinion on the question. In Opinion 87-127 (1987), the Pennsylvania ethics committee said that a lawyer may not allow a legal assistant to conduct a deposition even where the legal assistant has a series of attorney-approved questions. The basis for this opinion was that the legal assistant would not be qualified to answer any questions that might arise and may be called on to give legal advice. In 1996, the Iowa Bar issued a similar opinion indicating that paralegals may not ask questions at a deposition even when supervised by an attorney. (Iowa Bar Ethics Opinion 96-3.)

Legal assistants play an active role in the discovery and trial phases of the litigation process. Legal assistants are often the factual experts in cases and, as such, work with attorneys in preparing for depositions by assisting in identifying areas of questioning. Many legal assistants help to prepare clients for the experience of being deposed or testifying at trial. Some accompany clients to independent medical examinations. It is common for legal assistants to attend depositions and trials, taking notes, assisting with the introduction of evidence, and otherwise handling last-minute details or unanticipated matters that arise during trial.

In a Missouri case, a judge upheld the right of a legal assistant to attend a deposition with her supervising attorney and to assist similarly at trial. However, in an unusual case in South Dakota, a federal court judge issued an order prohibiting paralegals and other nonlawyer personnel from sitting at counsel table except by special prior permission.

The majority of legal assistants work in the litigation area. They find themselves involved in all phases of the litigation process, from legal research and drafting of pleadings and motions through the discovery process (including preparing and answering interrogatories, handling subpoenas duces tecum and document productions) and trial preparation to settlement, trial, and post-judgment matters.

3.   Pleadings

In addition to being restricted from representing clients in court and taking depositions, paralegals cannot sign a pleading or other document filed with the court on behalf of the client. A *pleading* constitutes a written "appearance" in court that only a licensed attorney can undertake.

4. Giving Legal Advice

A closely related but broader function within the exclusive purview of licensed attorneys is giving legal advice. This is one of three areas under the umbrella of the attorney-client relationship that the ABA Model Guidelines specifically prohibit a lawyer from delegating to a legal assistant. See Guideline 3 and comment. This prohibition against giving legal advice has its foundation in the same precepts as the prohibition against court appearances by nonlawyers. Formulating a substantive legal opinion that will guide a client's conduct is one of the most important and critical functions an attorney undertakes. The attorney's advice lies at the heart of his or her value in society and to the client. Arriving at the advice requires the application of the attorney's knowledge of law gained through formal education and experience, judgmental and analytical abilities, and understanding of the client's situation, context, and goals. Ethical Consideration 3-5 of the ABA Model Code perhaps states it best:

> [T]he essence of the professional judgment of the lawyer is his educated ability to relate the general body and philosophy of law to a specific legal problem of a client; and thus, the public interest will be better served if only lawyers are permitted to act in matters involving professional judgment.

The task of defining what constitutes giving legal advice is perhaps only slightly easier than defining the practice of law. At a minimum, any such definition would have to include: (1) directing a client how to proceed in a matter that potentially has legal consequences, and/or (2) explaining to a client his or her legal rights and responsibilities. The New Mexico Guidelines for the Use of Legal Assistant Services provide one excellent definition:

> Some activities which would involve the unauthorized practice of law if undertaken by the legal assistant include: (a) independently recommending a course of conduct or a particular action to a client; (b) evaluating for or speculating with a client on the probable outcome of litigation, negotiations or other proposed action; (c) independently outlining rights or obligations to a client; and, (d) independently interpreting statutes, decisions or legal documents to a client.

New Mexico Supreme Court Rules, 20-103.

In practice, many legal assistants and other nonlawyers in legal settings have frequent contact with clients, which opens the door to potential problems. Legal assistants often cite client contact as an area of their work that affords considerable job satisfaction. That an important role for legal assistants is acting as liaison with clients deserves no argument. The benefits to the firm and the client are many. Paralegals are often easier to reach by telephone than attorneys who are frequently unavailable because they are in court or meetings. Since most paralegals enjoy client contact, they may be more patient with clients than attorneys, especially with clients who need a lot of attention. Legal assistants are usually less likely than lawyers to use legal jargon and may be able to explain matters more clearly in simple language. Finally, it is more cost-efficient for the client and the firm to have the client speak with a legal assistant rather than a lawyer.

It is not uncommon for a client to develop an especially strong rapport with a legal assistant who works with the client over time, and for the client to ask questions of the legal assistant that would require the legal assistant to give legal advice in response. That the legal assistant may know the answer to the question further exacerbates this dilemma. To avoid breaching the rule, clearly the legal assistant must first consult with the attorney before relaying this advice to the client. The legal assistant may communicate such advice so long as it is the advice of the attorney. It must be the exact legal opinion of the attorney, however, without expansion or interpretation by the legal assistant.

One state ethics opinion is particularly instructive. The Michigan Bar emphasizes in its ethics opinion RI-128 (1992) that an attorney cannot avoid all client contact by delegating to the legal assistant responsibility for all fact gathering and drafting. Attorneys must maintain a "direct" relationship with clients and must exercise independent professional judgment. Overdelegation of client relations creates great potential for ethical problems to arise, especially if a client becomes dissatisfied.

One major exception to the prohibition against nonattorneys giving legal advice has been created in the criminal area for so-called jailhouse lawyers. In *Johnson v. Avery*, 393 U.S. 484 (1969), the Supreme Court held that a state may not bar inmates from helping one another to prepare post-conviction writs unless the state provides a reasonable alternative. However, it should be remembered that communications between persons and their nonlawyer advisors are not protected by the attorney-client privilege. This important proviso applies to all nonlawyer representatives. Courts have consistently refused to extend the privilege to communications between nonlawyers of all kinds and their "clients" or "customers."

The prohibition against nonlawyers giving legal advice has also been the basis for challenges to do-it-yourself legal kits, typing services, and independent paralegals. After years of state litigation over whether the sale of kits (such as divorce kits or books and forms to assist in preparing one's own will) is unauthorized practice, a few general rules have emerged. The kits and form books themselves do *not* constitute the unauthorized practice of law as long as they are not sold in conjunction with direct personalized assistance in completing the forms or procedures. This rule should extend to new methods of disseminating self-help materials using electronic technology, such as software for individuals handling their own bankruptcies, wills, and business tax matters.

Typing services that type legal documents for lay persons are not engaging in unauthorized practice unless they select forms for the customer or assist the customer in deciding how and what to fill in on the forms. Again, the line here is not always clear in practice and in the future may change with the growth of nonlawyer legal service providers. Read the cases at the end of this chapter for examples of independent nonlawyer legal service providers working on marital dissolutions, bankruptcy, and landlord-tenant matters.

There is a clear nationwide trend toward expanding the role of nonlawyers in providing legal advice to pro se litigants despite the unauthorized practice prohibitions. Most of the progress in this area has come about as the result of legislation that narrowly circumscribes the role of the nonlawyer to a particular area of law in which there is a great need for access to the legal system by persons who cannot afford attorneys and who therefore seek to represent themselves. In California, government-employed small claims advisers are authorized by statute to assist litigants in filling out and filing forms and preparing for trial. (C.C.P. §117.18). California and Maryland legislation permit private nonlawyer practitioners to assist litigants in unlawful detainer/summary eject proceedings. In Washington, court facilitators assist pro se litigants in child support proceedings. A similar program exists in Arizona and has been proposed in Vermont. Proposed legislation in several states allows nonlawyers to help pro se litigants in courts of limited jurisdiction, including small claims and justice courts. In Arizona, the state has hired paralegals to assist prisoners in preparing their habeas corpus writs since it is less expensive than providing a full law library to serve the prisons.

Finally, technological advances that are being used to increase access to legal information are posing new challenges to the traditional notions of what it means to give legal advice. A user-friendly computer program has been set up in kiosks in courthouses in several states, including California, Colorado, Florida, and Arizona. This program enables users to prepare court-approved forms in domestic relations, small claims, and landlord-tenant matters. Users answer a series of questions, and forms and instructions are printed out.

A related issue is the propriety of the dispensing of legal advice on electronic bulletin boards. Giving out general legal information, such as that given in a newspaper column on law, is not only considered ethical but is encouraged by ethics codes. However, advice that is too specific, incomplete, or inaccurate for another jurisdiction raises questions about the unauthorized practice of law as well as the attorney-client relationship and competence. These issues will undoubtedly be dealt with by the bar as the use of this technology spreads throughout society.

See the cases at the end of this chapter for examples of actual prosecutions or disciplinary actions for unauthorized practice/legal advice.

E. Paralegal Tasks That May Constitute the Unauthorized Practice of Law

Throughout this chapter, a number of legal tasks have been discussed as falling within or outside the boundaries of the unauthorized practice of law. Since the concept of unauthorized practice is somewhat amorphous and varies with time and place, creating a definitive list of functions that fall on either side of the boundary is not really possible. Such a list is likely to be quickly outdated or to be inaccurate for one locale or another.

1. General Guidelines

However, some general guidelines may help legal assistants who are faced with decisions about whether or not to perform a specific function. As indicated in the beginning of this chapter, a good general rule is the expansive one stated as follows in Guideline 2 of ABA Model Guidelines.

> Provided the lawyer maintains responsibility for the work product, a lawyer may delegate to a legal assistant any task normally performed by the lawyer except those tasks proscribed to one not licensed as a lawyer by statute, administrative rule or regulation, controlling authority, the ABA Model Rules of Professional Conduct, or these Guidelines.

The comment to this guideline discusses in some detail the importance of appropriate attorney supervision and lists the few functions traditionally forbidden to nonlawyers and discussed earlier in this chapter: representing

59

a client in a court proceeding (unless court rules authorize it), taking a deposition, and giving legal advice.

Guideline 3 cites three functions that a lawyer may not delegate:

What Paralegals Can not do!

A lawyer may not delegate to a legal assistant:

(a) Responsibility for establishing an attorney-client relationship.
(b) Responsibility for establishing the amount of a fee to be charged for a legal service.
(c) Responsibility for publishing a legal opinion to a client.

Guideline 3(c) is another way of saying that a legal assistant may not give legal advice; (a) and (b) relate to the responsibility of the lawyer to establish and maintain a direct relationship with a client. As noted in the comment to Guideline 3, the attorney-client relationship and fee arrangements between attorney and client are sacrosanct.* The ABA Model Rules and the predecessor Model Code both emphasize early on the importance of the attorney-client relationship. As noted in the comment, the NALA Model Standards and Guidelines and most state guidelines on working with legal assistants make reference to these matters. See NALA Guideline VI.1; NALA Code of Ethics Canon 3.

Some states provide lists of the kinds of tasks paralegals typically perform. (Some of these are cited in the comment to Guideline 2 of the ABA Model Guidelines.) NALA and NFPA also have lists of paralegal job functions. A short summary list not specific to any particular area of practice might read as follows:

Role of Paralegals

1. conduct legal and factual research and investigation;
2. draft memoranda, pleadings, and other legal documents;
3. prepare standard form documents;
4. prepare correspondence for attorney and legal assistant signature;
5. interview clients and witnesses, and act as liaison with clients and others outside the firm;
6. organize, analyze, and summarize legal documents;
7. file documents with courts and government agencies;
8. handle procedural, administrative, and scheduling matters.

---

*One distinction that needs to be made is between "setting" fees and "quoting" fees. Many state guidelines as well as the NALA Code and Guidelines prohibit legal assistants from "setting fees" or "accepting cases." This prohibition does not preclude a legal assistant from quoting standard fees to a prospective client or client, with the provision that only the attorney can actually contract with the client for legal services and determine the fee that will be charged to handle a client's case.

60

While there is little dispute over the appropriateness of legal assistants performing the above functions under attorney supervision, other very specialized tasks or functions have presented special ethical issues for legal assistants and the lawyers who utilize their services, as the rest of this section describes.

2. Will Executions

A *will execution* is a relatively simple but critical step in the process of estate planning. Whether by case law or statute, very specific rules exist in every state about the signing and witnessing of wills, including the number of witnesses, their relationship to the person(s) making the will, and their presence during the signing. In an early ethics opinion, the New York State Bar Association recommended against legal assistants handling these proceedings on their own. NYSBA Ethics Opinion 74-343 concludes that the delegation of the task of supervising a will execution is "tantamount" to "counseling a client" and constitutes the practice of law. The new Connecticut Guidelines for Lawyers Who Employ or Retain Legal Assistants indicate that a legal assistant may "attend will executions and act as a witness but may not provide legal advice. . . ."

Most states do not address the matter directly but some, such as Rhode Island in its Supreme Court Provisional Order No. 18 (1983) Guideline II, include among the permissible paralegal functions witnessing the execution of documents in general language. Others, like Colorado, include witnessing will executions in the job description adopted for an estate planning paralegal. See *In re Morin* at the end of this chapter for an example of the problems that arise when wills are not properly executed.

3. Real Estate Closings

Likewise, some states prohibit attorneys from allowing a legal assistant to appear at a real estate closing without the supervising lawyer present. For example, the Illinois State Bar Association reaffirmed its earlier opinion in a 1984 position paper with the following language:

> Attorney assistants may attend real estate closings of all types, but only in the company of the employing attorney and at such closings prepare computations, revisions of agreements and perform similar tasks, but only at the direction of, and under the supervision of, the employing attorney.

Position Paper of the Illinois State Bar Association Real Estate Section Council and Unauthorized Practice of Law Committee Re: Use of Attorney Assistants in Real Estate Transactions, Approved by the State Bar Board of Governors, May 16, 1984.

The rationale for this prohibition is that the legal assistant is likely to be asked by the client for legal advice, particularly for an explanation of the meaning and legal consequences of the various legal documents that must be signed. In addition, there is always the potential for last-minute disputes to arise over terms, such disputes requiring the services of the attorneys to resolve. A legal assistant who gives legal advice by means of explaining the legal consequences of documents or attempting to resolve a dispute over terms would likely be engaging in the unauthorized practice of law.

These concerns are addressed by bar association opinions that endorse the use of legal assistants to attend real estate closings unaccompanied by a lawyer. For example, in an advisory opinion issued in 1989, the Florida Bar stated that "[a] law firm may permit a paralegal or other trained employee to handle a real estate closing at which no lawyer in the firm is present if certain conditions are met." Florida Professional Ethics Committee Advisory Opinion 89-5 (1989). The conditions listed in the opinion include attorney supervision and review up to the time of the closing; attorney availability to give advice during the closing if needed; client consent; a determination that the closing will be purely ministerial and that the client understands the documents in advance; and a prohibition against the legal assistant giving legal advice or making legal decisions during the closing. The Florida bar believes that imposing these limitations on the functions of a legal assistant during a real estate closing protects the client's interests adequately and prevents the unauthorized practice of law.

The Virginia State Bar Unauthorized Practice of Law Committee issued a similar opinion in 1991 (Opinion No. 47), in which it endorsed the use of paralegal support companies providing real estate closing services under the supervision of attorneys. The opinion details specifically the division of functions in such a matter between the attorney and the paralegal. In 1995 and 1996, three bar associations issued opinions that are in accord with Virginia's and Florida's analyses, pointing to a trend to expand paralegal duties in this area of law practice. (See New York State Bar Association Ethics Opinion 95-677, Wisconsin Ethics Opinion 95-3, and Connecticut Bar Association Ethics Opinion 96-14.) In a contradictory ruling in Massachusetts, a court held that a closing company could not provide similar services; however, in this case, the company in question was providing services directly to the public as well as to attorneys.

4. Personal Injury Settlements

Special mention also needs to be made about one paralegal function that is fairly common in personal injury practices—negotiating settlements. Legal assistants in these firms frequently handle all the documentation of a case, typically called "working up" the case. This includes collecting medical bills, assisting the client with medical insurance claims, and discussing the case with insurance claims adjusters. The legal assistant often has extensive contact with adjusters and provides information on the nature of the client's injuries, his or her treatment, and property damage. The adjuster makes offers to settle to the legal assistant. The legal assistant, of course, must pass these offers on to the attorney, who discusses with the client whether or not to accept an offer. The legal assistant may, in turn, relay the decision to accept or reject to the adjuster and handle follow-up negotiations or settlement paperwork. But the legal assistant may not accept a settlement offer on behalf of a client, even if he or she knows that it is an offer the client should or will accept.

REVIEW QUESTIONS

1. When were the first rules limiting the practice of law passed in the United States? What did the rules limit? What were the purposes of these rules?
2. What was the role of bar associations in limiting the practice of law to licensed attorneys? Describe the ABA's Statements of Principle entered into with other professional associations. What happened to them?
3. What kinds of legal functions do most nonlawyer legal service providers perform? Whom do they serve? What areas of law do they work in?
4. Give the most complete and accurate definition of the practice of law that you can.
5. What are all the potential consequences of engaging in the unauthorized practice of law?
6. What are an attorney's responsibilities to prevent the unauthorized practice of law? What might happen to an attorney whose legal assistant engages in the practice of law?
7. Make a list of the specific functions that constitute the practice of law and are prohibited to legal assistants. What rationale lies behind each prohibition?
8. What are the exceptions to the general rule against a nonlawyer appearing in court on behalf of a client?

9. Give your best definition of what constitutes giving legal advice. Why are nonlawyers prohibited from giving legal advice?
10. What are two exceptions to the general prohibition against giving legal advice?
11. Does selling a self-help divorce kit constitute giving legal advice? What about answering legal questions on the Internet? Why, or why not?
12. What kinds of work can legal typing services perform without stepping into the area of unauthorized practice of law?
13. Why are legal assistants prohibited from setting legal fees? From accepting a case?
14. May a legal assistant supervise a will execution without an attorney present? Why, or why not?
15. May a legal assistant handle a real estate closing without the supervising attorney present? Why, or why not?
16. What titles do nonlawyer legal service providers use?
17. Are prosecutions for unauthorized practice of law increasing or decreasing? Why?
18. What are some of the functions that a lawyer may not delegate to a legal assistant?

DISCUSSION QUESTIONS

1. Make a list of all the reasons you can think of for limiting the practice of law to licensed attorneys. Next, list all the functions that are prohibited to nonlawyers. Do you agree that only licensed attorneys should be able to perform these functions? Why, or why not? How would you revise the unauthorized practice of law restrictions in view of their purposes?
2. Do you think that a sole practitioner lawyer who has ten legal assistants working in her or his office can adequately supervise these legal assistants? What office procedures and policies might ensure adequate supervision? What if the lawyer is in court every day and only spends a few hours a week in the office?
3. Do you think that an attorney who hires a legal assistant without any formal paralegal training is violating his or her duty to supervise? Why, or why not? Might this be appropriate or inappropriate depending on the circumstances? What factors would you consider in deciding?
4. Interview five litigation paralegals in your area and ask them what kinds of tasks they perform. Find out if they attend trials and depositions with the attorneys for whom they work.

5. Why should law students and not legal assistants be permitted to represent clients in court?

6. Based on *Faretta v. California,* do you think a constitutional argument could be made that citizens should be able to choose their representative in court, even if that person is a nonlawyer? Try to formulate that proposition and then develop the arguments against it.

7. Since it is essential for lawyers to have a direct relationship with their clients, and legal assistants are prohibited from giving legal advice, why are legal assistants allowed to have any client contact? Why do you think legal assistants like client contact?

8. Which of the following acts by a legal assistant would be permissible and which prohibited under the definitions of legal advice given in this chapter:

   a. interviewing a client to obtain the facts relating to an automobile accident;

   b. telling the client that the firm probably would be able to get a $10,000 recovery;

   c. explaining to the client what happens at a deposition;

   d. explaining to the client the meaning of an affidavit given to the client for signature;

   e. telling a client that his or her case is likely to settle;

   f. telling a client that he or she would be best off to file a small claims action;

   g. answering a client's questions about the meaning of terms in a contract;

   h. giving a client the legal opinion that she or he knows the attorney would give;

   i. relaying a message from the attorney to the client, which tells the client that it is okay to sign a contract.

9. Could you use *Johnson v. Avery* to make an argument that poor people who don't have access to legal services have a right to legal advice from whomever they choose unless the state provides an alternative? Is this argument convincing? Why, or why not?

10. The cases that hold self-help kits not to be prohibited by unauthorized practice of law statutes also hold that helping customers to use those kits does violate unauthorized practice of law statutes. Do you think this an appropriate place to draw this line? Do the *Brumbaugh* and *Furman* cases help you to see the difficulty of drawing the line here? Find out what happened when the Texas UPL Committee investigated Nolo Press.

11. What do you think the policy reasons are for permitting nonlawyers to give legal advice in small claims or unlawful detainer cases and

65

not in other kinds of legal matters? How do you reconcile this exception with the policy reasons why nonlawyers are prohibited from giving legal advice?

12. In a personal injury law firm that takes every case that comes to it and that charges the same contingency fee, why should it be necessary for the lawyer to set the fee and establish the relationship with the client? Should this be an ethical rule, or is it really a matter of good practice? Suppose the initial contact between the attorney and client is a five-minute meeting to formalize the relationship and the client never speaks to the attorney again because the legal assistant "works up" the case, negotiates the settlement, and has all the client contact. Is the attorney maintaining a direct relationship with the client? Does the *Lawless* case in Chapter 2 help you to decide?

13. What are the rules governing will executions in your state? Does the state or local bar association have an advisory opinion about legal assistants supervising will executions without the presence of an attorney? Interview three probate/estate planning paralegals and find out what the practice is in their firms.

14. Do parties to residential real estate transactions in your state usually utilize the services of lawyers? If not, who does? If so, are legal assistants who work for real estate lawyers permitted to handle closings without an attorney present? Is it common practice? Does the state or local bar have an opinion about it? Do you find the Illinois or the Florida rule most appropriate? Why?

15. What kinds of tasks not prohibited to legal assistants as unauthorized practice of law do you think might be made permissible in the future?

16. Has your state studied the problem of providing access to legal services?

F. Practice before Administrative Agencies

Administrative agencies are created by state and federal legislatures to provide for the regulation of certain highly specialized fields. A few examples of administrative agencies are the Immigration and Naturalization Service and Patent Office at the federal level, and workers' compensation, unemployment insurance, public utility and disability boards at the state level. Many administrative agencies handle an extremely large volume of cases that do not require much more than a mechanical application of rules.

The volume of cases and the specialized nonlegal subject matter involved make it impractical and inefficient to adjudicate disputes in these fields through regular court procedures.

Administrative agencies are quasi-judicial in nature, meaning that disputes before these agencies are resolved through a hearing similar to though less formal than a trial, before an administrative law judge or hearing officer or examiner, with advocates representing the parties. Procedures include the issuance of subpoenas, testimony under oath, admission of evidence, and oral and written arguments.

From even this brief description of administrative agencies, it should be fairly clear why practice before administrative agencies would constitute the practice of law without some specific exception carved out for it. Someone representing a client before an administrative agency requires the same or similar skills to those required of an attorney representing a client in a trial. The representative must have knowledge of the law and of the procedures used by the agency; must be able to apply this knowledge to the specific facts and context of the case, using the proper analytical and judgmental abilities in doing so; and must be able to advocate the client's case competently in an adversarial setting. While the area of law might be narrower and the rules of evidence and procedure more informal than in a court, the functions of the advocate-representative and the skills necessary for success in this setting are similar to a trial lawyer's.

Despite the similarities described above, lawyers and the organized bar have not fought very hard to keep administrative agencies within the exclusive domain of the practice of law. Why? The answer that many experts give is that most cases held before administrative agencies, especially those typically handled by nonlawyers, are small cases involving individuals from lower-income brackets and in which little money—by most lawyers' standards—is at stake. The fees in such cases are small and provide little economic incentive for a turf battle over unauthorized practice.

The federal government has long permitted nonlawyer practice before many of its administrative agencies. The purpose of doing so is twofold; to allow easy access to these agencies and to make the process as informal, efficient, and inexpensive as possible. The Administrative Procedure Act, 5 U.S.C. §555 (b) (1994), specifically authorizes individual federal administrative agencies to permit nonlawyer practice. It states that persons compelled to appear before an agency may be "accompanied, represented, and advised by counsel or, if permitted by the agency, by other qualified representative."

This provision leaves the decision about nonlawyer practice to the agency itself. Some agencies have set very specific criteria (for example, a specific degree such as a J.D., or a license as a lawyer or certified public accountant, the recommendation of others admitted to practice, or an exam that must be passed) for nonlawyers to practice before them. A few such federal agencies are the U.S. Patent Office, Internal Revenue Service, and Interstate Commerce Commission. Other agencies allow all nonlawyer representatives without requiring them to meet any specific standards. Examples of these agencies include the National Labor Relations Board, Small Business Administration, Social Security Administration, and Bureau of Indian Affairs.

There is no consistency among the states about nonlawyer practice before administrative agencies. Some state statutes authorize representation by nonlawyers before state administrative agencies and some do not. In states that have a strong judicial history supporting the inherent power of the court to oversee the practice of law, legislation authorizing nonlawyer practice before state administrative agencies has been struck down. See, for example, *Denver Bar Association v. P.U.C.*, 154 Colo. 273, 391 P.2d 467 (1964) and an opinion of the Illinois State Bar Association, which holds that employers cannot utilize nonattorney representatives in termination hearings held before the Illinois Department of Employment Security. An unusual way of limiting nonlawyer representation without actually banning it was adopted by the California legislature, which allows nonlawyers to appear before the Workers' Compensation Appeals Board but does not allow nonlawyers to collect fees. (California Labor Code Sections 4903 and 5710.) Finally, recall the case in Chapter 1, *UPL Committee v. State Department of Workers' Compensation*, at page 11, in which the court upheld legislation that created a job for nonlawyer advisors to assist persons filing claims.

Further debate revolves around whether or not paralegals employed by attorneys may represent clients before state administrative agencies that allow nonlawyer representation. Representing one view, an ethics opinion of the State Bar of California provides that "a law firm may delegate authority to a paralegal employee, provided that the employee is adequately supervised, to make appearances at Workers' Compensation Appeals Board hearings. . . ." Advisory Opinion 88-103 (1988).

Other states agree. In Michigan. Ethics Opinion RI-125 (1992) states that legal assistants employed by attorneys may appear before administrative proceedings where other nonlawyers may do so, and that the supervising attorney remains responsible for the legal assistant's conduct and work product. And in Alaska the bar reversed itself after first issuing an ethics opinion advising attorneys not to allow their legal assistants to represent clients in workers' compensation hearings. (See Ethics Opinion 84-7 (1984), later reversed.)

In addition to the lack of consistency among the states about allowing nonlawyer practice before their administrative agencies, there is a conflict between the states' authority to regulate the practice of law and the federal government's authority over its administrative agencies. The key case of *Sperry v. Florida,* 373 U.S. 379 (1963), would seem to have resolved this conflict when it held that the U.S. Patent Office regulations authorizing nonlawyer practice prevail over state law by virtue of the U.S. Constitution's Supremacy Clause. However, unauthorized practice charges are still brought occasionally against nonlawyer practitioners who appear before federal agencies. See *Unauthorized Practice Committee, State Bar of Texas v. Cortez,* 692 S.W.2d 47 (Tex. 1985).

G. Disclosure of Status as Legal Assistant and Job Titles

One of the main functions of many legal assistants is acting as liaison to persons outside the law firm—clients, witnesses, opposing law firms, courts, and so forth. This contact may take the form of telephone conversations, correspondence, or meetings in person. A key ethical aspect of the liaison role is ensuring that the person with whom the legal assistant is dealing is fully aware that the legal assistant is not a lawyer.

The discussion of disclosure of one's status as a legal assistant is appropriate in this chapter on unauthorized practice of law for two reasons. First, a nonlawyer may appear to be engaging in unauthorized practice if he or she seems to others to be an attorney. Not clearly identifying one's status as a legal assistant may mislead the other party into believing that the legal assistant is a lawyer. It is not difficult to see how someone, especially a lay person such as a client or witness, could misconstrue the status of a legal assistant if the legal assistant "sounds" like an attorney. To the other person, a paralegal's inadvertent lack of disclosure may appear to be intentional. If this conduct by the legal assistant later creates problems, the legal assistant could be charged with holding himself or herself out as an attorney. This claim could give rise under many state laws to a criminal charge of unauthorized practice of law against the legal assistant, against the legal assistant's attorney-employer, or both. (In many jurisdictions, misrepresenting oneself as an attorney is itself a misdemeanor.) Disciplinary action against the attorney may also arise, as state ethics codes all have rules prohibiting attorneys from aiding in the unauthorized practice of law. See ABA Model Rule 5.5; ABA Model Code DR 3-101.

The second reason that disclosure of the legal assistant's status relates to the unauthorized practice of law is that a legal assistant who is mistaken for an attorney may be called on to perform functions that are tantamount to unauthorized practice of law. If a client mistakenly believes that a legal assistant is an attorney, the client may ask for legal advice. This places the legal assistant in the uncomfortable position of having to backtrack in the conversation to explain his or her status and how that status makes giving a legal opinion unethical.

Guideline 4 of the ABA Model Guidelines holds attorneys responsible for informing clients and others that the legal assistant is not licensed to practice law. The comment to this guideline mentions several means by which this may be accomplished, including attorney communication orally or in writing to the third party and legal assistant disclosure. Most state guidelines on legal assistant utilization also cover disclosure. Many of the guidelines speak of "routine, early disclosure" or disclosure at the "outset" of the communication with the third party. Those guidelines that explain the rationale of this rule speak in terms of avoiding confusion or avoiding the misleading of clients or the public.

At least one state, New Mexico, specifically prohibits the use of the title "associate" for a legal assistant because law firms commonly use this title to identify their attorneys. "Legal assistant" and "paralegal" are the most commonly used titles, although their use and shades of meaning vary across the country. The Alabama Bar uses the titles "nonlawyer assistant" and "nonlawyer paralegal." Rhode Island Ethics Opinion 92-6 (1992) advises that the term "legal assistant" be used rather than "paralegal" to avoid confusion.

While the titles "legal assistant" and "paralegal" are usually used interchangeably, they carry different connotations in some regions of the country and one or the other appellation may be preferred within the local paralegal community. Frequently, a legal specialty is attached to one of these titles to indicate more specifically the area of practice in which the legal assistant works, for instance, probate legal assistant or litigation paralegal. As legal assistants have become more specialized and firms have developed career paths for them, new titles have been created, such as senior legal assistant and litigation support specialist. As a general rule, any title that does not potentially mislead a third party into believing that the legal assistant is an attorney is permissible.

One interesting twist on this rule is that in the state of Iowa, legal assistants may *not* sign correspondence using the title Certified Legal Assistant even though they are certified by the National Association of Legal Assistants (NALA). The Iowa ethics committee believes that using such a title may mislead clients and the public into believing that the legal assistant is state-licensed. Iowa State Bar Ethics Opinions 88-5 (1988) and 88-19 (1989). This opinion has been challenged by NALA.

Mississippi's and New York's bars arrived at the opposite conclusion to Iowa and held that the Certified Legal Assistant designation can be used on letterhead. (See Mississippi Ethics Opinion 95-223 and New York State Bar Association Ethics Opinion 97-695.) And in another twist, New York issued an opinion endorsing the terms *paralegal* and *senior paralegal,* but finding unacceptable and ambiguous the terms *paralegal coordinator, legal associate, public benefits advocate, family law advocate, housing law advocate, disability benefits advocate* and *public benefit specialist.* Ethics Opinion 64 (54-92) (1992).

It follows from the rule requiring legal assistants to fully disclose their status that the assistants must be able to sign correspondence with their appropriate job title. However, the bar has not always been so clear on this. Many states are silent on the subject, but some—Iowa, Kansas, Michigan, Missouri, New Mexico, North Carolina, and Rhode Island for instance—indicate that a legal assistant may sign correspondence so long as his or her status as a legal assistant is clear. In 1976, the ABA issued an informal ethics opinion that supported the practice, in recognition of the growing use of legal assistants:

> The lawyers' use of assistants to perform specialized tasks . . . is becoming increasingly common, and, indeed essential to the efficient practice of law. The Committee is of the opinion that it is appropriate for Legal Assistants to sign correspondence which is incident to the proper conduct of his or her responsibilities but care should be taken to identify accurately the capacity of the person who signs the letter so that the receiver is not misled.

ABA Comm. on Ethics and Professional Responsibility, Informal Op. 1367 (1976).

Likewise, state rules have varied on the use of business cards by legal assistants and on legal assistants' names being listed on firm letterhead. Business cards represent a special concern to the organized bar beyond the confusion that might be created about the status and permissible functions of a legal assistant. That concern is the unlawful solicitation of clients by legal assistants, discussed further in Chapter 6. In the recent past, many state and local bars balanced the benefits of disclosure from legal assistants having business cards against the risk of cards being used improperly and decided that the risk of unlawful solicitation was too great to permit them. However, most of these opinions were only advisory, and now every state that has addressed this issue permits legal assistants to have business cards so long as their status is clear. The ABA has long supported the use of business cards by legal assistants, as indicated in a 1971 opinion:

The term "legal assistant" appears to be coming into general use as connoting a lay assistant to a lawyer, as evidenced by its use in the title of the American Bar Association's Special Committee on Legal Assistants. . . . Informal Opinion 909 permits the designation on a business card of an employee of a law firm who does investigation work for the firm as an "Investigator." By the same reasoning, it would appear to be proper to designate a legal assistant as such on a business card, provided that the designation is accurate, and the duties involved are properly performed under the direction of the lawyer. . . .

ABA Comm. on Ethics and Professional Responsibility, Informal Op. 1185 (1971).

More troublesome yet has been the listing of legal assistants' names and titles on law firm letterheads. The ABA Model Code (in effect from 1969 to 1980), which had been adopted in whole or in part by nearly all jurisdictions, originally prohibited the listing on an attorney's letterhead of virtually anything other than attorneys' names and the firm's address and phone numbers. ABA Model Code DR 1-102(A)(4) (1969, amended 1980).

The decision of *Bates v. State Bar of Arizona,* 430 U.S. 350 (1977), raised questions about the constitutionality of these restrictions. This case, which appears in Chapter 6 at page 211, held that the state could not impose blanket restrictions on lawyer advertising. In its opinion, the Supreme Court emphasized that consumers need information about legal services in order to make legal services more accessible and to help consumers to select a lawyer.

Because of this case and several that followed it (in particular, see *Zauderer v. Office of Disciplinary Counsel,* 471 U.S. 626 (1985); *Shapero v. Kentucky Bar Association,* 486 U.S. 466 (1988); and *Peel v. Attorney Registration & Disciplinary Commission of Illinois,* 496 U.S. 91 (1990)), all states and the ABA have revised their rules limiting the kind of information that may appear on lawyers' letterheads, in announcements, and the like. Since the early 1980s, several states that had prohibited the listing of legal assistants' names on letterhead have adopted new rules permitting the practice. The states that address this issue and now permit the listing of legal assistants on letterhead include Arizona, Colorado, Connecticut, Florida, Hawaii, Illinois, Indiana, Kentucky, Michigan, Minnesota, Mississippi, Missouri, Nebraska, New Jersey, New York, South Dakota, Texas, Virginia, and Wisconsin. A few states—Georgia, Iowa, and Rhode Island, for instance—have either not reexamined their rules or are holding firm on the prohibition.

The ABA rewrote completely its rules on law firm letterheads for its Model Rules. Rules 7.1 and 7.5 do not prohibit anything from appearing on letterhead except for false and misleading statements that may create unjustified expectations; statements that compare the lawyer's services to another lawyer's; use of a misleading trade name; listing of an attorney holding public office who is not actively practicing with the firm; and anything implying that the attorneys are organized in a certain form if they are not. Finally, a firm with offices in more than one jurisdiction must identify the jurisdictional limits of those not licensed to practice in the jurisdiction where the office is located.

In keeping with the changes wrought by the momentous *Bates* case, the ABA also withdrew several earlier opinions about nonlawyer listings on letterhead and business cards in a 1989 opinion, which reads in part:

> The listing of nonlawyer support personnel on lawyers' letterheads is not prohibited by these [Model Rules 7.1 and 7.5] or any other Rules so long as the listing is not false or misleading. In order to avoid being misleading, the listing must make it clear that the support personnel who are listed are not lawyers. The listing of support personnel, such as the law firm administrator or office manager, administrative assistants, paralegals or others, appropriately designated may furnish useful information to the public in determining whether to engage the firm and in learning the status of members of the support staff with whom they have contact.
>
> A law firm also may list nonlawyer personnel on business cards, written advertisements and the like, provided the designation is not likely to mislead those who see it into thinking that the nonlawyers who are listed are lawyers or exercise control over lawyers in the firm.

ABA Comm. on Ethics and Professional Responsibility, Informal Op. 1527 (1989).

The ABA Model Guidelines also conform to this policy. Guideline 5 states that a lawyer "may identify legal assistants by name and title on the lawyer's letterhead and on business cards identifying the lawyer's firm."

It now seems clear that legal assistants may be listed with appropriate job titles on business cards, letterheads, firm announcements, in a firm newsletter, in telephone directory advertisements or listings, in print advertisements, and so forth. The rule is also likely to cover a listing of names on the door of the law firm and a directory in the lobby of the building in which the law firm is located.

In general, most law firms who have legal assistants on staff do provide them with business cards but do *not* list them on the firm letterhead or in other permissible places. Practice regarding paralegal listings on letterhead varies with the locale, the size of the firm, and the nature of its practice. Small and mid-sized firms are more likely to list legal assistants than are large firms for both practical and firm-culture reasons. Most large law firms do not list all their partners' names on the firm letterhead because they could not possibly do so with the number of partners running into the hundreds. Competition is strong in these firms for symbols of status, and legal assistants have many attorneys in line ahead of them for this kind of recognition. However, many mid-sized and small law firms do list legal assistants on their letterhead. And many firms have individualized letterhead for each attorney and legal assistant.

The NFPA Model Code addresses the issue of disclosure in Canon 6, which requires that titles be fully disclosed. The ethical considerations that follow spell out the details, including the use of titles on business cards, letterhead, brochures, and directories, and in advertisements. Canon 5 of the recently revised NALA Code also requires disclosure "at the outset of any professional relationship. . . ." The National Federation of Paralegal Associations has also issued an informal ethics opinion endorsing the use of paralegals' names on lawyers' letterhead and detailing the history and status of the rules nationwide. (See NFPA Informal Ethics Opinion 95-2.)

H. Legal Assistants as Independent Contractors

1. Background

During the late 1970s and the 1980s, a growing number of legal assistants began to offer their services as *independent contractors,* handling projects for attorneys on an as-needed basis. In the 1970s, most of these *freelance paralegals* worked in the probate area, which lends itself well to the effective use of legal assistants because the probate process is highly structured and procedural. In addition, many firms handle only a small amount of probate work, not enough to warrant having a full-time staff legal assistant to perform the paralegal functions in this specialized area of practice.

Gradually, freelance legal assistants began to offer their services in other areas of practice, especially litigation. Most freelance litigation paralegals became litigation support specialists, focusing on trial preparation, usually in large civil lawsuits. Freelance litigation paralegals assist law firms in organizing the sometimes massive numbers of documents in a case and in summarizing depositions and other documents.

As computers came to be used more effectively in litigation support, freelance paralegals added computer skills to their legal expertise. In some areas of the country, freelancers started their own businesses, hiring a staff of legal assistants and case clerks who worked on the more clerical aspects of this work.

The use of independent contractors in the legal field is not limited to legal assistants. Attorneys and a wide array of support services are now provided to firms in this fashion. The growing use of part-time and freelance workers is a major trend in our economy, and is likely to continue to grow during the rest of this decade.

2.   Advantages

Many legal assistants find that working as an independent contractor opens up an attractive career path. Freelance paralegals are working for themselves in the sense that they are running their own business. Legal assistants with an entrepreneurial spirit find this more rewarding than working the usual 9 to 5 (or longer) for a paycheck. They enjoy the added responsibility of working for themselves, the freedom and flexibility of choosing their own hours, and the power to decline an assignment if they choose. Not least important is the potential to earn top income albeit not without good marketing and public relations and a lot of very hard work.

In areas of the country where freelance paralegals are prevalent, law firms use their services in lieu of hiring additional staff when a new case or project comes into the firm. Many firms prefer using temporary paralegal help for several reasons. Many of the projects commonly given to independent contractors generate an intense amount of work for a limited period of time—a lawsuit that will go to trial or settle within a year, for instance. If a firm adds paralegals and case clerks to its regular staff to handle this work, it must invest the time and human resources in recruiting, training, and supervising; it must pay taxes and benefits; and ultimately it may have to discharge staff when work on the matter ends, a painful process with additional potential legal and financial consequences. A firm that instead hires independent contractors, either individually or through an agency, minimizes these costs. It pays an agreed-upon fee for the services and does not have to concern itself with the tax and other obligations as an employer. Independent contractors are experts in the areas in which they work and therefore require no training and little supervision. Because they are working on a temporary basis and do not expect to stay with the firm, they are not disturbed or disgruntled when the project ends. One final benefit, especially applicable in the case of litigation support, is that the freelance legal assistants generally do the most routine paralegal tasks (for example, sorting, labeling, and stamping documents), which keeps permanent staff legal assistants from having to perform the least challenging work.

3.   Freelance Paralegals and the Unauthorized Practice of Law

Working as a freelance paralegal has ethical ramifications in many areas—such as confidentiality and conflicts of interest—but problems have surfaced as well in the area of unauthorized practice of law. One concern of traditional legal assistants has been clarifying the difference between an independent contractor paralegal who provides legal services to an attorney and a nonattorney who provides legal services directly to the public. The latter often call themselves "independent paralegals," exacerbating the confusion between themselves and the legal assistants who are acting under the supervision of lawyers. This confusion greatly concerns freelance paralegals who work for attorneys as they do not want to find themselves categorized by the organized bar or local prosecutors as independent paralegals, who are subject to prosecution for the unauthorized practice of law and who in the future may be subject to regulation by a state agency.

A related concern arose in the early 1990s out of an ethics opinion in the state of New Jersey. In 1990, the New Jersey Committee on the Unauthorized Practice of Law issued Opinion No. 24, which found that freelance paralegals were engaged in the unauthorized practice of law in violation of state law. The committee found that a lack of adequate supervision was inherent in the relationship between a lawyer and a freelance paralegal. The paralegal community and other bar associations lobbied heavily for a retraction of the opinion and in 1992 the New Jersey Supreme Court modified the opinion, concluding that lawyers were obligated to supervise paralegals, whether as employees or independent contractors. The opinion also indicated that paralegals who found themselves in a situation in which they were not being adequately supervised should "withdraw" from the case. (In re Opinion No. 24 of the Committee on the Unauthorized Practice of Law, May 14, 1992.) Another state, South Carolina, more recently issued an ethics opinion that endorsed the use of freelance paralegal services so long as the lawyer supervises properly, retains responsibility for the work, and discloses the costs to the client. (South Carolina Ethics Opinion 96-13.)

It is clear that the ABA Model Rules of Professional Conduct allow attorneys to use the services of all kinds of independent contractors, including legal assistants. Rule 5.3, which outlines attorneys' ethical responsibilities regarding nonlawyer assistants, specifically includes non-lawyers "retained by" a lawyer as well as those employed by, a lawyer. The comment to Rule 5.3 further emphasizes that assistants may be "independent contractors."

The short history of the paralegal profession has seen a tremendous expansion in the nature of legal tasks that legal assistants perform. The trend is toward continued growth into new areas and functions that neither attorneys nor paralegals might have expected 20 years ago when the profession was just beginning. The pressures to expand the functions performed by supervised legal assistants and to allow some legal services to be delivered directly to the public by nonlawyers will undoubtedly continue. In the coming years, these social and economic forces will change the way we view the practice of law and will redefine the rules prohibiting the practice of law by nonlawyers.

REVIEW QUESTIONS

1. Why are nonlawyers allowed to practice before some administrative agencies?
2. Name five federal agencies that permit nonlawyer practice.
3. Do states allow nonlawyers to represent clients before their administrative agencies?
4. Can legal assistants working under the supervision of a lawyer represent clients before administrative agencies for their attorney-employers?
5. Can a state court prohibit a nonlawyer from practicing before a federal administrative agency within the state on grounds that such representation constitutes the unauthorized practice of law? Why, or why not?
6. Why must legal assistants be careful to disclose their status as a legal assistant?
7. Name three job titles that are appropriate for legal assistants to use in identifying their status. What did the New York bar opinion say about various titles?
8. May legal assistants sign correspondence on firm letterhead? What limitations might be placed on the form and content of such correspondence?

9. May legal assistants have business cards? How should a legal assistant's business card read? How might it be misused?
10. May legal assistants' names be listed on law firm letterhead? Why, or why not? Why have policies about this changed? Is this practice common?
11. Are freelance paralegals who work for lawyers engaging in the unauthorized practice of law? Why, or why not? What is the confusion over these independent contractors?
12. What are some of the benefits to legal assistants and law firms of legal assistants acting as independent contractors?
13. What ethical concerns arise in the utilization of independent contractor paralegals?

DISCUSSION QUESTIONS

1. How can the prohibition against nonlawyers representing clients in court be reconciled with nonlawyer representation of clients before administrative agencies? Do you think that the differences in these two settings are substantial enough to warrant the difference in policy?
2. Are there any state administrative agencies in your area that permit nonlawyer practice? Do nonlawyers appear before these agencies frequently or infrequently? What about legal assistants working under the supervision of lawyers? Are there any state or local bar ethics opinions on this matter?
3. Do any statutes in your state disallow fees for nonlawyer representatives in administrative agencies?
4. Contact ten local law firms, five large and five small, and find out if their legal assistants:

   a. have business cards;
   b. are listed on the law firm letterhead;
   c. are listed in advertisements or in firm brochures or newsletters;
   d. are listed on the door to the firm;
   e. are listed in the directory to the firm in the lobby of the building;
   f. sign correspondence to clients.

   Also ask what job titles are used by legal assistants.
5. Are independent contractor legal assistants widely used in your area? Interview five freelance paralegals and the attorneys who utilize their services. Ask them what special ethical problems they are faced with. Does the freelance paralegal work in the attorney's office or elsewhere? How does the attorney select an independent contractor? How does

the attorney supervise and review the work of the independent contractor?

6. How can independent paralegals who work under the supervision of lawyers distinguish themselves from those who serve the public directly? Would different job titles make a difference? For example, nonlawyer direct service providers have sometimes been called "legal technicians." Can a title be "forced" on the public and the occupation? Would it make a difference if the state regulated the occupation?

7. Do you think freelance paralegals who provide services to attorneys are engaged in the practice of law? Might lawyers who use the services of independent contractors be more likely to fail in their responsibility to select, train, supervise, and review the work of these legal assistants than legal assistants employed full-time by their firm? How would this happen? Are these risks significant enough to warrant a complete ban on independent contractor paralegals? What about other independent contractors who serve lawyers, for example, process servers, investigators, accountants, and experts?

CASES FOR ANALYSIS

The case that follows is a leading decision about a "typing service" that was assisting customers in preparing paperwork for uncontested divorces. Pay special attention to the court's definition of the practice of law and to its application of this definition to the defendant's actions.

Florida Bar v. Brumbaugh
355 So. 2d 1186 (Fla. 1978)

. . . Respondent, Marilyn Brumbaugh, is not and has never been a member of the Florida Bar, and is, therefore, not licensed to practice law within this state. She has advertised in various local newspapers as "Marilyn's Secretarial Service" offering to perform typing services for "Do-It-Yourself" divorces, wills, resumes, and bankruptcies. The Florida Bar charges that she performed unauthorized legal services by preparing for her customers those legal documents necessary in an uncontested dissolution of marriage proceeding and by advising her customers as to the costs involved and the procedures which should be followed in order to obtain a dissolution of marriage. For this service, Ms. Brumbaugh charges a fee of $50. . . .

With regard to the charges made against Marilyn Brumbaugh, this

Court appointed a referee to receive evidence and to make findings of fact, conclusions of law, and recommendations as to the disposition of the case. The referee found that respondent, under the guise of a "secretarial" or "typing" service prepares, for a fee, all papers deemed by her to be needed for the pleading, filing, and securing of a dissolution of marriage, as well as detailed instructions as to how the suit should be filed, notice served, hearings set, trial conducted, and the final decree secured. The referee also found that in one instance, respondent prepared a quit claim deed in reference to the marital property of the parties. The referee determined that respondent's contention that she merely operates a typing service is rebutted by numerous facts in evidence. Ms. Brumbaugh has no blank forms either to sell or to fill out. Rather, she types up the documents for her customers after they have asked her to prepare a petition or an entire set of dissolution of marriage papers. Prior to typing up the papers, respondent asks her customers whether custody, child support, or alimony is involved. Respondent has four sets of dissolution of marriage papers, and she chooses which set is appropriate for the particular customer. She then types out those papers, filling in the blank spaces with the appropriate information. Respondent instructs her customers how the papers are to be signed, where they are to be filed, and how the customer should arrange for a final hearing. . . .

This case does not arise out of a complaint by any of Ms. Brumbaugh's customers as to improper advice or unethical conduct. It has been initiated by members of the Florida Bar who believe her to be practicing law without a license. The evidence introduced at the hearing below shows that none of respondent's customers believed that she was an attorney, or that she was acting as an attorney in their behalf. Respondent's advertisements clearly addressed themselves to people who wish to do their own divorces. These customers knew that they had to have "some type of papers" to file in order to obtain their dissolution of marriage. Respondent never handled contested divorces. During the past two years respondent has assisted several hundred customers in obtaining their own divorces. The record shows that while some of her customers told respondent exactly what they wanted, generally respondent would ask her customers for the necessary information needed to fill out the divorce papers, such as the names and addresses of the parties, the place and duration of residency in this state, whether there was any property settlement to be resolved, or any determination as to custody and support of children. Finally, each petition contained the bare allegation that the marriage was irretrievably broken. Respondent would then inform the parties as to which documents need to be signed, by whom, how many copies of each paper should be filed, where and when they should be filed, the costs involved, and what witness testimony is necessary at the court hearing. Apparently, Ms. Brumbaugh no longer informs the parties verbally as to the proper procedures for the filing of the papers, but offers to let them copy papers described as "suggested procedural education."

The Florida Bar argues that the above activities of respondent violate the rulings of this Court in *The Florida Bar v. American Legal and Business Forms, Inc.,* 274 So. 2d 255 (Fla. 1973), and *The Florida Bar v. Stupica,* 300 So. 2d 683 (Fla. 1974). In those decisions we held that it is lawful to sell to the public printed legal forms, provided they do not carry with them what purports to be instructions on how to fill out such forms or how to use them. We stated that legal advice is inextricably involved in the filling out and advice as to how to use such legal forms, and therein lies the danger of injury or damage to the public if not properly performed in accordance with law. In *Stupica,* supra, this Court rejected the rationale of the New York courts in *New York County Lawyer's Association v. Dacey,* 28 A.D.2d 161, 283 N.Y.S.2d 984, *reversed and dissenting opinion adopted,* 21 N.Y.2d 694, 287 N.Y.S.2d 422, 234 N.E.2d 459 (N.Y.1967), which held that the publication of forms and instructions on their use does not constitute the unauthorized practice of law if these instructions are addressed to the public in general rather than to a specific individual legal problem. The Court in *Dacey* stated that the possibility that the principles or rules set forth in the text may be accepted by a particular reader as solution to his problem, does not mean that the publisher is practicing law. Other states have adopted the principle of law set forth in *Dacey,* holding that the sale of legal forms with instructions for their use does not constitute unauthorized practice of law. (Citations omitted.) However, these courts have prohibited all personal contact between the service providing such forms and the customer, in the nature of consultation, explanation, recommendation, advice, or other assistance in selecting particular forms, in filling out any part of the forms, suggesting or advising how the forms should be used in solving the particular problems.

Although persons not licensed as attorneys are prohibited from practicing law within this state, it is somewhat difficult to define exactly what constitutes the practice of law in all instances. This Court has previously stated that:

> . . . if the giving of such advice and performance of such services affect important rights of a person under the law, and if the reasonable protection of the rights and property of those advised and served requires that the persons giving such advice possess legal skill and a knowledge of the law greater than that possessed by the average citizen, then the giving of such advice and the performance of such services by one for another as a course of conduct constitute the practice of law.

81

Sperry, supra, 140 So. 2d at 591 [full citation deleted]. . . .

In determining whether a particular act constitutes the practice of law, our primary goal is the protection of the public. However, any limitations on the free practice of law by all persons necessarily affects important constitutional rights. Our decision here certainly affects the constitutional rights of Marilyn Brumbaugh to pursue a lawful occupation or business. Our decision also affects respondent's First Amendment rights to speak and print what she chooses. In addition, her customers and potential customers have the constitutional right of self representation and the right of privacy inherent in the marriage relationship. (Citations omitted.) All citizens in our state are also guaranteed access to our courts by Article I, Section 21, Florida Constitution (1968). Although it is not necessary for us to provide affirmative assistance in order to ensure meaningful access to the courts to our citizens, as it is necessary for us to do for those incarcerated in our state prison system, (citation omitted), we should not place any unnecessary restrictions upon that right. We should not deny persons who wish to represent themselves access to any source of information which might be relevant in the preparation of their cases. There are numerous texts in our state law libraries which describe our substantive and procedural law, purport to give legal advice to the reader as to choices that should be made in various situations, and which also contain sample legal forms which a reader may use as an example. We generally do not restrict the access of the public to these law libraries, although many of the legal texts are not authored by attorneys licensed to practice in this state. These texts do not carry with them any guarantees of accuracy, and only some of them purport to update statements which have been modified by subsequently enacted statutes and recent case law.

The policy of this Court should continue to be one of encouraging persons who are unsure of their legal rights and remedies to seek legal assistance from persons licensed by us to practice law in this state. However, in order to make an intelligent decision as to whether or not to engage the assistance of an attorney, a citizen must be allowed access to information which will help determine the complexity of the legal problem. Once a person has made the decision to represent himself, we should not enforce any unnecessary regulation which might tend to hinder the exercise of this constitutionally protected right. . . .

It is also important for us to consider the legislative statute governing dissolution of marriage in resolving the question of what constitutes the practice of law in this area. Florida's "no fault" dissolution of marriage statute clearly has the remedial purpose of simplifying the dissolution of marriage whenever possible. . . .

Families usually undergo tremendous financial hardship when they decide to dissolve their marital relationships. The Legislature simplified procedures so that parties would not need to bear the additional burden of expensive legal fees where they have agreed to the settlement of their property and the custody of their children. This Court should not place unreasonable burdens upon the obtaining of such divorces, especially where both parties consent to the dissolution. . . .

The legal forms necessary to obtain such an uncontested dissolution of marriage are susceptible of standardization. This Court has allowed the sale of legal forms on this and other subjects, provided that they do not carry with them what purports to be instructions on how to fill out such forms or how they are to be used. (Citation omitted.) These decisions should be reevaluated in light of those recent decisions in other states which have held that the sale of forms necessary to obtain a divorce, together with any related textual instructions directed towards the general public, does not constitute the practice of law. . . .

Although there is danger that some published material might give false or misleading information, that is not a sufficient reason to justify its total ban. We must assume that our citizens will generally use such publications for what they are worth in the preparation of their cases, and further assume that most persons will not rely on these materials in the same way they would rely on the advice of an attorney or other persons holding themselves out as having expertise in the area. The tendency of persons seeking legal assistance to place their trust in the individual purporting to have expertise in the area necessitates this Court's regulation of such attorney-client relationships, so as to require that persons giving such advice have at least a minimal amount of legal training and experience. Although Marilyn Brumbaugh never held herself out as an attorney, it is clear that her clients placed some reliance upon her to properly prepare the necessary legal forms for their dissolution proceedings. To this extent we believe that Ms. Brumbaugh overstepped proper bounds and engaged in the unauthorized practice of law. We hold that Ms. Brumbaugh, and others in similar situations, may sell printed material purporting to explain legal practice and procedure to the public in general and she may sell sample legal forms. To this extent we limit our prior holdings in *Stupica* and *American Legal and Business Forms, Inc.* Further, we hold that it is not improper for Marilyn Brumbaugh to engage in a secretarial service, typing such forms for her clients, provided that she only copy the information given to her in writing by her clients. In addition, Ms. Brumbaugh may advertise her business activities of providing secretarial and notary services and selling legal forms and general printed information. However, Marilyn Brumbaugh must not, in conjunction with her business, engage in advising clients as to the various remedies available to them, or otherwise assist them in preparing those forms necessary for a dissolution proceeding. More specifically, Marilyn Brumbaugh may not make inquiries nor answer questions from her clients as to the particular forms which might be necessary, how best to fill out such forms, where to properly file such forms, and how to present necessary evidence at the court hearings. Our specific holding with regard to the dissolution of marriage also applies to other unauthorized legal assistance such as the preparation of wills or real estate transaction documents. While Marilyn Brumbaugh may legally sell forms in these areas, and type up instruments which have been completed by clients, she must not engage in personal legal assistance in conjunction with her business activities, including the correction of errors and omissions.

Accordingly, having defined the limits within which Ms. Brumbaugh and those engaged in similar activities may conduct their business without engaging in the unauthorized practice of law, the rule to show cause is dissolved.

It is so ordered.

Questions about the Case

1. Was Brumbaugh holding herself out as an attorney? Did any of her customers mistakenly believe that she was an attorney? Did any of her customers complain to the bar about her? Who initiated this action, and why?
2. How does the court define the practice of law? Do you find this definition useful?
3. What does the court say is the primary goal of unauthorized practice rules? With what right or rights do these rules conflict in this case?
4. What does the court say about the sale of legal publications that include sample forms? Does this constitute the unauthorized practice of law? Explain the court's reasoning.
5. What does the court say about the operation of a typing service that prepares legal forms? What functions may Brumbaugh perform that do not violate the unauthorized practice rules? What is she forbidden from doing? Do these same restrictions apply to areas of law other than uncontested divorces?
6. What does the court say about the right of self-representation, about Brumbaugh's First Amendment rights, and about the goals of the state's no-fault marital dissolution statute? Do these interests reconcile with its holding?

The following is the most well-known of the early unauthorized practice cases involving nonlawyer legal service providers. Like *Brumbaugh,* it involves a secretarial service that prepared legal documents for laypersons.

Florida Bar v. Furman
376 So. 2d 378 (Fla. 1979)

PER CURIAM.

The Florida Bar has petitioned this Court to enjoin Rosemary W. Furman, d/b/a Northside Secretarial Service, from unauthorized practice of law in the State of Florida. . . . We find the activities of the respondent to constitute the practice of law and permanently enjoin her from the further unauthorized practice of law.

The Florida Bar alleged . . . that Furman, a non-lawyer, engaged in the unauthorized practice of law by giving legal advice and by rendering legal services in connection with marriage dissolutions and adoptions in the years 1976 and 1977. The bar specifically alleges that Furman performed legal services for at least seven customers by soliciting information from them and preparing pleadings in violation of Florida law. The bar further contends that through advertising in the *Jacksonville Journal,* a newspaper of general circulation, Furman held herself out to the public as having legal expertise in Florida family law and sold "do-it-yourself divorce kits." The bar does not contend that Furman held herself out to be a lawyer, that her customers suffered any harm as a result of the services rendered, or that she has failed to perform the services for which she was paid.

In describing her activities, Furman states that she does not give legal advice, that she does prepare pleadings that meet the desires of her clients, that she charges no more than $50 for her services, and that her assistance to customers is in aid of their obtaining self-representative relief from the courts. In general, the respondent alleges as a defense that the ruling of this court in *Florida Bar v. Brumbaugh,* 355 So. 2d 1186 (Fla. 1978), violates the first amendment to the United States Constitution by restricting her right to disseminate and the right of her customers to receive information which would allow indigent litigants access to the state's domestic relations courts. She alleges that our holding in Brumbaugh is so narrow that it deprives citizens who are indigent of equal protection of the laws as provided by the Florida and United States constitutions. . . .

. . . The Respondent admits that the customer returns with the intake sheet not completed, because the people are unfamiliar with the legal terms and some are illiterate and, of course, she then proceeds to ask questions to complete the intake sheet for preparing the Petition for Dissolution of Marriage. Then after she types the Petition for Dissolution of Marriage, she advises the customer to take the papers for filing to the Office of the Clerk of Circuit Court, and Respondent follows the progress of the case every step of the way until it is at issue. She then notifies the customer to come in for a briefing session preferably the day before the date set for trial. In the course of briefing Respondent furnishes the customer with a diagram of the Court chambers and where to find the Judge to which that particular case has been assigned. . . . She also explains the full procedure that will take place before the Judge, including the questions the customer should ask. . . . The facts in the record of this case establish very clearly that the Respondent performs every essential step in the legal proceedings to obtain a dissolution of marriage, except taking the papers and filing them in the Clerk's office and going with the customer to the final hearing and interrogating the witness.

Respondent admitted that she could not follow the guidelines as set forth in the *Florida Bar v. Brumbaugh,* for the reason that the customers who come to obtain her services are not capable for various and sundry reasons, mainly not being familiar with legal terminology or illiterate, and were unable to write out the necessary information. Therefore, she was compelled to ask questions and hold conferences with her customers. . . .

We do not write on a clean slate in this case. Last year we took the opportunity to clearly define to non-lawyers the proper realm in which they could operate without engaging in the unauthorized practice of law. In *Brumbaugh,* we clearly stated what services a similar secretarial business could lawfully perform. . . .

Before the referee and before this court, Furman admitted that she did not abide by the dictates of *Brumbaugh.* She says that it is impossible for her to operate her "do-it-yourself divorce kit" business in compliance with this court's ruling in that case. The bar alleges that Furman has engaged in the unauthorized practice of law as previously defined by this court. The referee so found. She so admits. We believe the referee's findings are supported by the evidence.

In other portions of the referee's report, he urges that as part of our disposition in this case we require the bar to conduct a study to determine how to provide effective legal services to the indigent. . . .

Therefore, we direct The Florida Bar to begin immediately a study to determine better ways and means of providing legal services to the indigent. We further direct that a report on the findings and conclusions from this study be prepared and filed with this court on or before January 1, 1980, at which time we will examine the problem and consider solutions.

Accordingly, we find that Rosemary Furman, d/b/a Northside Secretarial Service, has been guilty of the unauthorized practice of law by virtue of the activities recited herein and she is hereby permanently enjoined and restrained from further engaging in the unauthorized practice of law in the State of Florida.

It is so ordered.

Questions about the Case

1. Did Furman ever hold herself out as attorney? Did any of her customers believe she was an attorney? Did her customers complain about her services? Who brought this action against her, and what relief was sought?
2. Make a list of the services Furman performed for her customers. Did she perform the same functions as Brumbaugh? What did she do that Brumbaugh did not do?
3. How did the court use the *Brumbaugh* case in making its decision?
4. Do you think that Furman's conduct constituted the unauthorized practice of law as defined in *Brumbaugh?* Do you think that nonlawyers should be prohibited from performing these tasks? Why, or why not?
5. What does the effective delivery of legal services to the indigent have to do with this case? What did the referee recommend to the court about this? How did the court respond?

The following case involves a so-called paralegal service that assisted a person in filing for bankruptcy. The bankruptcy area has many published cases involving nonlawyer legal service providers. This one is unique in its broad use of remedies.

In re Anderson
79 B.R. 482 (Bankr. S.D. Cal. 1987)

. . . Katheryn Anderson, a Chapter 7 debtor, brings this motion for dismissal of her Chapter 7 case. She also asks this Court to order San Diego Paralegal Services to refund monies she paid them for assistance in filing, her bankruptcy petition. Finally, she asks that this Court enjoin

San Diego Paralegal Service from engaging in the unauthorized practice of law.

Factual Summary

When Ms. Anderson was having financial difficulties, she responded to an ad in a local newspaper by San Diego Paralegal Services, a sole proprietorship run by Tom Kavanaugh. She was attracted by the ad because it said that San Diego Paralegal would come to your home, and she was without transportation.

She telephoned San Diego Paralegal and spoke with Kavanaugh. Kavanaugh explained he was a paralegal and that San Diego Paralegal was a typing service. She indicated she was thinking about filing bankruptcy and asked him to come to her home because her car was inoperative.

Kavanaugh went to her house and questioned her about her assets, liabilities and financial affairs from a questionnaire which roughly parallels those questions asked by Official Form Nos. 6 and 7 prescribed by the Judicial Conference of the United States. Kavanaugh admits the answers to the questions were written down by him.

During the interview, Anderson asked Kavanaugh a number of questions concerning the consequences of filing bankruptcy. She asked him whether she would lose her car if she filed Chapter 7; he said, "yes." She asked him if she would be able to keep her income tax refund. He indicated probably. He told her that the income taxes which she owed would have to be paid after bankruptcy. She mentioned that she had a pending civil lawsuit which would bring in extra money and inquired whether she needed to report it. He advised her not to worry about it and that it did not need to be reported. . . .

When she inquired about a Chapter 13, he indicated that it would cost her more money for a Chapter 13; that she would have three years to pay it off and that the payments would be $150 per month. He did not tell her that a Chapter 13 plan could last up to five years. Based on his statements, she decided not to file Chapter 13.

Anderson paid Kavanaugh one-half of the $290 required, and signed an "Agreement and Guarantee" . . . which stated:

> I, the undersigned, hereby authorize San Diego Paralegal Clinic, a legal scrivener service, to transcribe the information submitted herewith, in order for them to complete the proper legal forms for me to file bankruptcy. I consider myself competent to represent myself in court and shall not expect said company to give me any legal advice or represent me in court or in any manner whatsoever.

The testimony conflicts as to who chose the exemptions claimed by Anderson in her Chapter 7 case. Kavanaugh states that it is his practice to hand lists of exemptions available under California Code of Civil Procedure . . . together with a copy of the statute to the client. to permit her to choose which exemption scheme to use when she files. . . . Ms. Anderson testified that Kavanaugh picked the exemptions for her; that she had no idea what she could keep under applicable exemption laws if she filed a Chapter 7. Her testimony is credible on this point.

After the Chapter 7 was filed, Ms. Anderson received an income tax refund of $1,050, rather than the $500 refund she was expecting and had scheduled. She called Mr. Kavanaugh when she got the larger refund and asked if she should amend her bankruptcy schedules. He told her not to worry about it. Consequently, no amendment was ever filed.

At the . . . hearing, Anderson, who was appearing in pro per, was questioned at length by the attorney for Mellon Bank. Mellon eventually filed an action to determine non-dischargeability of the debt she owed them. From a conversation she had with Mellon's attorney after the . . . hearing and other "free advice" given by our generous local counsel in the hallway outside the hearing room, she began to question whether she should have filed a Chapter 7 proceeding at all.

Indeed, an examination of the debtor's schedules supports her regret at having done so. She lists only $2,340 in unsecured debt and $533 in non-dischargeable debt to the IRS. Her only secured debt is that to Mellon Financial for $2,380, for which the collateral is a 1968 Dodge Dart valued at $250. She is employed as a sheet metal mechanic, earning net take home pay of $1,016 per month, and having net income over expenses of $156 per month. Further, her testimony indicated that although she was being pressured by some of her creditors when she filed her Chapter 7 case, she was current with Mellon and Citibank, her two largest creditors.

Issues

    I. Whether Tom Kavanaugh, doing business as San Diego Paralegal Service, is engaged in the unauthorized practice of law under California law.

    II. Whether Tom Kavanaugh, doing business as San Diego Paralegal Service, should be required to refund to Katheryn Anderson, all monies she paid to him to assist her in filing her bankruptcy.

    III. Whether an injunction against the unauthorized practice of law should issue against Tom Kavanaugh doing business as San Diego Paralegal Service.

    IV. Whether debtor's case should be dismissed.

Discussion

I

. . . It is not controverted that Kavanaugh is not a member of the State Bar. California law punishes the unlawful practice of law as a misdemeanor. . . .

Whether one is engaged in the practice of law or is merely a legal scrivener has long been settled under California law. In *People v. Sipper*, 61 Cal. App. 2d Supp. 844, 846 (1943), the court wrote:

> The term "practice law" or its equivalent, "the practice of law," has been repeatedly defined by our reviewing courts. They have uniformly said that "as the term is generally understood, the practice of law . . . includes legal advice and counsel and the preparation of legal instruments and contracts by which legal rights are secured although such matter may or may not be pending in a court.". . .

After considering the testimony of Kavanaugh and debtor in light of the *Landlords* and *Sipper* opinions [citations omitted], the conclusion that Kavanaugh is engaged in the unauthorized practice of law is inescapable. Kavanaugh held himself out to be qualified to give advice concerning bankruptcies. He interviewed debtor and solicited information from her, from which he selected and prepared bankruptcy schedules. He advised Anderson of her legal rights vis-a-vis secured collateral and of the differences between a Chapter 13 filing and one under Chapter 7. He further (incorrectly) advised her regarding the necessity to file amendments to her schedules to accurately reflect an increased tax refund. It also appears that he selected her exemptions. All of these acts require the exercise of legal judgment beyond the knowledge and capacity of the lay person.

II

California law has long held that a contract executed in violation of a statute which requires one of the parties to be licensed will not be enforced. The contract in the instant case recites that the fee paid by debtor is non-refundable; however, since the contract cannot be enforced under California law, this provision is of no effect. Inasmuch as the contract was executed in violation of a statute designed to protect the public, the contract is void and debtor is entitled to restitution of all monies paid under the contract. Cal. Civ. Code §1689(b)(6) authorizes rescission of a contract if the "public interest will be prejudiced by permitting the contract to stand.". . . Although not articulated in the moving papers, debtor's request for a refund from Kavanaugh, taken together with the motion to dismiss her case, indicates a desire to rescind the transaction. Since the transaction is void under California law, debtor is entitled to a refund of all monies paid to Kavanaugh.

III

Debtor has also requested that this Court enjoin Kavanaugh from future unauthorized practice of law. In support of this request, debtor cites O'Connell v. David, 35 B.R. 141 (Bankr. E.D. Pa. 1983). In *O'Connell,* a Chapter 13 trustee brought an action to enjoin several defendants from engaging in the unauthorized practice of law. After a trial of the matter, the court issued an injunction enjoining the defendants from preparing Chapter 13 petitions, statements, schedules or plans on a regular basis for a fee, soliciting debtors for such services or offering advice concerning the differences between a Chapter 13 case and one under Chapter 7. . . .

A similar situation arose in *In re Arthur,* [15 B.R. 541 (Bankr. E.D. Pa. 1981)], where the court, apparently on its own motion, entered a similar injunction *and* directed that the unauthorized practitioner refund all fees collected from any debtors. In each instance, the court granted relief upon its inherent authority as a court to determine what constituted the practice of law and "broad equity" powers under §105(a).

Although the *Arthur* court based its injunction on the "broad equity powers" of the court under §105(a), a statutory basis for such an injunction exists. Compensation of debtor's counsel must be disclosed under §329 and is subject to review by the Court for reasonableness and disgorging of all fees determined to be excessive to the Chapter 7 trustee. This process of disclosure and disgorgement involves the administration of the estate which is a "core proceeding" under 28 U.S.C. §157(b)(2)(A). Even though Kavanaugh is not licensed to practice law, §329 applies to non-lawyers who engage in the practice of law before bankruptcy courts. (Citation omitted.)

Accordingly, an injunction will issue barring Kavanaugh, doing business as San Diego Paralegal Services, from engaging in any of the following activities for a fee: Advising debtors regarding exemptions, dischargeability or the automatic stay; providing advice concerning the differences and/or relative advantages of filing a Chapter 13 or Chapter 7 case; and, from interviewing debtors with an eye towards preparing statements or schedules. Kavanaugh will also be barred from soliciting any such employment in accordance with the prohibition contained in Cal. Bus. & Prof. Code §6126.

IV

The only remaining issue to be resolved is whether debtor's case should be dismissed. Recent case authority indicates that a Chapter 7 debtor has no right to have his or her case dismissed. However, where debtor is a victim of someone engaged in the unauthorized practice of law, equity dictates that, under certain circumstances such as those before the Court, the motion to dismiss be granted. . . .

Questions about the Case

1. Who brought this action? What remedies were sought? In what ways does this case differ from *Brumbaugh* and *Furman?*
2. How does this court define the practice of law? Is this California definition more or less useful than the Florida definition in *Brumbaugh?*
3. What actions did Kavanaugh perform that constitute the practice of law? Did he hold himself out as an attorney?
4. Did Kavanaugh do a competent job for his client Anderson? What mistakes did he make? Do you think this made a difference to the court?
5. How did the court act on each of the four requests made by Anderson in this case? Do you agree with the court's decisions? Why, or why not?

Landlord-tenant law is another area in which nonlawyer legal service providers commonly work. In the following case an eviction service is prosecuted under the state unauthorized practice and consumer protection statutes.

People v. Landlords Professional Services
215 Cal.App.3d 1599, 264 Cal.Rptr. 548 (1989)

In 1982 the Orange County Apartment News carried an advertisement for the eviction services provided by LPS. The ad stated "Evictions as low as $65" and showed the picture of a purposeful and authoritative looking man, arms folded across his chest, stating: "One low price $65 plus costs uncontested or contested in pro per. Attorney for trial extra if needed." Below the picture were the words "Time to Act!" and

"Call & talk to us." The advertisement ended with an address and telephone number.

In 1982 Roberta Spiegel decided to evict the tenants of an apartment she owned. A friend recommended LPS. Roberta spoke to Bill Watts, an employee of LPS, who told her to come to the LPS office and bring all documentation related to the rental. On arrival Roberta was given a booklet with Mr. Watts's business card attached. The card was imprinted with the words "Landlord's Professional Services" and the name Bill Watts. Beneath Mr. Watts's name was the word "Counselor."

The booklet begins with a chronology of an unlawful detainer action as carried out by the eviction service. The chronology was generally factual. However, at the end of the chronology, this bit of advice is imparted concerning what to do after the tenants have been evicted: "*You must change the locks at that time.* If you do not change the locks you may have a problem. The defendant may re-enter and take possession, and the ball game starts from the beginning."

The following pages of the booklet contain examples of the types of forms used in an unlawful detainer action and provides a guide for how those forms should be completed. Often the guidance is purely factual, i.e., where a form requires the name of the city in which the subject property is located the guide states "enter city." The advice given, however, can be more useful. In discussing the "Notice to Pay Rent or Quit," for example, the guide states: "Acceptance of any money after service may void notice. You don't have to accept money after notice expires."

Bill Watts reviewed the normal routine in an unlawful detainer action with Roberta who was unfamiliar with eviction procedures. Roberta asked questions about the procedure and Bill answered them. Roberta told Bill she had already mailed the tenants a three-day notice. Bill told her this was insufficient and she would have to take another notice to the apartment. Bill asked Roberta questions and completed the documents and forms necessary for the unlawful detainer action and eventually filed them.

On December 7, 1982, Ralph Lopes, an investigator with the Orange County District Attorney's Office, called LPS and stated he was a property owner who was interested in eviction services. Lopes stated he was unfamiliar with the eviction process. The procedure for commencing and carrying through an unlawful detainer action was explained by Jacqueline Sutake, an LPS employee. Sutake explained Lopes would have to send LPS all documentation concerning the rental and they would handle the process. Lopes asked what it meant in the LPS ad when it stated "pro per." Sutake explained LPS was not an attorney and Lopes would be representing himself. Sutake stated LPS could not represent him in court. If an answer was filed by the tenant, LPS would type up Lopes's testimony and he could read it in court. Lopes asked if he would need an attorney. Sutake stated if an answer is filed by an attorney. LPS recommends its client obtain one as well but that it is possible to prevail without the assistance of counsel.

Lopes asked if he could turn off the utilities at the rental property. Sutake stated he could not. Lopes asked what would occur if he needed an attorney during the process. Sutake stated he could use his own attorney or "we have attorneys here."

Ms. Sutake testified she did not advise her clients on questions of law. She did, however, explain the unlawful detainer procedure and would share with clients her personal experiences as a landlord. If the case presented was more complex than the routine uncontested unlawful detainer action, she would suggest the client contact an attorney. Ms. Sutake explained her activities were always supervised by an attorney. When an unfamiliar situation arose she would ask an attorney for help and the attorney would determine if the complexity of the case required the services of a lawyer. In most cases her work was reviewed by an attorney before being filed.

In February 1983, the Orange County District Attorney filed a civil complaint against LPS and five other eviction services, alleging the unauthorized practice of law. (Bus. & Prof. Code. §§6125, 6126.) The complaint sought monetary penalties pursuant to Business and Professions Code sections 17200 (unfair competition) and 17500 (false or misleading statements) and injunctive relief. At the conclusion of the hearing below the trial court ordered LPS to pay $8.000 in civil penalties for eight violations of Business and Professions Code section 17200 and $9.000 for nine violations of Business and Professions Code section 17500. The finding of eight violations of section 17200 was based on evidence concerning services provided by LPS to seven clients, including Ms. Spiegel, and on the telephone conversation between Ms. Sutake and Investigator Lopes. The finding of nine violations of section 17500 was based on the same evidence with one additional violation based on the advertisement appearing in the Orange County Apartment News.

The trial court also granted the following permanent injunction: "Defendants, their agents, officers, employees and representatives are enjoined from engaging in or performing directly or indirectly any and all of the following acts: "1. the preparation, other than at the specific and detailed direction of a person in propria persona or under the direct supervision of an attorney, of written instruments relating to evictions such as: three day notices, summons and complaints, at issue memoranda, judgments, writs of execution or other legal documents relating to evictions.

94

"2. Explaining orally or in writing, except under the direct supervision of an attorney, to individual clients: (A) the effect of any rule of law or court; (B) advising such persons as to the requirements for commencing or maintaining a proceeding in the Courts of this state; or (C) advising or explaining to such clients the forms which are legally required or how to complete such forms.

"3. Holding themselves out or allowing themselves to be held out to newspapers, magazines, or other advertising, or representing themselves as being able to provide, except through an attorney, any of the following: legal advice, the preparation of legal documents (other than as a secretarial service), or any explanation of any rules of law or court in relation to evictions or as being qualified to do any of the above activities.

"4. Any employee, agent, officer, or representative of L.P.S., not a licensed member of the California Bar, is prohibited from practicing law in any form or holding themselves out as having the right to practice law in any form.". . .

Business and Professions Code section 6125 states: "No person shall practice law in this State unless he is an active member of the State Bar." Business and Professions Code section 6126, subdivision (a), provides: "Any person advertising or holding himself or herself out as practicing or entitled to practice law or otherwise practicing law who is not an active member of the State Bar, is guilty of a misdemeanor."

The code provides no definition for the term "practicing law." In *Baron v. City of Los Angeles* (1970) 2 Cal. 3d 535, 542 [86 Cal. Rptr. 673, 469 P.2d 353, 42 A.L.R.3d 1036], our Supreme Court noted that as early as 1922, before the passage of the State Bar Act, it had adopted a definition of "practice of law" used in an Indiana case: " ' "[A]s the term is generally understood, the practice of law is the doing and performing services in a court of justice in any manner depending therein throughout its various stages and in conformity with the adopted rules of procedure. But in a larger sense it includes legal advice and counsel and the preparation of legal instruments and contracts by which legal rights are secured although such matter may or may not be depending in court." ' " (Citations omitted.) . . .

The eviction service offered by LPS was designed to assist clients in the preparation, filing and resolution of unlawful detainer actions. LPS, therefore, offered to assist clients in advancing their legal rights in a court of law. We believe general California law and the approach taken by other states with respect to divorce services teach that such services do not amount to the practice of law as long as the service offered by LPS was merely clerical i.e., the service did not engage in the practice of law if it made forms available for the client's use, filled the forms in at the specific direction of the client and filed and served those forms as directed by the client. Likewise, merely giving a client a manual, even a detailed one containing specific advice, for the preparation of an unlawful detainer action and the legal incidents of an eviction would not be the practice of law if the service did not personally advise the client with regard to his specific case.

With these principles in mind, we conclude LPS was engaged in the unauthorized practice of law. The advertisement used by LPS implies its eviction services were not limited to clerical functions. The tenor of the advertisement was that the service accomplished evictions. The advertisement's statement "Call & talk to us" was a general invitation for clients to discuss the matter of eviction with LPS. Bill Watts's LPS business card listed his title as "Counselor." In short, LPS cast about itself an aura of expertise concerning evictions.

While an eviction may not be the most difficult of procedures, it is, nonetheless, a legal procedure carried out before a court with specific legal requirements for its accomplishment. As we have seen, some courts have held that providing advice as to which forms to use, which blanks to fill in with what information or in which courts an action must be filed is itself the practice of law. Here, of course, LPS's eviction advice went further. It provided specific information to its clients concerning eviction procedure. This it did in the context of personal interviews where it was able to provide additional information and advice addressed to the specific problems and concerns of its clients. . . . Given the aura of expertise created by the business practices of LPS such advice would undoubtedly be relied upon by its clients, perhaps to their serious detriment. . . .

The judgment is affirmed.

Questions about the Case

1. What specific conduct by LPS constituted unauthorized practice of law? What conduct constituted false or misleading advertising?
2. What definition of the practice of law does this court use? How does it compare to other definitions cited in this chapter?
3. How did the prosecutor's office investigate LPS?
4. Does it make any difference that an eviction is simple and many nonlawyers could file the appropriate papers without any help?
5. Did the court cite any instances where LPS customers were given bad advice or were harmed?

In recent years, preparing living trusts for consumers has become a popular business for lawyers and nonlawyer practitioners alike. In this case, an attorney working with paralegals was found to have violated several ethics rules in the conduct of his living trust practice.

In re Morin

319 Or. 547, 878 P.2d 393 (1994)

The facts relating to this case are undisputed. The accused was licensed to practice law in California in 1974 and was admitted to practice law in Oregon in 1984. During the spring of 1988, the accused began conducting "living trust" seminars and selling "living trust packages," which included pour-over wills and directives to physicians.

The accused and two of his employees, who were paralegals, travelled throughout Oregon and northern California, conducting seminars and preparing the living trust packages. If a person at a seminar indicated that he or she was interested in discussing a living trust package, the accused or one of the paralegals would make an appointment and return to meet with the client. The accused or the paralegal would gather information from the client and then prepare the documents for the living trust package in the accused's Medford office.

At trial, Monnett, a paralegal employed by the accused, testified that he usually travelled alone, conducted seminars before groups, collected information from prospective clients, and assisted clients in executing the documents contained in the trust packages. He testified that the questions that he answered at the seminars were general and did not apply to individual clients' problems.

Monnett also testified that, during meetings with individual clients, he read their wills and explained to them the operative parts of the will. He also testified that he inquired into the clients' assets and advised them whether or not they needed a trust. He reviewed the trusts and other legal documents with the clients. Some of the clients never met the accused and dealt only with Monnett throughout the process. Both Monnett and the other paralegal employed by the accused, Pesterfield, testified that the accused instructed them to call him if they had legal questions. Both also testified that they believed that the accused reviewed all the documents that were prepared because he signed all of them and because occasionally he discussed the contents of the documents with Monnett.

Ordinarily, after the documents were prepared, the accused or one of the paralegals scheduled an additional appointment with the client to execute the documents. . . .

97

The accused testified that clients in the Medford and Ashland area ordinarily executed the documents in the living trust packages in the accused's office, where the accused's office staff members served as witnesses. When the accused or the paralegals executed documents at seminar sites, however, it was difficult for them to have the wills and directives to physicians witnessed.

The accused and the paralegals began a practice of taking the wills and directives to physicians back to the accused's office in Medford after they were signed by the clients at the seminar sites and directing the office staff to sign the documents as witnesses. The signatures of the "witnesses" on the wills were notarized either by the accused or by one of his employees. The signatures on the directives to physicians were not notarized. The accused then mailed the signature pages back to the clients. . . .

. . . [T]he accused admitted that he had caused the wills and directives to physicians of approximately 300 clients to be executed outside the presence of the witnesses, who later signed the wills and directives to physicians.

The accused stated before the trial panel that he knew that a will is invalid unless it is either executed or affirmed by the testator in the presence of two witnesses. He also testified that part of the fee he charged his clients was for a valid will and that he understood that his clients believed that they were receiving valid wills as part of the living trust packages. . . .

Here, the accused charged his clients a fee for the performance of certain services, including the preparation and execution of a *valid* will and a valid directive to physicians. The accused intentionally failed to provide his clients with the valid documents for which they had paid. The accused intentionally charged clients for services that he knew he would not provide. Accordingly, the fee was excessive and the accused violated DR 2-106(A). . . .

There is insufficient evidence for us to conclude that the paralegals engaged in the unlawful practice of law by giving the seminars on living trusts and by answering general questions about the living trust packages. Disseminating information that is "directed to the general public and not to a specific individual" is not the practice of law. *Oregon State Bar v. Gilchrist,* 272 Or. 552, 558, 538 P.2d 913 (1975). Apparently, the seminars and questions answered by the paralegals in the seminars went to general information about the advantages of living trusts and about the contents of the packages. The dissemination of that information did not involve the practice of law.

It appears, however, that at least Monnett went beyond the mere dissemination of general information to the public. The Bar alleges that it was Monnett's interactions with individuals that constituted the practice of law. In *Gilchrist,* this court held that advertising and selling do-it-yourself divorce kits did not constitute the practice of law. 272 Or. at 557-60, 538 P.2d 913. This court also held, however:

> [A]ll personal contact between defendants and their customers in the nature of consultation, explanation, recommendation or advice or other assistance in selecting particular forms, in filling out any part of the forms, or suggesting or advising how the forms should be used in solving the particular customer's marital problems does constitute the practice of law. . . .

Id. at 563-64, 538 P.2d 913. . . .

This court set forth the test for ascertaining what conduct constitutes the practice of law in *State Bar v. Security Escrows, Inc.,* 233 Or. 80, 89, 377 P.2d 334 (1962): "[T]he practice of law includes the drafting or selection of documents and the giving of advice in regard thereto any time an informed or trained discretion must be exercised in the selection or drafting of a document to meet the needs of the persons being served."

In *State Bar v. Miller & Co.,* 235 Or. 341. 347. 385 P.2d 181 (1963), this court held that an insurance salesperson that assisted people in preparing estate plans could

> explain to his prospective customer alternative methods of disposing of assets . . . which are available to taxpayers *generally.* . . . He cannot properly advise a prospective purchaser with respect to his *specific* need for life insurance as against some other form of disposition of his estate, unless the advice can be given without drawing upon the law to explain the basis for making the choice of alternatives. (Emphasis in original.)

In this case, Monnett examined wills and interpreted them for chents of the accused. Moreover, Monnett discussed clients' individual assets with them to determine whether a living trust would be an appropriate device for the particular client to use. Monnett also told the accused's clients his opinion of the usefulness of another trust format, telling them that it "didn't do much." In short. Monnett advised clients and potential clients of the accused on legal decisions specific to them, and he used discretion in selecting between using a trust and a will and among trust forms. Accordingly, Monnett, a nonlawyer, practiced law.

The accused argues that, even if Monnett practiced law, he did not assist Monnett. He argues that he "took pains to tell these paralegals not to practice law at the seminars." He also told them to call him at the office or at home "[i]f any legal questions arose." Furthermore, the

99

accused argues that he did not know of Monnett's conduct nor did he aid in that conduct: therefore, he did not violate the rule.

This court's decision in *In re Jones,* 308 Or. 306, 779 P.2d 1016 1989), is instructive. In that case, the accused allowed a nonlawyer to use pleading paper and a letterhead stamp with the lawyer's name on it in the nonlawyer's dissolution-processing business, 308 Or. at 308, 779 P.2d 1016. The accused knew that the nonlawyer had been warned by the Bar not to practice law. Id. at 309. 779 P.2d 1016. The accused instructed her to bring any legal questions that she had to him. Id. This court held that the accused aided a nonlawyer in the practice of law because he "took no steps to enforce his instruction or to test her ability to determine when legal help was needed." Id. This court also found it to be important that the clients were never required to speak with the accused. Id.

Here, as in *Jones,* although the accused told his paralegals not to practice law, he did not tell them the precise contours of what constituted the practice of law, Moreover, the accused created the situation in which at least one of his paralegals had the opportunity to practice law. The accused sent the paralegals to meet with clients alone, and he failed to supervise them properly. Thus, even if the accused did not intend for the paralegals to practice law, he assisted in that unlawful practice by allowing them too much freedom in dealing with clients, thereby allowing at least Monnett to provide legal advice to those clients. Accordingly, we conclude that the accused assisted in the unlawful practice of law. . . .

Accordingly, considering the ABA Standards and the prior decisions of this court, we conclude that the trial panel's decision of disbarment is correct.

Questions about the Case

1. What exactly did the paralegals do in this case that constitutes unauthorized practice of law?
2. Could the attorney have run his practice the same way and avoided the ethical violations cited? How?
3. What was wrong with the way the wills were executed? What was the result for the client? Is this legal malpractice? (See Chapter 8.)
4. What did the court say about the attorney charging fees for the invalid wills?
5. Did the court condemn the activities of the paralegals as unauthorized practice of law?
6. What definition of the practice of law did this court use?

In the following case, a lawyer is disciplined for his work with a firm of nonlawyer legal service providers. Some independent paralegals have tried to avoid charges of unauthorized practice by associating with an attorney who answers questions and meets with clients if the paralegal determines it advisable. Most disciplinary authorities treat this arrangement the way the Florida court did here.

Florida Bar v. Beach
675 So. 2d 106 (Fla. 1996)

The alleged violations in this case concern Beach's legal practices during 1993 when he provided services as an independent contractor to King and King Paralegals (King and King). King and King was owned and operated by Kenneth and Cathy King. As the Kings' supervising attorney, Beach discussed their clients' legal issues, reviewed pleadings and other documents prepared by them, and offered thirty-minute consultations to Kings' customers. King and King paid Beach a $75 flat rate for his services rendered in each case.

On June 29, 1993, Margery Rose contracted with King and King to prepare legal documents, which would be reviewed by Beach. The contract also provided that Beach would have a thirty-minute consultation with Ms. Rose, but would not represent her unless she entered into a separate agreement with him. Pursuant to the contract, Ms. Rose paid King and King $675 as a nonrefundable retainer to prepare the paperwork, conduct research and additional interviews, and for attorney time. During her relationship with King and King, Ms. Rose received advice and guidance from Kenneth King regarding the various legal actions she considered pursuing. The guidance provided by King was the direct product of legal advice King had received from Beach.

Approximately two weeks after hiring the Kings, Ms. Rose requested they cease working on her case and provide her with the documents they had prepared up to that point. She also requested but was denied a refund. Ms. Rose then filed a pro se action seeking a refund and delivery of her file documents to determine whether the legal services she initially requested had been performed. The Kings defended that action pro se. After mediating the disagreement, the parties entered into a stipulation which provided the Kings would deliver the documents within seventy-two hours and pay Ms. Rose $47 on or before October 21, 1993. Subsequently, a dispute arose as to whether the Kings had exhibited good faith in attempting delivery of the documents within the required time period, and final judgment was entered awarding Ms. Rose $675 because of the Kings' breach of the stipulation.

Ms. Rose filed a grievance with The Florida Bar wherein she complained that Roy Beach had failed to meet with her or contact her pursuant to the King and King contract. Ms. Rose also stated in her complaint that the Kings had tried twice to deliver her documents to her former husband prior to actually delivering them to him at his place of business. Based upon his belief that Ms. Rose's statement was contradictory to her prior position that the Kings had violated the mediation agreement, Beach filed a motion on behalf of the Kings to vacate the final judgment. The court granted this motion and set the matter for a new final hearing but, prior to that date, Ms. Rose dismissed her action.

The Florida Bar filed a complaint against Roy Beach alleging violation of Rules Regulating The Florida Bar 4-5.4 (sharing legal fees with a nonlawyer), 4-5.5 (assisting a person who is not a member of the Bar to perform activities that constitute the practice of law), 4-1.7 (representing a client when the representation would be directly adverse to the interests of another client), 4-1.8 (using information relating to the representation of a client to the disadvantage of the client), and 4-1.9 (representing another person in the same or substantially related matter in which that person's interests are materially adverse to the interest of a former client).

After a hearing, the referee recommended that Beach be found guilty of violating rules 4-5.4 and 4-5.5 and that he be suspended from the practice of law for three months with automatic reinstatement at the end of the suspension period and all costs of the proceedings be charged to the defendant. The referee found for Beach on the other charges. . . .

In this case, the referee's finding that Beach assisted Mr. King in the unlicensed pratice of law is supported by the record. Beach never met with or consulted Ms. Rose. Rather, he met with Mr. King who passed on Beach's advice to Ms. Rose concerning what legal action she should pursue. While Beach did discuss Ms. Rose's case with Mr. King, he never monitored or participated in the subsequent discussions that Mr. King had with Ms. Rose concerning her legal problems. . . . Beach improperly allowed Mr. King to act as his conduit for giving legal advice by obtaining and relaying, without supervision, case-specific information to persons when Beach never actually met or consulted. . . . Consequently, we find the referee's conclusions, that Beach (1) assisted Mr. King in the unauthorized practice of law in violation of rule 4-5.5 and (2) shared a legal fee with a nonlawyer in violation of rule 4-5.4, to be supported by the record in this case.

The Bar contends the referee's legal conclusion that Beach triggered no conflict of interest by funneling legal advice to Ms. Rose through King and King and his subsequent representation of King and King in the civil action against Ms. Rose, was erroneous. The Bar argues that Ms. Rose became Beach's client, whether he was employed by her or not, when she disclosed confidential information to King who passed it on to Beach while seeking legal advice on Ms. Rose's behalf. . . . In this case, Ms. Rose specifically sought out assistance from a paralegal instead of an attorney. She entered into a contract with King and King and not with Beach. Although the contract stated that Beach would review her paperwork and give her a thirty-minute consultation, it also stated that she would not be represented by him. Ms. Rose dealt exclusively with Mr. King and she never even met with Beach. In view of these facts, we find the record supports the referee's conclusion that Beach did not establish an attorney-client relationship with Ms. Rose and consequently, was not guilty of representing clients with conflicting interests in violation of rules 4-1.7—4-1.9. Despite our conclusion, however, we acknowledge that a close question is presented and caution lawyers that they should be very careful in placing themselves in such difficult positions. . . .

Accordingly, Beach is hereby suspended from the practice of law for ninety days with automatic reinstatement at the end of the suspension period. . . .

Questions about the Case

1. How would you characterize the relationship between the lawyer and the King and King Paralegals? Were the paralegals working for the lawyer or was the lawyer working for the paralegals?
2. How would you characterize the relationship of the lawyer to the clients of the Kings' services? Was it direct? Did the attorney set the fee? Decide to accept the case?
3. What were the two violations of the ethics codes here? How are they related?
4. Why did the court find that the lawyer had aided in the unauthorized practice of law?
5. What did the court say about the conflict of interest? Do you agree? (Remember this case for Chapter 5.)

Confidentiality

This chapter explains why confidentiality is one of the most critical elements of legal ethics and how its importance is felt in practice every day. Chapter 4 covers:

- the foundations and basic principles of confidentiality
- the attorney-client privilege and the difference between the legal privilege and the ethics rules on confidentiality
- what information is privileged or protected by the rule of confidentiality
- how and when the privilege and the duty of confidentiality may be broken or waived
- the work product rule
- how the principles and rules of confidentiality come into play for legal assistants in practice
- how to protect confidentiality of information and records
- special problems in maintaining confidentiality with technology

A. The Principle of Confidentiality

Confidentiality is one of the oldest precepts of legal ethics, one that in theory is unquestioned in its importance. Despite this, it is also commonly abused in daily law practice. It is not unusual for ethical dilemmas concerning confidentiality to arise in all kinds of law practice.

The principle of confidentiality is based on the notion that an attorney must know all the facts if he or she is to best serve the client and that a client is not likely to provide such full disclosure without assurance that information that may be incriminating or embarrassing will not be revealed outside the attorney-client relationship. The principle of confidentiality is also based on agency law. A lawyer has a fiduciary relationship with the client that requires the lawyer's highest trust, which includes confidence, loyalty, and good faith.

The general duty of confidentiality encompasses both ethics rules and evidentiary rules relating to *attorney-client privilege* and *work product*. The attorney-client privilege is a rule of evidence that relates only to what confidential information may be divulged in litigation by way of discovery or testimony. The ethical rules of confidentiality are much broader than the attorney-client privilege, as they cover a lawyer's duty not to divulge information about a client in any context.

B. Attorney-Client Privilege

1. Defined Generally

All jurisdictions make provision for the attorney-client privilege by statute, court rule, or common law. The general rule is that a client who seeks a lawyer's advice or assistance may invoke an unqualified privilege not to testify and to prevent the lawyer from testifying as to communications made by the client in confidence to the lawyer. The privilege lasts indefinitely. The client is the holder of the privilege; only the client may waive it, thereby consenting to the disclosure of confidential communications. And although the client is the holder of the privilege, it is the attorney who must advise the client of the privilege. It should be noted that the privilege only extends to the attorney-client relationship and does not cover nonlawyer legal service providers or jailhouse lawyers.

Case law has further clarified the meaning of the attorney-client privilege: The privilege covers confidential communications between lawyer and client—whether oral or written—so long as the advice sought by the client is legal; other kinds of advice—personal or business, for instance—are not covered. It also covers initial consultations even if the lawyer does not undertake representation and includes an attorney-client communication whether or not the attorney charges a fee. The privilege does not cover material or information that is not classified as a communication. The privilege lasts after the representation of the client ends and even after the death of the client. There are very limited reasons for which the privilege will be waived, as noted below.

2. Disclosure to Parties Other Than Client's Lawyer

One of the key aspects of the privilege for legal assistants is that it covers communications made directly to or in the presence of the attorney's agents, a category that includes colleagues and employees in the law firm who are working or may be working on the client matter. This principle also covers experts, investigators, and outside agencies working with counsel on a case. For example, the privilege extends to an outside vendor, such as a data processing firm that stores confidential information.

Some state statutes on the privilege specifically extend its scope to employees of attorneys. Even without such statutory language, the privilege would be defeated were it not extended to persons other than attorneys who work on clients' matters as members of the legal services delivery team. In an important case, the Arizona Court of Appeals confirmed this principle in unequivocal language:

> We hold that a lawyer does not forfeit the attorney-client privilege by receiving otherwise privileged client communications through the conduit of a properly supervised paralegal employee.

Samaritan Foundation v. Superior Court, 844 P.2d 593 (Ariz. App. Div. 1 1992) at 599. This case is excerpted on page 128 at the end of this chapter.

Since this decision was handed down in 1992, the Arizona attorney-client privilege statute was amended to include paralegals along with other named law office personnel, such as secretaries and clerks. And wide publicity surrounding the case caused a heightened awareness about legal assistants being covered by the privilege. Many state and federal courts have arrived at the same conclusion as the Arizona court in cases decided in the early 1990s; no contrary decisions have been made.

Communications must be made in a confidential setting in order to merit the protection of the privilege. This means that the setting must be private—that is, one in which others cannot overhear—and there should not be any other persons present who would not otherwise be covered by the privilege—a friend of the client, for example. See *People v. Mitchell* on page 126 for a case in which the setting is determinative of the privilege.

Under contemporary rules, an eavesdropper who listens in on a confidential communication will not destroy the privilege. The client can waive the privilege by implication by repeating the communication to nonconfidential third parties or otherwise by expressing an intention to make the confidential information public. For example, if a client makes public disclosures of otherwise protected communications, the privilege will be waived. However, the waiver applies only to the communications revealed, not to other related protected communications.

It should be noted also that some disclosures are themselves protected and therefore do not result in a waiver of the privilege. Disclosures made during plea bargaining or settlement negotiations cannot later be admitted at trial to prove guilty or liability.

3. Matters Not Covered by the Privilege

The privilege usually does not extend to the identity of a client or to a client's whereabouts. In one well-known case, *Baird v. Koerner,* 279 F.2d 623 (9th Cir. 1960), the court held the identity of a client to be privileged when the attorney sent a payment to the Internal Revenue Service anonymously on the client's behalf for underpayment of federal taxes. Because revealing the identity of the client could have led to conviction of a federal crime, the client's identity was protected. Only a few other cases have followed this reasoning, and then only when revealing the client's identity would lead to a criminal prosecution.

The fee arrangement between a lawyer and client has historically not been privileged. The only exception to this rule is triggered when details of the fee arrangement would reveal the identity of a client and the identity itself is privileged. This exception has been used in recent years by government prosecutors, grand juries, and the Internal Revenue Service in order to identify and then seize legal fees paid to attorneys with money or assets obtained through illegal activity, particularly in the drug trade. Criminal defense attorneys generally object to the exception and are challenging the government on the basis of the privilege.

They contend that fee arrangements and records as well as client names are privileged and that the government's actions constitute harassment and interference with the right to counsel.

There is a split of authority in the courts that have decided cases on the issue, with some recent cases upholding the privilege and others finding that the client must be named. See, for example, *In re Grand Jury Subpoena for Attorney Representing Reyes-Requena;* 926 F.2d 1423 (5th Cir. 1991); *In re Grand Jury Matter,* 969 F.2d 995 (11th Cir. 1992); and *U.S. v. Goldberger & Dubin,* 935 F.2d 501 (2d Cir. 1991).

Protection of confidential communications about a client's whereabouts is almost never extended. Usually in such cases, the client is a fugitive so that the attorney's nondisclosure of the client's location would amount to assisting the client in committing a future crime.

A client cannot bring a preexisting document within the protection of the privilege simply by giving it to his or her attorney. Physical evidence of a client's crime is not protected by the privilege, and an attorney who comes into possession of such evidence is probably required to turn it over to the prosecutor. The attorney may or may not be compelled to testify about the source of the evidence, depending on the attorney's role in obtaining the evidence—if the lawyer obtained the evidence illegally, the court would be more inclined to force such testimony. Finally, if a preexisting document is covered by another privilege, such as the spousal privilege, it will continue to be privileged while in the attorney's possession.

4.   Inadvertent Disclosure of the Privilege

In addition to actual client consent to waiver of the privilege and consent implied from the actions of the client, inadvertent disclosure might destroy the privilege. For example, if a protected document is accidentally given to opposing counsel in a document production, there is often a dispute over whether the privilege is lost. The cases across the country are not uniform, with a few states consistently holding that such conduct constitutes a waiver of the privilege and the majority finding that inadvertent disclosure does not necessarily constitute waiver. Most cases hold that the disclosure is not tantamount to waiver so long as reasonable good-faith measures to prevent disclosure were made. Some courts also look at the extent of the disclosure, the timeliness of attempts to rectify it, and the issue of fairness. It has been argued that inadvertent disclosure by the attorney should not result in waiver of the privilege because the client is the holder of the privilege and would not actually or impliedly consent to the revealing of damaging protected information. However, obvious practical difficulties arise with continuing protection of information once it is revealed; even if not admissible at trial, opposing counsel will have the benefit of the knowledge. See the *Ocean Transportation* case at the end of this chapter for examples of the approach a court might take when faced with an inadvertent disclosure.

5. Exceptions to the Privilege

An exception to or waiver of the privilege may occur when the client calls into question the attorney's professional competence through criminal charges, a malpractice suit, disciplinary action, or a contention of ineffective counsel on appeal from a criminal conviction. When an attorney represents two clients who later become adversaries, otherwise privileged communications relating to the joint matter are not protected. However, pooled information shared by counsel who represent different clients with common interests generally is protected; although it may be used by the parties in later litigation in which the interests of the parties are adverse.

Also, confidential communications about a future crime or fraud a client is planning are not protected. (Note in the discussion of the ethical rules in section D that the rules provide more protection for this kind of information than does the privilege.) Under the important crime-fraud exception, privileged communications can be disclosed if they were made in furtherance of a crime or fraud. What communications fall into this exception varies from jurisdiction to jurisdiction, but the trend seems to be toward more court-ordered disclosure for plaintiffs in civil lawsuits and prosecutors in criminal cases. In one recent case, the court concluded that the privilege would not be applied to attorney-client communications even though the attorney was unaware of a continuing crime and gave no legal advice related to that crime. *In re Grand Jury Proceedings,* 87 F.3d 377 (9th Cir. 1996). And in the well-publicized tobacco litigation, the crime-fraud exception was used successfully in several cases to gain access to incriminating documents between the companies and their lawyers. See, for example, *Haines v. Liggett Group Inc.,* 975 F.2d 81 (3d Cir. 1992), and *American Tobacco Co. v. State of Florida,* 1997 WL 40852 (4th D. Fla. App.).

6. The Privilege with a Corporate Client

Special problems in applying the attorney-client privilege inhere in the representation of corporations. While the privilege does apply to corporate clients, questions arise as to who the client is and what communications are protected. Different jurisdictions use different tests to determine the application of the privilege. On one end of the spectrum is the *control group test,* which limits the privilege to confidential communications between the attorney and the management personnel responsible for acting in the legal matter being discussed. The broader *subject matter test* followed in other jurisdictions prevailed in one critical case. *Upjohn Co. v. United States,* 449 U.S. 383 (1981). The Supreme Court in that case extended the privilege to all corporate employees who communicate in confidence with the attorney for the purpose of enabling the attorney to render legal services to the corporation. However, many states continue to follow the control group test in state litigation.

Another issue that arises in corporate representation relates to the holder of the privilege. The corporation, not the employee, is the client and thus the holder of the privilege; only the corporation may waive it. The employee who communicates the information may not object to the corporation's waiver of the privilege. The current board of directors controls the exercise of the privilege; this leadership obviously changes over time and with modifications in the corporate structure. Such changes may alter the corporate policy on waiver as to any particular communication.

Finally, an issue that arises in the corporate setting is whether an internal audit or investigation conducted by a corporation's attorneys is protected under the attorney-client privilege. Whether or not a court will extend the protection of the privilege to such audits varies from state to state and depends to a large extent on how carefully the lawyers and their client constructed the audit to preserve the privilege.

7. Court-Ordered Disclosure

If protected communications are sought, the attorney must respond to the court and invoke the privilege. If the court orders the attorney to testify or to produce documents, the attorney may do so or may refuse and appeal the ruling. Sometimes, a court will order an in camera examination to determine whether or not to order disclosure in open court. If an attorney breaks the privilege without client consent or court order, the client may seek to enjoin or suppress the attorney's testimony or seek dismissal of the case. And, of course, the client may sue the attorney for malpractice or file a complaint with the appropriate disciplinary authorities.

C. Work Product

Federal and state rules of evidence and discovery provide for the protection of materials prepared by lawyers in anticipation of litigation. This *work product doctrine* derives from the 1947 case of *Hickman v. Taylor,* 329 U.S. 495, in which the Court created a qualified immunity from discovery for a lawyer's trial preparation so as to allow each side to prepare fully and in private. This case identified two kinds of trial preparation material: informational and mental impression. *Mental impressions,* which are covered by an unqualified privilege, are the lawyer's ideas on how to conduct the case—that is, strategies and theories. *Informational material,* which is protected by a qualified privilege, covers factual research material such as witness statements. When the opposition finds such informational material critical to its case and does not have an effective substitute, it may break the privilege and obtain the material. The work product doctrine as enunciated in *Hickman* is codified in the Federal Rules of Civil Procedure and provides the model for many state rules as well.

Because only material prepared in anticipation of litigation is protected under the work product doctrine, some material, like investigator's reports, prepared before there was a clear indication that a lawsuit would be filed, may be discoverable. This creates special problems in litigation with insurance companies. Cases in this area vary widely, some lending protection whenever an insurance investigation is made, some only after an attorney becomes involved and orders the investigation or reports.

The work product doctrine has become increasingly critical with the advent of computerized litigation support systems. Discovery under the information prong of the rule is generally permitted if documents are input verbatim. However, paraphrased or summarized documents, selectively input documents, and documents sorted topically by means of an index of issues prepared by an attorney and staff generally are protected because such information relates to case preparation, usually representing both strategic and legal theories the lawyer is developing. See the *Bloss* case at the end of this chapter for an example of a dispute over an index.

The life of the work product protection varies with the jurisdiction. Some states hold that the protection terminates with the litigation; others continue it indefinitely; still others terminate it with the end of the litigation except as to future related litigation.

As with the attorney–client privilege, work product protection can be waived by actual or implied consent of the client.

112

REVIEW QUESTIONS

1. What is the basis for the principle of confidentiality?
2. Define the attorney-client privilege.
3. A client seeks advice from an attorney. Give three examples of advice that would be covered by the attorney-client privilege. Give three examples of advice that would not. What's the difference?
4. Are initial consultations covered by the privilege if the attorney does not undertake representation?
5. Are conversations that take place in the presence of law firm employees covered by the privilege? What might change your answer?
6. Do privileged communications that are relayed to outside vendors hired by a lawyer lose their protection?
7. Does the privilege cover communications in cases in which the attorney does not charge a fee?
8. Are conversations protected by the privilege if they take place in the reception areas? Lobby? Elevator? A restaurant? A cocktail party?
9. Name three ways in which a privilege may be destroyed.
10. Does the privilege cover information about a client's identity? A client's whereabouts? The fee arrangement made with the attorney? Name the exceptions to these rules.
11. When are a client's written papers protected by the privilege? When are they not?
12. What does an attorney do when a court requests disclosure of information that the attorney believes to be privileged?
13. What happens when privileged information is inadvertently disclosed to opposing counsel?
14. Name three general kinds of circumstances under which an attorney may disclose privileged information.
15. What two kinds of complications in applying the privilege arise when an attorney's client is a corporation?
16. Define the work product doctrine. What is the reasoning behind this rule?
17. Is the data base in a computerized litigation support program protected as work product? Explain why or why not.
18. Is a nonlawyer who helps a friend prepare divorce papers covered by the privilege?

DISCUSSION QUESTIONS

1. Find the source of the attorney-client privilege in your state. Is it in the statutes? A case or series of cases? A court rule? How does it

113

compare with the general definition of the privilege given in this chapter?

2. Are there any cases in your state relating to the legal assistant and the privilege?

3. Find the rule for the work product doctrine in your state. How does it compare with the provision in the Federal Rules of Civil Procedure?

4. Do you think that the identity of or fee arrangement with a client should be privileged? How does allowing the government access to such information affect the attorney-client relationship and the purpose of the privilege as spelled out at the beginning of this chapter?

5. You discover that opposing counsel has included clearly privileged documents in a document production. What would you do? What rule does your state follow in deciding whether an inadvertent disclosure destroys the privilege?

6. What would you suggest if your firm, which had just gotten computers, instructed you to have all the information on a litigated matter input verbatim in full text?

7. Find the cases related to Independent Counsel Kenneth Starr's investigation into the Whitewater and other matters relating to President Bill Clinton. In particular, look for the case in which a court allowed the production of notes of privileged conversations between Vincent Foster and his attorney relating to the White House travel office scandal. On what grounds does the court base its decision? Is the court carving out a new exception for deceased clients? What would this do to the underlying purpose of the privilege?

D. Ethics Rules of Confidentiality

Broad protection for client confidentiality was included in the earliest codes governing attorney conduct and is now included in the ethics rules in every state. In addition to requiring lawyers to protect client confidences, these rules also provide part of the foundation for conflict of interest rules, discussed in Chapter 5.

Canon 4 of the ABA Model Code of Professional Responsibility (ABA Model Code) provides that "[a] lawyer should preserve the confidences and secrets of a client." DR 4-101 spells out the specifics of this requirement, including exceptions. This rule is worthy of some examination since it differs from the newer ABA Model Rules of Professional Conduct (ABA Model Rules) covering confidentiality.

DR 4-101 defines "confidences" as information protected by the attorney-client privilege. It defines "secrets" as "other information gained in the professional relationship that the client has requested to be held inviolate or the disclosure of which would be embarrassing or would likely to be detrimental to the client." Extending the rule of confidentiality to secrets defined in this fashion clearly calls for protection that goes beyond the testimonial attorney-client privilege. Potentially, any information learned in the course of the attorney-client relationship is covered by this protection, without regard to the source of the information or the setting in which the attorney learns the information. (Remember the requirement of a private setting to invoke the attorney-client privilege.) Further, since either client request or potential embarrassment or detriment to the client will bring the protection into play, the best practice must be to reveal nothing about a client. Even if the client has not requested confidentiality, much of the information learned in the course of a client's dealings with a lawyer may have the potential to harm or embarrass the client. Whereas the identity and whereabouts of a client generally are not protected by the attorney-client privilege, they are protected by ethics rules of confidentiality. Finally, it should be noted that the protection afforded by the rule extends beyond termination of the case and the attorney-client relationship.

DR 4-101 (B) goes on to spell out the prohibitions, stating that in addition to being protected from release, confidences and secrets may not be used to the disadvantage of the client and may not be used to the advantage of the attorney or a third person without client consent after full disclosure. Section (C) spells out the four conditions under which the rule of confidentiality may be broken: (1) client consent; (2) when required by the Model Code, law, or court order; (3) to prevent the commission of a crime; and (4) to establish or collect a fee or to defend against an accusation of wrongful conduct.

Finally, section (D) of DR 4-101 requires a lawyer to exercise reasonable care to ensure that employees and others involved in client matters do not disclose or use client confidences or secrets. This section emphasizes the attorney's duty to supervise employees and others; this special admonition in the area of confidentiality is undoubtedly included because the staff of an attorney's office necessarily has easy access to much confidential information, providing the potential for unauthorized disclosures. EC 4-2 further emphasizes this aspect of the rule in the following language:

> It is a matter of common knowledge that the normal operation of a law office exposes confidential professional information to non-lawyer employees of the office, particularly secretaries and those having access to files; and this obligates a lawyer to exercise care in selecting and training

115

his employees so that the sanctity of all confidences and secrets of his clients may be preserved. . . .

EC 4–5 also reminds the attorney to be "diligent in his efforts to prevent the *misuse* of such information by his employees or associates" (emphasis added). Misuse of information includes conduct beyond revealing information for the benefit of a third party, for example, using information for one's own benefit by making an investment, buying stock, or buying property.

Rule 1.6 of the ABA Model Rules has an even broader statement of the attorney's obligation of confidentiality. It eliminates the distinction between confidences and secrets contained in the ABA Model Code and has a general prohibition against revealing "information relating to representation of a client." Setting the parameters of what is confidential in this way means that virtually all information is covered, regardless of when and how it was learned by the attorney. No private setting is required; the information need not have been communicated directly by the client; information learned before or after the representation is covered. Further, the client need not request confidentiality, and the attorney must abstain from revealing information, whether or not it has potential to harm or embarrass the client. Finally, while a lawyer may reveal confidential information pursuant to a court order under the Model Code, the Model Rules allow judicially ordered disclosure only in accordance with exceptions to the attorney-client privilege or work product rule.

The exceptions to the general rule not to reveal confidential information are also narrower in the Model Rules than in the predecessor Model Code. For example, confidential information becoming public does not relieve the attorney of responsibility not to reveal the information under the ethics rule while it does under the privilege. Section (a) of Rule 1.6 provides for disclosure only if the client consents after full consultation, unless implied authorization exists because the disclosures are necessary to carry out representation. Rule 1.6(b) supplies two exceptions: (1) to prevent certain criminal acts, and (2) to establish an attorney's claim or defense in dispute between the attorney and client. The latter is similar to the Model Code's exception, which permits disclosure of confidential information to collect a fee from the client (revealing the minimum amount of confidential information necessary) and to defend against a malpractice suit brought by a client, a criminal case initiated by a client complaint, or a disciplinary action in which the attorney's conduct has been called into question. There is some question as to whether confidential information may be revealed when an attorney must do so to defend himself or herself in an action by a third party.

While some have argued against revealing information under these circumstances, the Model Code and Model Rules both permit it.

Rule 1.6(b)(1)'s exception that allows an attorney to reveal confidential information to prevent a crime is substantially narrower than the equivalent exception in the Model Code. Rule 1.6(b)(1) permits disclosure to prevent the client from committing a crime, only if "the lawyer believes [the act] is likely to result in imminent death or substantial bodily harm." The Model Code's DR 4-101(B)(3) includes a broad exception for future crimes, without modifying language about the seriousness of the crime or the lawyer's certainty that the client is going to act. The handling of future crimes is the most controversial aspect of Rule 1.6 and is one that many states have chosen to modify in adopting the Model Rules. Some *require* an attorney to reveal information to prevent the commission of a crime likely to result in death or substantial bodily harm. Some follow the Model Code's exception *permitting* revelation of information to prevent commission of a crime, without provision that the crime be serious. Some allow the attorney discretion to reveal confidential information to prevent future crimes or fraud, or acts that are likely to result in substantial injury to the financial or property interests of another. Other variations have also been made.

Other rules also relate to this exception. Rule 1.2(d) prohibits a lawyer from counseling a client to engage in or from assisting a client to commit a crime. Rule 3.3(a)(4) prohibits a lawyer from offering false evidence before a tribunal and requires the lawyer to take remedial measures if the lawyer later learns that he or she has offered material false evidence. This dilemma comes up most frequently when an accused in a criminal case commits perjury and the attorney knows it. The comments to Rule 3.3 offer attorneys the following alternative solutions, listed in their order of preference: (1) convince the client to retract the false testimony; (2) withdraw from the case; and finally (3) make disclosure if neither (1) nor (2) remedy the situation. State ethics rules vary considerably on how attorneys should rectify client perjury.

Rule 1.6 does not contain a warning to the attorney to supervise employees to ensure they do not reveal or misuse confidential information, such as that contained in DR 4-101(D). However, Rule 5.3 and its comment call special attention to the attorney's duty to supervise legal assistants and other nonlawyer employees to ensure that their conduct is compatible with the attorney's professional obligations, "particularly regarding the obligation not to disclose information relating to representation of the client."

E. Confidentiality and the Legal Assistant

1. Application of the Rule to Legal Assistants

Every state that has guidelines on the utilization of legal assistants requires attorneys to ensure that legal assistants preserve client confidences. The ABA Model Guidelines for the Utilization of Legal Assistant Services (ABA Model Guidelines) cover confidentiality in Guideline 6: "It is the responsibility of a lawyer to take reasonable measures to ensure that all client confidences are preserved by a legal assistant." Most state guidelines speak in terms of the attorney "instructing" the legal assistant to preserve client confidences or to "exercise care" to ensure that legal assistants preserve client confidences. One state, Illinois, is more detailed in its statement, calling on the lawyer to ensure that the legal assistant's work product "does not benefit the client's adversaries." Illinois State Bar Association Recommendations to Attorneys for the Use of Legal Assistants, Recommendation (A)(3) (1988). The Iowa guidelines remind attorneys that the confidentiality duty covers "casual disclosure (for example, by common gossip) as well as intentional misuse (for example, by such things as insider trading)." Ethical Guidelines for Legal Assistants in Iowa, V.A. (1988). Finally, at least one state has issued an opinion endorsing the use of freelance paralegals' services so long as the supervising attorney exercises care to prevent disclosure or use of client confidences. Maryland Ethics Opinion 86-83 (1986). The ABA reached a similar conclusion about attorney supervision of freelance lawyers in its Formal Ethics Opinion 88-356 (1988).

NALA Model Guideline IV requires legal assistants to preserve confidences and secrets, using the terminology of the ABA Model Code. Canon 7 of the recently revised NALA Code calls for legal assistants to protect client confidentiality and to uphold the laws on the attorney-client privilege. The new NFPA Model Code in Canon 5 requires paralegals to "preserve all confidential information provided by the client or acquired from other sources, before, during, and after the course of the professional relationship." The ethical considerations that accompany this canon set out exceptions, cover the misuse of information, and establish a prohibition against "indiscreet" communications. See also NFPA's publication *Attorney-Client and Attorney Work Product Privileges: Their Application to Paralegals,* March 1997.

More than other nonlawyer employees in the law firm, legal assistants have access to confidential information about clients. Legal assistants are frequently included in client conferences in which privileged information is revealed, are privy to confidential written communications from and to clients, and are working on highly sensitive and private matters for clients.

2.   Protecting Confidentiality in Daily Practice

Law firms need well-established policies and procedures to help prevent inadvertent disclosure of confidential information. Some firms include these in their written manuals, orientation programs, or training videos.

Policies should deny unauthorized personnel access to files and to the file room. Code numbers can be used on client files instead of names. Old files and paper (even scratch paper) concerning clients should be disposed of properly, preferably by shredding, so that no one outside the firm will have access to them. Computer screens should not be visible to those walking through the office. Conversations over the intercom and speaker phone should be limited to nonconfidential matters to prevent unauthorized personnel, clients, or others visiting the office from overhearing. Privileged documents should be labeled as such when they are created to lessen the risk that they will not be handled carefully. Privileged documents should also be segregated from nonconfidential documents in separate files whenever possible. Procedures should limit who has access to any privileged documents.

The most common kind of disclosure of confidential information takes place in conversations about work outside the firm offices. Like everyone else, lawyers and legal assistants enjoy talking about their work. Casual conversations concerning clients that are held with coworkers and friends outside the firm offices are potentially serious breaches of ethics. Not only are the other participants in such conversations receiving confidential information, but these participants may repeat the confidences to others or the conversations may be overheard. While such improper disclosures take place often and rarely result in sanctions, the consequences—losing a client, having a court deny protection to the information, having a client bring a malpractice suit or initiate a disciplinary action—are serious and should provide a sufficient incentive to legal assistants to exercise great discretion when discussing client matters.

There are many common sense practices that legal assistants and others in the law firm should live by to prevent disclosure. One group of rules centers on the importance of keeping communications between the client and the lawyer and staff sufficiently private to withstand a challenge under the attorney-client privilege that the communication was not intended to be confidential. This means not carrying on a conversation in the presence of parties who are not necessary to the representation. Conversations with clients should take place in the privacy of a closed office or conference room, not the reception or secretarial area, lunchroom, hallway, or elevator.

The presence of others should be limited to those attorneys and nonlawyer employees who are working on the client's case. This automatically excludes such law firm employees as receptionists, file clerks, and mailroom personnel. Legal assistants should not take calls from a client while meeting with another client since the client present might overhear the legal assistant's half of a potentially confidential conversation. Likewise, when seeing a client or anyone else from outside the firm, a legal assistant should not have any other clients' files or an active computer screen visible to the visitor.

The work product rule is the primary means of protecting information in data bases, especially those used for litigation support. To ensure that the data base is protected, lawyers must be involved in the design and planning of the data base. Headnotes should include their legal theories, opinions, conclusions, and strategies. Clients, witnesses, and others should not have access to the data base. Full-text data bases are most likely to be found discoverable. To prevent this, only selected material should be included and headings or annotations to assist with searches should be developed cooperatively by attorneys and legal assistants. See *Bloss v. Ford Motor Co.* on page 130 for an example of an index that was found to be discoverable.

Confidentiality agreements are another means to protect against disclosures of protected information. A confidentiality agreement should require the signer not to disclose and to prevent any disclosure of confidential information. It should require the signer to return all documents acquired or developed during the course of work and admonish the signer not to remove any documents from the workplace. Such agreements should be signed by all employees, independent contractors, and outside agencies with access to privileged information. Access to extremely sensitive confidential information should be limited to as few employees as possible, preferably permanent staff members.

Finally, legal assistants may have access to confidential information that they could misuse for their own gain. For example, if a legal assistant learns that a real estate development being handled by a firm will result in dramatic increases in property values in the surrounding areas, the legal assistant should not misuse this information to buy property. Similarly, using confidential information to benefit on the stock market is forbidden by insider trading rules. In addition to the individual's liability under securities law, the firm is also liable. Under the Insider Trading and Securities Fraud Enforcement Act of 1988, fines of up to $1 million may be levied against a law firm whose employee uses confidential or inside information to engage in unlawful securities transactions if the firm did not exercise appropriate supervision to prevent the unlawful trading. Many large firms that handle securities work screen paralegal employees very carefully and require them to sign agreements not to misuse confidential client information in trading. Several well-publicized cases of paralegals involved in insider trading have raised awareness in the legal community about this important ethical problem.

3. Special Issues Relating to Technology

Technological advances that have changed the way law is practiced have also created new problems in protecting the confidentiality of information. Electronic records are more portable and accessible than paper; are easier to retrieve, copy, and transmit; are easier to alter and intercept; and are more difficult to delete. Firms must take special security measures to preserve confidentiality and to protect against potential claims that the privilege has been waived because communications were not treated as private and confidential.

Facsimile machines pose special risks to confidentiality. Generally, faxing confidential communications should be avoided; if time is short, courier service or overnight mail could be used. If faxing is necessary, steps should be taken to ensure that the client is on the receiving end, to guard against third parties who are not covered by the privilege reading the communication. A notice of confidentiality should accompany the material on the cover sheet, the word "confidential" or "privileged" stamped on every page.

Calls made on cellular and cordless telephones may be intercepted by special scanners, making them less secure for sensitive conversations than ordinary land-based telephone lines. Under the Federal Electronic Communications Privacy Act and some state statutes, an interception of any kind of communication made through these media does not destroy the privilege if the communication is otherwise protected by a privilege, such as the attorney-client privilege. Despite these statutes, caution should be exercised when using cordless or cellular telephones for privileged communications. The use of this kind of phone may be a breach of the duty of confidentiality, even if the privilege is not considered waived by a court. Many state and local bar associations have issued opinions recommending that lawyers not use such telephones for confidential communications because of the risk of interception and the lowered expectation of privacy. These opinions also suggest that lawyers inform their clients of the risks involved and obtain their consent to use this means of communication to discuss confidential matters. The safest practice is obviously to limit the conversations on such phones and to communicate about sensitive and privileged matters only on a secure land-based phone.

Special protections must be in place to ensure that privileged material on computers is not vulnerable. Physical security of computers and network servers is essential. Servers should be in a secure, locked room and should be secured to the furniture or floor. Access to these areas should be restricted to those who must have it to service the equipment. All computers should also be bolted and have screen savers and panels that prevent anyone passing by from viewing the screen.

The system should be protected by requiring everyone to log in with passwords, which should be carefully chosen so that they are not obvious (like initials, birthdates, and the like) and are frequently changed. Obviously, passwords should not be written down and left in an accessible place and employees should be admonished not to reveal their passwords to anyone except their supervisor. As the technology is improving, more firms are starting to use electronic identification cards ("smart cards") in conjunction with passwords. Everyone using the system should be required to log out if they leave their computer unattended. Some firms even restrict what passwords can log on at different locations. A list of who logged on and when should be maintained. Anti-virus software must be used and back-up tapes should be kept. Disks and back-up tapes should be kept in secure locations. Special software must be used to delete material; otherwise it may be subject to retrieval. The number of persons serving as network administrators should be small and these persons especially screened and trained, with policies that prohibit their access to materials except to service the network. Finally, laptop computers should require passwords and protective software as well so that if they are stolen confidential information and/or the firm network cannot be accessed.

Electronic mail is such an efficient way to communicate that it has become commonplace in law firms and other businesses in the last five years. Because it is so new, there are few cases and statutes to guide the conduct of those working in a legal environment. E-mail communications are protected by federal and some state law, just as other communications are as noted above. But this is not adequate assurance that one can communicate freely with clients over e-mail. Because e-mail can be intercepted, firms must take steps to ensure security of these communications. Two excellent ways to protect confidentiality are firewalls and closed networks with the client that use land-based phone lines. Firms should use the following procedures to protect confidentiality in addition to those noted above that apply to computers generally:

122

- Inform clients about the concerns over electronic communications and obtain their written consent to use electronic mail.
- Mark all confidential communications as privileged and include a statement telling the reader what to do if the communication is inadvertently sent to the wrong person (i.e., not to read it and to contact the sender).
- Limit the recipients of a privileged e-mail to those who are absolutely essential to the privileged communication and warn recipients not to send such communications on to other persons.
- Use encryption software that locks the message into unreadable form until it is unlocked by the intended recipient who has the only "key" to decrypt the message.

In addition, firms should have internal policies that employees are informed of and agree to in writing. Policies should prohibit employees from misusing e-mail to send personal, sexually explicit, or harassing material; prohibit accessing another person's e-mail; stress the importance of sending confidential material only to those who need to have it; remind employees not to leave their e-mail access open and unattended or to share their passwords; and establish procedures for the use of encryption in sending and storing privileged material.

4. More on Inadvertent Disclosure

Incidents of inadvertent disclosure are rising, in large part because of the increase in multiparty litigation, the large scale of discovery, and the use of fax machines and electronic communications. Some examples of recent reports of damaging inadvertent disclosure have involved a lawyer in a large law firm accidentally releasing sealed documents to a magazine, another firm that inadvertently placed sealed records in an appellate file to find them later published in a magazine, privileged documents produced to opposing counsel when post-it notes marking them as privileged fell off the papers, and finally, a case in which the defendant's lawyer's staff accidentally sent a seven-page memorandum outlining legal strategy to the plaintiff's lawyer. In 1991, a trial judge in Baltimore dismissed a panel of prospective jurors in a major asbestos case when a temporary secretary working for the defense firm inadvertently faxed a secret document on jury selection strategy to the plaintiff's firm.

Legal assistants often have extensive responsibility for discovery, including responding to subpoenas duces tecum and handling document productions. When hundreds of documents are requested by opposing counsel, the legal assistant is often the one to review, organize, and examine these documents and to see that they are purged of privileged material before they are copied and provided to the opposing counsel. In addition to needing guidance from the supervising attorney as to what documents to look for, the legal assistant needs a clear understanding of the privilege so that he or she can flag documents that may be protected and bring them to the attorney's attention. Two cases at the end of this chapter, *Ocean Transportation* and *Berg Electronics* (which begin on pages 132 and 135), illustrate how privileged documents may be inadvertently disclosed during the discovery process and how different courts deal with this situation.

While most court cases on inadvertent disclosure center on whether the privilege has been waived, another important concern is the conduct of a lawyer or legal assistant who comes into possession of privileged documents through the error of the opposition. There is not yet an ethics rule that governs the conduct of lawyers and others in this situation but the American Bar Association has issued two ethics opinions on the matter (ABA Formal Ethics Opinions 92-368 and 94-382). The second rule, which expands the options of the lawyer who is the unintended recipient over the earlier opinion, states:

> A lawyer who receives on an unauthorized basis materials of an adverse party that she knows to be privileged or confidential should, upon recognizing the privileged or confidential nature of the materials, either refrain from reviewing such materials or review them only to the extent required to determine how appropriately to proceed: she should notify her adversary's lawyer that she has such materials and should either follow instructions of the adversary's lawyer with respect to the disposition of the materials, or refrain from using the materials until a definitive resolution of the proper disposition of the materials is obtained from a court.

Because of the lack of guidance through codes for lawyers who find themselves on the receiving end of inadvertently disclosed material, there is likely to be litigation over this ethical dilemma in the coming years and, one hopes, movement toward a consensus that will ultimately be incorporated into the ethics rules.

REVIEW QUESTIONS

1. Compare and contrast Model Code DR 4-101 and Model Rule 1.6. Which rule provides greater protection for confidential information?
2. What is the difference between the attorney-client privilege and the

rules relating to confidentiality found in the state ethics codes for lawyers? Which is broader?

3. Under what circumstances may an attorney reveal protected information pursuant to the ethics rules?

4. What are a lawyer's responsibilities to prevent disclosure of confidential information by his or her employees?

5. Compare DR 4-101(D) with Model Rule 5.3 and its comment. Is one stricter than the other? Provide better guidance than the other?

6. What do the state guidelines for the utilization of legal assistants say about the paralegal role in client confidentiality? What do the ABA Guidelines for the Utilization of Legal Assistants Services say? What about the paralegal associations' rules?

7. Name ten procedures or policies that would help a firm prevent disclosure of confidential information.

8. How can inadvertent disclosure of confidential information be avoided? What should you do if you receive privileged information in error?

9. What kinds of threats to the security of confidential information are posed by computers, faxes, and cellular phones? How should a firm guard against disclosure?

10. What are the special risks concerning e-mail? How should these communications be protected?

11. What is a confidentiality agreement? Who should use them? What provisions should they contain?

12. What is meant by a legal assistant's "misuse" of confidential information? Give several examples. What might be the ramifications of such misuse?

DISCUSSION QUESTIONS

1. Find the ethics rule of confidentiality in your state. Is it based on the ABA Model Code or Model Rule? Does it vary from the ABA model? How?

2. Which formulation of the ethical rule of confidentiality do you think is best, the Model Code's DR 4-101 or Model Rule's Rule 1.6? Why?

3. Do you think that the provisions relating to confidentiality found in the state guidelines for utilization of legal assistants are adequate? Does your state mention confidentiality in its guidelines? In any ethics opinions?

4. What would you do as a legal assistant if an attorney at your firm introduced you during the company's Christmas party to a client,

who then proceeded to tell you the whole sordid story that led to his being represented by the firm?

5. What would you do if while attending a local paralegal association meeting you overheard a group of legal assistants talking about a case on which you worked for opposing counsel? Would your answer be any different if you weren't working on the opposite side of the case?
6. What would you do if you overheard a legal assistant in your firm discussing confidential information about a client with a legal assistant in another firm? Would your answer be different if an attorney were doing the talking?
7. You happen to know that on Tuesdays and Fridays the file room personnel always have their friends eat lunch with them in the file room. What should you do? Would your answer be different if the friends were employees of another firm?
8. What would you do if you caught a client going through other clients' files on your desk while you were momentarily out of the room?
9. What should you do with handwritten notes of a confidential conversation once they had been typed up and put into a client's file?
10. What would you do if you were assigned to respond to a document production but knew nothing about the case?
11. Contact five local law firms and find out what written policies they have to protect the confidentiality of information. Be sure to ask about confidentiality agreements and protections for e-mail.
12. Have any cases on inadvertent disclosure been decided in your jurisdiction? What about ethics opinions issued by the bar?

CASES FOR ANALYSIS

In the following case, statements that would otherwise have been protected by the attorney-client privilege were held to be admissible because of the setting in which they were made and the persons present. As you read, think about what you would have done as the legal assistant.

People v. Mitchell
86 A.D.2d 976, 448 N.Y.S.2d 332 (1982)

MEMORANDUM:

Defendant appeals from his conviction for murder, second degree. The autopsy of the victim's body revealed 11 stab wounds on the face, chest, and back, four of which penetrated the aortic arch, liver, and heart. While the charge to the jury that "a person is presumed to intend the natural and probable consequences of his act, and, accordingly, if the consequences are natural and probable, he will not be heard to say that he did not intend them" was error, we find the error to have been harmless. The evidence of defendant's guilt was overwhelming, and the question of intent was not a "vital issue at trial."

There was no error in the court's finding admissible the testimony of two secretaries and a paralegal concerning statements made by defendant to them in the common waiting room shared by defendant's attorney with another lawyer. Defendant made the statements while his attorney was away from his office and before defendant had had an opportunity to consult with him on this matter. Under the circumstances, defendant could not reasonably have expected that the communication would be confidential nor could the communication have been for the purposes of securing legal advice or assistance. We have considered defendant's other arguments and find them to be without merit.

Judgment affirmed.

All concur, except CALLAHAN, J., who dissents and votes to reverse and grant a new trial in the following Memorandum:

I view existing precedent to mandate reversal and a new trial. . . .

Furthermore, I disagree with the majority that there was no error in the trial court's ruling with respect to the admission of certain statements made by defendant to personnel in the waiting room of his attorney's office. The record reveals that defendant telephoned the office of an attorney who was representing him on another pending charge and went to the office at their request. The trial court erroneously concluded that the attorney–client relationship did not exist until defendant's attorney arrived at his office. Contrary to the majority's view, it appears to be clear that defendant had gone to the attorney's office for the purpose of securing legal advice or assistance. Since the attorney-client privilege applies to "a confidential communication made between the attorney or *his employee* and the client in the course of professional employment" (CPLR 4503, subd. [a], emphasis added), I would remit for a further in camera hearing to determine (1) whether the two secretaries and a paralegal were, in fact, "employees" of defendant's attorney and (2) whether such statements were made in the "presence of strangers" (there being unsubstantiated claims that an unnamed third party was present) which would take the statements outside the privilege. Although the burden of proving each element of the claimed privilege rests upon the defendant, the trial court's erroneous ruling precluded defendant from offering proof to support his claim of privilege.

Questions about the Case

1. Where did the defendant make the statements in question? Who was present?
2. What is the basis for the court's decision that the statements were admissible? Do you agree or disagree? Why?
3. What does the dissenting justice say? Do you find his reasoning convincing?
4. What would you do if you were the legal assistant in such an office, and a client came in and began telling his whole story to you and the staff in the reception area?

This well-known case clearly confirms the extension of the attorney-client privilege to paralegals who work on litigated matters. It should be noted that this Court of Appeals opinion was vacated in part on other grounds in *Samaritan Foundation v. Goodfarb,* 862 P.2d 870 (Ariz. 1993).

Samaritan Foundation v. Superior Court
844 P.2d 593 (Ariz. App. Div. 1 1992)

In February of 1988, a child suffered a cardiac arrest in surgery and emerged revived but neurologically impaired. This special action arises from discovery disputes in the medical malpractice suit brought by the child and her parents against the hospital and two physicians.

Shortly after surgery, at the direction of the hospital's legal department, a nurse paralegal interviewed four operating room witnesses. The witnesses now claim at depositions to recall little or nothing of the event. Though the paralegal's summaries might refresh the witnesses' recollection, the hospital declines to provide these summaries to the witnesses or release them to plaintiffs' counsel.

Plaintiffs (real parties in interest) moved to compel disclosure. The hospital and its fellow petitioners responded that the summaries are absolutely protected by the attorney-client privilege and immune from discovery under the work product doctrine. The trial court ordered the summaries to be produced for inspection *in camera,* found only portions to be privileged, and ordered the remainder—"the functional equivalent of a witness statement"—disclosed. . . .

Petitioners and amici argue that, even if work product immunity might yield to plaintiffs evidentiary needs, the attorney-client privilege absolutely bars disclosure of communications by Samaritan or PCH employees to a member of Samaritan's legal staff. This argument poses several subordinate issues:

(1) Does the attorney-client privilege apply when, as here, the conduit of communications is a paralegal? . . .

Arizona's attorney-client privilege statute provides that

an attorney shall not, without the consent of his client, be examined as to any communication made by the client to him, or his advice given thereon in the course of professional employment. An attorney's *secretary, stenographer or clerk* shall not, without the consent of his employer, be examined concerning any fact the knowledge of which was acquired in such capacity.

Ariz. Rev. Stat. Ann. ("A.R.S.") §12-2234 (1982) (emphasis added). Paralegals are not mentioned in the statute.

Plaintiffs argue that paralegals are an omitted and, therefore, unprotected conduit for attorney-client communications. See *Church of Jesus Christ,* 159 Ariz. at 29, 764 P.2d at 764 ("Privilege statutes, which impede the truth-finding function of the courts, are restrictively interpreted."). Although we accept the precept of restrictive construction and will have more to say about it later in this opinion, we find plaintiffs' construction too restrictive in this instance.

. . . [O]ur legislature recognized that lawyers often communicate with clients through agents. . . . We believe that the legislature intended by reference to "secretary, stenographer or clerk" to list a representative, not exclusive, group of agents through whom a lawyer and client might confidentially confer.

The law has recognized in other contexts that an attorney may properly and efficiently act through a paralegal. This Court, for example, has found paralegal services compensable in attorneys' fee awards, reasoning that lawyers should not devote time to tasks more economically assigned to legal assistants, "solely to permit that time to be compensable [in a fee award]." *Continental Townhouses East Unit One Ass'n v. Brockbank,* 152 Ariz. 537, 544, 733 P.2d 1120, 1127 (App. 1986); accord *Missouri v. Jenkins ex rel. Agyei,* 491 U.S. 274, 288 & n.10, 109 S. Ct. 2463, 2471 & n.10, 105 L. Ed. 2d 229 (1989). Similarly, lawyers should not retain information-gathering tasks more efficiently delegated to paralegals, solely to protect the client's privilege. We hold that a lawyer does not forfeit the attorney-client privilege by receiving otherwise privileged

129

client communications through the conduit of a properly supervised paralegal employee.[8]

We caution that this holding does not create an automatic "paralegal-chent privilege." There may be circumstances in which a nominal paralegal serves an investigative function independent of the attorney-client relationship. . . . Such circumstances, however, are not established here. Ms. Fraiz was an employee of Samaritan's Legal Department, acting solely at its direction, in anticipation of litigation against PCH. Her paralegal status did not strip the communications she received of whatever attorney-client privilege might otherwise attach. . . .

Although the interview summaries are protected by both the work product doctrine and by a qualified attorney-client privilege, plaintiffs have made the requisite showing that their need for disclosure outweighs the corporation's interest in confidentiality. Because the trial court did not abuse its discretion in ordering limited disclosure, the relief that petitioners have requested is denied.

Questions about the Case

1. Why are the plaintiffs seeking the nurse-paralegal's interview summaries?
2. Does the Arizona attorney-client privilege statute cover paralegals?
3. What are the arguments for and against paralegals being covered by the privilege?
4. What does footnote 8 in the case remind us?
5. Did the court provide full protection for the paralegal interview summaries? What did the court protect and not protect, and why?

This next case involves the discoverability of a set of document indexes. As you read, remember what was said in the text about the work product rule protection of trial preparation materials.

Bloss v. Ford Motor Co.
126 A.D.2d 804, 510 N.Y.S.2d 304 (1987)

HARVEY, Justice.
Appeal from an order of the Supreme Court at Special Term

8. An attorney is ethically responsible for the conduct of a nonlawyer employed by, retained by, or associated with the lawyer. 17A A.R.S. Sup. Ct. Rules, Rules of Professional Conduct, Rule 42, ER 5.3 (1988). The Rules of Professional Conduct require the lawyer

(Walsh, Jr., J.), entered January 24, 1986, in Fulton County, which denied defendant's motion to strike plaintiffs' demand for discovery and granted plaintiffs' cross motion to compel discovery.

In May 1981, plaintiffs commenced this action against defendant seeking damages caused when the jeep plaintiff Edward Bloss was driving, while employed by the United States Army, overturned. Defendant allegedly designed, manufactured and sold the jeep to the Army. In preparation for the instant lawsuit, and others pending against it, defendant retained a law firm in Detroit, Michigan, to review and index the approximately 76 boxes of documents relating to the design and development of the vehicle in question. An attorney from the Detroit firm, along with two or three paralegals, spent approximately a month reviewing the documents. As part of this review, two indexes of the documents were prepared.

In January 1985, Jeffrey Anderson, an attorney from the law firm representing plaintiffs, traveled from Troy, New York, to Dearborn, Michigan, to review the aforementioned documents. . . . Anderson's cursory review of the documents revealed that they had been indexed. He was subsequently informed that between 25 to 30 boxes of documents had been removed as defendant claimed they were either attorney's work product or contained confidential attorney-client information.

Plaintiffs subsequently served a discovery notice upon defendant seeking production of its indexes. Defendant moved for a protective order and plaintiffs cross-moved to compel production of the indexes. Special Term granted plaintiffs' cross motion and ordered defendant to produce the indexes in question. The court permitted defendant to redact any information which it, in good faith, believed to contain conclusions or opinions of its attorney. Defendant appealed.

Defendant asserts that the indexes are privileged matter (CPLR 3101[b]), attorney's work product (CPLR 3101[c]) or material prepared for litigation (CPLR 3101[d]). . . .

Turning first to whether the indexes constituted attorney's work product, the term "work product" has been narrowly construed to include only material prepared in an attorney's professional capacity and which necessarily involved professional skills. Documents which could have been prepared by a layman are not covered (Siegel, Practice Commentaries, McKinney's Cons. Laws of N.Y., Book 7B, CPLR C3101:28, p.33). Here, plaintiffs seek only indexes of the documents relating to the design and development of the subject vehicle. No opinions, strategy or legal

---

with direct supervisory control over the nonlawyer to "make reasonable efforts to ensure that the [nonlawyer's] conduct is compatible with the professional obligations of the lawyer." *Id.* Those obligations include client confidentiality. *Id.* ER 5.3 cmt.

conclusions are sought. Defendant has not shown that the indexing of the documents was accomplished by using any particular legal skills.

Nor has defendant shown that the indexes are immune from disclosure under CPLR 3101(b). To be immune under that section, defendant must establish that the information sought would divulge confidential attorney-client communications. There is no indication in the record that the indexes contained confidential communications between defendant and its attorneys. In any event, Special Term specifically allowed defendant to redact any legal opinions from the indexes.

Defendant's further contention that the indexes are protected from discovery as material prepared for litigation has been considered and found meritless. We conclude that it was within Special Term's discretion to order defendant to produce redacted copies of the indexes.

Order affirmed, with costs.

Questions about the Case

1. What was it that the plaintiff's attorney Anderson was seeking in this case? What were the defendant's grounds for not producing this material?
2. Why did the court deny the defendant's assertion that the index was protected by the work product rule?
3. Why did the court deny the defendant's assertion that the index was protected by the attorney-client privilege?
4. Based on your reading of the material on work product in this chapter, under what conditions could the rule protect an index? Could the defendants in this case have created such a protected index?

The following two cases involve inadvertent disclosure of privileged information, a not uncommon event in which legal assistants often play a role. In the first case, note carefully the facts relating to the disclosure and assertion of the privilege.

In re Grand Jury Investigation of Ocean Transportation
604 F.2d 672 (D.C. Cir. 1979)

PER CURIAM:

The District Court denied a motion of Sea-Land Services, Inc. ("Sea-Land") for the return of various documents which Sea-Land alleges are protected by the attorney-client privilege but which were inadvertently disclosed to the Antitrust Division of the United States Department of Justice in the course of responding to a grand jury duces tecum subpoena. Sea-Land appeals. In response, the Government questions this Court's jurisdiction and asserts that, in any event, the District Court's order must be sustained because any privilege that existed as to these documents has been effectively waived. Accepting jurisdiction, we affirm.

A brief recital of the facts is all that is necessary. It is undisputed that the United States has acted from the outset in complete good faith. Upon receipt of the subpoena in August 1976, Sea-Land instructed its counsel ("original counsel") to withhold from production all documents which were felt might be covered by the attorney-client privilege. On September 30, 1976, said counsel responded to the subpoena and turned over two groups of documents which Sea-Land's current counsel are now claiming were protected by the privilege.

One group need not detain us any further. For whatever reason, original counsel did not mark these papers as potentially privileged and voluntarily turned them over. This must be deemed a complete waiver. Original counsel's responsibility was to determine the privileged status of Sea-Land's documents. Its decisions in this regard were binding on its client. Privilege claims cannot be reopened by retaining new counsel who read the privilege rules more broadly than did their predecessor.

The second group of documents was marked by original counsel with a "P." When the Antitrust Division received them it thought something might be amiss and promptly asked original counsel whether the set had been disclosed by mistake, Counsel investigated and explicitly, even though mistakenly, advised that the documents were intended to be disclosed and that no privilege was accordingly claimed. It was not until March 1977 that original counsel discovered their mistake, so advised the Antitrust Division, and indicated that a formal demand for return would be forthcoming. No such demand was made, however, until early 1978 after new counsel had been retained by Sea-Land. Sea-Land itself was first advised of the inadvertent disclosure in December of 1977. Since September 1976, the documents have been copied, digested and analyzed by the Antitrust Division, as well as periodically used in connection with the grand jury investigation. Several witnesses have been asked questions concerning the documents, including Mr. Halloran, a high official of Sea-Land who was represented by personal counsel and testified with respect to the documents pursuant to a related order of the District Court.

Assuming that these documents were in fact privileged prior to their disclosure to the Government—an issue not before this Court—it is clear that the mantle of confidentiality which once protected the documents has been so irretrievably breached that an effective waiver of the privilege has been accomplished. Because of the privilege's adverse effect on the full disclosure of the truth, it must be narrowly construed. An intent to waive one's privilege is not necessary for such a waiver to occur. . . . Moreover, "[a]ll involuntary disclosures, in particular, through the loss or theft of documents from the attorney's possession, are not protected by the privilege, on the principle . . . that . . . the law . . . leaves to the client and attorney to take measures of caution sufficient to prevent being overheard by third persons. The risk of insufficient precautions is upon the client." 8 Wigmore, Evidence §2325 (McNaughton rev. 1961). Perhaps this latter rule should not be strictly applied to all cases of unknown or inadvertent disclosure; this, however, is not a case where any such exception would be appropriate. Here, the disclosure cannot be viewed as having been inadvertent in all respects. Original counsel knew that some papers marked "P" had been divulged. This production was brought to their attention on at least one occasion; each time, however, said counsel declined to assert the privilege. Similarly, the Government cannot be said in any way to have "compelled" Sea-Land or original counsel to produce privileged documents; and there certainly was here an adequate opportunity in September 1976 to claim the privilege.

To be sure, in the final analysis, the privilege is for the client, not the attorney, to assert. McCormick, Evidence §92 (Cleary ed. 1972). Original counsel, however, acted as Sea-Land's agent in determining which documents would be produced pursuant to the subpoena and which documents would be withheld under the attorney-client privilege. Original counsel acted within the scope of authority conferred upon it, and Sea-Land may not now be heard to complain about how that authority was exercised.

Most importantly, it would be unfair and unrealistic now to permit the privilege's assertion as to these documents which have been thoroughly examined and used by the Government for several years. The Government attorneys' minds cannot be expunged, the grand jury is familiar with the documents, and various witnesses' testimony regarding the papers has been heard. This is not a case of mere inadvertence where the breach of confidentiality can be easily remedied. Here, the disclosure cannot be cured simply by a return of the documents. The privilege has been permanently destroyed.

Affirmed.

Questions about the Case

1. What were the two categories of documents that Sea-Land's counsel now claims are privileged? Explain why the court treats these two groups of documents differently. Do you agree with this analysis? Why, or why not?
2. What did the government attorneys do when they received the documents marked "P"? Why? How did the Sea-Land's counsel respond?
3. How much time passed between the inadvertent disclosure and the demand that the documents be returned? What did the Antitrust Division legal staff do with the documents in the interim? How did this figure into the court's analysis?
4. Did Sea-Land waive its privilege as to the documents in question? What is the court's analysis about why the privilege is waived? Is this based on sound legal principles, practical considerations, or both?

In the following case, the court determines that inadvertent disclosure does not constitute waiver. Note the good explanation of the approaches that different courts take in handling inadvertent disclosures and the lessons to be learned about how to identify, mark, and separate privileged documents when preparing materials for a document production.

Berg Electronics, Inc. v. Molex, Inc.
875 F.Supp. 261 (D.Del. 1995)

In presenting the motion, Molex's trial counsel reported that during the process of gathering and copying approximately 15,000 documents to be produced to Berg, copies of documents to be withheld as privileged or not relevant were marked with a yellow tab. However, somewhere in the process from tabbing, to copying, to producing, the tabs fell off or were removed. As a result, these documents were copied and the copies were delivered to Berg's counsel. Molex's counsel learned of this problem when certain of the documents were identified and used in a deposition. The next day Molex's counsel asked Berg's counsel to return the documents. Berg has declined to return the documents and contends that the vast majority of them are not privileged.

Molex has moved for an order directing Berg's counsel to return the documents that were inadvertently produced and striking the testimony taken when the documents surfaced.

The Supreme Court has recognized that the privilege forbidding the discovery and admission of evidence relating to communications between an attorney and a client is intended to ensure the client remains free from apprehension that consultations with a legal advisor will be disclosed. *See Hunt v. Blackburn,* 128 U.S. 464, 470, 9 S.Ct. 125, 127, 32 L.Ed. 488 (1888). If we intend to serve the interests of justice by encouraging clients to consult with counsel free from the apprehension of disclosure, then courts must work to apply the privilege in ways that are predictable and certain.

Courts have followed three general approaches in deciding whether the inadvertent production of a document that contains a confidential attorney-client communication waives the privilege. Some courts have found that inadvertently producing the document does waive the privilege. . . .

A disadvantage of this traditional approach is that it divests the client of the opportunity to protect communications he or she intended to maintain confidential. The privilege for confidential communications can be lost if papers are in a car that is stolen, a briefcase that is lost, a letter that is misdelivered, or in a facsimile that is missent. This approach takes from the client the ability to control when his or her privilege is waived, and is inconsistent with the Supreme Court's admonition that courts should apply the privilege to ensure a client remains free from apprehension that consultations with a legal advisor will be disclosed.

Other courts have looked to the general circumstances surrounding the disclosure of the documents to determine whether finding a waiver would be fair and reasonable. Those courts consider factors such as the reasonableness of the precautions taken to prevent inadvertent disclosure, the number of inadvertent disclosures, the extent of the disclosure, measures taken to rectify the disclosure, any delay in taking those measures, and whether the overriding interests of justice would or would not be served by relieving a party of its error. (Citations omitted.)

This balancing approach results in an uncertain privilege. That is, the protection of the privilege will depend on courts reviewing and making judgments on a broad array of facts, such as what procedures were put in place to identify and copy the documents, whether there was a written description of the procedure to be followed, and what were the time pressures present in the production. In addition, courts might ask such questions as was the person doing the copying given specific instructions not to copy the privileged documents, who reviewed the photocopying, were five hundred pages of documents copied or five thousand, and is two days, three days, or ten days too long a delay in taking steps to rectify the error?

This approach also has the disadvantage of inviting parties to litigate almost every dispute where there is a claim of an inadvertent waiver, as it suggests the decision on whether the protection of the privilege has been lost will be made on a case by case basis and will depend on a particular court's judgment on whether it would be reasonable to find a waiver in the context of the facts and circumstances of that case.

Still other courts have found that the mere inadvertent production of documents by counsel does not waive the privilege. (Citations omitted.) These cases look to the factual basis for the claim the disclosure was inadvertent to determine whether the client intended to disclose the document or communication, whether the disclosure was inadvertent, or whether the disclosure was unintentional but was so negligent or reckless that the court should deem it intentional. (Citations omitted.)

The court finds the rule of law established by these cases that look to intent best serves the interests of the attorney-client privilege, as it protects the client from the apprehension that consultations with their legal advisors will be inadvertently disclosed and applies the privilege in a way that is predictable and certain.

In this case, Molex has identified a sufficient factual basis for the court to find it inadvertently produced these documents. That is, it has shown (and Berg has not disputed) that Molex's counsel identified the documents to be withheld, marked those documents, and someone at counsel's law firm nevertheless copied and produced them. It is clear that Molex and its counsel did not intend to produce these documents; on the contrary, they intended not to produce them, and the documents were produced by mistake.

As the court has found the production was inadvertent, it concludes Molex has not waived the privilege that protects these documents from disclosure in discovery. The court will enter an Order directing Berg to return to Molex all copies of the documents Molex has identified as inadvertently produced. With regard to each document produced and returned, Molex will prepare a log identifying the document and the basis for its claim the document is protected from discovery by the attorney-client privilege.

Questions about the Case

1. How did the privileged documents get into the set of documents produced for the opposing side? How could this have been avoided? How do you think a client would react to this kind of mistake?
2. What is the purpose of the privilege?
3. What are the three approaches taken by courts in handling such inadvertent disclosures, as stated by this court?

4. Why does the court disapprove of the middle ground analysis that takes several factors into account? Do you agree?
5. Why does the court choose the approach that provides the most protection for the privilege?
6. What additional work does the firm that inadvertently disclosed the privileged documents have to do in response to this order? Where do you think this might lead?

5

Conflicts of Interest

This chapter explains why conflicts of interest have become increasingly common in today's dynamic legal environment, and why legal assistants are more and more often confronted with potential conflicts. Chapter 5 covers:

- the foundation on which conflict of interest rules rest
- the rules governing simultaneous and successive representation and their application to legal assistants
- exposure to the rules governing special conflict situations and their application to legal assistants

  - an attorney being called as a witness
  - business transactions with clients
  - publication rights
  - financial assistance to clients
  - lawyer's interest in litigation
  - gifts from clients
  - agreements with clients limiting lawyer malpractice liability
  - payment of attorney's fees by third persons
  - conflicts involving family members or relatives of lawyers and legal assistants

- disqualifications caused by individual conflicts of interest that are imputed to an individual's firm
- client consent to conflicts
- screens to protect against disqualification
- the use of conflicts checks and paralegals' responsibility to maintain records

A. Introduction

In the past 20 years, conflicts of interest have become one of the most troublesome areas of ethics for law firms and their clients. The growth in the size of law firms, the development of branch offices, the merger of firms, the increase in attorney mobility from firm to firm, and greater legal specialization have made the potential for conflicts of interest an ever-present concern. The traditional strict, straightforward rules governing conflicts don't seem to work anymore; they fail to address certain kinds of conflicts and, in fact, in some situations act as an undue hardship on law firms, law firm employees, and clients.

The ethical rules governing conflicts of interest are based on the duties of loyalty and confidentiality. Both of these duties are threatened when an attorney has an interest that is adverse to a client's. This is true whether the attorney's adverse interest is a personal or business one, or relates to the current or past representation of a client. For example, an attorney who has received confidential information from one client that may help another client may feel obligated to use that information to help the second client. An attorney who represents two clients, even if in different matters, may not represent them both with equal zeal, especially if one is a favored client (perhaps because this client brings more business to the attorney).

Ethical rules governing conflicts of interest have existed since the first codes of lawyer conduct came into being, and conflicts are included in the ethics rules of every jurisdiction. While these rules form the basis for attorney discipline, they are supplemented by court interpretations in cases in which a party has moved to disqualify a law firm because of a conflict of interest. The courts have seen many more conflict dilemmas than have disciplinary bodies and have had to flesh out the rules to apply them to increasing numbers of complicated conflict situations.

The ABA Model Code of Professional Responsibility (ABA Model Code) and Model Rules of Professional Conduct (ABA Model Rules), and the state and local rules that are based on them, cover several different kinds of conflict situations including:

- simultaneous representation of adverse interests;
- representation that is adverse to a former client;
- representation of clients whose interests are aligned; and
- lawyer's financial, personal, or business interests that are or may be adverse to a client.

Finally, the rules and cases cover imputed or vicarious disqualification, a general rule under which the conflict of interest of one lawyer in a firm is imputed to all the firm's lawyers, causing the whole firm to be disqualified. Legal assistants must pay special attention to this rule because under it legal assistants may "taint" a firm and cause its disqualification.

Guideline 7 of the ABA Model Guidelines for the Utilization of Legal Assistant Services (ABA Model Guidelines) advises attorneys to take measures to prevent conflicts resulting from a legal assistant's other employment or interests. The comment to this guideline makes it clear that personal and financial interests are covered, as well as employment interests. The comment also discusses the screening of a legal assistant from any case in which a conflict exists, a matter covered later in this chapter in section F. About half of the states that have guidelines on legal assistants refer to paralegal conflicts of interests and call on the lawyer generally to ensure against conflicts impinging on the services rendered to the client. See, for example, Indiana Guideline 9.10(g); Kansas Guideline X; Michigan Guideline 5; New Mexico Guideline VI; North Carolina Guideline 7; South Dakota Guideline 9.

The NFPA Model Code includes an extensive section on conflicts of interest (Canon 8). NFPA has also issued an ethics opinion describing the use of ethical screens and highlighting key cases and ethics opinions throughout the country (NFPA Ethics Opinion 95-3). The NALA Code of Ethics and Professional Responsibility does not refer directly to conflicts of interest although general language about confidentiality and adherence to ethical codes for lawyers would cover conflict situations. (See Canon 3(c) and Canon 7.) The NALA Model Guidelines refer to conflicts under Guideline I, citing to the California *Asbestos Litigation* case found on page 175 at the end of this chapter.

B. Simultaneous Representation

The most clearcut case of a conflict of interest is an attorney's concurrent or *simultaneous representation* of two clients whose interests are adverse to one another. The most obvious and absurd example of this is an attorney attempting to represent both the plaintiff and the defendant in the same case. However, simultaneous representation problems arise in other less blatant situations, such as in nonlitigated matters and when the adverse representation involves the same client or clients, but a different case.

ABA Model Code DR 5-105 contains the rules governing such conflicts. DR 5-105(C) permits such representation "if it is obvious that [the attorney] can adequately represent the interest of each [client] and if each consents to the representation after full disclosure of the possible effect of such representation on the exercise of his independent professional judgment on behalf of each."

ABA Model Rule 1.7(a) contains similar language and allows simultaneous representation in cases involving direct adverse interests only if "(1) the lawyer reasonably believes the representation will not adversely affect the relationship with the other client; and (2) each client consents after consultation."

Both configurations have a twofold test: first, an assurance of adequate representation of both clients and, second, client consent after full disclosure or consultation. Adequate representation of two adverse clients is no small hurdle; it is quite difficult for an attorney to demonstrate objectively how he or she can be equally loyal to and zealous on behalf of two clients who oppose each other. Even if the attorney believes that this is possible, it is easy to see how a client would question an attorney's loyalty if the attorney were fighting hard against him or her in another case.

The courts generally have treated simultaneous representation as improper on its face and start with the presumption that disqualification is required. The more remote the adverseness, however, the less stringently the rule is applied. For example, it is not considered a conflict of interest per se for an attorney to represent business competitors simultaneously in unrelated matters.

Determining whether there has been client consent (called "waiver" by many firms) is also critical. The ABA Model Code calls for consent after full disclosure; the ABA Model Rules require consent after "consultation." Consultation is defined in the Model Rules as "communication of information reasonably sufficient to permit the client to appreciate the significance of the matter in question." Whether or not a court honors a client's consent depends on a number of circumstances, including

- the extent of the attorney's disclosure and discussions with the client about the implications of the dual representation;
- whether the consent was truly voluntary and not given under pressure from the attorney or others;
- when the attorney raised the issue with his or her client;
- the capacity of the client to understand fully the implications of the dual representation and consent;
- whether or not the client consulted with and relied upon independent counsel; and
- whether or not the consent is in writing and signed.

142

These factors suggest some guidelines that attorneys should follow to ensure that consents will be upheld. Thorough written disclosures are highly recommended and should cover the circumstances giving rise to the potential conflict and the actual and reasonably foreseeable consequences to the client if the lawyer undertakes or continues the representation. To qualify as independent, consulting counsel should not be from the same firm or be recommended by the firm. Consents should also include

- consideration for the consent (i.e., future or continued representation);
- procedures to screen appropriately to protect confidentiality;
- procedures to follow if a client decides to withdraw consent.

It should be noted that some states — California, Washington, and Wisconsin, for instance — have varied from the ABA Model Code and Model Rules by requiring consent to be in writing. Finally, it should be kept in mind that courts sometimes will not honor a consent if the two clients' interests are so clearly adverse that the court believes the attorney cannot adequately represent them.

Sometimes an attorney will attempt to avoid the strict rule against simultaneous representation by dropping one client in order to represent the other, more favored client. This may seem desirable for the attorney because the rules governing representation of interests that are adverse to former clients are not as strict (see Section C below). However, a court may not allow this to stand. It will look to see if representation was concurrent at any time. Improper simultaneous representation generally results in disqualification of the attorney from representing *either* client unless, of course, there is disclosure and/or consultation and consent.

Imputed disqualification rules are applied strictly in cases of simultaneous representation. These rules have been held to apply to branch offices of the same firm. And a screen to protect against improper access to confidential information will not overcome the rule, as it might in cases involving former clients. Fortunately for legal assistants, the courts have been more lenient in applying these rules to situations in which the legal assistant carries the simultaneous conflict to a new firm. See Sections C and F in this chapter.

One area of concern in simultaneous representation that comes up frequently in practice, but that neither the ABA Model Code nor the Model Rules addresses thoroughly, is that of *issue conflicts*. An issue conflict occurs when an attorney is representing two clients in unrelated cases and urging a legal position in one case that, if the attorney prevails, will have negative consequences for the other client. The comment to Model Rule 1.7 provides the only guidance. It generally condones lawyer representation of clients with antagonistic legal positions and says that "it is ordinarily not improper to assert such positions in cases pending in different trial courts, but it may be improper to do so in cases pending at the same time in appellate court." The American Law Institute's draft of the Restatement of the Law Governing Lawyers expands on this comment, stating that "indirect precedential effect" on another client does not constitute a conflict. California Ethics Opinion 108 (1989) also refuses to apply prohibitions against conflicts to the issue conflict situation even where the attorney would be arguing opposite positions before the same judge. Philadelphia Bar Association Ethics Opinion 89-27 (1990) recommends disclosure of an issue conflict and consent from both clients, and recommends against lawyers handling cases that present issue conflicts at the appellate level. Arizona also recommends consent after full disclosure in positional conflicts.

Related to issue conflicts is the representation of competitors. While neither the ABA Model Code nor the Model Rules prohibit it, some firms have policies against representing direct competitors in the same industry. The American Law Institute may also make a proposal to amend the Model Rules to include some limits on representation of competitors.

The Model Rules further prohibit simultaneous representation when a lawyer's responsibilities to one client may materially limit the attorney's ability to represent the other client. In this scenario, the interests of the two clients are not adverse, but the attorney's loyalty or zeal may be impaired because of the demands of a case. For example, an attorney representing two criminal defendants with conflicting trial dates will have to delay one trial, possibly to the detriment of that client.

Simultaneous conflicts of interests may arise in litigation in various ways. One of the most common and controversial is dual representation of a husband and wife in a marital dissolution. Many dissolutions that begin amiably, and so seem to lend themselves to resolution by one attorney for reasons of cost and efficiency, end up in court. Although the courts are not in agreement throughout the country, it is certainly risky for an attorney to attempt to represent both parties to a dissolution. Similar problems can arise in representation of co-parties in litigation. While aligned initially, co-parties may become adversaries during the course of litigation if cross-claims are filed or another party seeks to realign the parties. For example, a passenger and driver who sue a third party may find themselves as adversaries if the passenger sues the driver. Some jurisdictions, like California, have decided cases that prohibit any joint representation of a driver and a passenger as an inherent conflict of interest.

Both ABA Model Code DR 5-106(A) and ABA Model Rule

1.8(g) prohibit a lawyer who is representing multiple clients from making an aggregate settlement of civil claims or a collective plea in a criminal case unless all clients consent after full disclosure. Representing seemingly aligned defendants in criminal cases is especially dangerous as the interests of the defendants are often potentially adverse. In addition to the ethical concerns, multiple representation may deprive one or both of the defendants of effective assistance of counsel, which constitutes grounds to overturn a conviction.

Other less obvious conflict traps arise in litigation and can result in further litigation and serious sanctions, including disqualification. For example, a firm may be disqualified for retaining an expert witness who was previously interviewed by the opposing counsel if confidential information was disclosed to the expert during the course of the interview. Representing both present and future claimants in class action suits may also result in an allegation of a conflict if a settlement seems to favor one group over another.

While litigation is the most obvious setting for conflicts of interest, many other kinds of cases can pose conflicts. An attorney may represent more than one party to a negotiation if the parties' interests seem aligned but should be aware of the potential for adverse interests to arise if negotiations fail or the contract becomes the subject of a dispute. If litigation is the result, the attorney may not represent either of the parties against the other and may be sued by a former client for malpractice because of the conflict. For example, entertainment law firms that represent producers, directors, writers, and actors have been accused of favoring wealthier and more prestigious clients in negotiations on film deals, resulting in less advantageous positions for other clients. Clients of these firms do sign consent forms to the multiple representation, but later, when deals fall apart, complain that there was not full disclosure or that they would have been frozen out of deals if they had sought independent counsel.

Conflicts may arise in the drafting of wills for members of the same family if the family members are not in complete agreement about the disposition of the estate. Consents to such joint representation are essential. Similarly, conflicts between an estate and the heirs of the estate may prohibit representation of both parties. For other conflicts in a probate setting, see Section E.5, on gifts from clients.

An attorney who represents a corporation and serves on its board of directors may face conflicts if the corporation's and board's interests become adverse, such as in a derivative suit. The comment to ABA Model Rule 1.7 suggests that an attorney who is asked to serve on a corporate client's board should consider several factors, including the likelihood of a conflict arising, and should not serve as a director if there is a "material risk that the dual role will compromise the lawyer's independence of professional judgment." Serving on a corporate board increases an attorney's risk of being sued for malpractice and threatens the attorney-client privilege as well. Even without serving on a corporate client's board, a lawyer may find that the interests of the board, management, and shareholders often diverge. These interests become quite problematic in derivative suits, especially in cases of self-dealing, when there are allegations of fraud, and in corporate takeovers. While the attorney is bound to represent the corporate entity, it is not always clear who the attorney represents or how to act in the best interests of that entity. Conflicts may also occur in the corporate setting if an attorney represents several entities within the corporate family (e.g., parent, subsidiary, "sister" companies) and these entities find themselves in an adversarial position.

Finally, the potential for a conflict of interest exists whenever a lawyer acts as an intermediary between or among clients. Under the ABA Model Code, the general rule governing representation of multiple clients applies. DR 5-105(C). The ABA Model Rules have a specific Rule, 2.2., which permits an attorney to act as an intermediary if (1) all the clients consent after full disclosure and consultation, (2) the lawyer reasonably believes the best interests of the clients will be served with little risk of "material prejudice" if the matter is not successfully resolved, and (3) the lawyer reasonably believes that he or she can act impartially and without violating any other duties to any of the clients. Rule 2.2 also provides that the attorney must withdraw from representing any of the clients in matters relating to the subject matter if any client so requests or if the other conditions stated in the rule can no longer be satisfied.

A lawyer may be acting as an intermediary or representing multiple clients whenever he or she represents more than one party to a transaction, such as a real estate sale, a mortgage, a loan, or a contract. For example, one Michigan law firm was recently found to have committed malpractice when it represented both a school district and the underwriters in a school bond issuance. Several states now have advisory opinions on the issue of representing both sides in a real estate transaction. Most opinions recommend against dual representation except in purely ministerial matters. See, for example, Virginia State Bar Advisory Opinion 1401 (1991) and South Carolina Advisory Opinion 91-30 (1991). Some states, such as New Jersey, prohibit dual representation in any complex commercial real estate transaction because of the great potential for conflicts.

As mentioned above, representing both spouses in a divorce settlement is generally not acceptable because the interests of the parties are inherently adverse, and the potential for a real dispute necessitating litigation is too great. It should be noted that this rule does not apply

146

to situations in which an attorney is acting as a neutral arbitrator or mediator between or among parties who are not the attorney's clients, such as in a bar-sponsored divorce mediation program or in a court-appointed arbitration.

C. Successive Representation

The rules governing the conduct of lawyers who desire to represent a client in a matter that may be adverse to a former client — so-called *successive representation* — have been steadily evolving over the past two decades, in large part because of the growth and complexity of law practice as a business. The ability of clients to be represented by the counsel of their choice and the increasing mobility of lawyers have been significant factors in recent court decisions that apply the conflict rules in cases of successive representation with a good deal more flexibility than ever before.

The general rule is that an attorney will be disqualified from successive representation only if the interests of the former and current client are truly adverse and if the past and current matters are substantially related. This formulation presupposes an attorney-client relationship with the former client within which the attorney would have learned confidential information. If the current representation relates to the same or a closely related matter, the attorney would be in a position to breach his or her duty of confidentiality to the former client by revealing the confidential information to assist the current client. (Remember from Chapter 4 that the duty of confidentiality continues after the termination of the attorney-client relationship.) Further, the duty of loyalty would be breached if the attorney opposes a client in the same matter in which the attorney earlier represented the client.

The ABA Model Code has no specific provision covering conflicts of interest in successive representation. DR 5-105(A) states the general rule that "[a] lawyer shall decline . . . employment . . . if it would be likely to involve him in representing differing interests." The exception that applies is the general exception found in DR 105-5(C), which permits representation if it is obvious the attorney could represent both clients adequately and both clients consent.

Not providing a more specific rule for successive representation has led some courts to rely on Canon 9 of the ABA Model Code in deciding whether or not to disqualify an attorney or firm from successive representation. Canon 9 calls on lawyers to avoid even the appearance of impropriety. Most circuits and states, however, do not order disqualification solely on the basis of an appearance of impropriety, but determine whether the former client's rights of confidentiality and loyalty from the attorney are in jeopardy. Most commentators disfavor disqualification predicated solely on Canon 9 because an appearance of impropriety is only that — an appearance. It does not mean that anything improper, like revealing of confidential information, has or will take place; it does not address directly the conflict problem; and disqualification can seriously harm the interests of the current client as well as the attorney.

The ABA Model Rules contain a clearer and more complete statement than the ABA Model Code. Rule 1.9(a) states the general rule that has been followed by most courts: A lawyer may not represent a person in a matter that is the *same* or *substantially related* to the representation of a former client in which the interests of the potential client are materially adverse to the former client. Such representation is permitted if the former client consents after consultation. Paragraph (b) of Rule 1.9 covers the situation in which a lawyer changing firms is faced with the question of whether to represent a new client in a matter that is adverse and substantially related to a matter of a former client of the attorney's former firm. Such representation is prohibited if the attorney learned confidential information about the former client in his or her past employment. Again, representation is permitted with former client's consent after consultation. Rule 1.9(c) reiterates the lawyer's duty not to reveal confidential information of a former client under any circumstances, unless other rules permit or require it or the information has become generally known. (This prohibition is also contained in the rules relating to confidentiality, Rules 1.6 and 3.3, discussed in Chapter 4.) A few states have modified Rule 1.9 in adopting the ABA Model Rules. The modifications are slight but varied; a growing number of states require client consent to be in writing, which is always the best practice.

A separate ABA Model Rule applies to government lawyers. Model Rule 1.11 allows a former government lawyer to represent a private client in a matter that the lawyer previously participated in or obtained confidential information about while in government service, *with* the government agency's consent after consultation. It further allows a screen to prevent firm disqualification in such a representation. A lawyer who moves from private practice to government service is prohibited from switching sides or from negotiating for private employment with a party or an attorney with whom the lawyer is dealing on a matter. ABA Model Code DR 9-101(B), (which falls under Canon 9 regarding the avoidance of any appearance of impropriety) prohibits a former public employee from accepting "private employment in a matter in which he had substantial responsibility as a public employee." The more flexible approach for government lawyers who wish to move into private practice is predicated on the policy of not discouraging lawyers from entering less lucrative government and civil service.

As the courts have heard an increasing number of motions for disqualification, they have been faced with the challenge of applying these rules consistently to factual situations. In ruling on these disqualification cases, the courts have been somewhat inconsistent in deciding the question of whether a *substantial relationship* exists between the former and current clients' representations. Some courts have examined the *facts* of the two matters to see whether it is likely that the attorney would have learned confidential information that relates to both matters. Others look to the *legal issues* and require a clear or even identical congruence of the issues before ordering disqualification. If the court finds that the matters are not substantially related, the attorney and the attorney's firm will not be disqualified. If the matters are found to be substantially related, a presumption that confidential information was disclosed arises. Some courts have held that this presumption is irrebuttable, precluding evidence to the contrary such as evidence that the attorney did not learn any confidential information on the prior matter or has been screened, in which case disqualification is automatic. Other courts have held that this presumption is rebuttable and that the attorney may provide evidence to overcome the presumption that confidential information has been or will be revealed. The latter rule applying a rebuttable presumption in successive disqualification is the trend among the courts.

CONFLICTS OF INTEREST INVOLVING PARALEGALS

When legal assistants move from one firm to another, they may find that they are faced with a conflict of interest. While successive conflicts generally are not as serious as concurrent ones, legal assistants must alert their present employer to any potential conflicts so that the firm can take measures to obtain client consent, to screen the "tainted" legal assistant if necessary, or both. See the cases at the end of this chapter for lessons on how to avoid conflicts and what to do when they arise.

D. Attorney as Witness

Another kind of conflict of interest arises when an attorney or someone in the attorney's firm is called on to testify in a case in which the attorney is acting as an advocate.

149

The rationale for prohibiting a lawyer from testifying in a case in which he or she is an advocate is to protect the client's interest because the potential exists for such testimony to harm the client's case. This harm may come about in a variety of ways, depending on the nature of the attorney's testimony. If the testimony is in the client's favor, opposing counsel could discredit it based on the assumption that the attorney is biased in the client's favor. In this situation, winning for the client also means winning for the lawyer. The attorney may have an unfair advantage as a witness with the jury, which may give the attorney undue credibility. There is also some concern that opposing counsel would not examine a colleague attorney-witness vigorously out of professional courtesy. Finally, the conflict and harm to the client are clear if the attorney's testimony is not in the client's favor.

Ethical rules prohibit the lawyer-advocate conflict, as do cases in which lawyers have been disqualified when such conflicts were present. ABA Model Code DR 5-101(B) prohibits a lawyer from accepting a case that will be litigated, or in which litigation is contemplated, in which the lawyer knows or "it is obvious" that he or she may be called on to testify. Exceptions are permitted if the testimony relates to an uncontested matter, a formality that is unlikely to be challenged with opposing testimony, or the nature and value of the legal services rendered in the case by the attorney and his or her firm. Further, an exception is provided if the attorney's not handling the case would cause a "substantial hardship" to the client because of the attorney's or firm's "distinctive value." Note that client consent is not mentioned as a means of evading the rule. It also should be noted that such conflicts under the ABA Model Code are imputed to other members of the attorney's firm.

ABA Model Rule 3.7 attempts to clarify and to alleviate the strictness of the old advocate-witness rule. Paragraph (a) prohibits a lawyer from acting as an "advocate at a trial in which the lawyer is likely to be a necessary witness." The meaning of *necessary witness* is crucial to deciding whether the dual role is prohibited. If testimony would be useful but is not critical to the client's case, or if other credible evidence could be used to prove the same point, the attorney's testimony is not "necessary." This rule also limits its application to trial situations, which enables the lawyer to represent the client in nonlitigated matters as well as in pre-trial and post-trial matters.

The Model Rules also provide exceptions for testimony that relates to an uncontested issue, to the nature and value of legal services, and when the disqualification would work substantial hardship on the client. Note that the exception for substantial hardship in the ABA Model Rules does not require the legal services to be of "distinctive value" as does the Model Code. This makes proving substantial hardship easier;

having to get a new lawyer at the time of trial would alone constitute substantial hardship in most cases.

Imputed disqualification resulting from an advocate-witness conflict is limited under ABA Model Rule 3.7(b), which permits an attorney to "act as an advocate in a trial in which another lawyer in the lawyer's firm is likely to be called as a witness." This permission is limited by the other conflicts prohibitions found in Rule 1.7 (the general conflict of interest rule on simultaneous representation described in the preceding section of the chapter) and Rule 1.9 (the rule governing conflicts involving successive representation).

In practice, an attorney should withdraw from representation as soon as it becomes likely that he or she will be called as a witness and that the attorney's testimony will not fall into one of the exceptions. If the lawyer does not withdraw early on, a court or disciplinary body will find the attorney's conduct more egregious. Motions for disqualification on the basis of this kind of conflict may be made by the attorney's adversary. This is sometimes done for tactical reasons, for instance, to disqualify the presumably able opposing counsel of choice, thereby delaying the trial or handicapping the opposition. When the adversary calls the attorney as a witness, the judge likely will inquire first as to the nature of and necessity for the testimony, and may find that the attorney need not be called. If a motion for disqualification is made, the attorney may object and, in most courts, may appeal immediately if it is granted.

LEGAL ASSISTANT AS WITNESS

These rules are also applicable to legal assistants, who are sometimes potential witnesses in litigation. Under the ABA Model Code's sweeping rule of imputed disqualification, DR 5-101(B), an attorney may be disqualified if another attorney in his or her firm must testify. If strictly interpreted, this rule could be extended to nonlawyer employees of the firm as well. However, the rationale regarding testimony in the client's favor would not be applicable to a legal assistant since it is based on the advantage an *attorney* has because of his or her professional status and role as an advocate. The advocate role cannot be attributed personally to a legal assistant-employee who does not argue the client's case in court. A more convincing argument could be made for disqualification if the legal assistant's testimony would harm the client's case. The ABA Model Rules' more flexible standard, found in Rule 3.7(b), probably will not force disqualification if a legal assistant must testify since it allows attorneys in the same firm to act as witnesses unless other kinds of conflicts are present. While there have been no cases applying the advocate-witness rule to legal assistants, it seems unlikely that a firm would be disqualified because of a legal assistant's having to testify.

One local advisory opinion, Ohio Ethics Opinion 87-7 (1987), states that in-house counsel is not required to withdraw because the corporation's legal assistant is called as a witness. The opinion specifically cites as a reason that the legal assistant's role is not that of advocate. And remember that neither lawyer nor legal assistant can be called on to divulge information protected by the attorney-client privilege or the related work product rule.

REVIEW QUESTIONS

1. On what principles are the conflicts of interest rules based?
2. Why are conflicts problems becoming more common?
3. What is the general rule about simultaneously representing two clients whose interests are adverse?
4. Can clients consent to a simultaneous conflict of interest? Under what circumstances may client consent? Why might a court not honor this consent?
5. What are the requirements for a client consent? What should be disclosed in a letter to a client regarding the potential conflict?
6. What do NALA and NFPA ethical rules say about conflicts?
7. What is an issue conflict? What does the ABA Model Code have to say about handling cases that present issue conflicts? The ABA Model Rules?
8. On what basis would it be a conflict of interest for an attorney to represent two clients whose interests were not adverse but whose trial dates conflicted? Would it be a conflict of interest at all if the attorney could successfully obtain a postponement of one of the trials? Why, or why not?
9. Is it ethical for a lawyer to represent both the husband and the wife in an amiable uncontested divorce? Why, or why not?
10. Is it ethical for an attorney to represent the passenger and the driver in a lawsuit against another driver? Why, or why not?
11. Is it ethical for an attorney to represent codefendants in a criminal case? Why, or why not?
12. Can a firm represent more than one party to a business transaction?
13. Can a firm represent all the family members in creating an estate plan?
14. Can a lawyer with a conflict withdraw from representing one client and continue representing the other client?

15. What is the general rule about representing a client whose interests may be adverse to a former client?
16. What does the ABA Model Code say about successive representation of conflicting interests? The ABA Model Rules? How do they differ?
17. How and why has Canon 9 been applied in cases of successive representation?
18. How does a court decide if matters in successive representation are "substantially related"? If a court finds that matters are substantially related, is the attorney or firm automatically disqualified? In what two ways might the attorney or firm rebut a presumption that the confidentiality of information is at risk?
19. Why is a lawyer generally prohibited from handling a litigated matter in which he or she will be called to testify? Name the exceptions to the general rule.
20. Do the rules applied to lawyer-witnesses apply equally to legal assistants? Explain any differences.

DISCUSSION QUESTIONS

1. If you worked in a law firm and were getting a divorce, would you find it acceptable to have two different lawyers in your firm represent you and your spouse? What if you were getting married and needed a prenuptial agreement?
2. Do you think firms should be bound by ethics rules against representing matters that create issue conflicts? Explain your reasoning.
3. What would you do if you worked for an attorney who had such a heavy court calendar that she or he was constantly rescheduling court dates and delaying motions and trials?
4. Should a firm be disqualified because one of its legal assistants might be called on to testify against a client in a case? What else might the firm do besides withdrawing from representation?
5. What would you do if you knew that your firm had a conflict of interest problem that it was not addressing internally? Would it make any difference in your actions if the firm was knowingly ignoring the problem?
6. Draft a letter to a client explaining a recently discovered potential conflict based on your previous employment and include the consent form for the client to sign.
7. Contact five local law firms and ask them to provide you with a model client consent form.

E. Other Conflicts in Relationships with Clients

1. Business Transactions with Clients

Business transactions between a lawyer and client contain tremendous potential for a conflict of interest in which a lawyer's interests will conflict with the client's and/or with the lawyer's role in representing the client. In addition to this inherent conflict in business dealings, clients rely on the lawyer's superior legal knowledge and are generally in a weaker bargaining position. The attorney's duties of loyalty, trust, and zealous representation are clearly implicated whenever a lawyer enters into a business transaction with a client.

Both the ABA Model Code and Model Rules prohibit business transactions between lawyers and clients but provide for an exception with client consent. The general provision in the ABA Model Code is DR 5-101(A), which provides that "[e]xcept with the consent of his client after full disclosure, a lawyer shall not accept employment if the exercise of his professional judgment on behalf of his client will be or reasonably may be affected by his own financial, business, property, or personal interests." DR 5-104(A) prohibits the lawyer from entering into a business transaction with an existing client when the lawyer and client have differing interests and the client expects the lawyer to exercise professional judgment to protect the client, except with client consent after full disclosure.

ABA Model Rule 1.8(a) is a bit more specific and affords greater protection for the client in consenting. It prohibits a lawyer from entering into a business transaction with a client or "knowingly acquiring an ownership, possessory, security or other pecuniary interest adverse to a client." An exception may be made only if (1) the transaction and term are fair and reasonable to the client; (2) the terms are fully and clearly disclosed to the client; (3) the client is given a reasonable opportunity to seek the advice of independent counsel; and (4) the client consents in writing. Some jurisdictions have modified the consent provisions by requiring only the consent, and not the disclosure of terms, to be in writing. A few more states have made other modifications. With regard to the independent counsel provision, it should be noted that a "reasonable opportunity to seek the advice of independent counsel" means that the attorney should recommend and encourage the client to seek such advice. Even under the ABA Model Code, which does not require this, consent is more likely to be upheld if independent counsel has been recommended to and consulted by the client. In addition to these requirements, it is good practice to allow the client a reasonable amount of time within which to sign the consent so that the client has enough time to reflect on the matter and to obtain the opinion of independent counsel.

In practice, lawyers and clients have many opportunities to enter into business transactions, not all of which are prohibited. Commercial transactions that clients in their business capacities may provide to the public—as well as to law firms—such as banking, medical services, products, and utilities are not prohibited. The comment to ABA Model Rule 1.8 points out that in these transactions the attorney has no advantage over the client. Obviously the representation of the client is itself a business transaction, one that is not covered by these prohibitions.

Examples of business transactions that are generally prohibited include: (1) a lawyer purchasing real estate from a client while also drafting the documents relating to the sale; (2) a lawyer advising clients to make investments in businesses in which he or she has an interest; (3) a lawyer borrowing money from a client while failing to advise the client how to perfect the client's security interest; and (4) a lawyer going into business with a client, forming a corporation for the business that gives the lawyer an ownership interest, and continuing to represent the corporation as its attorney.

BUSINESS TRANSACTION CONFLICTS WITH LEGAL ASSISTANTS

Conflicts based on business transactions may arise also for legal assistants. For example, a legal assistant may be invited to invest in a client's business or may own stock in a client's company. Such conflicts are not as likely to be as incurable for a legal assistant as they are for an attorney. Because it is the attorney who is relied on by the client for legal advice, it is the attorney who is more likely to have an unfair advantage over the client. However, legal assistants should be aware of the general prohibition on business transactions with clients and take care to avoid dual roles that might create a conflict. If such a conflict arises, the legal assistant should consult with the supervising attorney about obtaining client consent.

2. Publication, Literary, and Media Rights

Both the ABA Model Code and Model Rules prohibit an attorney from entering into an agreement that grants the attorney publication, literary, or media rights relating to the subject matter of his or her employment prior to the conclusion of the representation. See ABA

Model Rule 1.8(d); ABA Model Code DR 5-104(B). This rule protects against conflicts that might arise during the representation between what is best for the client and what would enhance the value of the "story," that is, the value of the lawyer's interests in the literary or media rights.

In addition to disciplinary action for violation of this rule (which is rare), this kind of conflict may be the basis of a motion to disqualify counsel or of an appeal in a criminal case based on ineffective counsel.

3. Financial Assistance to Clients

Whenever a lawyer loans funds to a client, a new dimension—that of creditor and debtor—is imposed on the attorney-client relationship. Because of the inherent conflict in both representing the client and being the client's creditor, the ABA Model Code and Model Rules prohibit most kinds of financial assistance to clients.

DR 5-103(B) prohibits a lawyer from giving a client financial assistance except for advancing or guaranteeing "the expense of litigation, including court costs, expenses of investigation, expenses of medical examination, and costs of obtaining and presenting evidence, provided the client remains ultimately liable for such expenses." ABA Model Rule 1.8(e) is more liberal in that it allows repayment of the advanced costs of litigation to be contingent on the outcome of the litigation and allows an attorney to pay litigation costs outright for an indigent client. Several states have adopted the ABA Model Rules without adopting these two notable exceptions.

It should be noted that advancing a client funds for living expenses is not covered by the rules allowing advances for "costs." Doing so is generally regarded as unethical conduct; however, a loan from attorney to client for living expenses may be evaluated separately under the rules relating to business transactions, rather than under the rules about advancing costs.

4. Lawyer's Interest in Litigation

Lawyers are prohibited from acquiring a proprietary interest in litigation in which they are involved. See ABA Model Code DR 5-103(A); ABA Model Rule 1.8(j). Contingency fees in civil cases and liens to secure fees or expenses are excepted.

The rule prohibiting an attorney from obtaining an interest in litigation derives from the old prohibitions on maintenance, champerty, and barratry. Under English common law these were crimes concerned with "stirring up litigation." Champerty was obtaining a financial interest in the litigation. It was long felt that such conduct encouraged unmeritorious litigation and dishonesty in the courtroom.

Obviously, attitudes have changed dramatically. The approval by the organized bar and the widespread use of contingency fees made a major inroad against these rules, and certainly the more recent changes in rules relating to attorney advertising have further diminished whatever strength remained in these principles. The current rules against obtaining an interest in litigation are all that seems to remain of the old principles. These modern rules are founded not so much on concerns about "stirring up litigation," but on the conflict that arises when an attorney "owns" a lawsuit and may be tempted to favor his or her own financial interests in the outcome over the best interests of the client.

5.   Gifts from Clients

Because of the inherent conflict in a lawyer's dual role of adviser to a client and recipient of a gift from a client, a longstanding rule strongly disfavors such gifts made from clients to their lawyers. This rule is especially pertinent when a lawyer drafts a document under which he or she then receives a gift, such as in a will or trust. The courts have long held that this scenario is rife with potential for undue influence, fraud, and overreaching, especially because clients in such cases are frequently elderly and may be more vulnerable to overreaching by their attorneys. Courts frequently void both inter vivos and testamentary gifts in such cases, even without an affirmative showing of undue influence. Some courts will allow the attorney-beneficiary to present evidence showing the legitimacy of the gift. To do so, the attorney usually must show that the gift was fair and fully intended by the client, who had the requisite capacity and was not subject to undue influence by the lawyer. One serious additional problem sometimes results from such a gift: It may raise the question of the client's testamentary capacity, potentially voiding the entire estate plan including the gift to the attorney.

In an example of this kind of conflict that shocked a community, an Orange County, California attorney who represented hundreds of wealthy retirees living in a retirement community was found in 1992 to have received millions of dollars in testamentary gifts under wills and estate plans he drafted. As a result, the California legislature adopted statutes invalidating instruments that purport to make such gifts except for gifts to blood relatives and when independent counsel certifies that there was no fraud or undue influence.

In addition to voiding a gift, an attorney may be subject to

157

discipline under the jurisdiction's version of the ABA Model Code or Model Rules. The ABA Model Code contains no specific disciplinary rule prohibiting gifts from clients, but a rather detailed ethical consideration, EC 5-5, warns lawyers against accepting gifts from clients. Many jurisdictions have disciplined attorneys based on EC 5-5. A few jurisdictions have refrained from imposing sanctions because the ethical considerations are intended to be aspirational, not mandatory-EC 5-5 says (1) that lawyers should not suggest to a client that the client make a gift to the lawyer; (2) that clients who voluntarily offer a gift to a lawyer should seek independent advice (although not necessarily legal advice); and (3) that another lawyer should draft the document in which any gift is given.

The ABA Model Rules do contain a specific provision, Rule 1.8(c), that prohibits a lawyer from preparing a document in which the lawyer or a close relative (parent, child, sibling, or spouse) is given a gift. An exception is permitted if the client is also a relative of the attorney-donee or beneficiary. The comment to Rule 1.8 also clarifies that "simple gifts," such as a holiday present or token of appreciation, are permitted and advises that in cases that require the attorney-donee to draft a document, independent counsel should be consulted.

Two issues remain unresolved by even the improved version of Rule 1.8: gifts that do not require a conveyance document and situations in which the attorney is nominated in the document he or she drafts to perform additional services, such as those of executor or trustee. This second practice is common and rarely questioned; more questionable is an attorney nominated to such a position in a document he or she drafts who also acts as his or her own counsel, or who has another attorney in the same firm act as his or her counsel. Some states prohibit this arrangement unless the court approves it upon a finding that it is in the best interests of the estate.

GIFTS MADE TO LEGAL ASSISTANTS

Legal assistants should also be aware of the potential conflict created when a client gives him or her a gift. As with business transactions, there is less risk of undue influence when a gift is bestowed on a legal assistant than on a lawyer, but the appearance of impropriety may be present nonetheless. In the case of a substantial gift, especially by an elderly or otherwise vulnerable client, it would be most cautious for the legal assistant to see that the supervising attorney recommends independent counsel and to refrain from working on the gift document in any way. For example, see the *Estate of Divine* case in Chapter 2 page 36.

6. Agreements with Clients Limiting the Attorney's Malpractice Liability

Both case law and the ethical rules prohibit attorneys from attempting to limit their liability for malpractice. The conflict in this situation is clear: The attorney is attempting to protect his or her own interests at the expense of the client. A few cases deal with attorneys who attempt to limit their liability by asking their clients to sign a disclaimer before representation even begins; most cases deal with attorneys who exercise undue influence to pressure a client into signing a release after the malpractice has taken place.

The applicable ABA Model Code provision is found in DR 6-102, which prohibits lawyers from attempting to exonerate themselves from or to limit their liability to clients for malpractice. EC 6-6 allows an attorney who is a member of a professional corporation to limit his or her liability for the malpractice of his or her associates. ABA Model Rule 1.8(h) is both more specific and more flexible. It prohibits a lawyer from attempting to limit his or her liability up front unless the law so permits and the client is represented by independent counsel in making the agreement. It also prohibits a lawyer from settling a malpractice claim unless the client has representation. If a client does not have representation, the attorney must advise the client in writing that it is appropriate for the client to be represented in settling the matter. Rule 1.8(h) is an improvement on the ABA Model Code as it allows malpractice claims to be settled out of court while providing protection for the client in the form of independent counsel.

Lawyers have occasionally attempted to circumvent the rule against limiting liability by including in a retainer agreement provisions that relieve them from responsibility if the client takes certain actions. One such provision, for example, might relieve the attorney from further responsibility if the client fails to inform the attorney of a new address or phone number. Both case law and bar ethics opinions have consistently disallowed such provisions. Equally unacceptable as a means to limit liability would be returning a client's fee with an endorsement releasing the attorney from liability.

7. Payment of Attorney's Fees by a Third Party

If someone other than the client pays the attorney's fees, a conflict may arise over who is guiding the representation, the client or the payor.

The attorney's loyalty and sense of responsibility may be divided and judgment clouded if the person paying the fee wants to be involved in making decisions about the case. The potential for harm to the client is greatest when the interests of the client and the one paying for the representation diverge. Some common instances of this kind of conflict are a parent paying the fee for a child, a spouse for another spouse, a corporation for a director, and an employer for an employee.

There have also been instances in which the legal fees for the representation of criminal defendants in drug cases were paid by an unknown third party, very probably the operator of the criminal enterprise. It is likely that the unnamed third party sought to guide the defense by keeping the client quiet about matters that may have mitigated guilt or lessened the sentence imposed. This situation would not only result in an ethical breach, subjecting the attorney to a civil suit and disciplinary action, but constitutes grounds for appeal based on ineffective assistance of counsel.

Generally, the ethics rules permit third-party payment of attorney's fees so long as the third party does not interfere with the exercise of the attorney's independent professional judgment or does not otherwise interfere with the attorney-client relationship and the duties of the attorney that arise from the relationship.

DR 5-107(A) prohibits attorneys from accepting compensation or any other item of value from a third party to compensate for legal services except with client consent after full disclosure. EC 5-21 recommends that an attorney withdraw from representing a client if he or she believes that third-party influence will impair effective representation.

EC 5-23 and 5-24 address in detail the concerns that arise when an attorney is employed by an organization, such as a legal aid organization, in which nonlawyers serve on the governing board. These ethical considerations advise the attorney to make certain that the board sets only broad policies and does not intervene in the legal decision-making process, and recommend that the attorney have a written agreement with the organization guaranteeing the attorney's professional independence.

Likewise, ABA Model Rule 1.8(f) prohibits an attorney from accepting compensation from a third party unless the client consents after consultation and the arrangement does not result in the third party's interference with the attorney's exercise of independent judgment or with the attorney-client relationship. The rule adds that protection of confidential information must not be threatened by third-party payment. The comment reiterates that the arrangement also must not violate ABA Model Rule 1.7 on conflicts of interest. ABA Model Rule 5.4(c) also addresses the topic of a lawyer's professional independence, emphasizing that a lawyer shall not permit the one who pays his or her fees "to direct or regulate" his or her professional judgment.

These seemingly straightforward and understandable rules on third-party payment of fees have been the source of some difficulty as the means of delivering legal services have changed. For example, the salary of an attorney in a public defender's office is paid by a government entity, not the indigent client the attorney represents. The courts have upheld this arrangement so long as those who have interests that may conflict with the client's do not control either the attorney's professional judgment and conduct or compensation. The issue is more complicated when a legal advocacy organization that has a political agenda of its own is representing a client whose personal interests may at some time clash with that of the organization. The U.S. Supreme Court has endorsed the activities of such organizations and struck down the application of state statutes and ethics regulations that attempted to limit their activities. *NAACP v. Button,* 371 U.S. 415 (1963). The basis of the *NAACP* decision and the cases that follow it is the First Amendment right of free association. The Court held in *NAACP* that only a compelling state interest could justify regulation that would limit activities of the organization in bringing lawsuits to redress grievances.

8.   Relatives of Lawyers

During the last three decades, the number of women entering law school has increased dramatically. Prior to 1970, most law schools had fewer than 10 percent female students; now most have at least 40 percent. As more women have graduated and become lawyers, and married their male colleagues, the potential for conflicts based on family relationships has greatly multiplied. When married or other closely related attorneys represent adverse interests, the possibility of a conflict that may harm a client clearly exists. Husbands and wives naturally discuss their work with one another, giving rise to the risk of disclosure of confidential information, which is especially harmful if the spouse who learns the information represents an adversary. Duties of loyalty and zealous representation are also implicated; an attorney-spouse may not fight as zealously for a client when the opposing counsel is his or her spouse. Lastly, because spouses have a financial interest in one another's income, the potential to increase the marital funds from a large fee may also influence an attorney-spouse's sense of loyalty or independent judgment.

When the ABA Model Code was written in 1969, conflict problems caused by familial relationships between attorneys were so rare that no specific provision, either in the form of a disciplinary rule or an ethical consideration, addressed them directly. The drafting of the ABA Model Rules remedied this gap by formulating Rule 1.8(i), which prohibits attorneys who fall into specifically named categories of relatives from opposing one another without client consent after consultation. The only family relationships named in the rule are parents, children, siblings, and spouses. The rule also makes plain that the two clients' interests must be directly adverse for the rule to apply. The comment to Rule 1.8(i) adds two important provisos: that this rule applies only to attorneys in different firms and that disqualification based on this rule is not imputed to other members of a firm. Some states with stricter rules on imputed disqualification have extended a taint based on a spousal relationship to the partners and associates of the spouses.

Some states are following the lead of California in expanding the scope of this rule to specified nonrelatives. The California rule covers persons who live with the lawyer or have an intimate personal relationship with the lawyer. Informed written consent is also required in California.

Prior to the adoption of the ABA Model Rules and in those states that continue to follow the ABA Model Code, the general conflict and confidentiality rules apply to conflict situations involving closely related attorneys. The Model Code's Canon 9 prohibition against appearances of impropriety has been used to supplement these two main concerns. Some cases have concluded that attorney-spouses representing directly adverse interests is a per se violation of the code. More frequently, courts examine the specifics of the situation to determine if the duties of confidentiality and loyalty are likely to be breached.

RELATIVES OF LEGAL ASSISTANTS

The ethical rules governing conflicts based on family relationships are also applicable to legal assistants. The potential for conflicts and disclosure of protected information is great between married legal assistants or legal assistants married to lawyers or other law firm employees when the spouses are working on opposite sides of a case. Family conflicts should be screened for by the employing firms, and the legal assistant and his or her spouse should be certain to inform their firms fully of their family situation that might give rise to a conflict.

Two state ethics opinions have addressed the problems created when a legal assistant is related to another person involved in a representation. Vermont Ethics Opinion 87-15 (1987) recommended that a law firm could represent clients in a real estate transaction in which the adverse party was the spouse of one of the firm's paralegals so long as the situation was fully disclosed to the client, the paralegal did not work on the matter, and the paralegal was admonished not to reveal client confidences or secrets. Similarly, Michigan Ethics Opinion CI-1168 (1986) found that a legal services organization could represent a plaintiff in an action in which a potential defendant was about to be married to the organization's paralegal and in another action in which the fiance's father (and paralegal's future father-in-law) was a defendant. The opinion required full disclosure and consent by the client-plaintiffs. Absent consent, the organization would be required to withdraw from representation or to terminate the paralegal's employment.

F. Imputed Disqualification

1. Introduction

As mentioned above, the disqualification of one lawyer in a firm may cause the entire firm to be disqualified from representing a client—that is, the disqualification of the lawyer with the conflict is imputed to the firm. *Imputed* or *vicarious disqualification* is based mainly on the rather outdated idea that all the lawyers in a firm know everything about all the clients and cases being handled by the firm. Particularly the partners in a firm (rather than other employees, whether lawyers or nonlawyers) are believed to share confidential information about clients in order to best represent their interests. While collegial sharing to this extent no longer characterizes large law firms, consideration of financial incentives still supports the application of imputed disqualification rules in some conflict situations. While confidential information can be protected by careful screening, it is much more difficult to protect against the actual or perceived pressure to handle a case in a manner that will most benefit the firm and not necessarily be the most ethical or beneficial for the client. It should be noted that when a firm is disqualified by a court it may be required to disgorge fees paid for the legal services during the representation. This remedy is most often applied when the firm knew or should have known of the conflict and failed to disclose it to the client. A disqualification may also be the basis for a malpractice case against the lawyer and firm for breach of fiduciary duty.

The strict application of imputed disqualification rules has created severe problems for law firms, individual lawyers, and clients in this age of lawyer mobility and clients' choosing representation on a matter-by-matter basis. Vicarious disqualification also poses special concerns for legal assistants, whose job mobility is also threatened by an overly rigid application of the rules.

2.   ABA Rules on Imputed Disqualifications

The ABA Model Code in DR 5-105(d) contains a strict rule on imputed disqualification that states if a lawyer cannot represent a client under the code because of a conflict or any other reason, neither can any other lawyer affiliated with the tainted lawyer's firm, whether partner, associate, or of counsel. This sweeping rule does not allow screening or client consent to overcome the disqualification.

The ABA Model Rules provide for more flexibility. Rule 1.10, which was amended in 1989, does not apply the imputed disqualification rule equally to all kinds of conflicts situations. Paragraph (a) prohibits lawyers currently associated in a firm from representing a client if any of them individually would be prohibited from representing the client because of (1) a conflict in simultaneous representation (Rule 1.7); (2) the prohibition against drafting a document under which the attorney is given a gift (Rule 1.8(c)); (3) a conflict in successive representation (Rule 1.9); and (4) the rules governing a lawyer acting as an intermediary (Rule 2.2). By listing the specific kinds of conflicts that will trigger disqualification, the rule excludes the others—for example, business trans-actions, familial relationships, and attorney-witnesses. Rule 1.10(b) covers the situation in which, after a lawyer leaves a firm, the firm wishes to represent a client whose interests are adverse to a client of the formerly associated lawyer. The rule permits the firm to represent the new client so long as the matter in question is not the same or substantially related to the matter handled by the lawyer who left and no lawyer still with the firm has confidential information about the new matter. Paragraph (c) of Rule 1.10 provides for an exception to firm disqualification by means of client consent after consultation if a lawyer has a reasonable belief that the relationship with the client will not be adversely affected.

Rule 1.10 is supplemented by Rule 1.11. which covers government lawyers. Rule 1.11(a) allows a former government lawyer to represent a client in a matter in which the lawyer participated while employed by the government, with the agency's consent after consultation. It further allows another lawyer in the firm to undertake representation when such a conflict exists, provided the former government lawyer is screened from the case and receives no part of the fee, and written notice is given to the government agency. Paragraph (b), mentioned above in Section C on successive representation, prohibits a former government lawyer from representing a client against a person about whom the lawyer has damaging confidential information obtained while the lawyer was in government service.

Screening and disallowing fee participation in the case are permitted to enable another lawyer in the former government lawyer's firm to represent such a client. Rule 1.11(c) covers lawyers who are currently employed by the government. It prohibits them from participating in matters in which they were previously involved in private practice and from negotiating for private employment with an opposing attorney or party in a current case.

3. Court Rulings on Imputed Disqualifications

Most court decisions on vicarious disqualification were made during the time that the ABA Model Code was followed by nearly all jurisdictions. As a result, the courts have frequently applied a per se rule of imputed disqualification. The trend, however, is toward a more flexible approach, under which the presumption of imputed disqualification may be rebutted by evidence that the disqualified lawyer did not have access to confidential information or that the disqualified lawyer is being properly screened from any involvement in the matter in question. Not all courts are in favor of this trend. A change to the Model Rules has been proposed by the drafters of the Restatement of the Law Governing the Conduct of Lawyers that would allow a job-hopping lawyer to be screened in conflict situations in which the lawyer had no knowledge of confidential information or only insignificant knowledge about the case in question. Several courts have already criticized the proposal and are continuing to follow "bright-line" rules requiring disqualification of lawyers and nonlawyers in all simultaneous conflicts where there is not client consent. See, for example, *Ciaffone v. District Court* at the end of this chapter at page 190.

4. Use of Screens to Avoid Imputed Disqualifications

The use of screening in the law firm to overcome imputed disqualification of the entire firm first arose in cases involving former government lawyers. See ABA Formal Opinion 342 (1975). While the risk of conflicts involving former government lawyers is especially high because of their perceived inside knowledge, connections, and influence, the legal community has been concerned especially about the ability of government lawyers to move into private practice. If disqualification rules are strictly applied, and screens are not allowed to overcome them, government lawyers' employment options are quite limited. Going into government service would become a "permanent" career choice, a significant deterrent to entering government service in which salaries are substantially lower than in private practice.

Screening in private law firms, in cases involving attorney and nonlawyer employees not previously in government service, has become common practice. A *screen* (also called a *Chinese wall* or *cone of silence*) isolates the disqualified attorney or legal assistant by setting up office procedures to prevent the disqualified person from having access to information, including case files and other documents relating to the matter in question. These procedures should include a memorandum to the staff, files and documents marked with stickers to indicate the limitations on access, and programmed computer warnings or blocks to prevent screened employees' access to documents on the firm's computer network. The wall must be erected by the time the disqualified person begins employment with the firm or work on the new matter is commenced. In addition, others in the firm are admonished in writing not to discuss the matter with the disqualified personnel, who must also maintain a blanket of silence. Physical separation of the disqualified person from those working on the case is also advisable. The firm may also require the disqualified person to sign an agreement in which he or she vows not to disclose any confidential information about the matter and not to discuss the matter with anyone at the firm. An attorney who is disqualified is also not permitted to share in fees generated by the matter; this part of the screen is designed to prevent the disqualified lawyer from having a financial stake in the case.

Proving the effectiveness of a screen can be problematic. For the most part, a court evaluating the procedures must accept what the firm says by way of affidavits and testimony about the thoroughness and care of the measures taken and the extent to which they are observed. Screening procedures should be routine and careful records kept. A court will examine not only the specific procedures in place, but the context of the situation. Is the firm large or small? Does the disqualified attorney or legal assistant work in the same department or physical area of the office as the team representing the client in question? Where are the files relating to the case kept? Do the disqualified person and the staff handling the representation work on other matters together? Does the firm have sanctions for breaking the rules relating to the wall? How many other persons in the firm have access to the confidential information?

The potentially disqualified firm sometimes benefits from the fact that disqualification motions are used to delay or harass the opposition. Courts look askance at such motions, especially if they are not made as early as possible in the proceedings or are based more on appearance of impropriety than on any real danger of harm to a client or a likely breach of confidentiality or loyalty.

166

Firms and clients have also been known to use the disqualification rules as a strategy to prevent another firm from being able to represent a specific client on a specific matter. For example, a large corporate client may give minor matters to all the competitor firms in town so that, in the event of litigation, there is no qualified attorney available without a conflict to represent the opposing party—that is, all the attorneys are "conflicted out."

SCREENING LEGAL ASSISTANTS AND NONLAWYER EMPLOYEES

Recently, much discussion has centered around the extent to which conflict rules apply to legal assistants and whether a screen will prevent a firm from being disqualified because a paralegal has worked on the opposite side of a case. In 1988, the ABA issued Informal Opinion 88-1521, which endorsed the screening of a legal assistant.

> A law firm that employs a nonlawyer who formerly was employed by another firm may continue representing clients whose interests conflict with the interests of clients of the former employer on whose matters the nonlawyer has worked, as long as the employing firm screens the nonlawyer from information about or participating in matters involving those clients and strictly adheres to the screening process described in this opinion and as long as no information relating to the representation of the clients of the former employer is revealed by the nonlawyer to any person in the employing firm. In addition. the nonlawyer's former employer must admonish the nonlawyer against revelation of information relating to the representation of clients of the former employer.

The opinion distinguishes between the application of a screen to an attorney's conflicts and those of a legal assistant. When a lawyer moves to another firm, the new firm is disqualified from representing an adverse interest of the attorney's former firm; a screen would not protect the firm from disqualification under the ABA Model Rules. However, a legal assistant who previously worked on a matter adverse to the legal assistant's former firm may be screened effectively, thereby preventing the legal assistant's new firm's disqualification. The rationale for the more flexible application of screens in cases involving legal assistants is expressed in the opinion as follows:

> It is important that nonlawyer employees have as much mobility in employment opportunity as possible consistent with the protection of clients' interests. To so limit employment opportunities that some nonlawyers trained to work with law firms might be required to leave the careers for which

they are trained would disserve clients as well as the legal profession. Accordingly, any restrictions on the nonlawyer's employment should be held to the minimum necessary to protect confidentiality of client information.

The ABA Model Guidelines for the Utilization of Legal Assistant Services (ABA Model Guidelines) in the comment to Guideline 7 also endorse the use of screens for conflicts involving legal assistants. The American Law Institute endorses the principle that disqualification rules for lawyers should not limit legal assistants' job mobility. Restatement (Third) of The Law Governing the Conduct of Lawyers, Conflicts of Interest, ch. 8, §203, comment f (Tentative Draft No. 3, 1990). This comment suggests that adequate protection of confidentiality can be given to clients by prohibiting the nonlawyer from using or disclosing information and leaving responsibility to ensure that confidentiality is maintained to the supervising lawyer.

In a recent, well-publicized California case, *In re Complex Asbestos Litigation,* the plaintiff's attorney, a sole practitioner, was disqualified from a number of asbestos cases because his legal assistant had previously worked for a firm representing several of the defendants in the case, and he had made no attempt to screen the legal assistant. The California Court of Appeal clearly endorsed the use of a screening procedure for paralegals to rebut the presumption that confidential information was shared. See this case at the end of this chapter.

Two additional recent cases involving legal assistants are included at the end of this chapter. The Texas Supreme Court also endorsed the use of screens for legal assistants in ongoing litigation in the case of *Phoenix Founders, Inc. v. Marshall,* 887 S.W.2d 831 (Tex. 1994) at page 182. In other cases, courts approved the use of screens but found the procedures employed by the firms to be inadequate. See *Grant v. Thirteenth Court of Appeals,* 38 Tex. Sup. Ct. J. 12 (1994) and *Smart Industries Corp. v. Superior Court,* 876 P.2d 1176 (Ariz. App. Div. 1 1994), which is also included at the end of this chapter. Finally see *Ciaffone v. District Court,* 945 P.2d 950 (Nev. 1997) at the end of this chapter at page 190 for the minority view holding that legal assistants cannot be screened in simultaneous conflict situations.

Several other ethics opinions have addressed the issue. Alabama Ethics Opinion 89-94 (1989) states that a lawyer may continue to represent a client when the lawyer's secretary previously worked for opposing counsel if the secretary gained no confidences or secrets about the opposing party during the previous employment. Florida Advisory Opinion 86-5 (1986) states that firms that hire a nonlawyer employee who is "switching sides" are not automatically disqualified but must ensure against breaches of confidentiality. This opinion imposes duties on the former firm to admonish the employee not to reveal confidences or secrets and to advise the client involved if the employee had a close relationship with the client. Kentucky Bar Association Ethics Opinion E-308 (1985) imposes eight different steps (including an effective screen) on the former and employing firm to ensure against breaches of confidentiality and calls for disqualification of the hiring firm if it fails to comply. North Carolina Ethics Opinion 74 (1989) endorsed the use of a screen in a case where a paralegal had previously worked directly with plaintiffs and later went to work for the firm representing the defendants. More recently, North Carolina issued another opinion stating that imputed disqualification rules do not apply to legal assistants but that lawyers have an obligation to use careful screening measures. (North Carolina Bar Association Ethics Opinion 176 (1994)). Philadelphia Ethics Opinion 80-77 (1980) similarly endorses screening—both the former and employing firm must take reasonable steps to ensure that confidences or secrets gained by the paralegal while employed by the lawyer are not disclosed or used to the disadvantage of the client. Vermont Bar Association Opinion 78-2 (1978) endorses screens for legal assistants and emphasizes the importance of not inhibiting paralegal job mobility.

Most jurisdictions with contrary advisory opinions are abandoning the strict position prohibiting a legal assistant from changing employment where a current conflict exists. For example, the New Jersey Supreme Court Advisory Committee on Professional Ethics modified earlier opinions by allowing such employment with appropriate "monitoring" and "prohibitions." N.J. Ethics Opinion 665 (1992). Michigan also moved away from disapproval of screening in a conflict that involved a legal secretary. Michigan Ethics Opinion R-115 (1992). Kansas, Nevada, and Nebraska remain firm in prohibiting the use of screen for lawyers and nonlawyers alike. Kansas Bar Association Ethics Opinion 90-005 (1990), Nebraska Supreme Court Advisory Committee Opinion 94-4 (1994), *Ciaffone v. District Court* at page 190.

As the courts are faced with more cases involving legal assistant conflicts, it seems likely that they will apply the conflicts rules with some care and flexibility. As is evident from the cases in this chapter, the courts have shown sensitivity to the different roles of the lawyer and legal assistant and to the problems of job changing in an increasingly mobile legal business.

G.   Conflicts Checks

Conducting a conflicts check when a firm is considering hiring a new employee or handling a new matter is critical to identify and address potential and real conflicts. The comment to ABA Model Rule 1.7 calls for every lawyer to "adopt reasonable procedures, appropriate for the size and type of firm and practice, to determine in both litigation and non-litigation matters the parties and issues involved and to determine whether there are actual or potential conflicts of interest."

When a prospective client seeks representation by a firm, the attorney or legal assistant should obtain first all the information necessary to conduct the conflicts check before the prospective client reveals confidential information about the matter for which representation is sought. This gives greater protection of the confidential information in the event that the firm does not undertake representation. The new client information obtained should relate to the client's activities and the nature of representation sought. If the client is a business client, such as a corporation or partnership, the information should include the names of subsidiaries and other related businesses as well as principal shareholders, officers, directors, partners, and the like. The lawyer and client should discuss the nature of the legal services sought—for instance, whether representation is needed for a single matter such as a lawsuit or negotiation of a business deal or is it needed for an array of ongoing legal matters. If a lawsuit is contemplated, the names of potential adversaries should be obtained. Finally, if the client has other legal matters pending, basic information about these matters (such as the names of adversaries) should be obtained. When an existing client seeks representation on a new matter, information relating to the nature of this matter and potential adversaries should always be obtained. Finally, it is good practice to update client information on existing clients regularly—names of officers and directors, and the nature of business activities, for instance—to ensure the accuracy and currency of all information.

Similarly, prospective employees, including both attorneys and nonattorneys, must provide the firm with basic information about matters on which they worked in previous employment, major business or financial interests that have the potential to create conflicts, and personal and family relationships that may give rise to conflicts.

The firm then must process the information to determine if any conflicts or potential conflicts exist that would preclude representation or require the erection of a screen to isolate the disqualified employee. Many firms have computer programs that enable searches to be conducted quickly and more thoroughly than with manual systems that often list only client names and the names of adversaries in lawsuits. Firms need an established procedure for evaluating conflicts that have been identified through the search to decide how the firm should deal with them. Many firms have an ethics or conflicts committee or an ethicist-attorney to act on these matters. Prompt action on new clients and matters is essential to prevent a client or prospective client from delay in securing counsel. The conflicts committee should evaluate each new client, new matter, and new prospective employee—along with any potential conflicts they carry with them—applying the relevant ethical rules, case law, and firm policies that may impact their decision.

Increasingly, firms have their own policies on conflicts that may be stricter than the policies codified into the local ethics rules or controlling case law. For example, as a matter of policy a firm may decide not to represent the main competitors of key clients or to take cases that present an issue conflict with an existing client's case.

If a possible conflict exists, the firm examines the information relating to the new client, matter, or prospective employee to determine whether the conflict is one that could disqualify the firm. It may need to decide, for example, whether an apparent conflict with a former client concerns a "substantially related" matter. Once it is clear that a potential conflict of some type exists, the firm may recommend declining the representation. Or it may recommend accepting the representation while seeking consent from the appropriate party or parties and/or creating a screen.

Avoiding conflicts of interest is a critical matter for legal assistants. Legal assistants have an ethical responsibility to keep good records of the matters on which they work and to be forthcoming with this information when appropriate. Generally, this information becomes pertinent when the legal assistant prepares to make a job change, begins work on a new matter, or engages in freelance work, which in essence is a job change with every new assignment. Freelancing greatly increases the potential for greater numbers of conflicts. While it has become common practice for freelance legal assistants and lawyers to handle assignments on a temporary, as-needed basis, this practice does necessitate careful monitoring. ABA Formal Opinion 88-356 (1988) endorses the use of temporary lawyers and the agencies that place them in firms but warns that special care is required to ensure against conflicts and breaches of confidentiality. In providing prospective employers with information that enables them to conduct a conflicts check, legal assistants must take care to protect client confidentiality as well. Information about matters that the legal assistants has worked on should not be revealed until the firm is ready to make a firm job offer and should be limited to the minimum information necessary to conduct the check.

The NFPA Model Code recognizes the importance of conflicts checks by calling on paralegals to "create and maintain an effective record keeping system" to enable the paralegal to identify conflicts, to reveal such information as is necessary to evaluate the existence of an actual conflict, and to comply with screening procedures. Canon 8, EC–8.4 through 8.7.

REVIEW QUESTIONS

1. What is the general rule about business transactions between lawyers and clients? Why do the ABA ethics rules prohibit them? Name two conditions necessary for a business transaction to override the rules' prohibitions.
2. What is the general rule about an attorney being granted publication rights? What is the rationale behind it?
3. Are attorneys prohibited from paying clients' costs in a matter? Loaning a client money? Why? Are there any circumstances under which a lawyer may cover a client's costs?
4. Why are lawyers prohibited from obtaining an ownership interest in a lawsuit they are handling?
5. Under what circumstances are gifts from clients prohibited? Explain the rationale. What steps should be taken to legitimize a gift to an attorney?
6. May an attorney attempt to limit his or her malpractice liability to a client? Settle a malpractice claim with a client?
7. What potential conflicts arise when a third party pays a client's legal fees? How can an attorney ensure against such conflicts? How do these rules affect legal aid organizations? Public defender's offices?
8. What do the ABA Model Code and ABA Model Rules say about closely related attorneys representing adverse interests? What family relationships are covered? How do these rules apply to legal assistants? Do any state's rules cover relationships outside of blood or marriage?
9. What is imputed disqualification? What is the basis for this rule? How does the rule apply to legal assistants?
10. What do the ABA Model Code and ABA Model Rules say about imputed disqualification?
11. Why were screens first used to prevent disqualification in the case of former government lawyers?
12. Describe how to create an effective screen that will withstand judicial scrutiny.
13. Why might a court look with disfavor on disqualification motions?
14. What does the ABA say about the use of screens in conflicts cases involving legal assistants? Is this policy more flexible than that applied to attorneys? Why?

15. What do local ethics opinions say about using screens in cases involving legal assistants?
16. How should a conflicts check be conducted when a firm has a new client? A new matter or case? A new employee?
17. Describe a legal assistant's obligation to avoid conflicts when changing positions. How does this differ for a freelance legal assistant?
18. Do the ABA Model Guidelines for the Utilization of Legal Assistant Services extend conflicts rules to legal assistants? What do the state guidelines say? How do NALA and NFPA address paralegal conflicts in their ethics codes?

DISCUSSION QUESTIONS

1. What is your state's ethics rule on conflicts of interest?
2. Does your state or local bar have any special guidelines or ethics opinions to the application of conflict rules to legal assistants?
3. Are there any cases in your state involving firm disqualification because of a paralegal conflict of interest?
4. Do you think legal assistants should be subject to the same rules on conflicts as those governing lawyers? Why or why not? Make a list of the reasons on each side of this argument.
5. Do you think the rules on conflicts of interest are antiquated? Why or why not? How would you change them to make them more responsive to the current and future legal environment?
6. Do you think that different conflicts rules should control government lawyers and paralegals than those governing lawyers and paralegals who work in private law firms? Should there be different rules for lawyers who work for political advocacy groups? For legal aid lawyers?
7. What would you do as a legal assistant if a client of an attorney with whom you work asked you to invest in his or her business? Buy property from him or her? Do you think that entering into these transactions would create a conflict of interest?
8. Do you think that a legal assistant obtaining the rights to a current client's story creates a conflict of interest?
9. Would you loan a client money for living expenses? Would your answer be different if lending the money would keep your client from accepting a low settlement offer because of the client's dire financial condition?
10. What would you do if an elderly client wanted to leave you a substantial gift in his or her will? Would it make any difference if the client had no other living relatives? If the client wanted to do

173

this because of an estranged relationship with his or her children?

11. What would you do if a client gave you a valuable piece of jewelry? Would it make a difference if the gift were in thanks for your work on a case? What if the client promised to give you a personal "bonus" if your firm prevailed in the case?

12. What would you do if you worked for a firm that had all new clients sign an agreement limiting the firm's malpractice liability?

13. Do you think the rules prohibiting conflicts among relatives should be limited to parents, children, siblings, and spouses? What about roommates? Long-term live-in relationships? In-laws? Is it any "safer" for closely related lawyers and paralegals to work in the same firm? What kinds of problems might this create?

14. Interview paralegals at five local law firms and ask them about their policies and procedures for establishing screens and conducting conflicts checks. Also find out how effective they think screens are.

15. List all the reasons you can think of to justify imputed disqualification. Do these reasons also apply to legal assistants? Should the same rules of imputed disqualification apply to legal assistants?

16. Knowing how people love to talk about their work, do you think an internal memorandum telling the staff not to discuss a particular case with certain employees is really an effective method to protect confidentiality? What other measures or sanctions would be more effective?

17. Do you think it is possible to screen an employee in a small law firm, for example, a firm with one lawyer, one paralegal, and one secretary? What if the firm had two lawyers, two paralegals, and two secretaries?

18. Make a list of all the information you would want to conduct a conflicts check on the following: (1) a new client; (2) a new matter for an existing client; (3) a prospective paralegal employee; (4) a prospective attorney employee; (5) a prospective partner.

19. Who do you think should conduct conflicts checks and decide on conflicts matters within a law firm? Does it make a difference if the firm is a national, multibranch firm or a small, local firm?

20. What kinds of conflicts policies (going beyond the legal ethical rules) do you think a law firm should ideally have? Consider the economic implications of policies that may impose limits on a firm's accepting cases.

21. What kind of information should a legal assistant keep on his or her own career conflict list? When should a legal assistant give this information to prospective employers? Does supplying this information in itself violate confidentiality rules? What should you do if a firm that has offered you a job does not request this information?

22. Should agencies that place legal assistants on temporary or freelance jobs do conflicts checks before they send a legal assistant to a job? Should a legal assistant work for an agency that fails to do this? What would you do if you went out on a freelance job and discovered after two days that you had worked on the opposing side of the case the previous week?

CASES FOR ANALYSIS

In this California case of first impression, a sole practitioner was disqualified from handling several asbestos cases when a legal assistant who had previously worked for the defense firm involved came to work for him.

In re Complex Asbestos Litigation
232 Cal.App.3d 670, 283 Cal.Rptr. 732 (1991)

Attorney Jeffrey B. Harrison, his law firm, and their affected clients appeal from an order disqualifying the Harrison firm in nine asbestos-related personal injury actions. The appeal presents the difficult issue of whether a law firm should be disqualified because an employee of the firm possessed attorney-client confidences from previous employment by opposing counsel in pending litigation. We hold that disqualification is appropriate unless there is written consent or the law firm has effectively screened the employee from involvement with the litigation to which the information relates. . . .

Michael Vogel worked as a paralegal for the law firm of Brobeck, Phleger & Harrison (Brobeck) from October 28, 1985, to November 30, 1988. Vogel came to Brobeck with experience working for a law firm that represented defendants in asbestos litigation. Brobeck also represented asbestos litigation defendants, including respondents. At Brobeck, Vogel worked exclusively on asbestos litigation.

During most of the period Brobeck employed Vogel, he worked on settlement evaluations. . . .

Vogel also monitored trial events, received daily reports from the attorneys in trial, and relayed trial reports to the clients. . . .

In 1988, Vogel's duties changed when he was assigned to work for a trial team. With that change, Vogel no longer was involved with the settlement evaluation meetings and reports. Instead, he helped prepare specific cases assigned to the team. Vogel did not work on any cases in which the Harrison firm represented the plaintiffs. . . .

. . . Brobeck gave Vogel two weeks' notice of his termination, though his termination date was later extended to the end of November.

Vogel contacted a number of firms about employment, and learned that the Harrison firm was looking for paralegals. The Harrison firm recently had opened a Northern California office and filed a number of asbestos cases against respondents. Sometime in the second half of November 1988, Vogel called Harrison to ask him for a job with his firm.

In that first telephone conversation, Harrison learned that Vogel had worked for Brobeck on asbestos litigation settlements. Harrison testified that he did not then offer Vogel a job for two reasons. First, Harrison did not think he would need a new paralegal until February or March of 1989. Second, Harrison was concerned about the appearance of a conflict of interest in his firm's hiring a paralegal from Brobeck. Harrison discussed the conflict problem with other attorneys, and told Vogel that he could be hired only if Vogel got a waiver from the senior asbestos litigation partner at Brobeck.

Vogel testified that he spoke with Stephen Snyder, the Brobeck partner in charge of managing the Northern California asbestos litigation. Vogel claimed he told Snyder of the possible job with the Harrison firm, and that Snyder later told him the clients had approved and that Snyder would provide a written waiver if Vogel wanted. In his testimony, Snyder firmly denied having any such conversations or giving Vogel any conflicts waiver to work for Harrison. The trial court resolved this credibility dispute in favor of Snyder.

While waiting for a job with the Harrison firm, Vogel went to work for Bjork, which represented two of the respondents in asbestos litigation in Northern California. Vogel worked for Bjork during December 1988, organizing boxes of materials transferred from Brobeck to Bjork. While there, Vogel again called Harrison to press him for a job. Vogel told Harrison that Brobeck had approved his working for Harrison, and Harrison offered Vogel a job starting after the holidays. During their conversations, Harrison told Vogel the job involved work on complex, nonasbestos civil matters, and later would involve processing release documents and checks for asbestos litigation settlements. Harrison did not contact Brobeck to confirm Vogel's claim that he made a full disclosure and obtained Brobeck's consent. Nor did Harrison tell Vogel that he needed a waiver from Bjork.

Vogel informed Bjork he was quitting to work for the Harrison firm. Vogel told a partner at Bjork that he wanted experience in areas other than asbestos litigation, and that he would work on securities and real estate development litigation at the Harrison firm. Initially, Vogel's work for the Harrison firm was confined to those two areas.

However, at the end of February 1989, Vogel was asked to finish another paralegal's job of contacting asbestos plaintiffs to complete client questionnaires. The questionnaire answers provided information for discovery requests by the defendants. Vogel contacted Bjork and others to request copies of discovery materials for the Harrison firm. Vogel also assisted when the Harrison firm's asbestos trial teams needed extra help.

In March 1989, Snyder learned from a Brobeck trial attorney that Vogel was involved in asbestos litigation. In a March 31 letter, Snyder asked Harrison if Vogel's duties included asbestos litigation. Harrison responded to Snyder by letter on April 6. In the letter, Harrison stated Vogel told Snyder his work for the Harrison firm would include periodic work on asbestos cases, and that Harrison assumed there was no conflict of interest. Harrison also asked Snyder to provide details of the basis for any claimed conflict. There were no other communications between Brobeck and the Harrison firm concerning Vogel before the disqualification motion was filed.

In June, a Harrison firm attorney asked Vogel to call respondent Fibreboard Corporation to see if it would accept service of a subpoena for its corporate minutes. Vogel called the company and spoke to a person he knew from working for Brobeck. Vogel asked who should be served with the subpoena in place of the company's retired general counsel. Vogel's call prompted renewed concern among respondents' counsel over Vogel's involvement with asbestos litigation for a plaintiffs' firm. On July 31, counsel for three respondents demanded that the Harrison firm disqualify itself from cases against those respondents. Three days later, the motion to disqualify the Harrison firm was filed; it was subsequently joined by all respondents.

The trial court held a total of 21 hearing sessions on the motion, including 16 sessions of testimony. During the hearing, several witnesses testified that Vogel liked to talk, and the record indicates that he would volunteer information in an effort to be helpful.

A critical incident involving Vogel's activities at Brobeck first came to light during the hearing. Brobeck's computer system access log showed that on November 17, 1988, Vogel accessed the computer records for 20 cases filed by the Harrison firm. On the witness stand, Vogel at first flatly denied having looked at these case records, but when confronted with the access log, he admitted reviewing the records "to see what kind of cases [the Harrison firm] had filed." At the time, Vogel had no responsibilities for any Harrison firm cases at Brobeck. The date Vogel reviewed those computer records was very close to the time Vogel and Harrison first spoke. The access log documented that Vogel opened each record long enough to view and print copies of all the information on the case in the computer system.

Vogel, Harrison, and the other two witnesses from the Harrison firm denied that Vogel ever disclosed any client confidences obtained while he worked for Brobeck. However, Harrison never instructed Vogel not to discuss any confidential information obtained at Brobeck. Vogel did discuss with Harrison firm attorneys his impressions of several Brobeck attorneys, After the disqualification motion was filed, Harrison and his office manager debriefed Vogel, not to obtain any confidences but to discuss his duties at Brobeck in detail and to assess respondents' factual allegations. During the course of the hearing, the Harrison firm terminated Vogel on August 25, 1989.

The trial court found that Vogel's work for Brobeck and the Harrison firm was substantially related, and that there was no express or implied waiver by Brobeck or its clients. The court believed there was a substantial likelihood that the Harrison firm's hiring of Vogel, without first building "an ethical wall" or having a waiver, would affect the outcome in asbestos cases. The court also found that Vogel obtained confidential information when he accessed Brobeck's computer records on the Harrison firm's cases, and that there was a reasonable probability Vogel used that information or disclosed it to other members of the Harrison firm's staff. The court refused to extend the disqualification beyond those cases where there was tangible evidence of interference by Vogel, stating that on the rest of the cases it would require the court to speculate.

The trial court initially disqualified the Harrison firm in all 20 cases Vogel accessed on November 17, 1988, which included 11 cases pending in Contra Costa County. However, on further consideration, the trial court restricted its disqualification order to the 9 cases pending in San Francisco. . . .

Our statutes and public policy recognize the importance of protecting the confidentiality of the attorney-client relationship. . . . The obligation to maintain the client's confidences traditionally and properly has been placed on the attorney representing the client. But nonlawyer employees must handle confidential client information if legal services are to be efficient and cost-effective. Although a law firm has the ability to supervise its employees and assure that they protect client confidences, that ability and assurance are tenuous when the nonlawyer leaves the firm's employment. If the nonlawyer finds employment with opposing counsel, there is a heightened risk that confidences of the former employer's clients will be compromised, whether from base motives, an excess of zeal, or simple inadvertence.

Under such circumstances, the attorney who traditionally has been responsible for protecting the client's confidences—the former employer—has no effective means of doing so. The public policy of protecting the confidentiality of attorney–client communications must depend upon the attorney or law firm that hires an opposing counsel's employee. Certain requirements must be imposed on attorneys who hire their opposing counsel's employees to assure that attorney–client confidences are protected. . . .

Hiring a former employee of an opposing counsel is not, in and of itself, sufficient to warrant disqualification of an attorney or law firm. However, when the former employee possesses confidential attorney-client information, materially related to pending litigation, the situation implicates " '. . . considerations of ethics which run to the very integrity of our judicial process.' [Citation]" (Citations omitted.) Under such circumstances, the hiring attorney must obtain the informed written consent of the former employer, thereby dispelling any basis for disqualification. (Citations omitted.) Failing that, the hiring attorney is subject to disqualification unless the attorney can rebut a presumption that the confidential attorney–client information has been used or disclosed in the new employment. . . .

An inflexible presumption of shared confidences would not be appropriate for nonlawyers, though, whatever its merits when applied to attorneys. There are obvious differences between lawyers and their nonlawyer employees in training, responsibilities, and acquisition and use of confidential information. These differences satisfy us that a rebuttable presumption of shared confidences provides a just balance between protecting confidentiality and the right to chosen counsel.

The most likely means of rebutting the presumption is to implement a procedure, before the employee is hired, which effectively screens the employee from any involvement with the litigation, a procedure one court aptly described as a " 'cone of silence.' " (See *Nemours Foundation v. Gilbane, Aetna, Federal Ins.* (D. Del. 1986) 632 F. Supp. 418, 428.) Whether a potential employee will require a cone of silence should be determined as a matter of routine during the hiring process. It is reasonable to ask potential employees about the nature of their prior legal work; prudence alone would dictate such inquiries. Here, Harrison's first conversation with Vogel revealed a potential problem—Vogel's work for Brobeck on asbestos litigation settlements. . . .

Two objectives must be achieved. First, screening should be implemented before undertaking the challenged representation or hiring the tainted individual. Screening must take place at the outset to prevent any confidences from being disclosed. Second, the tainted individual should be precluded from any involvement in or communication about the challenged representation. To avoid inadvertent disclosures and to

179

establish an evidentiary record, a memorandum should be circulated warning the legal staff to isolate the individual from communications on the matter and to prevent access to the relevant files. . . .

We decline to adopt the broader rule urged by respondents and applied by other courts, which treats the nonlawyer employee as an attorney and requires disqualification upon the showing and standards applicable to individual attorneys. . . .

Respondents' alternative formulation, that a substantial relationship between the type of work done for the former and present employers requires disqualification, presents unnecessary barriers to employment mobility. Such a rule sweeps more widely than needed to protect client confidences. We share the concerns expressed by the American Bar Association's Standing Committee on Ethics and Professional Responsibility: "It is important that nonlawyer employees have as much mobility in employment opportunity as possible consistent with the protection of clients' interests. To so limit employment opportunities that some nonlawyers trained to work with law firms might be required to leave the careers for which they are trained would disserve clients as well as the legal profession. Accordingly, any restrictions on the nonlawyer's employment should be held to the minimum necessary to protect confidentiality of client information." (Imputed Disqualification Arising from Change in Employment by Nonlawyer Employee, ABA Standing Com. on Ethics & Prof. Responsibility, Informal Opn. No. 88-1526 (1988) p.3.) Respondents' suggested rule could easily result in nonlawyer employees becoming "Typhoid Marys," unemployable by firms practicing in specialized areas of the law where the employees are most skilled and experienced.

Absent written consent, the proper rule and its application for disqualification based on nonlawyer employee conflicts of interest should be as follows. The party seeking disqualification must show that its present or past attorney's former employee possesses confidential attorney–client information materially related to the proceedings before the court. The party should not be required to disclose the actual information contended to be confidential. However, the court should be provided with the nature of the information and its material relationship to the proceeding. (Citations omitted.)

Once this showing has been made, a rebuttable presumption arises that the information has been used or disclosed in the current employment. The presumption is a rule by necessity because the party seeking disqualification will be at a loss to prove what is known by the adversary's attorneys and legal staff. (Citations omitted.) To rebut the presumption, the challenged attorney has the burden of showing that the practical effect of formal screening has been achieved. The showing must satisfy the trial court that the employee has not had and will not have any involvement with the litigation, or any communication with attorneys or coemployees concerning the litigation, that would support a reasonable inference that the information has been used or disclosed. If the challenged attorney fails to make this showing, then the court may disqualify the attorney and law firm. . . .

There can be no question that Vogel obtained confidential attorney-client information when he accessed the Harrison firm's case files on Brobeck's computer. . . .

The Harrison firm also argues that there was no evidence that Vogel disclosed any confidences to any member of the firm, or that any such information was sought from or volunteered by Vogel. Harrison testified that he never asked Vogel to divulge anything other than impressions about three Brobeck attorneys. Harrison and his office manager also testified that Vogel was not involved in case evaluation or trial tactics discussions at the Harrison firm. However, this evidence is not sufficient to rebut the presumption that Vogel used the confidential material or disclosed it to staff members at the Harrison firm. Moreover, there was substantial evidence to support a reasonable inference that Vogel used or disclosed the confidential information.

Despite Harrison's own concern over an appearance of impropriety, Harrison never told Vogel not to discuss the information Vogel learned at Brobeck and did not consider screening Vogel even after Brobeck first inquired about Vogel's work on asbestos cases. The evidence also amply supports the trial court's observation that Vogel was "a very talkative person, a person who loves to share information." Further, Vogel's willingness to use information acquired at Brobeck, and the Harrison firm's insensitivity to ethical considerations, were demonstrated when Vogel was told to call respondent Fibreboard Corporation and Vogel knew the person to contact there. . . .

The order of the trial court is affirmed. . . .

Questions about the Case

1. Did Vogel actually work on any of the cases from which his employer Harrison is being disqualified? Did Vogel possess any confidential information about these cases? How did he obtain it and why?
2. Did Harrison do a conflicts check on Vogel? Did he attempt to screen Vogel from working on cases that he had worked on at Brobeck? Did he admonish Vogel not to reveal any confidential information about these cases?

3. Did Vogel get a consent from the clients involved? From the Brobeck firm?
4. Was Vogel cautious in accepting assignments to work on cases he may have worked on previously at Brobeck? Was he careful about what he said to other employees about his previous employment?
5. Does the court provide guidance to lawyers who hire legal assistants who may carry potential conflicts? How would you state this rule?
6. Did the court's flexible application of screening rules to legal assistants help Vogel? Why, or why not?
7. What should Vogel have done to ensure against this disqualification? What about Harrison?

The following case is another example of the trend in the courts to permit the use of screens of legal assistants in conflict situations that arise when a legal assistant changes jobs.

Phoenix Founders, Inc. v. Marshall
887 S.W.2d 831 (Tex. 1994)

In this original proceeding, we consider whether a law firm must be disqualified from ongoing litigation because it rehired a legal assistant who had worked for opposing counsel for three weeks. We hold that disqualification is not required if the rehiring firm is able to establish that it has effectively screened the paralegal from any contact with the underlying suit. Because this standard had not been adopted in Texas prior to the trial court's disqualification order, we deny mandamus relief without prejudice to allow the trial court to reconsider its ruling in light of today's opinion.

The present dispute arises from a suit brought by Phoenix Founders, Inc. and others ("Phoenix") to collect a federal-court judgment against Ronald and Jane Beneke and others. The law firm of Thompson & Knight represented Phoenix in the original federal-court suit, which began in 1990 and ended in 1991, and has also represented them in the collection suit since its commencement in 1992. The Benekes have been represented in the latter suit by the firm David & Goodman.

In July of 1993, Denise Hargrove, a legal assistant at Thompson & Knight, left her position at that firm to begin working for David & Goodman as a paralegal. While at David & Goodman, Hargrove billed six-tenths of an hour on the collection suit for locating a pleading. She also discussed the case generally with Mark Goodman, the Benekes' lead counsel.

182

After three weeks at David & Goodman, Hargrove returned to Thompson & Knight to resume work as a paralegal. At the time of the rehiring, Thompson & Knight made no effort to question Hargrove in regard to potential conflicts of interest resulting from her employment at David & Goodman.

Three weeks after Hargrove had returned, counsel for the Benekes wrote to Thompson & Knight asserting that its renewed employment of Hargrove created a conflict of interest. The letter demanded that the firm withdraw from its representation of Phoenix.

Hargrove resigned from Thompson & Knight the next week, after having been given the option of either resigning with severance pay or being terminated. The firm itself, however, refused to withdraw from the case. The Benekes then filed a motion to disqualify.

After an evidentiary hearing, the trial court initially overruled the Benekes' motion, stating that it found no evidence that confidential client information was actually provided to Hargrove. On motion for reconsideration, however, the trial court granted the Benekes' motion and disqualified Thompson & Knight from further representation of Phoenix. The disqualification order states that Hargrove possesses confidential information relating to the Benekes, and that all such confidential information was imputed to the firm of Thompson & Knight at the time she was rehired.

This Court has not previously addressed the standards governing a disqualification motion based on the hiring of a nonlawyer employee. With respect to lawyers, however, this Court has adopted a standard requiring disqualification whenever counsel undertakes representation of an interest that is adverse to that of a former client, as long as the matters embraced in the pending suit are "substantially related" to the factual matters involved in the previous suit. (Citation omitted.) This strict rule is based on a conclusive presumption that confidences and secrets were imparted to the attorney during the prior representation. (Citation omitted.)

The Benekes argue that the standards applied to the hiring of lawyers should also apply to the hiring of paralegals. . . . [T]he Benekes urge that the entire firm of Thompson & Knight must be automatically disqualified because of the confidences Hargrove obtained while working at David & Goodman.

We agree that a paralegal who has actually worked on a case must be subject to . . . a conclusive presumption that confidences and secrets were imparted during the course of the paralegal's work on the case. . . .

We disagree, however, with the argument that paralegals should be conclusively presumed to share confidential information with members of their firms. The Disciplinary Rules require a lawyer having direct supervisory authority over a nonlawyer to make reasonable efforts to ensure that the nonlawyer's conduct is compatible with the professional obligations of the lawyer. Tex. Disciplinary R. Prof. Conduct 5.03(a). If the supervising lawyer orders, encourages, or even permits a nonlawyer to engage in conduct that would be subject to discipline if engaged in by a lawyer, the lawyer will be subject to discipline. R. 5.03(b). Thus, to the extent that the Disciplinary Rules prohibit a lawyer from revealing confidential information, R. 1.05(b)(1), they also prohibit a supervising lawyer from ordering, encouraging, or permitting a nonlawyer to reveal such information.

This view is consistent with the weight of authority in other jurisdictions. The American Bar Association's Committee on Professional Ethics has considered whether a law firm that hires a paralegal may continue representing clients whose interests conflict with interests of the former employer's clients on whose matters the paralegal has worked. ABA Comm. on Ethics and Professional Responsibility, Informal Op. 1526 (1988). After surveying case law and ethics opinions from a number of jurisdictions, the Committee concluded that the new firm need not be disqualified, as long as the firm and the paralegal strictly adhere to the screening process set forth in the opinion, and as long as the paralegal does not reveal any information relating to the former employer's clients to any person in the employing firm. Id. A number of courts have since relied on the ABA's opinion to allow continued representation under similar conditions. (Citations omitted.)

Underlying these decisions is a concern regarding the mobility of paralegals and other nonlawyers. A potential employer might well be reluctant to hire a particular nonlawyer if doing so would automatically disqualify the entire firm from ongoing litigation. This problem would be especially acute in the context of massive firms and extensive, complex litigation. Recognizing this danger, the ABA concluded that "any restrictions on the nonlawyer's employment should be held to the minimum necessary to protect confidentiality of client information." ABA Op. 1526 at 2. (Citations omitted.)

We share the concerns expressed by the ABA, and agree that client confidences may be adequately safeguarded if a firm hiring a paralegal from another firm takes appropriate steps in compliance with the Disciplinary Rules. See ABA Op. 1526 at 3. Specifically, the newly-hired paralegal should be cautioned not to disclose any information relating to the representation of a client of the former employer. The paralegal should also be instructed not to work on any matter on which the paralegal worked during the prior employment, or regarding which the paralegal has information relating to the former employer's representation. Additionally, the firm should take other reasonable steps to ensure that the paralegal does no work in connection with matters on which the paralegal worked during the prior employment, absent client consent after consultation. See id.

Each of these precautions would tend to reduce the danger that the paralegal might share confidential information with members of the new firm. Thus, while a court must ordinarily presume that some sharing will take place, the challenged firm may rebut this presumption by showing that sufficient precautions have been taken to guard against any disclosure of confidences. . . .

Absent consent of the former employer's client, disqualification will always be required under some circumstances, such as (1) when information relating to the representation of an adverse client has in fact been disclosed, or (2) when screening would be ineffective or the nonlawyer necessarily would be required to work on the other side of a matter that is the same as or substantially related to a matter on which the nonlawyer has previously worked. . . .

In reconsidering the disqualification motion, the trial court should examine the circumstances of Hargrove's employment at Thompson & Knight to determine whether the practical effect of formal screening has been achieved. The factors bearing on such a determination will generally include the substantiality of the relationship between the former and current matters; the time elapsing between the matters; the size of the firm; the number of individuals presumed to have confidential information; the nature of their involvement in the former matter; and the timing and features of any measures taken to reduce the danger of disclosure.

The ultimate question in weighing these factors is whether Thompson & Knight has taken measures sufficient to reduce the potential for misuse of confidences to an acceptable level. As with any disqualification motion, the trial court must adhere to an exacting standard so as to discourage any use of a disqualification motion as a dilatory tactic. . . .

Because we have modified the controlling legal standard, the writ of mandamus is denied without prejudice to allow the trial court to reconsider the disqualification motion in light of today's opinion. The stay order previously issued by this Court remains in effect only so long as necessary to allow the trial court to act.

Questions about the Case

1. Was the paralegal Hargrove aware of the potential conflict of interest? Did she work on the Phoenix Founders matter at Thompson & Knight either before she went to David & Goodman, or after?

2. Did David & Goodman do a conflicts check?
3. Did Thompson & Knight attempt to screen Hargrove from the Phoenix Founders matter upon her return to the firm?
4. What is the standard applied to lawyers in disqualification motions in Texas courts? Does the court apply this same standard to legal assistants?
5. What authority does the Texas Supreme Court rely on to make this new rule?
6. What specific steps does the court prescribe to establish an acceptable safeguard against the disclosure of client confidences?
7. Did the Texas Supreme Court here decide whether or not to disqualify Thompson & Knight?

Like the California asbestos case above, the Arizona appeals court found that screening a paralegal would protect a firm from a disqualification, but then found that the facts here warranted disqualification.

Smart Industries Corp. v. Superior Court
876 P.2d 1176 (Ariz. App. Div. 1 1994)

Petitioner Smart Industries, a defendant in the underlying personal injury suit, seeks review of the trial court's denial of its motion to disqualify plaintiff's lawyer after defendant's counsel's former legal assistant was hired by plaintiff's lawyer. This special action requires us to decide whether the same rules of imputed disqualification that apply to lawyers also apply to nonlawyer personnel who change employment between law firms. . . .

In December 1990, real parties in interest Darryl and Marilyn St. Germaine (collectively, "the St. Germaines" or "plaintiffs"), through their former lawyer Richard D. Engler, filed a personal injury suit alleging products liability and premises liability against Smart and other defendants. The St. Germaines subsequently retained their present counsel, Don B. Engler, the brother of Richard D. Engler, to represent them in this action. Don Engler is a sole practitioner in Yuma.

Smart retained the law firm of Mower, Koeller, Nebeker, Carlson & Haluck ("Mower, Koeller") to defend it in that litigation. The Yuma office of Mower, Koeller consists of two lawyers and three support staff. Co-counsel Constance Miller and William A. Nebeker of that firm worked on the case. Ms. Miller also worked with her secretary, Janet Gregston, who has been employed "in a secretarial/paralegal capacity" at Mower, Koeller since September 1991. According to Ms. Miller's affidavit, Ms. Gregston's paralegal duties involved extensive work on the St. Germaine/Smart litigation:

> [Ms. Gregston] worked extensively [on this case] in numerous confidential settings. . . . [She] was privy to exhaustive client confidences, correspondences between counsel and clients, strategic planning, litigation preparation and documentation, pretrial conferences with clients, lay and expert witnesses. She participated in the preparation of trial exhibits and is shown in one test video which may be presented at trial.

> . . . Ms. Gregston participated in numerous discussions with co-defendants, clients, and experts, involving strategic planning for a cooperative defense.

On October 8, 1993, approximately 60 days prior to the firm trial date, Ms. Gregston suddenly terminated her employment at Mower, Koeller. On October 18, 1993, she began new employment as a legal secretary for plaintiffs' lawyer Don Engler. According to Mr. Engler's avowal to the court:

> [C]ontrary to Mrs. Gregston's duties while in Ms. Miller's employ . . . her duties [in Engler's employ] do not include a broad spectrum of "paralegal" tasks. To the contrary, Mrs. Gregston was employed to perform the specific professional duties of a legal secretary.
> This means that Mrs. Gregston is responsible only to prepare those pleadings, motions and correspondence which [Engler] dictates, in conformance with [his] directions. Mrs. Gregston's contact with clients generally, and in this case in particular, is limited to receipt of telephone messages and placing of telephone calls for the undersigned.

Mr. Engler also avowed that he had given "specific and segregated authority" to a separate paralegal with her own secretary for "[a]ll matters relating to discovery, client conferences, preparation of discovery motions for final review . . . . trial exhibits, and pretrial statements . . ." and that "Mrs. Gregston has no responsibility in regards to these matters whatsoever." Similarly, Ms. Gregston's affidavit states that, prior to her employment with Mr. Engler, she was informed that she would not be asked to reveal any confidences she had learned in her prior employment, and to report to Mr. Engler if she were ever questioned by anyone in the office regarding her knowledge gained from her employment at Mower, Koeller. However, Ms. Gregston's initials and signature appear on several pleadings in this case, both in the underlying litigation and in special action papers filed in this court. Thus, it is apparent she is presently performing secretarial work on this case. . . .

187

The trial court's quandary in this case . . . was that the disqualification motion was based on the conduct of a nonlawyer, over whom the Model Rules have no effect in a disciplinary setting. However, as both Smart and the St. Germaines point out, the operation of ER 1.10(b) may be extended to the conduct of nonlawyers through ER 5.3. This duty imposes on a lawyer the duty to supervise a nonlawyer employee, which includes "reasonable efforts to ensure that the person's conduct is compatible with the professional obligations of the lawyer. . . ." ER 5.3(b). The duty of supervision also includes lawyer responsibility for any nonlawyer conduct "that would be a violation of the rules of professional conduct if engaged in by a lawyer," if the lawyer orders, has knowledge of, or ratifies such conduct. ER 5.3(c). . . .

Arizona law does not recognize screening devices to avoid imputed disqualification of the new law firm to which a lawyer moves when that lawyer possesses client confidences and the new firm has interests adverse to that client. . . .

Because Arizona does not recognize the "cone of silence" or other screening mechanisms as an exception to a lawyer's imputed disqualification of the new firm, we do not find persuasive cases from those jurisdictions that have adopted the opposite rule, such as the seventh circuit.

We are also reluctant, however, to adopt the reasoning of those jurisdictions that have declined to adopt the "cone of silence" screening defense for lawyers, but then have blindly applied this rule to the analogous nonlawyer situation without first examining whether any distinction exists between the two situations. . . .

We believe that this reason for treating government lawyers differently in the context of imputed disqualification cases applies equally to nonlawyer assistants, who, unlike lawyers in private practice, generally have neither a financial interest in the outcome of a particular litigation, nor the choice of which clients they serve. Moreover, in our opinion, the public perception of what is expected of lawyers as compared to nonlawyers is different, probably based on the "independent contractor" status enjoyed by lawyers as compared to the "master/servant" role of nonlawyer assistants. Our analysis, thus, is directed to determining the scope and extent of a supervising lawyer's ethical duty under ER 5.3, to insure that a nonlawyer's conduct in this "master/servant" setting is compatible with other ethical obligations. . . .

We conclude that the screening requirements articulated above are sufficient to satisfy a lawyer's duty under ER 5.3 to supervise a nonlawyer employee in a manner that will assure conduct "compatible" with the lawyer's ethical obligations. Thus, satisfaction of these requirements will prevent disqualification of the firm based on a nonlawyer's potential conflict even though a stricter standard is imposed on lawyers by operation of ER 1.10(b). . . . We reach this result because we agree with the concerns of ABA Informal Opinion and the cases cited therein regarding the employment of nonlawyer assistants within the legal community, and because we perceive that, once a supervising lawyer in the employment relationship has properly instructed and screened such an employee, the danger is small of a disclosure of a former client's confidences.

Applying these concepts to this case, however, we conclude that Smart is entitled to disqualification of plaintiffs' counsel under the undisputed facts before us. First, there is no question that Ms. Gregston obtained client confidences in her former employment; the St. Germaines do not contend that her involvement in the case was any less than lawyer Miller has alleged. Second, there is no question that these client confidences are substantially related to the representation by her current employer; indeed she is now on the other side of the same lawsuit, which is pending trial. It is also clear on this record that Smart did not consent to her employment by opposing counsel, nor did Smart waive its objection to her new employment.

We understand that plaintiffs' counsel instructed Ms. Gregston not to divulge any client confidences gained in her former employment, and, as previously mentioned, we accept as true counsel's avowals, in both this court and the trial court, that he has insulated himself from any possible disclosure. However, this instruction and insulation do not necessarily satisfy the minimum requirements necessary under ER 5.3 to prevent disqualification. In this case, counsel does not dispute that Ms. Gregston has not been screened from participation in the actual litigation with which she was intimately involved in her former employment; rather, she has initialed and signed pleadings and correspondence in this record. She has also submitted personal affidavits as evidence, in both the trial court and in this court. Counsel's avowal that Ms. Gregston's duties are limited to typing and taking phone messages is not sufficient to remove her from involvement in the case in a manner that would significantly decrease the likelihood of a prohibited disclosure, even inadvertently. . . . Furthermore, we observe that counsel's refusal, after a strong suggestion by the trial court to withdraw, to even offer to screen this employee from working on the very matter which gave rise to the problem shows an apparent insensitivity by counsel to the valid concerns of the adverse client that confidences may be disclosed by the nonlawyer who had such a significant involvement on the other side of the case for over two years. . . .

For the foregoing reasons, we hold that the trial court abused its discretion in denying Smart's motion to disqualify. We remand this matter to the trial court for entry of an order consistent with this opinion.

Questions about the Case

1. Did the paralegal Gregston work on both sides of the St. Germaine/ Smart litigation? What kind of duties did she have in her two positions with the two law firms? Do you think it is likely that she was privy to confidential information in both jobs?
2. Was there any attempt to screen Gregston? Was any consent given by the former client or law firm? Was she warned not to divulge confidential information about the case?
3. Did the court think that it was relevant that her duties at the Engler firm were primarily secretarial?
4. Is it certain that confidential information was disclosed by Gregston?
5. Does Arizona allow screening of attorneys in conflict cases based on imputed disqualification? What are the reasons the court gives for applying different rules to legal assistants?
6. What would a firm have to do to create a sufficient screen of a conflict-tainted paralegal in Arizona after this case?

In this case, the Nevada Supreme Court decides the issue of screens for legal assistants differently. As you read, try to ascertain why the similar facts and rules can result in a different conclusion.

Ciaffone v. District Court
945 P.2d 950 (Nev. 1997)

On May 27, 1993, petitioners Linda Ciaffone, Joseph Ciaffone, and Carla Ciaffone, individually, and Kathleen Hornbrook as Special Administratrix, on behalf of the estate of Joseph Ronald Ciaffone, the deceased, ("Ciaffones") filed a wrongful death action against Skyline Restaurant & Casino ("Skyline") for the shooting of Joseph Ciaffone. The law firm of Gillock, Koning, Markley & Killebrew, P.C. ("Gillock firm") represented the Ciaffones while Skyline retained the law firm of Thorndal, Backus, Armstrong & Balkenbush ("Thorndal firm"). The case was scheduled for trial in April 1996, but was continued until December 30, 1996.

On February 11, 1995, Ingrid Decker ("Decker") was employed by the Thorndal firm through a "temp" agency and worked in the word processing unit. On March 25, 1995, Decker was hired directly by the Thorndal firm to serve as a legal secretary to attorney David Clark ("Clark"). Although Clark was not assigned to the *Ciaffone v. Skyline*

Restaurant & Casino ("Ciaffone v. Skyline") litigation, Decker admits that she performed some work on *Ciaffone v. Skyline* in a limited "overflow" secretarial capacity.

After Clark left the Thorndal firm, Decker remained for several months. Decker sat from March 18, 1996, to March 25, 1996, as a floating secretary to attorney of record in *Ciaffone v. Skyline,* Janice Marshall ("Marshall"). Although Decker claims she did not do any work on *Ciaffone v. Skyline* while working for Marshall, she does admit that she may have done some work on *Ciaffone v. Skyline* in her brief duties as a word processor at the Thorndal firm.

On September 9, 1996, Decker began her employment at the Gillock firm as a secretary to Julie A. Mersch ("Mersch"), attorney of record in *Ciaffone v. Skyline.* The Gillock firm made efforts to screen Decker from any involvement in the *Ciaffone v. Skyline* case; the trial court found these efforts sufficient, despite some minor involvement by Decker with the case.

On November 25, 1996, the Thorndal firm moved to disqualify the Gillock firm based on Decker's involvement in *Ciaffone v. Skyline* and the absence of any authority in Nevada recognizing nonlawyer screening. Judge Sobel, based on written motions, affidavits, and an informal hearing, ruled as follows:

> The Motion to Disqualify poses at least two significant issues.
>
> First, should "screening" be allowed where a nonlawyer is involved? I think it should be permitted, but there is a complete absence, as far as I can tell, of applicable Nevada law permitting it. . . .
>
> Second, was the screening effective with respect to Ingrid Decker? I believe that the screening was effective in this case, and that Decker did not, after taking her new employment, have the significant participation in the case that the nonlawyer had in [*Smart Industries Corp. v. Superior Court,* 179 Ariz. 141, 876 P.2d 1176 (Ariz.Ct.App. 1994)].
>
> However, I feel constrained as a trial judge to find that neither by rule or case has our state yet recognized screening. . . .
>
> I believe if screening is to take place with respect to nonlawyers in Nevada, in the face of rules that apparently do not permit it, it should be the Supreme Court, the maker of Supreme Court rules, and not me, who gives permission for screening.
>
> The Motion to Disqualify is therefore granted reluctantly.

Ciaffones then petitioned this court for a writ of mandamus ordering the district court to reinstate the Gillock firm as attorneys of record. . . .

Skyline argues that regardless of the efforts taken by the Gillock firm to screen Decker from participation in *Ciaffone v. Skyline,* no statute or case law exists in Nevada permitting nonlawyer screening. Skyline further contends that because Nevada law does not authorize screening when lawyers move from one private firm to another, nonlawyers should be held to the same standard. . . .

Although Nevada has not addressed the problem of nonlawyer screening, this court has taken the position in SCR 160(2) that *lawyer screening* is prohibited. In part, SCR 160(2) provides:

> When a lawyer becomes associated with a firm, the firm may not knowingly represent a person in the same or a substantially related matter in which that lawyer, or a firm with which the lawyer was associated, had previously represented a client whose interests are materially adverse to that person and about whom the lawyer had acquired information protected by Rules 156 and 159(2) that is material to the matter.

SCR 156 and 159(2) address the disclosure of confidential and privileged information between the attorney and client.

Additionally, SCR 187 requires lawyers to hold nonlawyer employees to the same professional standards. In relevant part, SCR 187 states:

> With respect to a nonlawyer employed or retained by or associated with a lawyer:
>
> 1. A partner in a law firm shall make reasonable efforts to ensure that the firm has in effect measures giving reasonable assurance that the person's conduct is compatible with the professional obligations of the lawyer;
> 2. A lawyer having direct supervisory authority over the nonlawyer shall make reasonable efforts to ensure that the person's conduct is compatible with the professional obligations of the lawyer. . . .

When SCR 187 is read in conjunction with SCR 160(2), nonlawyer employees become subject to the same rules governing imputed disqualification. To hold otherwise would grant less protection to the confidential and privileged information obtained by a nonlawyer than that obtained by a lawyer. No rationale is offered by Ciaffones which justifies a lesser degree of protection for confidential information simply because it was obtained by a nonlawyer as opposed to a lawyer. Therefore, we conclude that the policy of protecting the attorney–client privilege must be preserved through imputed disqualification when a nonlawyer employee, in possession of privileged information, accepts employment with a firm who represents a client with materially adverse interests. . . .

In contrast, Ciaffones cite *Smart Industries Corp. v. Superior Court,* 179 Ariz. 141, 876 P.2d 1176 (App.1994), for the proposition that jurisdictions may expressly prohibit lawyer screening while allowing nonlawyer screening. In justifying this seemingly contradictory position, the *Smart Industries* court adopted the rational [sic] of ABA Informal Opinion 88-1526. . . .

The reasoning of *Smart Industries* implicitly recognizes that a non-lawyer's employment opportunities or mobility must be weighed against client confidentiality before disqualification occurs. While this approach may appear fairer to the paralegal/secretary, it has been roundly criticized for ignoring the realities of effective screening and litigating that issue should it ever arise. For example, one commentator explained that *a majority of courts have rejected screening* because of the uncertainty regarding the effectiveness of the screen, the monetary incentive involved in breaching the screen, the fear of disclosing privileged information in the course of proving an effective screen, and the possibility of accidental disclosures. M. Peter Moser, *Chinese Walls: a Means of Avoiding Law Firm Disqualification When a Personally Disqualified Lawyer Joins the Firm,* 3 Geo. J.Legal Ethics 399, 403, 407 (1990). Accordingly, we conclude that adherence to the existing SCR scheme is the better rule. We, therefore, refrain from creating an exception to the imputed disqualification rule embodied in SCR 160. Thus, we conclude a writ of mandamus is not warranted.

Questions about the Case

1. What were the duties of the nonlawyer, Ingrid Decker, in the case of *Ciaffone v. Skyline*?
2. Did Decker perform work for attorneys on opposite sides of the case? Was this a simultaneous or successive conflict?
3. Did the Gillock firm make any effort to screen Decker from involvement in the case?
4. What did the trial court decide?
5. What two ethical rules did this court cite? Are these the same or similar to the provisions cited by the courts in the previous cases in this chapter from California, Texas, and Arizona?
6. Why does the Nevada court conclude differently from the majority of states that have had to decide this issue?

Advertising
and Solicitation

This chapter traces how the rules governing attorney advertising have changed radically in the last two decades, and how they are still evolving. Chapter 6 covers:

- the key U.S. Supreme Court cases affecting the ways that lawyer advertising is regulated
- the current status of legal advertising and marketing
- the ethics rules governing advertising
- how advertising rules apply to legal assistants
- ethics rules prohibiting direct solicitation of clients
- how the limits on solicitation apply to legal assistants
- advertising and solicitation on the Internet

A. Advertising

In 1977, the landmark case of *Bates v. State Bar of Arizona,* 433 U.S. 350, upset decades of ethics rules prohibiting lawyer advertising. These rules date back to the first state codes and first American Bar Association (ABA) model rules, the 1908 Canons. The early rules prohibited virtually every form of advertising except business cards. Later, inclusion of biographical information on approved lists of lawyers was permitted.

The political and social environment surrounding the *Bates* decision was one of growing consumer awareness. Part of this general awareness was a recognition that most citizens did not have access to legal services while, at the same time, the cost of legal services was rising dramatically. During the late 1960s and throughout the 1970s, new nontraditional methods of increasing access to legal services were being developed. Legal aid and public interest law firms began opening their doors. The first prepaid legal insurance plans were established. Storefront legal clinics that handled common legal problems at lower cost than traditional firms began to crop up. The organized bar and the public shared the realization that not only were most middle- and lower-middle income citizens unable to afford an attorney, most did not know how to go about finding one.

The ABA Code of Professional Responsibility (ABA Model Code) adopted in 1969 contained the traditional restrictions on lawyer advertising. Only business cards, announcements of attorney personnel changes within the firm or of a new address, and Christmas cards to existing clients were permitted. The ABA had made some slight modifications in these rules in the mid-1970s to accommodate the special needs of legal aid organizations and prepaid legal insurance plans. But it was not until *Bates* that sweeping changes were made in the ethics codes of every jurisdiction.

In the *Bates* case, two Arizona lawyers advertised low-cost legal services in a local newspaper and were disciplined by the state bar. Their challenge to restrictions on lawyer advertising was ultimately heard by the U.S. Supreme Court, which struck down such restrictions as violative of the First Amendment. The Court held that lawyer advertising—like other forms of commercial speech—was protected, and states could prohibit advertisements only in limited ways—for example, for false, misleading, or deceptive ads; by means of reasonable time, place, and manner restrictions.

The *Bates* case is included at the end of this chapter at page 211. Reading it is especially valuable not only because of its important holding but because it outlines so well all the arguments on both sides of the lawyer advertising issue. The legal profession's resistance to lawyer advertising was tremendous, based mainly on the notion that it would deprofessionalize and commercialize law practice. Strong support for these beliefs still exists in many segments of the legal community; however, recent studies have shown that at least half of the lawyers in the country engage in some form of advertising.

The ABA Commission on Advertising released a report in 1995 after conducting a year-long study of lawyer advertising. The Commission found that advertising and marketing had become pervasive. Trends identified in the study included: more firms using advertising as part of a marketing effort; varied levels and frequency of advertising in different regions of the country; and the use of advertising to create a firm image.

The study also found that, while lawyers themselves attribute the declining image of the legal profession to advertising, the public does not. The public considers advertising as a source of information and only begins to perceive it as objectionable when it becomes "invasive." Finally, the report found that an increasing number of people find a lawyer through advertising.

Legal marketing has become a small support industry to the legal profession. Consultants and legal marketing firms abound. Many larger firms have their own in-house legal marketing personnel. A new organization, the National Association of Law Firm Marketing Administrators, was established in the 1980s. Firms have on their own become sophisticated marketers, using marketing jargon to describe their efforts to attract clients in ways never dreamed of when *Bates* was decided.

Legal advertising and marketing have taken many forms and have been designed to target many different kinds of potential clients. Larger traditional law firms have strategic marketing plans, identifying potential clients and developing ways to attract their business. Most have firm brochures, describing the backgrounds of attorneys and the nature of their practice. Many also have regularly published newsletters for clients, updating them in the latest firm triumphs and informing them of changes in the law that may encourage them to have legal work done. Many hold social events and educational seminars for clients and send press releases to the media to announce significant events in the firm, for example, when the firm wins an important case or a prestigious new partner joins the firm.

Combined with the increased competition for corporate clients, the phenomenon of advertising has created a new atmosphere in larger law firms. New value is placed on attorneys who can bring in business (called "rainmakers"); a lawyer's ability to work well with clients and keep them satisfied is essential to success in a firm. Law firms try to establish a high public profile by donating funds to worthy causes, partici-

197

pating in community and civic activities, taking pro bono cases that will generate favorable publicity, and encouraging their lawyers to participate in a wide variety of organizational activities outside the firm, both professional and civic in nature. Some firms sponsor in-house seminars to train lawyers how to better market their services and to enhance client relations. Many firms give seminars at trade shows in industries from which they draw clients, an example of "niche marketing."

In the past few years, large firms have begun to use client surveys to assess the attitudes, needs, and levels of satisfaction of their clients. Surveys, conducted either orally through structured interviews or in writing, aim to identify the importance of various factors in meeting clients' needs and to find out how the firm's responsiveness, communication, services, and fee structure are perceived. Theoretically, client relations are improved simply by virtue of conducting the survey, and the information gained may be used to enhance services and to remedy weaknesses. Sophisticated research surveys are also being used by a few major firms, sometimes in conjunction with a client, to gain information about a particular industry or trend. The firms then use the results to sponsor firm events for clients and prospective clients, and to craft press releases and articles for publication in bar, industry, or general-interest periodicals.

Smaller firms also engage in advertising. The more traditional firms use the same kinds of marketing activities as large firms. But many small firms are specialized, handling one or two kinds of legal matters and seeking a clientele that might not otherwise have a ready referral to an attorney. Personal injury firms have led the way in lawyer advertising, most visibly with television and radio spots, but also with billboards, flyers placed on cars or doorknobs, posters on telephone poles, and even ads on the back of grocery store receipts. Firms that handle immigration, family law, workers' compensation. Social Security matters, and bankruptcy frequently utilize these techniques as well. Direct-mail advertising of targeted persons who may need a specific kind of legal service is employed by some firms. A few attorneys have 900 numbers to dispense legal advice and others have catchy 800 numbers that are included in print, radio, or television ads.

Legal assistants can play an important role in marketing by serving clients efficiently, emphasizing the cost savings to the client from the use of legal assistants, identifying sources for referrals, alerting attorneys to opportunities for rainmaking, and working with attorneys to develop a marketing plan and client surveys.

As the Internet has become such an important means of disseminating information, more and more lawyers are using various kinds of Internet communications to reach prospective clients. Large law firms and many mid- and small-sized firms have their own home pages on the World Wide Web, which, like firm brochures, provide background information on lawyers in the firm and areas in which the firm practices, and may include newsworthy articles about legal issues of interest to clients. Some lawyers participate in chat groups and have used e-mail for direct solicitation of clients. Many lawyers post advertisements and articles to bulletin boards and newsgroups and participate in trade group seminars on-line.

This new form of communication has raised unanticipated ethical issues that fall in many areas of the ethics rules. Is direct e-mail of prospective clients advertising or solicitation, and which rules apply? Is a website more like a television ad or a firm brochure? If an attorney states a legal opinion in a chat group, is the attorney forming an attorney-client relationship with the person posing the question? Is the attorney violating unauthorized practice rules in states in which he or she is not licensed to practice but where the opinion is read? Is it inherently misleading to advertise on the Internet when the attorney is not licensed in all the states where the ad may be read?

Only a handful of states have issued ethic opinions on how ethics rules on advertising and solicitation rules apply to Internet communications and no jurisdiction has adopted changes to its ethics code. An example of a state that has tried to address the issue recently is Utah, whose bar issued an opinion indicating that it is ethical to operate a firm website and to post ads to newsgroups so long as the material complies with existing rules on advertising, including those prohibiting false and misleading statements and requiring the lawyer to maintain copies of the material for review by disciplinary authorities. On the other hand, the Utah bar found that chat groups are akin to in-person solicitation and are subject to the restrictions that apply to that kind of communication. (See section B of this chapter for a description of those restrictions.) The Utah bar also examined direct e-mail advertising and found that it is not direct solicitation since it is not "live" and the reader can choose not to read it or to reflect on its contents before responding (Utah Bar Association Ethics Opinion 97-10). Florida requires lawyers with home pages on the Web to file a copy with the bar and to pay a filing fee. Tennessee was the first to discipline a lawyer for soliciting on the Internet when an immigration lawyer sent direct e-mail to more than 10,000 Internet users including users in jurisdictions in which the lawyer was not licensed to practice. The Arizona bar's ethics committee, however, has determined that e-mail to potential clients does not generally constitute an improper solicitation since it lacks the immediacy and confrontational aspects of in-person and telephone communications. (Arizona Ethics Opinion 97-04.) Iowa lawyers are not permitted to be listed in lawyers' directories on the Internet and several states classify fee-charging directories as profit-making referral services that lawyers are prohibiting from using.

Many commentators are calling for uniform national ethics rules concerning Internet communications. The great variation among states in their handling of advertising and solicitation exacerbates this already difficult new area of ethics. A lawyer may be in compliance with the local jurisdictional rules but will clearly be in violation of the rules in another state where the communication is read. Further, the lawyers in states with more restrictive advertising rules are at a competitive disadvantage because they are more limited in what they can say, how they can say it and where they can say it. Differences in rules on advertising in directories, how one's areas of expertise can be described, and whether extensive disclaimers are required make advertising on the Internet especially challenging for lawyers in restrictive jurisdictions.

Several Supreme Court decisions that followed *Bates* made it clear that the Court will not look favorably at restrictions on lawyer advertising. In *In re R.M.J.,* 455 U.S. 1991 (1982), the Court held that a practitioner could advertise the areas of law in which he practiced in language other than that specified in the state ethics code because the language the lawyer used was not misleading and the code was unnecessarily restrictive. The court also allowed the lawyer to advertise the jurisdictions in which he was licensed to practice. In *Zauderer v. Office of Disciplinary Counsel of Supreme Court of Ohio,* 471 U.S. 626 (1985), the Supreme Court reversed the state supreme court's ruling that disciplined a personal injury attorney for placing a newspaper ad that pictured the intrauterine device that was the subject of litigation. The Court held that the attorney had the right to publish ads directed at readers with specific legal problems so long as the ads were accurate and not misleading. In 1988, the Supreme Court in *Shapero v. Kentucky Bar Association,* 486 U.S. 466, held that state ethics codes could not prohibit truthful and nondeceptive direct-mail advertising. The language it found unconstitutional in the Kentucky code was identical to ABA Model Rule 7.3, which has since been revised. Prior to this case, ethics rules had classified direct-mail advertising with telephone and in-person solicitation and had prohibited it. In *Peel v. Attorney Registration and Disciplinary Commission of Illinois,* 496 U.S. 91 (1990), the Court struck down state prohibitions on statements carried on a lawyer's letterhead that indicated the lawyer's certification as a specialist. While the certifying agency here—the National Board of Trial Advocacy—was not one authorized by the state, it had objective and verifiable criteria for the certification of a civil trial specialist. This ruling has resulted in changes in several state codes that had restrictions similar to those of Illinois. The *Peel* case is included at the end of this chapter at page 220.

Peel was followed by another case endorsing the use of a designation by an organization not approved by a state agency. In *Ibanez v. Florida Dept. of Business and Professional Regulation*, 512 U.S.136 (1994), the Court held that an attorney/certified public accountant who advertised her certified public accountant (CPA) and certified financial planner (CFP) designations could not be reprimanded by the Florida Board of Accountancy for false, deceptive, and misleading advertising since the ad was truthful and the CFP designation was publicly recognized by potential clients.

The pattern of the court striking down state prohibitions on lawyer advertising was finally broken in 1995 in the case of *Florida Bar v. Went For It, Inc.*, 515 U.S. 618 (1995). In this landmark case, the Supreme Court upheld restrictions on targeted direct mail advertising sent to accident and disaster victims. The Florida bar, like many other jurisdictions, had adopted a rule prohibiting such ads from being sent within 30 days of the incident. In upholding the prohibition, the Court cited heavily to bar studies that showed how negatively such letters were viewed by the public who saw the lawyers' conduct as an invasion of privacy designed to take advantage of vulnerable people in tragic circumstances. The case could be viewed as marking a change in the way that restrictions on lawyer advertising are treated by the court or as one in a series of cases that are defining permissible limits since the *Bates* decision.

The ABA Model Code was amended after *Bates* to comply with that decision. Its last revisions appear in DR 2-101 through 2-105. DR 2-101(A) prohibits false, fraudulent, misleading, deceptive, self-laudatory, or unfair statements or claims in public communications. Paragraph (B) delineates the specific information that may be used in print or broadcast media advertisements. The list includes basic background information about the firm and its lawyers as well as fee information. It also requires that the ads be "dignified." DR 2-101(C) provides for a means for lawyers to seek authorization to expand the information that may be included in ads. Paragraph (D) contains special rules on making and retaining copies of broadcast ads. Paragraphs (E), (F), and (G) obligate a lawyer who advertises fees to abide by the advertised fee for specified periods. DR 2-101(H) permits a lawyer's name to be used in certain public documents or announcements, and Paragraph (I) prohibits a lawyer from compensating anyone in the media for giving him or her publicity. This version of DR 2-101 is known as Proposal A and is considered a "regulatory" approach because it restricts ads to specific information. Another version of DR 2-101, Proposal B, was adopted in some states.

This version is called a "directive" approach because it permits any advertising except that which is false, fraudulent, misleading, or deceptive.

DR 2-102 contains restrictions on the contents of business cards, announcements, letterheads, and signs. The information designated is quite limited and probably would not withstand the constitutional test as applied in the *Peel* case cited above. DR 2-105 further restricts any attorney from holding himself or herself out as a specialist except if admitted to practice before the U.S. Patent and Trademark Office or if certified by a designated organization of the state agency governing lawyer specialization. This limitation would also not meet the test of *Peel*. Finally, another questionable section of the rule requires lawyers to use only state-approved designations and definitions when disclosing that their practice is limited to a specific area of law.

ABA Model Rules 7.1, 7.2, 7.3(c), and 7.4 follow a less restrictive and less specific approach to advertising. Rule 7.1 prohibits lawyers from making false or misleading communications about themselves or their services. It specifically includes in this category three kinds of statements: (1) those that contain a material misrepresentation of fact or law, or that omit a fact which results in a statement being materially misleading; (2) those that create an unjustified expectation about results or imply that results can be achieved by violating the law or ethics rules; and (3) those that compare the lawyer's services to other lawyers' unless factually substantiated. The comment to ABA Model Rule 7.1 states that this rule "ordinarily" precludes ads about results obtained in cases, such as the amount of an award, the lawyer's record, or testimonials or endorsements by clients.

Several states specifically prohibit testimonials, contending that they are inherently misleading, create unjustified expectations, or are self-laudatory. A growing number of jurisdictions allow testimonials, usually with the requirement that they include information about payment to the endorser and/or the status of the endorser as a client, or have disclaimers to avoid unjustified expectations. The U.S. Supreme Court in 1987, and again in 1990, refused to review a case in which a California lawyer was disciplined for using a testimonial. For the time being, each jurisdiction will have to decide this issue for itself. Despite the organized bar's apparent distaste for testimonials, a list of clients' names, with their approval, may be used in advertising under both the ABA Model Code and ABA Model Rules and in all jurisdictions. Dramatizations in radio and television ads are also disfavored by many in the organized bar, but are becoming increasingly common and tolerated. Several states permit them, usually with disclaimers that advise the viewers that the ad is a dramatization and does not guarantee similar results.

It is worthy of note that ABA Model Rule 7.1 does not require ads to be "dignified," as does DR 2-101(B). The evaluation of what is "dignified" is completely subjective, and would not meet the tests established by *Bates* and its progeny. However, the ABA still encourages dignity in lawyer advertising through its Aspirational Goals for Lawyer Advertising adopted in 1988 and its annual awards for Dignity in Lawyer Advertising. Among the goals included in this statement is one that recommends against "the use of inappropriately dramatic music, unseemly slogans, hawkish spokespersons, premium offers, slapstick routines or outlandish settings," which undermine public confidence in the legal profession.

Many states' rules are more restrictive than the ABA Model Rules. Some prohibit all lawyer comparison advertising. Other states prohibit statements regarding past performance on the grounds that they are inherently misleading and create false expectations. Several states specifically prohibit predictions of success; these claims would probably be found to be misleading even without a specific prohibition in the code. Claims about quality are generally prohibited as they are incapable of objective measurement. Fee information and comparisons are generally permissible, although some states have adopted specific language that may or may not be used to describe fees.

ABA Model Rule 7.2 was amended in 1989 after *Shapero v. Kentucky Bar Association*. Paragraph (a) permits lawyers to advertise through "public media," giving the examples of telephone directories, legal directories, newspapers, periodicals, outdoor advertising, radio, television, and written or recorded communication. Related ABA Model Rule 7.3(c) was also amended in 1989 after *Shapero*. This rule requires lawyers to include the words "Advertising Material" at the beginning and end of targeted direct-mail and recorded communications, and on the outside of the envelope of a direct-mail ad. Most states have similar rules about labeling on direct-mail advertising pieces. Paragraph (b) of Rule 7.3 requires lawyers to keep copies of ads and records on when and where they were used, whatever the method of advertising, for two years. Some states require ads to be kept for longer periods, as long as six years, and some require copies of ads to be sent to a specific state agency. Others require specifically worded disclaimers in ads. ABA Model Rule 7.3(c) also prohibits payment to a person for recommending legal services except for the cost of ads, charges for legal service organizations or lawyer referral services, or payment when a lawyer buys another lawyer's practice.

ABA Model Rule 7.4, covering statements about a lawyer's area(s) of practice, was amended in 1992 after the U.S. Supreme Court decision in *Peel v. Attorney Registration and Disciplinary Commission of Illinois,* which, as mentioned earlier, struck down prohibitions on specialty designations by organizations other than state-approved ones.

The rule now permits attorneys to advertise their certification by an organization not approved by a state regulatory authority, so long as appropriate disclaimers are included. Unchanged by the 1992 amendments are provisions permitting attorneys to advertise that they do or do not practice in a particular field, are state certified as specialist in a field, and are licensed as patent attorneys or are engaged in admiralty practice. This rule covers these two traditionally recognized kinds of specialties, and acknowledges the recent growth of state specialty certification programs and the trend toward legal specialization in practice. Most Model Rule jurisdictions have adopted 7.4 but some jurisdictions prohibit the use of the word "specialize" to describe an attorney's area of expertise and allow terms such as "limited to" or "concentrated in" in particular areas of practice.

The final ABA Model Rule that relates to advertising is 7.5, which covers firm names and letterheads. Under this rule, a lawyer's letterhead must meet the standards set forth in Model Rule 7.1, that is, not be false or misleading, create unjustified expectations, or contain unsubstantiated comparisons. Trade names are permitted under this rule so long as they do not imply a connection to a government agency or legal services organization. Some states have strict limits on the use of trade names. Firms with multijurisdictional practices may use the same firm name but must show limits on listed lawyers' licenses to practice. Lawyers in public office cannot be listed in the firm name or on its letterhead unless the lawyer is actively and regularly practicing with the firm. Finally, lawyers cannot state or imply that they practice with a partnership or organization unless they do in fact. For example, lawyers who share office space but are not partners cannot hold themselves out as partners by means of their firm name or letterhead.

The ABA Model Code provisions on letterheads are found in DR 2-102. This Disciplinary Rule is more specific than the Model Rule in limiting the information that can be included on cards and letterheads and prohibits the use of trade names in private practice. Some of its provisions would not hold up against a challenge under the *Peel* case.

As was indicated in Chapter 3, legal assistants' names and titles may be listed on letterhead and business cards in most jurisdictions. Earlier restrictions on nonlawyers being listed on letterhead and having business cards have been revised in most jurisdictions because of changes in the rules on lawyer advertising brought about by *Bates* and the cases that followed it.

For example, Indiana and South Dakota guidelines adopted in the early 1990s as well as the opinion of a 1994 New Jersey Committee on Attorney Advertising condone the use of legal assistants' names and titles on letterhead and in newspaper advertisements (Opinion 16 issued in

1994). The NFPA Model Code's Canon 6 also endorses this practice. Two recent ethics opinions specifically endorse the use of "CLA" and CCLAS" on letterhead and business cards. (Mississippi Bar 95-223 and New York State Bar Association 97-695.)

Legal assistants in New York were surprised in 1992 by New York State Bar Association Committee on Professional Ethics Opinion 640 (1992), the first opinion issued by a bar on which titles may be used by legal assistants. While the committee endorsed the use of "paralegal" and "senior paralegal," which it believed unambiguously convey the nonlawyer status of the legal assistant, it forbids the use of several other titles: legal associate, paralegal coordinator, public benefits specialist, legal advocate, family law advocate, housing law advocate, disability advocate, and public benefits advocate. The committee objects to these titles on the ground that they are likely to be confusing to the public, which would be misled about the nonlawyer status of someone with one of these titles. No other jurisdiction has followed suit, but the debate over titles will undoubtedly continue as legal assistants and legal assistant managers seek to develop new job titles that reflect accurately status, function, and specialty.

A final concern about letterhead and business cards relates to their use, which should be carefully monitored by the law firm. Several ethics opinions advise against allowing clients to use lawyers' letterhead to send correspondence without attorney review. Business cards, of course, must not be used for unethical solicitation.

Ethics rules on advertising and solicitation continue to be among the most hotly debated issues in legal ethics. At one end of the opinion spectrum are attorneys who favor a wide-open and unrestricted environment in order to demystify the legal profession and to encourage a more competitive climate among lawyers. At the other end are more traditional lawyers who believe that strong prohibitions are essential to preserve the good reputation and status of the legal profession and to protect the public from unscrupulous practitioners. Many jurisdictions continue to adopt rules restricting certain kinds of advertising only to find these being challenged in court.

Several kinds of advertising are being restricted in the latest flurry of rules in at least a dozen states. These include the use of testimonials, dramatizations using actors to portray attorneys on television and radio ads, claims about quality of service, and emotional appeals. Many of these proposed restrictions are aimed specifically at television and radio ads, which some members of the bar contend are particularly misleading and more likely to exploit vulnerable people. In many surveys, it is reported that most attorneys believe that lawyer advertising is a major cause of the poor public image of lawyers. So far, only conflicting evidence is available. Some studies report that lawyers who advertise do not fare as well with juries; other studies show that advertising does improve access to information about legal services and that the public does not find the ads as distasteful as lawyers do.

B. Solicitation

The changes in ethics rules and practice relating to advertising have not had much impact on the rules restricting the conduct of lawyers in soliciting clients directly, either in person or by telephone. The foundation for these restrictions is strong and virtually unquestioned by the profession. The rules reflect concerns about the intimidation, undue influence, and unfair bargaining position that a lawyer may have when he or she confronts a prospective client face-to-face or on the phone. Related is the longstanding prohibition against "ambulance chasers" or "runners and cappers," agents of lawyers who prey on accident victims by soliciting them directly at the scene of an accident or while they are in a hospital as the result of an accident. This kind of overreaching conduct, especially when it is directed toward clients who are vulnerable and not in a position to make a rational or well-thought-out choice about selecting counsel, clearly offends most lawyers and the public alike.

Several cases have addressed this issue. The leading case upholding restrictions on direct solicitation is *Ohralik v. Ohio State Bar Association,* 436 U.S. 447 (1978), included at the end of this chapter at page 228. This case involved an attorney who solicited an accident victim both by telephone and in person. Aggravating the solicitation violation was the attorney's refusal to stop the solicitation after the potential "client" refused representation.

The U.S. Supreme Court case of *Edenfield v. Fane,* 507 U.S. 761 (1993), has caused a great deal of speculation that the Court might strike down some of the restrictions against direct solicitation by lawyers. In that case, a Florida certified public accountant sought relief from regulations that prohibited direct solicitation of clients. The Court held that such restrictions are a violation of free speech in a business context where prospective clients are sophisticated and experienced business executives.

An exception to rules against direct solicitation of clients is made in cases involving organizations that seek to represent plaintiffs in cases that further a specific political principle, such as freedom of speech or association, or civil rights. Examples of such organizations are the National Association for the Advancement of Colored People and American Civil Liberties Union. The leading cases in this area are *NAACP v. Button,* 371 U.S. 415 (1963), and *In re Primus,* 436 U.S. 412 (1978).

ABA Model Code DR 2-103 prohibits lawyers from recommending their own or their firm's employment to a layperson who has not sought advice. DR 2-104 prohibits lawyers from representing clients to whom they have given unsolicited advice. Exceptions are carved out for close friends, relatives, former clients or persons reasonably believed to be clients; participation in activities to educate the public or to provide legal services through a qualified organization; and speaking or writing about legal matters so long as not emphasizing one's own experience or reputation or giving individual advice.

ABA Model Rule 7.3, substantially revised in 1989 after the *Shapero* decision, prohibits direct solicitation two ways. Paragraph (a) prohibits a lawyer from soliciting in person or by phone any prospective client "with whom the lawyer has no family or prior professional relationship, when a significant motive for the lawyer's doing so is the lawyer's pecuniary gain." This statement encompasses the ABA Model Code exceptions for family and former clients as well as solicitations motivated by political or public interest concerns. Paragraph (b) prohibits lawyers from soliciting either by written or recorded communication or by phone or in person when the prospective client has asked not to be solicited or when "the communication involves coercion, duress or harassment."

Several states have adopted an alternative to ABA Model Rule 7.3, which takes a different approach to the exception for politically motivated solicitations. This version of the rule allows personal contact with the prospective client if "under the auspices of a public or charitable legal services organization; or . . . a bonafide political, social, civic, fraternal, employee or trade organization" whose purposes include providing or recommending legal services. Generally, courts have also carved out an exception for attorneys seeking to contact members of a class in a class action suit. This is usually done by mail and is additionally protected under *Shapero.*

Some states have also adopted additional wording for Rule 7.3(b) that prohibits any direct or written solicitation of persons who are in a vulnerable physical, emotional, or mental state. California, for example, adds that communications transmitted at the scene of an accident or en route to a health care facility are presumed to violate rules against solicitation.

Finally, there is a split in the jurisdictions over the use of prerecorded telephone messages. Some states classify these messages as direct telephone solicitation and prohibit them while others find this method to be more like direct-mail advertising and do not per se prohibit them.

A lawyer who attempts to use agents or intermediaries to circumvent rules against solicitation will be held responsible in a disciplinary action for the conduct of his or her agents, under general principles of agency law as well as ethics rules. ABA Model Code DR 1-102(A)(2); ABA Model Rule 8.4(a). Despite these very clear rules, instances of unethical solicitation are not that uncommon, especially by lawyers using agents. For example, agents of lawyers, including accident investigators, have been found soliciting business at the scene of several recent airline crashes.

Two recent ethics opinions addressed situations in which nonlawyers were soliciting legal work for lawyers. The Illinois State Bar Association found it improper for an attorney's employee, designated a "tax representative," to conduct work independently, referring back to the attorney clients that he believed needed further assistance from a lawyer (Illinois State Bar Association 94-8). And the Rhode Island Bar found fee-splitting and unlawful solicitation in a collection agency owned by a nonlawyer who sold forms and legal services, paying the attorney who provided the legal services a percentage of the fees collected (Rhode Island Bar 95-47). Some personal injury lawyers offer a referral fee to anyone who brings a new case to the firm, often accomplished through the agent's unethical in-person or telephone solicitation. In this case, the violation is coupled with the unethical practice of paying a fee for the referral (see Chapter 7). These violations are not often the subject of discipline since only the parties involved are aware of them, and none are willing to report them and thus lose their source of income.

Some states are attempting to overcome the difficulties inherent in stopping unlawful solicitation by creating disaster response teams of volunteer and staff lawyers who go the scenes of major accidents and disasters to warn victims about unlawful solicitation and to deter lawyers from engaging in such conduct.

The NALA and NFPA ethics codes do not address advertising and solicitation directly but prohibit a legal assistant from engaging in any act that is unethical. (See NALA Canon 3(c), NALA Guidelines, 1.3 and NFPA Canon 3 and E.C. 3.3.) Likewise, the ABA Model Guidelines for the Utilization of Legal Assistant Services require the lawyer to ensure that the paralegal's conduct is compatible with ethical rules. (See Guidelines 1 and ABA Model Rule 5.3.)

Legal assistants who work in firms that engage in unlawful solicitation should be aware of the fact that they do violate professional ethics and may subject the lawyer to discipline. They may also indicate a loose attitude toward ethics generally. The best option for a legal assistant is to avoid working for such a firm.

REVIEW QUESTIONS

1. When were prohibitions on lawyer advertising lifted? Under what leading U.S. Supreme Court case?
2. How did the recognition in the 1960s and 1970s that many Americans do not have access to legal services affect the movement toward acceptance of lawyer advertising?
3. What kinds of lawyer advertising were permitted under the 1969 ABA Model Code?
4. What kinds of restrictions may states place on lawyer advertising after the *Bates* case?
5. Why do many lawyers dislike lawyer advertising?
6. What kinds of advertising do lawyers most commonly use?
7. Do large traditional firms do advertising?
8. What do the key court decisions since *Bates* say about lawyer advertising?
9. What does the revised ABA Model Code say generally about lawyer advertising? What do the ABA Model Rules say?
10. What kinds of restrictions are some states enacting now? Will they be upheld by the courts?
11. Do lawyer ads have to be "dignified" under the ABA Model Code? The ABA Model Rules?
12. List the media in which lawyers may advertise under the ABA Model Rules.
13. What are the rules governing lawyer advertising of specializations and certifications under the ABA Model Code? The ABA Rules? The *Peel* case?
14. What are the rules pertaining to time restrictions on direct mail ads to accident victims?
15. Are law firms allowed to use trade names? Under what circumstances?
16. What information about legal assistants may law firms include on their letterhead? Their business cards?
17. Are lawyers prohibited from soliciting clients in person? On the telephone? Why?
18. What are the exceptions to the direct solicitation rule?
19. May lawyers use legal assistants to solicit clients directly?
20. How common are violations of the ban on direct solicitation?
21. What job titles for legal assistants are and are not acceptable?

22. What role can a legal assistant play in marketing?
23. What kinds of advertising and solicitation are being done on the Internet? What do ethics rules say about it?
24. What do NALA's and NFPA's ethics codes say about advertising and solicitation?

DISCUSSION QUESTIONS

1. Locate the rules governing advertising and solicitation in your jurisdiction. Compare them to the ABA Model Code and ABA Model Rules.
2. Using the *Bates* case, make a list of the reasons that support banning lawyer advertising and of those that support little restriction of lawyer advertising. Which side of the argument do you find more persuasive?
3. Collect examples of as many different kinds of lawyer ads as you can find in your area. Check the Yellow Pages, billboards, television, radio, and so on. Rate these ads according to their (1) usefulness and information value; (2) effectiveness in recruiting clients to a firm; and (3) degree of dignity or offensiveness.
4. Call five local law firms and find out what they are doing to bring in clients, including what methods of advertising they use. Collect their firm brochures, newsletters, and other advertising materials and rate them the same way you did the ads in question 3.
5. Do you think advertising has hurt or helped the public image of lawyers? Has it made legal services more accessible?
6. Do you think that dramatizations should be restricted? Why or why not? How?
7. Do you think testimonials should be prohibited? Why or why not?
8. Is there anything objectionable about an ad that states that an attorney is an experienced trial attorney and an expert in personal injury cases when the attorney has only been in practice a year and all his or her cases have settled out of court?
9. An ad says. "No recovery, no fee." The fact is that the client is liable for the costs even if he or she loses. Is this objectionable? Under what rule?
10. May an ad say that an attorney is an "expert"? "Highly qualified"? "Competent"? Why, or why not?
11. May an ad say that a firm specializes in "quickie divorces"? "Guaranteed visas"? Why, or why not?
12. May an ad say the fee is $150 an hour without any additional information? Why, or why not?

13. May a firm in a jurisdiction that allows trade names have the name "Public Law Firm"? "Legal Defenders"?
14. May a law firm print its name and phone number on pens that are given out to clients? On shirts donated to the local Little League team? On city maps sent to new residents?
15. Does your jurisdiction have any ethics opinions on advertising and solicitation on the Internet?
16. Write an ethics rule that covers advertising and solicitation on the Internet and is constitutional under *Bates* and its progeny.
17. How is in-person solicitation different from advertising? How is telephone solicitation different from advertising? Is targeted, personalized, direct-mail advertising more like a newspaper print ad or a telephone call? Why, or why not?
18. Do you think restrictions on in-person and telephone solicitation are appropriate? Can you think of a way to allow direct solicitation while addressing concerns about overreaching and intimidation? Read the *Edenfield v. Fane* case for guidance.
19. Should political and public interest organizations be excused from restrictions on in-person solicitation? Why, or why not?
20. Suppose a corporation called "Foreclosure Fighters" was organized to represent people (for a fee) whose homes were being foreclosed on. Would it be allowed to solicit clients directly under the exception for public interest causes?
21. What would you do if you were asked to go to the hospital to visit a friend who had been in a car accident to try to get the friend to hire your firm to represent him or her?
22. Can a criminal defense lawyer have flyers about her services handed out at the courthouse?

CASES FOR ANALYSIS

In the following landmark case, the U.S. Supreme Court struck down restrictions in lawyer advertising under the First Amendment. As you read, take note of the arguments for and against such restrictions and how the Court deals with each one.

Bates v. State Bar of Arizona
433 U.S. 350 (1977)

Justice BLACKMUN delivered the opinion of the Court.
As part of its regulation of the Arizona Bar, the Supreme Court

of that State has imposed and enforces a disciplinary rule that restricts advertising by attorneys. This case presents two issues: whether §§1 and 2 of the Sherman Act, 15 U.S.C. §§1 and 2, forbid such state regulation, and whether the operation of the rule violates the First Amendment, made applicable to the States through the Fourteenth.

I

Appellants John R. Bates and Van O'Steen are attorneys licensed to practice law in the State of Arizona. As such, they are members of the appellee, the State Bar of Arizona. After admission to the bar in 1972, appellants worked as attorneys with the Maricopa County Legal Aid Society.

In March 1974, appellants left the Society and opened a law office, which they call a "legal clinic," in Phoenix. Their aim was to provide legal services at modest fees to persons of moderate income who did not qualify for governmental legal aid. In order to achieve this end, they would accept only routine matters, such as uncontested divorces, uncontested adoptions, simple personal bankruptcies, and changes of name, for which costs could be kept down by extensive use of paralegals, automatic typewriting equipment, and standardized forms and office procedures. More complicated cases, such as contested divorces, would not be accepted. Because appellants set their prices so as to have a relatively low return on each case they handled, they depended on substantial volume.

After conducting their practice in this manner for two years, appellants concluded that their practice and clinical concept could not survive unless the availability of legal services at low cost was advertised and, in particular, fees were advertised. Consequently, in order to generate the necessary flow of business, that is, "to attract clients," appellants placed an advertisement (reproduced in the Appendix to this opinion, infra, at 219), in the Arizona Republic, a daily newspaper of general circulation in the Phoenix metropolitan area. As may be seen, the advertisement stated that appellants were offering "legal services at very reasonable fees," and listed their fees for certain services.

The issue presently before us is a narrow one. First, we need not address the peculiar problems associated with advertising claims relating to the *quality* of legal services. Such claims probably are not susceptible of precise measurement or verification and, under some circumstances, might well be deceptive or misleading to the public, or even false. Appellee does not suggest, nor do we perceive, that appellants advertisement contained claims, extravagant or otherwise, as to the quality of services. Accordingly, we leave that issue for another day. Second, we also need not resolve the problems associated with in-person solicitation of clients—at the hospital room or the accident site, or in any other situation that breeds undue influence—by attorneys or their agents or "runners." Activity of that kind might well pose dangers of overreaching and misrepresentation not encountered in newspaper announcement advertising. Hence, this issue also is not before us. Third, we note that appellee's criticism of advertising by attorneys does not apply with much force to some of the basic factual content of advertising: information as to the attorney's name, address, and telephone number, office hours, and the like. The American Bar Association itself has a provision in its current Code of Professional Responsibility that would allow the disclosure of such information, and more, in the classified section of the telephone directory. DR 2-102(A)(6) (1976). We recognize, however, that an advertising diet limited to such spartan fare would provide scant nourishment.

The heart of the dispute before us today is whether lawyers also may constitutionally advertise the *prices* at which certain routine services will be performed. Numerous justifications are proffered for the restriction of such price advertising. We consider each in turn:

1. *The Adverse Effect on Professionalism.* Appellee places particular emphasis on the adverse effects that it feels price advertising will have on the legal profession. The key to professionalism, it is argued, is the sense of pride that involvement in the discipline generates. It is claimed that price advertising will bring about commercialization, which will undermine the attorney's sense of dignity and self-worth. The hustle of the marketplace will adversely affect the profession's service orientation, and irreparably damage the delicate balance between the lawyer's need to earn and his obligation selflessly to serve. Advertising is also said to erode the client's trust in his attorney: Once the client perceives that the lawyer is motivated by profit, his confidence that the attorney is acting out of a commitment to the client's welfare is jeopardized. And advertising is said to tarnish the dignified public image of the profession.

We recognize, of course, and commend the spirit of public service with which the profession of law is practiced and to which it is dedicated. . . . But we find the postulated connection between advertising and the erosion of true professionalism to be severely strained. At its core, the argument presumes that attorneys must conceal from themselves and from their clients the real-life fact that lawyers earn their livelihood at the bar. We suspect that few attorneys engage in such self-deception. And rare is the client, moreover, even one of modest means, who enlists the aid of an attorney with the expectation that his services will be rendered free of charge. In fact, the American Bar Association advises that an attorney should reach "a clear agreement with his client as to

213

the basis of the fee charges to be made," and that this is to be done "[a]s soon as feasible after a lawyer has been employed." (Citation omitted.) . . .

Moreover, the assertion that advertising will diminish the attorney's reputation in the community is open to question. Bankers and engineers advertise, and yet these professions are not regarded as undignified. In fact, it has been suggested that the failure of lawyers to advertise creates public disillusionment with the profession. The absence of advertising may be seen to reflect the profession's failure to reach out and serve the community: Studies reveal that many persons do not obtain counsel even when they perceive a need because of the feared price of services or because of an inability to locate a competent attorney. Indeed, cynicism with regard to the profession may be created by the fact that it long has publicly eschewed advertising, while condoning the actions of the attorney who structures his social or civic associations so as to provide contacts with potential clients.

It appears that the ban on advertising originated as a rule of etiquette and not as a rule of ethics. Early lawyers in Great Britain viewed the law as a form of public service, rather than as a means of earning a living, and they looked down on "trade" as unseemly. Eventually, the attitude toward advertising fostered by this view evolved into an aspect of the ethics of the profession. But habit and tradition are not in themselves an adequate answer to a constitutional challenge. In this day, we do not belittle the person who earns his living by the strength of his arm or the force of his mind. Since the belief that lawyers are somehow "above" trade has become an anachronism, the historical foundation for the advertising restraint has crumbled.

2. *The Inherently Misleading Nature of Attorney Advertising.* It is argued that advertising of legal services inevitably will be misleading (a) because such services are so individualized with regard to content and quality as to prevent informed comparison on the basis of an advertisement, (b) because the consumer of legal services is unable to determine in advance just what services he needs, and (c) because advertising by attorneys will highlight irrelevant factors and fail to show the relevant factor of skill.

We are not persuaded that restrained professional advertising by lawyers inevitably will be misleading. Although many services performed by attorneys are indeed unique, it is doubtful that any attorney would or could advertise fixed prices for services of that type. The only services that lend themselves to advertising are the routine ones: the uncontested divorce, the simple adoption, the uncontested personal bankruptcy, the change of name, and the like—the very services advertised by appellants. Although the precise service demanded in each task may vary slightly, and although legal services are not fungible, these facts do not make advertising misleading so long as the attorney does the necessary work at the advertised price. . . .

The second component of the argument—that advertising ignores the diagnostic role—fares little better. It is unlikely that many people go to an attorney merely to ascertain if they have a clean bill of legal health. Rather, attorneys are likely to be employed to perform specific tasks. Although the client may not know the detail involved in performing the task, he no doubt is able to identify the service he desires at the level of generality to which advertising lends itself.

The third component is not without merit: Advertising does not provide a complete foundation on which to select an attorney. But it seems peculiar to deny the consumer, on the ground that the information is incomplete, at least some of the relevant information needed to reach an informed decision. The alternative—the prohibition of advertising—serves only to restrict the information that flows to consumers. Moreover, the argument assumes that the public is not sophisticated enough to realize the limitations of advertising, and that the public is better kept in ignorance than trusted with correct but incomplete information. We suspect the argument rests on an underestimation of the public. . . .

3. *The Adverse Effect on the Administration of Justice.* Advertising is said to have the undesirable effect of stirring up litigation. The judicial machinery is designed to serve those who feel sufficiently aggrieved to bring forward their claims. Advertising, it is argued, serves to encourage the assertion of legal rights in the courts, thereby undesirably unsettling societal repose. There is even a suggestion of barratry.

But advertising by attorneys is not an unmitigated source of harm to the administration of justice. It may offer great benefits. Although advertising might increase the use of the judicial machinery, we cannot accept the notion that it is always better for a person to suffer a wrong silently than to redress it by legal action. As the bar acknowledges, "the middle 70% of our population is not being reached or served adequately by the legal profession." ABA, Revised Handbook on Prepaid Legal Services 2 (1972). Among the reasons for this underutilization is fear of the cost, and an inability to locate a suitable lawyer. Advertising can help to solve this acknowledged problem: Advertising is the traditional mechamsm in a free-market economy for a supplier to inform a potential purchaser of the availability and terms of exchange. The disciplinary rule at issue likely has served to burden access to legal services, particularly for the not-quite-poor and the unknowledgeable. A rule allowing restrained advertising would be in accord with the bar's obligation to "facilitate the process of intelligent selection of lawyers, and to assist in making legal services fully available." ABA Code of Professional Responsibility EC 2-1 (1976).

4. *The Undesirable Economic Effects of Advertising.* It is claimed that advertising will increase the overhead costs of the profession, and that these costs then will be passed along to consumers in the form of increased fees. Moreover, it is claimed that the additional cost of practice will create a substantial entry barrier, deterring or preventing young attorneys from penetrating the market and entrenching the position of the bar's established members.

These two arguments seem dubious at best. . . . The ban on advertising serves to increase the difficulty of discovering the lowest cost seller of acceptable ability. As a result, to this extent attorneys are isolated from competition, and the incentive to price competitively is reduced. Although it is true that the effect of advertising on the price of services has not been demonstrated, there is revealing evidence with regard to products: where consumers have the benefit of price advertising, retail prices often are dramatically lower than they would be without advertising. It is entirely possible that advertising will serve to reduce, not advance, the cost of legal services to the consumer.

The entry-barrier argument is equally unpersuasive. In the absence of advertising, an attorney must rely on his contacts with the community to generate a flow of business. In view of the time necessary to develop such contacts, the ban in fact serves to perpetuate the market position of established attorneys. Consideration of entry-barrier problems would urge that advertising be allowed so as to aid the new competitor in penetrating the market.

5. *The Adverse Effect of Advertising on the Quality of Service.* It is argued that the attorney may advertise a given "package" of service at a set price, and will be inclined to provide, by indiscriminate use, the standard package regardless of whether it fits the client's needs.

Restraints on advertising, however, are an ineffective way of deterring shoddy work. An attorney who is inclined to cut quality will do so regardless of the rule on advertising. And the advertisement of a standardized fee does not necessarily mean that the services offered are undesirably standardized. Indeed, the assertion that an attorney who advertises a standard fee will cut quality is substantially undermined by the fixed-fee schedule of appellee's own pre-paid Legal Services Program. Even if advertising leads to the creation of "legal clinics" like that of appellants'—clinics that emphasize standardized procedures for routine problems—it is possible that such clinics will improve service by reducing the likelihood of error.

6. *The Difficulties of Enforcement.* Finally, it is argued that the wholesale restriction is justified by the problems of enforcement if any other course is taken. Because the public lacks sophistication in legal matters, it may be particularly susceptible to misleading or deceptive advertising

by lawyers. After-the-fact action by the consumer lured by such advertising may not provide a realistic restraint because of the inability of the layman to assess whether the service he has received meets professional standards. Thus, the vigilance of a regulatory agency will be required. But because of the numerous purveyors of services, the overseeing of advertising will be burdensome.

It is at least somewhat incongruous for the opponents of advertising to extol the virtues and altruism of the legal profession at one point, and, at another, to assert that its members will seize the opportunity to mislead and distort. We suspect that, with advertising, most lawyers will behave as they always have: They will abide by their solemn oaths to uphold the integrity and honor of their profession and of the legal system. For every attorney who overreaches through advertising, there will be thousands of others who will be candid and honest and straightforward. And, of course, it will be in the latter's interest, as in other cases of misconduct at the bar, to assist in weeding out those few who abuse their trust.

In sum, we are not persuaded that any of the proffered justifications rise to the level of an acceptable reason for the suppression of all advertising by attorneys. . . .

In holding that advertising by attorneys may not be subjected to blanket suppression, and that the advertisement at issue is protected, we, of course, do not hold that advertising by attorneys may not be regulated in any way. We mention some of the clearly permissible limitations on advertising not foreclosed by our holding.

Advertising that is false, deceptive, or misleading of course is subject to restraint. See *Virginia Pharmacy Board v. Virginia Consumer Council,* 425 U.S., at 771-772, and n.24. . . . For example, advertising claims as to the quality of services—a matter we do not address today—are not susceptible of measurement or verification; accordingly, such claims may be so likely to be misleading as to warrant restriction. Similar objections might justify restraints on in-person solicitation. We do not foreclose the possibility that some limited supplementation, by way of warning or disclaimer or the like, might be required of even an advertisement of the kind ruled upon today so as to assure that the consumer is not misled. In sum, we recognize that many of the problems in defining the boundary between deceptive and nondeceptive advertising remain to be resolved, and we expect that the bar will have a special role to play in assuring that advertising by attorneys flows both freely and cleanly.

As with other varieties of speech, it follows as well that there may be reasonable restrictions on the time, place, and manner of advertising. See *Virginia Pharmacy Board v. Virginia Consumer Council,* 425 U.S., at 771. Advertising concerning transactions that are themselves illegal obviously may be suppressed. And the special problems of advertising on the electronic broadcast media will warrant special consideration.

The constitutional issue in this case is only whether the State may prevent the publication in a newspaper of appellants' truthful advertisement concerning the availability and terms of routine legal services. We rule simply that the flow of such information may not be restrained, and we therefore hold the present application of the disciplinary rule against appellants to be violative of the First Amendment.

The judgment of the Supreme Court of Arizona is therefore affirmed in part and reversed in part.

It is so ordered.

Questions about the Case

1. Examine the ad that is the subject of this litigation and evaluate whether it:

   a. is false or misleading;
   b. is undignified;
   c. is offensive to you personally;
   d. denigrates the image of the legal profession;
   e. would be helpful to someone seeking a lawyer.

2. Make a list of the bar's justifications for prohibiting advertising and summarize how the court refutes each one. Do you agree with the bar's arguments or the court's rationale on each?
3. What kinds of restrictions may be placed on lawyer advertising after *Bates?*

APPENDIX TO OPINION OF THE COURT

The *Peel* case is one of the recent cases on lawyer advertising decided by the U.S. Supreme Court. As you read, think about how this ruling might affect legal assistants. What information about legal assistants might an attorney wish to include on firm letterhead? Would it be permissible based on the ruling in this case?

Peel v. Attorney Registration and Disciplinary Commission of Illinois
496 U.S. 91 (1990)

Justice STEVENS announced the judgment of the Court and delivered an opinion in which Justice BRENNAN, Justice BLACKMUN, and Justice KENNEDY join.

The Illinois Supreme Court publicly censured petitioner because his letterhead states that he is certified as a civil trial specialist by the National Board of Trial Advocacy. We granted certiorari to consider whether the statement on his letterhead is protected by the First Amendment, 492 U.S.—, 109 S. Ct. 3240, 106 L. Ed. 2d 588 (1989). . . .

Petitioner practices law in Edwardsville, Illinois. He was licensed to practice in Illinois in 1968, in Arizona in 1979, and in Missouri in 1981. He has served as president of the Madison County Bar Association, and has been active in both national and state bar association work. He has tried to verdict over 100 jury trials and over 300 nonjury trials, and has participated in hundreds of other litigated matters that were settled. NBTA issued petitioner a "Certificate in Civil Trial Advocacy" in 1981, renewed it in 1986, and listed him in its 1985 Directory of "Certified Specialists and Board Members."

Since 1983 petitioner's professional letterhead has contained a statement referring to his NBTA certification and to the three States in which he is licensed. It appears as follows:

> Gary E. Peel
> Certified Civil Trial Specialist
> By the National Board of Trial Advocacy
> Licensed: Illinois, Missouri, Arizona

In 1987, the Administrator of the Attorney Registration and Disciplinary Commission of Illinois (Commission) filed a complaint alleging that petitioner, by use of this letterhead, was publicly holding himself out as a certified legal specialist in violation of Rule 2-105(a)(3) of the Illinois Code of Professional Responsibility. That Rule provides:

A lawyer or law firm may specify or designate any area or field of law in which he or its partners concentrates or limits his or its practice. Except as set forth in Rule 2-105(a), no lawyer may hold himself out as "certified" or a "specialist."

The complaint also alleged violations of Rule 2-101(b), which requires that a lawyer's public "communication shall contain all information necessary to make the communication not misleading and shall not contain any false or misleading statement or otherwise operate to deceive," and of Rule 1-102(a)(1), which generally subjects a lawyer to discipline for violation of any Rule of the Code of Professional Responsibility. Disciplinary Rule 2-101(b), 1-102(a)(1) (1988). . . .

In *Bates v. State Bar of Arizona,* 433 U.S. 350, 97 S. Ct. 2691, 53 L. Ed. 2d 810 (1977), this Court decided that advertising by lawyers was a form of commercial speech entitled to protection by the First Amendment. Justice Powell summarized the standards applicable to such claims for the unanimous Court in *In re R.M.J.,* 455 U.S. 191, 102 S. Ct. 929, 1 L. Ed. 2d 64 (1982):

> Truthful advertising related to lawful activities is entitled to the protections of the First Amendment. But when the particular content or method of the advertising suggests that it is inherently misleading or when experience has proved that in fact such advertising is subject to abuse, the States may impose appropriate restrictions. Misleading advertising may be prohibited entirely. *But the States may not place an absolute prohibition on certain types of potentially misleading information, e.g., a listing of areas of practice, if the information also may be presented in a way that is not deceptive.* . . .
>
> Even when a communication is not misleading, the State retains some authority to regulate. But the State must assert a substantial interest and the interference with speech must be in proportion to the interest served.

Id., at 203, 102 S. Ct., at 937 (emphasis added). In this case we must consider whether petitioner's statement was misleading and, even if it was not, whether the potentially misleading character of such statements creates a state interest sufficiently substantial to justify a categorical ban on their use.

The facts stated on petitioner's letterhead are true and verifiable. It is undisputed that NBTA has certified petitioner as a civil trial specialist and that three States have licensed him to practice law. There is no contention that any potential client or person was actually misled or deceived by petitioner's stationery. Neither the Commission nor the State Supreme Court made any factual finding of actual deception or misunderstanding, but rather concluded, as a matter of law, that petitioner's claims of being "certified" as a "specialist" were necessarily misleading absent an official state certification program. Notably, although petitioner was originally charged with a violation of Disciplinary Rule 2-101(b), which aims at misleading statements by an attorney, his letterhead was not found to violate this rule.

In evaluating petitioner's claim of certification, the Illinois Supreme Court focused not on its facial accuracy, but on its implied claim "as to the quality of [petitioner's] legal services," and concluded that such a qualitative claim " 'might be so likely to mislead as to warrant restriction.' " 126 Ill. 2d, at 406, 128 Ill. Dec., at 540, 534 N.E. 2d, at 984 (quoting *In re R.M.J.,* 455 U.S., at 201, 102 S. Ct., at 936). This analysis confuses the distinction between statements of opinion or quality and statements of objective facts that may support an inference of quality. A lawyer's certification by NBTA is a verifiable fact, as are the predicate requirements for that certification. Measures of trial experience and hours of continuing education, like information about what schools the lawyer attended or his or her bar activities, are facts about a lawyer's training and practice. . . .

We must assume that some consumers will infer from petitioner's statement that his qualifications in the area of civil trial advocacy exceed the general qualifications for admission to a state bar. Thus if the certification had been issued by an organization that had made no inquiry into petitioner's fitness, or by one that issued certificates indiscriminately for a price, the statement, even if true, could be misleading. In this case, there is no evidence that a claim of NBTA certification suggests any greater degree of professional qualification than reasonably may be inferred from an evaluation of its rigorous requirements. . . .

We are satisfied that the consuming public understands that licenses—to drive cars, to operate radio stations, to sell liquor—are issued by governmental authorities and that a host of certificates—to commend job performance, to convey an educational degree, to commemorate a solo flight or a hole in one—are issued by private organizations. . . .

Even if petitioner's letterhead is not actually misleading, the Commission defends Illinois' categorical prohibition against lawyers' claims of being "certified" or a "specialist" on the assertion that these statements are potentially misleading. In the Commission's view, the State's interest in avoiding any possibility of misleading some consumers with such communications is so substantial that it outweighs the cost of providing other consumers with relevant information about lawyers who are certified as specialists.

We may assume that statements of "certification" as a "specialist," even though truthful, may not be understood fully by some readers. However, such statements pose no greater potential of misleading consumers than advertising admission to "Practice before: The United States Supreme Court," *In re R.M.J.,* 455 U.S. 191, 102 S. Ct. 929, 71 L. Ed. 2d 64 (1982), of exploiting the audience of a targeted letter, *Shapero v. Kentucky Bar Assn.,* 486 U.S. 466, 108 S. Ct. 1916, 100 L. Ed. 2d 475 (1988) or of confusing a reader with an accurate illustration, *Zauderer v. Office of Disciplinary Counsel,* 471 U.S. 626, 105 S. Ct. 2265, 85 L. Ed. 2d 652 (1985). In this case, as in those, we conclude that the particular State rule restricting lawyers' advertising is " 'broader than reasonably necessary to prevent the' perceived evil." The need for a complete prophylactic against any claim of specialty is undermined by the fact that use of titles such as "Registered Patent Attorney" and "Proctor in Admiralty," which are permitted under Rule 2-105(a)'s exceptions, produces the same risk of deception. . . .

Petitioner's letterhead was neither actually nor inherently misleading. There is no dispute about the bona fides and the relevance of NBTA certification. The Commission's concern about the possibility of deception in hypothetical cases is not sufficient to rebut the constitutional presumption favoring disclosure over concealment. Disclosure of information such as that on petitioner's letterhead both serves the public interest and encourages the development and utilization of meritorious certification programs for attorneys. As the public censure of petitioner for violating Rule 2-105(a)(3) violates the First Amendment, the judgment of the Illinois Supreme Court is reversed and the case is remanded for proceedings not inconsistent with this opinion.

It is so ordered.

Questions about the Case

1. What rule did attorney Peel violate and how?
2. What narrow issue does the Court say it must decide?
3. Do you agree with the Court's conclusion that the certification in question is a verifiable fact and not a claim of quality? Why, or why not?
4. Can you imagine circumstances under which a certification would not be permitted?
5. What information about a legal assistant could a firm include on its letterhead after this case?

The following is the most recent case decided by the Supreme Court on lawyer advertising. Note the difference in the approach to these ethical restrictions and to those in the previous cases where the restrictions were struck down.

Florida Bar v. Went For It, Inc.
515 U.S. 618 (1995)

In 1989, the Florida Bar completed a 2 year study of the effects of lawyer advertising on public opinion. After conducting hearings, commissioning surveys, and reviewing extensive public commentary, the Bar determined that several changes to its advertising rules were in order. In late 1990, the Florida Supreme Court adopted the Bar's proposed amendments with some modifications. *The Florida Bar: Petition to Amend the Rules Regulating the Florida Bar—Advertising Issues*, 571 So. 2d 451 (Fla. 1990). Two of these amendments are at issue in this case. Rule 4-7.4(b)(1) provides that "[a] lawyer shall not send, or knowingly permit to be sent, . . . a written communication to a prospective client for the purpose of obtaining professional employment if: (A) the written communication concerns an action for personal injury or wrongful death or otherwise relates to an accident or disaster involving the person to whom the communication is addressed or a relative of that person, unless the accident or disaster occurred more than 30 days prior to the mailing of the communication." Rule 4-7.8(a) states that "[a] lawyer shall not accept referrals from a lawyer referral service unless the service: (1) engages in no communication with the public and in no direct contact with prospective clients in a manner that would violate the Rules of Professional Conduct if the communication or contact were made by the lawyer." Together, these rules create a brief 30-day blackout period after an accident during which lawyers may not, directly or indirectly, single out accident victims or their relatives in order to solicit their business.

In March 1992, G. Stewart McHenry and his wholly owned lawyer referral service, Went For It, Inc., filed this action for declaratory and injunctive relief in the United States District Court for the Middle District of Florida challenging Rules 4.7-4(b)(1) and 4.7-8 as violative of the First and Fourteenth Amendments to the Constitution. McHenry alleged that he routinely sent targeted solicitations to accident victims or their survivors within 30 days after accidents and that he wished to continue doing so in the future. Went For It, Inc. represented that it wished to contact accident victims or their survivors within 30 days of accidents and to refer potential clients to participating Florida lawyers. In October 1992, McHenry was disbarred for reasons unrelated to this suit, *The Florida Bar v. McHenry*, 605 So. 2d 459 (Fla. 1992). Another Florida lawyer, John T. Blakely, was substituted in his stead. . . .

The District Court . . . entered summary judgment for the plaintiffs. . . .

The Eleventh Circuit affirmed. . . . We granted certiorari. . . . In *Bates v. State Bar of Arizona, supra,* the Court struck a ban on price advertising for what it deemed "routine" legal services: "the uncontested divorce, the simple adoption, the uncontested personal bankruptcy, the change of name, and the like." *Id.,* at 372. Expressing confidence that legal advertising would only be practicable for such simple, standardized services, the Court rejected the State's proffered justifications for regulation.

Nearly two decades of cases have built upon the foundation laid by *Bates.* It is now well established that lawyer advertising is commercial speech and, as such, is accorded a measure of First Amendment protection. (Citations omitted.) . . . .

Such First Amendment protection, of course, is not absolute. We have always been careful to distinguish commercial speech from speech at the First Amendment's core. " '[C]ommercial speech [enjoys] a limited measure of protection, commensurate with its subordinate position in the scale of First Amendment values,' and is subject to 'modes of regulation that might be impermissible in the realm of noncommercial expression.' " . . .

Mindful of these concerns, we engage in "intermediate" scrutiny of restrictions on commercial speech, analyzing them under the framework set forth in *Central Hudson Gas & Electric Corp. v. Public Service Comm'n of N.Y.,* 447 U.S. 557 (1980). Under *Central Hudson,* the government may freely regulate commercial speech that concerns unlawful activity or is misleading. *Id.,* at 563-564. Commercial speech that falls into neither of those categories, like the advertising at issue here, may be regulated if the government satisfies a test consisting of three related prongs: first, the government must assert a substantial interest in support of its regulation; second, the government must demonstrate that the restriction on commercial speech directly and materially advances that interest; and third, the regulation must be " 'narrowly drawn,' " *id.,* at 564-565.

The Florida Bar asserts that it has a substantial interest in protecting the privacy and tranquility of personal injury victims and their loved ones against intrusive, unsolicited contact by lawyers. . . . This interest obviously factors into the Bar's paramount (and repeatedly professed) objective of curbing activities that "negatively affec[t] the administration of justice." . . . Because direct mail solicitations in the wake of accidents are perceived by the public as intrusive, the Bar argues, the reputation of the legal profession in the eyes of Floridians has suffered commensurately. . . . The regulation, then, is an effort to protect the flagging reputations of Florida lawyers by preventing them from engaging in conduct that, the Bar maintains, " 'is universally regarded as deplorable and beneath common decency because of its intrusion upon the special vulnerability and private grief of victims or their families.' " . . .

We have little trouble crediting the Bar's interest as substantial. On various occasions we have accepted the proposition that "States have a compelling interest in the practice of professions within their boundaries, and . . . as part of their power to protect the public health, safety, and other valid interests they have broad power to establish standards for licensing practitioners and regulating the practice of professions." (Citations omitted.) Our precedents also leave no room for doubt that "the protection of potential clients' privacy is a substantial state interest." (Citations omitted.) . . .

Under *Central Hudson*'s second prong, the State must demonstrate that the challenged regulation "advances the Government's interest 'in a direct and material way.' " (Citations omitted.) . . . The Florida Bar submitted a 106-page summary of its 2 year study of lawyer advertising and solicitation to the District Court. That summary contains data—both statistical and anecdotal—supporting the Bar's contentions that the Florida public views direct mail solicitations in the immediate wake of accidents as an intrusion on privacy that reflects poorly upon the profession. . . . A survey of Florida adults commissioned by the Bar indicated that Floridians "have negative feelings about those attorneys who use direct mail advertising." . . . Fifty four percent of the general population surveyed said that contacting persons concerning accidents or similar events is a violation of privacy. . . . A random sampling of persons who received direct mail advertising from lawyers in 1987 revealed that 45% believed that direct mail solicitation is "designed to take advantage of gullible or unstable people"; 34% found such tactics "annoying or irritating"; 26% found it "an invasion of your privacy"; and 24% reported that it "made you angry." . . . Significantly, 27% of direct mail recipients reported that their regard for the legal profession and for the judicial process as a whole was "lower" as a result of receiving the direct mail. (Citations omitted.)

The anecdotal record mustered by the Bar is noteworthy for its breadth and detail. . . . In light of this showing—which respondents at no time refuted, save by the conclusory assertion that the rule lacked "any factual basis," (citation omitted) we conclude that the Bar has satisfied the second prong of the *Central Hudson* test. . . .

Passing to *Central Hudson*'s third prong, we examine the relationship between the Florida Bar's interests and the means chosen to serve them. (Citation omitted.) With respect to this prong, the differences between commercial speech and noncommercial speech are manifest. . . . "What our decisions require" . . . "is a 'fit' between the legislature's ends and the means chosen to accomplish those ends,' a fit that is not necessarily perfect, but reasonable; that represents not necessarily the single best disposition but one whose scope is 'in proportion to the interest served,' that employs not necessarily the least restrictive means but . . . a means narrowly tailored to achieve the desired objective." (Citations omitted.) . . . We find little deficiency in the ban's failure to distinguish among injured Floridians by the severity of their pain or the intensity of their grief. Indeed, it is hard to imagine the contours of a regulation that might satisfy respondents on this score. Rather than drawing difficult lines on the basis that some injuries are "severe" and some situations appropriate (and others, presumably, inappropriate) for grief, anger, or emotion, the Florida Bar has crafted a ban applicable to all postaccident or disaster solicitations for a brief 30-day period. Unlike respondents, we do not see "numerous and obvious less burdensome alternatives" to Florida's short temporal ban. (Citation omitted.) The Bar's rule is reasonably well tailored to its stated objective of eliminating targeted mailings whose type and timing are a source of distress to Floridians, distress that has caused many of them to lose respect for the legal profession. . . .

We believe that the Florida Bar's 30-day restriction on targeted direct mail solicitation of accident victims and their relatives withstands scrutiny under the three part *Central Hudson* test that we have devised for this context. The Bar has substantial interest both in protecting injured Floridians from invasive conduct by lawyers and in preventing the erosion of confidence in the profession that such repeated invasions have engendered. The Bar's proffered study, unrebutted by respondents below, provides evidence indicating that the harms it targets are far from illusory. The palliative devised by the Bar to address these harms is narrow both in scope and in duration. The Constitution, in our view, requires nothing more.

The judgment of the Court of Appeals, accordingly, is *reversed.*

Questions about the Case

1. Why does the court open its opinion with the recitation of the bar study of lawyer advertising and the resulting changes in the code? What does this tell you about where the court is going to go?
2. Does the court in any of the previous cases on lawyer advertising use the *Central Hudson* analysis that the court uses here? How does

this analysis impact the decision? What is the three-prong test of *Central Hudson?*

3. Do you find the Florida bar study on lawyer advertising persuasive? Could the bar have adopted a different and less restrictive approach to addressing the problem of lawyers preying on accident and disaster victims?
4. What is the primary interest of the state in adopting this restriction? Do you think it is an adequate justification to restrict commercial speech?

The following case was decided just after *Bates.* In it, the Court addresses the question of restrictions on in-person solicitation of clients by attorneys. Pay close attention to the Court's reasons for the distinction between advertising and solicitation.

Ohralik v. Ohio State Bar Association
436 U.S. 447 (1978)

Justice POWELL delivered the opinion of the Court.

In *Bates v. State Bar of Arizona,* 433 U.S. 350 (1977), this Court held that truthful advertising or "routine" legal services is protected by the First and Fourteenth Amendments against blanket prohibition by a State. The Court expressly reserved the question of the permissible scope of regulation of "in-person solicitation of clients—at the hospital room or the accident site, or in any other situation that breeds undue influence—by attorneys or their agents or 'runners.' " Id., at 366. Today we answer part of the question so reserved, and hold that the State—or the Bar acting with state authorization—constitutionally may discipline a lawyer for soliciting clients in person, for pecuniary gain, under circumstances likely to pose dangers that the State has a right to prevent.

I

Appellant, a member of the Ohio Bar, lives in Montville. Ohio. Until recently he practiced law in Montville and Cleveland. On February 13, 1974, while picking up his mail at the Montville Post Office, appellant learned from the postmaster's brother about an automobile accident that had taken place on February 2 in which Carol McClintock, a young woman with whom appellant was casually acquainted, had been injured. Appellant made a telephone call to Ms. McClintock's parents, who informed him that their daughter was in the hospital. Appellant suggested that he might visit Carol in the hospital. Mrs. McClintock assented to the idea, but requested that appellant first stop by at her home.

During appellant's visit with the McClintocks, they explained that their daughter had been driving the family automobile on a local road when she was hit by an uninsured motorist. Both Carol and her passenger, Wanda Lou Holbert, were injured and hospitalized. In response to the McClintocks' expression of apprehension that they might be sued by Holbert, appellant explained that Ohio's guest statute would preclude such a suit. When appellant suggested to the McClintocks that they hire a lawyer, Mrs. McClintock retorted that such a decision would be up to Carol, who was 18 years old and would be the beneficiary of a successful claim.

Appellant proceeded to the hospital, where he found Carol lying in traction in her room. After a brief conversation about her condition, appellant told Carol he would represent her and asked her to sign an agreement. Carol said she would have to discuss the matter with her parents. She did not sign the agreement, but asked appellant to have her parents come to see her. Appellant also attempted to see Wanda Lou Holbert, but learned that she had just been released from the hospital. He then departed for another visit with the McClintocks.

On his way appellant detoured to the scene of the accident, where he took a set of photographs. He also picked up a tape recorder, which he concealed under his raincoat before arriving at the McClintocks' residence. Once there, he re-examined their automobile insurance policy, discussed with them the law applicable to passengers, and explained the consequences of the fact that the driver who struck Carol's car was an uninsured motorist. Appellant discovered that the McClintocks' insurance policy would provide benefits of up to $12,500 each for Carol and Wanda Lou under an uninsured-motorist clause. Mrs. McClintock acknowledged that both Carol and Wanda Lou could sue for their injuries, but recounted to appellant that "Wanda swore up and down she would not do it." The McClintocks also told appellant that Carol had phoned to say that appellant could "go ahead" with her representation. Two days later appellant returned to Carol's hospital room to have her sign a contract, which provided that he would receive one-third of her recovery.

In the meantime, appellant obtained Wanda Lou's name and address from the McClintocks after telling them he wanted to ask her some questions about the accident. He then visited Wanda Lou at her home, without having been invited. He again concealed his tape recorder and recorded most of the conversation with Wanda Lou. After a brief, unproductive inquiry about the facts of the accident, appellant told Wanda Lou that he was representing Carol and that he had a "little tip" for Wanda Lou: the

McClintocks' insurance policy contained an uninsured-motorist clause which might provide her with a recovery of up to $12,500. The young woman, who was 18 years of age and not a high school graduate at the time, replied to appellant's query about whether she was going to file a claim by stating that she really did not understand what was going on. Appellant offered to represent her, also, for a contingent fee of one-third of any recovery, and Wanda Lou stated "O.K."

Wanda's mother attempted to repudiate her daughter's oral assent the following day, when appellant called on the telephone to speak to Wanda. Mrs. Holbert informed appellant that she and her daughter did not want to sue anyone or to have appellant represent them, and that if they decided to sue they would consult their own lawyer. Appellant insisted that Wanda had entered into a binding agreement. A month later Wanda confirmed in writing that she wanted neither to sue nor to be represented by appellant. She requested that appellant notify the insurance company that he was not her lawyer, as the company would not release a check to her until he did so. Carol also eventually discharged appellant. Although another lawyer represented her in concluding a settlement with the insurance company, she paid appellant one-third of her recovery in settlement of his lawsuit against her for breach of contract.

Both Carol McClintock and Wanda Lou Holbert filed complaints against appellant with the Grievance Committee of the Geauga County Bar Association. The County Bar Association referred the grievance to appellee, which filed a formal complaint with the Board of Commissioners on Grievances and Discipline of the Supreme Court of Ohio. After a hearing, the Board found that appellant had violated Disciplinary Rules (DR) 2-103 (A) and 2-104 (A) of the Ohio Code of Professional Responsibility. The Board rejected appellant's defense that his conduct was protected under the First and Fourteenth Amendments. The Supreme Court of Ohio adopted the findings of the Board, reiterated that appellant's conduct was not constitutionally protected, and increased the sanction of a public reprimand recommended by the Board to indefinite suspension.

The decision in *Bates* was handed down after the conclusion of proceedings in the Ohio Supreme Court. We noted probable jurisdiction in this case to consider the scope of protection of a form of commercial speech, and an aspect of the State's authority to regulate and discipline members of the bar, not considered in *Bates*. 434 U.S. 814 (1977) . . .

II

The solicitation of business by a lawyer through direct, in-person communication with the prospective client has long been viewed as inconsistent with the profession's ideal of the attorney-client relationship and as posing a significant potential for harm to the prospective client. It has been proscribed by the organized Bar for many years. . . .

Appellant contends that his solicitation of the two young women as clients is indistinguishable, for purposes of constitutional analysis, from the advertisement in *Bates*. Like that advertisement, his meetings with the prospective clients apprised them of their legal rights and of the availability of a lawyer to pursue their claims. . . .

In-person solicitation by a lawyer of remunerative employment is a business transaction in which speech is an essential but subordinate component. While this does not remove the speech from the protection of the First Amendment, as was held in *Bates* and *Virginia Pharmacy,* it lowers the level of appropriate judicial scrutiny.

As applied in this case, the Disciplinary Rules are said to have limited the communication of two kinds of information. First, appellant's solicitation imparted to Carol McClintock and Wanda Lou Holbert certain information about his availability and the terms of his proposed legal services. In this respect, in-person solicitation serves much the same function as the advertisement at issue in *Bates*. But there are significant differences as well. Unlike a public advertisement, which simply provides information and leaves the recipient free to act upon it or not, in-person solicitation may exert pressure and often demands an immediate response, without providing an opportunity for comparison or reflection. The aim and effect of in-person solicitation may be to provide a one-sided presentation and to encourage speedy and perhaps uninformed decision-making; there is no opportunity for intervention or countereducation by agencies of the Bar, supervisory authorities, or persons close to the solicited individual. The admonition that "the fitting remedy for evil counsels is good ones" is of little value when the circumstances provide no opportunity for any remedy at all. In-person solicitation is as likely as not to discourage persons needing counsel from engaging in a critical comparison of the "availability, nature, and prices" of legal services, cf. *Bates,* 433 U.S., at 364; it actually may disserve the individual and societal interest, identified in *Bates,* in facilitating "informed and reliable decisionmaking." Ibid.

It also is argued that in-person solicitation may provide the solicited individual with information about his or her legal rights and remedies. In this case, appellant gave Wanda Lou a "tip" about the prospect of recovery based on the uninsured-motorist clause in the McClintocks' insurance policy, and he explained that clause and Ohio's guest statute to Carol McClintock's parents. But neither of the Disciplinary Rules here at issue prohibited appellant from communicating information to these young women about their legal rights and the prospects of obtaining a monetary recovery, or from recommending that they obtain counsel. DR 2-104 (A) merely prohibited him from using the information as bait with which to obtain an agreement to represent them for a fee. The Rule does not prohibit a lawyer from giving unsolicited legal advice; it proscribes the acceptance of employment resulting from such advice. . . .

The substantive evils of solicitation have been stated over the years in sweeping terms: stirring up litigation, assertion of fraudulent claims, debasing the legal profession, and potential harm to the solicited client in the form of overreaching, overcharging, underrepresentation, and misrepresentation. . . .

The State's perception of the potential for harm in circumstances such as those presented in this case is well founded. The detrimental aspects of face-to-face selling even of ordinary consumer products have been recognized and addressed by the Federal Trade Commission, and it hardly need be said that the potential for overreaching is significantly greater when a lawyer, a professional trained in the art of persuasion, personally solicits an unsophisticated, injured, or distressed lay person. Such an individual may place his trust in a lawyer, regardless of the latter's qualifications or the individual's actual need for legal representation, simply in response to persuasion under circumstances conducive to uninformed acquiescence. Although it is argued that personal solicitation is valuable because it may apprise a victim of misfortune of his legal rights, the very plight of that person not only makes him more vulnerable to influence but also may make advice all the more intrusive. Thus, under these adverse conditions the overtures of an uninvited lawyer may distress the solicited individual simply because of their obtrusiveness and the invasion of the individual's privacy, even when no other harm materializes. Under such circumstances, it is not unreasonable for the State to presume that in-person solicitation by lawyers more often than not will be injurious to the person solicited.

The efficacy of the State's effort to prevent such harm to prospective clients would be substantially diminished if, having proved a solicitation in circumstances like those of this case, the State were required in addition to prove actual injury. Unlike the advertising in *Bates,* in-person solicitation is not visible or otherwise open to public scrutiny. Often there is no witness other than the lawyer and the lay person whom he has solicited, rendering it difficult or impossible to obtain reliable proof of what actually took place. This would be especially true if the lay person were so distressed at the time of the solicitation that he could not recall specific details at a later date. If appellant's view were sustained, in-person solicitation would be virtually immune to effective oversight and regulation by the State or by the legal profession, in contravention of the State's strong interest in regulating members of the Bar in an effective, objective, and self-enforcing manner. It therefore is not unreasonable, or violative of the Constitution, for a State to respond with what in effect is a prophylactic rule.

On the basis of the undisputed facts of record, we conclude that the Disciplinary Rules constitutionally could be applied to appellant. . . . Under our view of the State's interest in averting harm by prohibiting solicitation in circumstances where it is likely to occur, the absence of explicit proof or findings of harm or injury is immaterial. The facts in this case present a striking example of the potential for overreaching that is inherent in a lawyer's in-person solicitation of professional employment. They also demonstrate the need for prophylactic regulation in furtherance of the State's interest in protecting the lay public. We hold that the application of DR 2-103(A) and 2-104(A) to appellant does not offend the Constitution.

Accordingly, the judgment of the Supreme Court of Ohio is affirmed.

Questions about the Case

1. Why do you think the court felt compelled to decide this case?
2. What exactly did attorney Ohralik do to break the ethics rules? Did you find his conduct objectionable?
3. What is the basis for the different rules on in-person solicitation and advertising? Do you find this reasoning convincing?
4. What general rule can you derive from this case? Do the ethics rules in your state comport with this decision? Do they carve out any exceptions?

Fees and Client Funds

This chapter examines the role that financial matters play in the attorney-client relationship, and how these matters can be a source of difficulty and dispute. Legal assistants are involved in financial matters in many of their functions, from handling client trust funds to billing clients for their time. Chapter 7 covers:

- the various kinds of fee arrangements made with clients, including fixed fees, contingency fees, and hourly fees
- the growing use of alternative kinds of fee arrangements
- factors considered in determining if a fee is unethically excessive
- unethical billing practices
- the communication of fee agreements with clients
- the terms included in fee agreements
- the awarding of attorney's fees under fee-shifting statutes
- the inclusion of paralegals' fees in statutory fee awards
- ethics rules prohibiting fee-splitting and referral fees, and how these apply to legal assistants
- ethics rules prohibiting lawyers from entering into partnerships with legal assistants, and recent innovations in this area
- duties in handling client funds and client trust accounts

A. Fee Arrangements with Clients

Several different methods are used to charge clients for legal services. The method selected depends mostly on the nature of the services being rendered. The most common methods of billing are fixed fees, contingency fees, and hourly fees.

1. Fixed Fees

Fixed fees (also known as *flat fees*) usually are used for routine legal services, ones for which the attorney knows the length of time needed to complete the work. In this instance, the client is paying for the attorney's expertise as much as for the time expended. Typical services for which a fixed or flat fee is charged are filing a default divorce, forming a corporation, or handling a simple wage-earner bankruptcy.

A variation on the fixed fee is a fee that is based on the percentage of the worth of the matter being handled, either by statute or by practice. In probate matters, for example, the fee usually is based on a percentage of the value of the estate, according to statute. It is common practice in some states for an attorney to charge a percentage of the value of a real estate transaction. Although calculated as a percentage, these kinds of fees are not to be confused with contingency fees, in which the attorney is taking the risk of not collecting a fee in the event he or she loses the case.

2. Contingency Fees

Contingency fees are usually based on a percentage of the recovery in a case. Sometimes a fixed fee is made contingent on the outcome in a case, giving it the most important attribute of a contingency fee—risk. Contingency fee arrangements typically are utilized by plaintiffs' attorneys in civil litigation like personal injury. The risk to the attorney in handling a case on contingency is that he or she will lose the case, thus receiving no compensation for the time spent on the case.

Although the contingency fee is now well accepted in the United States (it is not utilized in England or Canada), it was resisted by the American bar until early in this century. Contingency fees were thought to stir up litigation and to encourage attorneys to engage in unethical conduct to win cases. Gradually, the bar came to recognize the value of the contingency fee as a means to provide access to legal services to those who have a legal claim but who cannot otherwise afford legal services.

Despite the widespread use of contingency fees in personal injury and medical malpractice cases, ethics rules still place some limitations on their use. Contingency fee arrangements are not permitted in any state in criminal cases because they are thought to encourage corruption and to discourage plea bargaining. ABA Model Code DR 2-106(c); ABA Model Rule 1.5(d) (2). Most jurisdictions also have rules prohibiting contingency fees in marital dissolution, divorce, and separation cases, again because they discourage reconciliation and settlement. In addition, a contingency arrangement in such cases may not be necessary to provide access to legal services since the court may award attorney's fees to the spouse without the means to pay them. ABA Model Rule 1.5(d) (1) prohibits contingency fees in domestic relations cases; ABA Model Code EC 2-20 says that they are "rarely justified" in such cases.

Other limitations on contingency fee arrangements have been codified into state ethics rules or statutes that restrict the percentage of the fee. For example, the Federal Torts Claims Act, 28 U.S.C.A. §2678, places the maximum fee at 25 percent. Some state statutes, including California's Business and Professions Code §6146, limit the percentage that can be charged in medical malpractice cases.

Some jurisdictions have special ethics rules relating to the communication with the client of the terms of a contingency fee arrangement. Many of these rules require contingency fee agreements to be in writing even though other fee agreements are not required to be in writing. See, for example, ABA Model Rule 1.5(c). (Communication of fee agreements is discussed in the next section of this chapter.) State rules requiring ads that mention contingency fees to disclose that clients are liable for costs even if they lose their case were upheld in *Zauderer v. Office of Disciplinary Counsel of the Supreme Court of Ohio,* 471 U.S. 626 (1985). Finally, contingency fees are subject to special judicial scrutiny for reasonableness and are disallowed if the percentage is considered exorbitant or the fee is well out of proportion to the work done or the risk taken by the attorney.

Contingency fees are a perpetual subject of debate within the legal profession. There are regular initiatives to prohibit them altogether in some jurisdictions or to limit the amount of fees if a case is uncontested or settles before trial. Despite this controversy, contingency fees are gaining in popularity in some areas as clients explore alternative fee arrangements. For example, more corporate clients are requesting contingency arrangements in business litigation, including on the defense side, and some states are studying the possible use of contingency fees for lawyers working to collect overdue child support.

While a typical contingency fee in a personal injury matter is one-third of the recovery, some lawyers charge on a sliding scale that reflects both the amount of risk to the attorney and the time and effort expended by the attorney as the case moves forward. For example, an attorney might charge 25 percent if the case settles before trial, 33⅓ percent if it goes to trial, and 40 percent if it is appealed.

3. Hourly Fees

Hourly fees are the most common method of billing in matters other than plaintiff civil litigation. Charging for time was not always so common in the legal profession but has become deeply ingrained in law practice during the past 20 years. Most large firms bill mainly by means of hourly rates, with every lawyer and legal assistant keeping close track of the time spent on client matters, usually in increments of either six or ten minutes.

Hourly rates are based on the expertise and other qualifications of the person billing, the nature and complexity of the services performed and, of course, the market. For example, a senior partner in a major law firm who handles complex securities transactions may have a billing rate of $500 an hour. The time of a mid-level associate with five years' experience, however, may be charged at $200 an hour, while that of a five-year legal assistant may be charged at $85 an hour.

Recently, there has been some movement away from hourly billing as the norm. Part of the impetus for this move is attributed to the increased efficiency of law firms through specialization and the use of technology. Firms that have developed highly valuable expertise and means of producing documents quickly and efficiently want to avoid being penalized for their efficiency and to be fairly compensated not just for their time but for the "value" of their services. Clients are also calling for changes in the way that legal services are priced as they seek ways to lower legal fees and to structure fee agreements in ways that allow them to plan and budget more accurately and to assess the value and productivity of the services provided.

Many firms are beginning to utilize alternative methods of structuring fee arrangements, such as charging a percentage of the value of a transaction, charging a premium for achieving results that are especially beneficial to a client, or charging a fixed fee that reflects the value of the services to the client without regard to the time expended. Capping of fees at a predetermined amount, discounted hourly rates for major clients, blended hourly rates arrived at by averaging rates for all firm lawyers and legal assistants, contingency fees in defense matters, and hybrids of several different billing methods are all commonly used now. One of the innovations that is catching on is task-based billing, in which clients are charged a predetermined flat fee for a specific function, such as taking a deposition or representing a client at a particular kind of hearing.

More changes in billing practices are on the horizon as law practice changes in response to the market and the new technology. The effect on legal assistants is significant: paralegals must be proficient in technology and demonstrably efficient and productive in all their work. Legal assistant managers and lawyers who supervise paralegals must be certain that legal assistants are well trained and are assigned to perform work that matches their degree of expertise.

It is well accepted that paralegal time may be charged directly to clients just as attorney time is. When utilized properly, legal assistants are engaged in legal work that, were it not for the legal assistant, would have to be done by an attorney. And because paralegal time is billed to clients at lower rates than attorney time is, the cost to the client is lower. Guideline 8 of the ABA Model Guidelines for the Utilization of Legal Assistant Services (ABA Model Guidelines) provides that lawyers may charge for paralegal services. Most state guidelines also endorse this customary practice, which was validated by the U.S. Supreme Court in *Missouri v. Jenkins,* 491 U.S. 274 (1989) (with regard to statutory fee awards). The comment to NALA Model Guideline 5 also discusses the practice of billing clients for paralegal time and fee awards that include compensation for paralegal work. (Section C below discusses this topic further.)

4. Ethics Violations in Fee Setting

The ethics rules covering fees prohibit fees that are illegal, excessive, unconscionable, or unreasonable. A fee is usually found illegal if it exceeds statutory limits such as those set by the Federal Torts Claims Act, mentioned above. The ABA Model Code, which speaks in terms of "clearly excessive," and the ABA Model Rules, which prohibit "unreasonable" fees, contain the same eight factors used to determine whether a fee is unethically high:

(1) the time and labor required, the novelty and difficulty of the questions involved, and the skill requisite to perform the legal service properly;
(2) the likelihood, if apparent to the client, that the acceptance of the particular employment will preclude other employment by the lawyer;

239

    (3) the fee customarily charged in the locality for similar legal services;
    (4) the amount involved and the results obtained;
    (5) the time limitations imposed by the client or by the circumstances;
    (6) the nature and length of the professional relationship with the client;
    (7) the experience, reputation, and ability of the lawyer or lawyers performing the services; and
    (8) whether the fee is fixed or contingent.

ABA Model Code DR 2-106(B); ABA Model Rule 1.5(a)(1)-(8). Some states, such as California, set the standard for excessive fees at the "unconscionable" level.

The reasonableness of fees has been litigated extensively, mainly in cases involving statutory fee awards (discussed below in Section C). Guidelines can be drawn from litigation over fees and from disciplinary cases. While all the factors on the ABA list are generally considered by courts and disciplinary bodies in determining if a fee is unethical, the amount of time spent still tends to be the most important. In fee dispute cases and disciplinary matters, the client's understanding of the fee agreement is also a critical factor.

Probably the most widespread ethical problem relating to fees is one that is not addressed directly by either ethics codes or case law. It is also one that legal assistants are likely to face during the course of their careers. It is the practice of inflating the figures for time spent on client matters.

In firms that depend on hourly billing for their revenue, the pressure to bill an ever-increasing number of hours is tremendous. The value of a fee-generating attorney or legal assistant is measured largely by how much revenue that biller produces for the firm. Expectations of billable hours rose dramatically in the 1980s. In the early 1980s, 1200 billable hours a year was common in a large firm; now, the expectation is closer to 2000 hours a year in many large firms. Studies show that associates in large law firms in metropolitan areas bill an average of 1650 to 1900 hours a year and partners bill an average of 1500 to 1850 hours a year.

While most of the pressure to bill falls on highly compensated associates trying to make partner, legal assistants feel it too. During the early 1990s many firms learned that their paralegals were not as profitable as they had once thought. Now, particularly in large firms, there are strict guidelines on paralegal billable hours too, usually in the range of 1200 to 1500 a year. This pressure to bill has created an incentive to engage in improper billing practices, such as double billing, billing full rates for recycled work product, overbilling, overstaffing, billing for overhead costs, padding hours, doing unnecessary work for clients, and spending excessive amounts of time on matters that do not warrant it.

In the past decade, several cases of prominent attorneys who engaged in overbilling and billing of personal expenses to clients have given this issue a high profile. Some cases involved padding hourly bills in corporate, insurance defense, and criminal defense cases; others have involved charging personal expenses, including clothes, travel, meals, and gifts, to clients. Examples abound in the press, with new scandals coming to light with some frequency. The most highly publicized case involved Webster Hubbell, a former advisor to President Clinton and law partner of Hillary Rodham Clinton, who was convicted of defrauding his former law firm and its clients of nearly one-half million dollars by improperly billing for work not done and charging for unreimbursable expenses. Another large law firm became the target of United States Senators for its billing of the government for work on a securities fraud case. The bill in question was more than $23 million and included hourly rates for attorneys ranging from $270 to $600 an hour, and paralegal rates at $85 an hour. In the last year or two, dozens of lawyers have been disciplined for unethical billing, a violation which has historically been quite rare. Reported cases have involved overcharging for legal research and driving time to an unnecessarily distant library, doubling the costs of process servers and independent contractors, billing clients more than 24 hours a day, charging fees and costs that were agreed in advance not be charged, and multiplying the time spent by specific factors to ensure a profit. These incidents have caused much speculation about the actual prevalence of abuses and the extent to which they can be attributed to fraud, overzealousness, or sloppy timekeeping or oversight practices.

Finally, it should be noted that corporate clients have taken proactive steps to prevent themselves from becoming the victims of unscrupulous billing practices and high legal bills. Many such clients have requested firms to make proposals for services, established budgets beyond which a firm may not bill, and demanded task billing, which provides detailed information on the cost of services from which clients can evaluate services and negotiate future billing arrangements. Some corporations have restricted the costs they will pay. For example, corporations reimburse for coach air fare only and refuse to pay surcharges on computerized legal research or for secretarial overtime or computer use. Some corporate clients and some law firms are conducting audits of their billing to turn up errors and improper practices.

The ABA issued a formal ethics opinion addressing billing practices in 1994. The practices highlighted as objectionable in the opinion were double-billing (that is, billing more than one client for the same hours—such as making court appearances for more than one client in the same day), surcharges on services contracted with outside vendors, such as expert witnesses, and charges beyond reasonable costs for in-house services like photocopying and computer searches. The opinion calls for full disclosure of the basis for charges when the fee agreement is made and subsequently when the client is billed. Further, the opinion emphasizes that the charges must also be reasonable, i.e., no charges for unnecessary work or for hours not actually expended. ABA Formal Opinion 93-379 (1993). Also see California State Board Ethics Opinion 147 (1996), which is in accord. One local bar association has publicly recognized the inherent hazards in judging performance by the amount of time billed. The Los Angeles County Bar Association issued an ethics opinion in which it stated that measuring attorney productivity on the basis of billable hours was acceptable, but that a firm that employs this method must "carefully analyze and evaluate the effects of such standard . . ." being cognizant of the incentive to pad bills, to bill for work not done, and to cause attorneys to work under extreme pressure and while fatigued. Los Angeles County Bar Association Ethics Opinion 479 (1995). For more on the hourly billing dilemma, see William G. Ross, The Honest Hour: The Ethics of Time Based Billing by Attorneys, Carolina Academic Press (1996).

Paralegals have been implicated in many highly publicized cases. For example, paralegals in one case billed deposition summaries at the rate of four to five pages an hour, about a fourth the average speed. In another case, a paralegal billed 43 hours in one day. In some cases, paralegal billing rates have been double the market rate or the time was billed for routine clerical work such as copying and filing. A few well-publicized cases in the insurance industry have forced insurance defense firms to rethink what work they assign to paralegals because their clients refuse to pay paralegal rates for work they consider to be clerical.

Billing abuses are not only inherently dishonest and unethical but also detrimental in the long term to both the one who engages in them and the firm. Good firms do not send bills to clients without first examining them to see that the amount fairly reflects the services rendered. If the bill is excessive, the partner who is responsible for billing the client will adjust it down, "writing off" excessive time. The written-off time will be allocated back to the one who billed it and deducted from his or her total billable hours.

The firm that does not review bills or adjust them in this fashion is running the risk of having a dissatisfied client or of losing a client in these days of greater and greater competition for clients. Egregious abuses may result in disbarment and malpractice suits. Some commentators believe that excessive legal fees caused by dishonest billing practices have been a leading factor in the revolt by clients against the high cost of legal services and in the lowered esteem in which lawyers are held by the public.

242

Legal assistants should not themselves engage in such unethical billing practices and have an obligation to report others' such conduct to a supervising attorney. A legal assistant should not continue to work in a firm that encourages such conduct. The NFPA Model Code calls attention to the proper paralegal role in billing under Canon 2. EC-2.3 advises paralegals to prepare thorough, accurate, and honest timekeeping and billing records. Also see NFPA Ethics Opinion 95-4, which discusses the ethics of billing for tasks that may be considered nonprofessional clerical work.

B. Terms and Communication of Fee Arrangements with Clients

As soon as possible after a lawyer and client agree to representation, the lawyer should fully explain the terms of the fee agreement to the client. It is good practice—required in some cases—to put the agreement in writing.

The ABA Model Code has no Disciplinary Rule requiring written fee agreements but advises in EC 2-19 that lawyers reach a "clear agreement" about fees, reduce it to writing especially in the case of contingency fees, and fully explain the reasons for the fee arrangement. The ABA Model Rules expand this guidance in Rule 1.5(b) and (c). Model Rule 1.5(b) states that when a lawyer "has not regularly represented a client," the fee basis or rate be communicated promptly to the client, "preferably in writing." Rule 1.5(c) requires that contingency fee agreements be in writing and that the writing include the method and percentage(s) by which the fee is to be calculated, as well as provision for payment of costs (that is, whether they are deducted before or after calculation of the fee). A written statement showing the calculations is required at the conclusion of the matter. Note that the ABA Model Rules emphasize the communication of the fee agreement only for new clients and contingency case clients. This may indicate a traditional reluctance to discuss financial matters with clients, or the longstanding distaste for contingency agreements. Some states have more stringent requirements about what kind of fee agreements must be in writing. For example, New Jersey and others have eliminated the singling out of contingency fees and require all fee agreements with new clients to be in writing.

Written fee agreements are favored because they promote clear communication between the attorney and client and prevent disputes over the fee later on. In addition, they protect both parties in the event of a dispute, especially attorneys who will have any misunderstanding about the fee arrangements construed against them. Some state bars have standard forms that attorneys are encouraged to use.

As indicated in Chapter 3 on unauthorized practice of law, legal assistants should be alert to the dangers of discussing fees directly with new clients. Only an attorney can agree to represent a client and in doing so determine the appropriate fee arrangement and meet the ethical obligation to explain it fully to the client. The role of the legal assistant as a liaison to the client may include answering questions about fees and costs but cannot include entering into the contractual agreement with the client on the lawyer's behalf.

The ABA Model Guidelines state that establishing a fee is one of the few specified functions that a lawyer cannot delegate to a legal assistant. Guideline 3(b) advises that a lawyer may not delegate "responsibility for establishing the amount of a fee to be charged for a legal service." The comment emphasizes the importance of attorney-client communication and cites state guidelines that also prohibit paralegals from "setting fees" or accepting cases. (See also ABA Informal Opinion 875 (1965), which provides that lay employees may not make fee arrangements or agree to undertake representation on the lawyer's behalf.) The National Association of Legal Assistants (NALA) Code of Ethics and Professional Responsibility provides in Canon 3(b) that "a legal assistant must not . . . establish an attorney-client relationship [or] set fees. . . ."

Fee arrangements should cover fully the scope of the firm's services: the responsibilites of the client and the firm; all the details regarding the method of determining the fee (that is, hourly, fixed, contingency, or some other method); what costs the client is obligated to pay and when (that is, out of client's recovery after the attorney's fee is calculated in the case of contingency arrangements or at specified regular billings); termination rights for both parties; the method and time of fee payment; and procedure for and frequency of billings, if applicable. The agreement should contain a provision indicating that it is privileged. It is also wise to include language indicating that the firm is not guaranteeing a particular result. If the client does not speak or read English proficiently, the agreement should be in a language that the client does understand. The signature clause should include an acknowledgment that the client has read and understood the terms of the agreement. And the client should be given sufficient time to read and reflect on the agreement before signing it.

In some instances, attorneys may require a *retainer* or *advance,* which is paid at the commencement of the agreed-upon work. While frequently called retainers. advance fees are usually refundable, in that the attorney earns the fee as the work progresses and will refund to the client whatever portion is unearned when, for whatever reason, the services stop. Retainer fees are in whole or in part nonrefundable, in essence acting as a minimum fee regardless of the amount of work done and as a guarantee that the attorney will be available to handle the representation. A nonrefundable retainer is ethically acceptable so long as the client fully understands the arrangement and the fee is not excessive, considering the factors previously discussed. Advances must be deposited into the client trust account until earned while nonrefundable retainers may be deposited directly into a firm operating account. (Client trust accounts are discussed below in Section E.)

Matters for which an hourly fee is charged represent potential problems because, without an estimate of the number of hours a project will take, the client will have no idea what the ultimate bill for services might be. It is good practice for the attorney to provide the client with an estimate if at all possible and to update the estimate if it changes as the matter proceeds.

Payment of costs requires special clarity in fee agreements as clients may not expect to pay or may resent paying many small charges when they are already paying what they believe are high fees. What kinds of costs are billed directly to clients varies somewhat from firm to firm. As a rule, all lawyers expect clients to pay direct expenses that the firm pays to an entity outside the firm. These costs include filing fees with courts and government bodies, transcripts of depositions and trials, expert reports and testimony, out-of-the-area travel expenses, outside printing, and messengers. Most firms also charge for copying done within the firm and long-distance telephone calls. Some firms also charge the client for costs that might ordinarily be thought of as part of overhead, such as secretarial overtime, computer use, and even air conditioning, in the event the firm must work extra evening and weekend hours for a particular client. Generally, costs are itemized on a client's bill. (Also see Chapter 5, for conflicts of interest rules relating to advancing costs and other expenses for clients.)

Finally, fee agreements may contain provisions indicating how fee disputes and malpractice claims will be handled, for example, by mediation or arbitration.

While not in widespread use, over thirty jurisdictions permit lawyers to accept payment of legal fees by credit card. This practice was first approved by the ABA in its Formal Opinion 338 (1974) with several limitations, including one that the attorney not increase fees to cover expenses of participating in such a plan. Some states also permit attorneys to help clients work out financing for the payment of fees with a bank. This practice was also approved by ABA Formal Opinion 338 (1974).

245

Some attorneys will accept property in payment of fees. When doing so, attorneys must pay special attention to the value of the property and reasonableness of the fee.

C. Statutory Fees

As a general rule, litigants in the United States must pay their own attorney's fees. This practice is contrary to that of England, Canada, and most other European countries, all of which have some form of fee-shifting. In England and Canada, for example, all or part of the attorney's fees in litigation are awarded to the prevailing party.

Efforts have been made to reform the American system, and some progress has been made by way of court decisions, contracts, and legislation. Courts have awarded attorney's fees in cases in which a common fund that benefits persons other than the parties was created as a result of the litigation; in which the litigation resulted in a common benefit to the public or some portion of the public even though no fund was created; similarly, in which the plaintiff acted as a "private attorney general" vindicating a legal right that also benefits others and for which the plaintiff's actual damages are relatively small; and, finally, in actions for malicious prosecution, for abuse of civil process, or those taken in bad faith. This last category of fee-shifting is also supported by legislation in some states. Contract provisions for attorney's fees are relatively common and will generally be enforced by the courts.

Fee-shifting statutes have proliferated in recent years, and now hundreds of state and federal statutes provide for the award of attorney's fees in specified kinds of litigation. These fee-shifting statutes generally apply to the kinds of litigation that the legislature wants to encourage as a matter of public policy (for example, protecting civil rights) and award fees only to prevailing plaintiffs, not defendants. Like contingency fees, statutory fees enable plaintiffs who might not otherwise be able to afford an attorney to bring legal action to vindicate their rights. And like contingency fees, the attorney is accepting the risk of not being compensated if he or she does not prevail.

Conflict of interest problems may arise in cases involving statutory fees when the interests of the client clash with the interest of the attorney in maximizing the fee award. For example, an offer to settle may satisfy the client but not include sufficient fees for the attorney, or may satisfy the attorney as to the fee award but not the client because the recovery to the client is too low. Lawyers must always be aware of the potential for this kind of conflict and keep the client's best interests in mind when advising whether to accept an offer.

Most important to legal assistants in the area of statutory fees is the landmark decision of *Missouri v. Jenkins,* 491 U.S. 274 (1989), in which an award of attorney and paralegal fees under the federal civil rights statute was upheld. The lower court had awarded fees that included compensation for paralegal time at hourly market rates. The state of Missouri contended, first, that the statute provided only for attorney's fees, not paralegals'; second, that if paralegal time were to be compensable, it should be compensated at cost, not at a market rate that included a profit to the law firm. In upholding the award, the Court construed the attorney's fee statute broadly, finding that it did include paralegals' fees, and followed the longstanding measure of market value as the appropriate one for setting paralegals' fees. This case is included at the end of this chapter and followed by several other cases in which paralegal fees were at issue.

This was a critical decision for legal assistants; a court decision that had gone the other way would have acted as a disincentive to the utilization of legal assistant services by firms that work in statutory fee cases and may have called into question the common practice of billing for paralegal time at market rates. Thousands of cases awarding paralegal fees as part of attorney's fee awards have been decided in state and federal trial courts since *Missouri v. Jenkins.* It was also the first U.S. Supreme Court decision in which the role of legal assistants was discussed at any length and endorsed as a praiseworthy innovation and an effective means of containing the costs of legal services. Finally, it gave guidance in what had been in dispute throughout the country; several state and some federal appeals courts had interpreted attorney's fees award statutes contrary to the holding in *Missouri v. Jenkins,* some finding the statutes not to include paralegal fees at all, some applying the cost, not market measure, to calculate the award.

As a result of these earlier court decisions denying the award of paralegals' fees at market rates, several states have amended statutes and/ or court rules to clarify that attorney's fee awards include paralegals' fees at market rates (e.g., Alaska, Arizona, California, Florida, New Jersey, Illinois, Indiana, New York, Oklahoma, and Ohio). A few states have continued to resist interpreting state statutes the way the court did in *Missouri v. Jenkins.* For example, see *Joerger v. Gordon* at the end of this chapter at page 274. Other state cases of note in which courts have determined that attorney's fee statutes or court rules do not include compensation for paralegal time are *Hines v. Hines,* 129 Idaho 847, 934 P.2d 20 (Idaho 1997) and *F.D.I.C. v. Singh,* 148 F.R.D. 6 (D. Me. 1993) interpreting the laws of Maine on attorney's fees. (A different result was reached without explanation in another case decided by the Maine Supreme Court. See *First NH Banks Granite State v. Scarborough*, 615 A.2d 248 (Me. 1992).) Note that the courts in *Joerger* and *Hines* do not object conceptually to the notion that paralegal time is compensable but believe that the legislature, not the courts, should make the determination of whether attorney's fees should also cover paralegal work.

Several federal attorney fee statutes have been amended to provide for the award of paralegal fees, including the Federal Bankruptcy Law (11 U.S.C. §330); the Employee Retirement Income Security Act of 1974 (29 U.S.C. §100); the Sherman Anti-Trust Act and Clayton Act (15 U.S.C. §1); and the Surface Mining Control and Reclamation Act of 1977 (30 U.S.C. §1270).

An important issue in statutory fee cases involves the kind of information that must be supplied to the court to justify the award of paralegals' fees. Some trial courts have denied paralegals' fees on the grounds that the work done by legal assistants was clerical in nature, and not the kind of work intended to be covered by an award of attorney's fees, or because there was inadequate information as to the qualifications of the legal assistants; the nature of their work, the customary practice of billing separately for their services, and the market rates charged for their services. Other courts have reduced the amounts requested for paralegals' fees because they were not sufficiently documented and justified or they contained what appeared to the court to be too high a profit margin. Documentation supplied to the court when seeking fees should include: the credentials and experience of the legal assistants; detailed descriptions of the work performed, including the number of hours spent; information on paralegal compensation, overhead allocated to legal assistants, and hourly rates; and comparison data on practices and rates in the legal community. Additionally, it is preferable for a firm to have a range of rates for legal assistants, depending on their experience and the level of work they are performing. As with attorney work, not all paralegal work requires the same level of sophistication and expertise.

Finally, a few courts have reduced fee awards for attorney time when the work billed at the attorney's rate could have been done by a legal assistant. This line of cases demonstrates the growing appreciation within the judiciary of the contribution legal assistants can make to improving the cost-effectiveness of and access to legal services. See the cases following *Missouri v. Jenkins* at the end of this chapter for examples of how various courts deal with these issues.

In 1993 the American Bar Association House of Delegates adopted a resolution "support[ing] the award of legal assistant/paralegal fees to law firms or attorneys who represent prevailing parties in a lawsuit where statutes or current case law allow for the recovery of attorney fees."

This resolution supports Guideline 8 of the ABA Model Guidelines for the Utilization of Legal Assistant Services, which endorses both recovery for paralegal time in statutory attorney fee matters and the billing of clients for paralegal time.

REVIEW QUESTIONS

1. What are fixed fees? For what kinds of work are they typically used?
2. What are contingency fees? When are they usually used?
3. What are the traditional objections to contingency fees? What are the most important modern limitations on contingency fees? What is a sliding-scale contingency fee?
4. What are hourly fees? In what kinds of legal matters are they typically used?
5. What is the authority for paralegal time to be billed separately to clients? What is the advantage to the client?
6. Why are some firms starting to use alternatives to hourly billing? What kinds of new fee arrangements are being developed as firms move away from hourly billing? How do these affect legal assistants?
7. What factors may be taken into account in determining if a fee is excessive?
8. What is an example of an illegal fee?
9. What kinds of billing abuses sometimes take place in law firms, and why? What are some of the risks of these abuses?
10. What is double billing? Is it ethical?
11. What are a lawyer's duties relating to the fee arrangement when he or she undertakes representation?
12. Under what circumstances must a fee arrangement be in writing?
13. Can a legal assistant tell a client what the firm's fee schedule is? Can a legal assistant negotiate a fee arrangement with a client?
14. What is the difference between a retainer and an advanced fee? How are they treated differently when received by the firm?
15. What provisions should a written fee agreement contain?
16. What kinds of costs are usually charged directly to the client?
17. What is the purpose of "fee-shifting"?
18. Give some examples of fee-shifting statutes.
19. What was the holding in *Missouri v. Jenkins?* Why is this decision so important for legal assistants?
20. What information should be included in a request to the court for paralegal's fees as part of an award of attorney's fees?
21. What will a court do if it sees that a lawyer did paralegal work at

249

attorney billing rates? If two paralegals did the same work and requested fees for all the time spent?

22. Would a court award paralegal fees for time spent filing documents? organizing documents? drafting documents? summarizing documents?

DISCUSSION QUESTIONS

1. Contact five local law firms and find out

    a. what kinds of fee arrangements they use for legal work (for example, contingency for personal injury, fixed to form a corporation, hourly to negotiate a deal);
    b. their hourly rates for lawyers and legal assistants;
    c. what costs they bill directly to clients; and
    d. whether they require fee agreements to be in writing (ask if you can have a copy of a standard fee agreement if the firm has one).

2. Do you believe that the special restrictions on contingency fees (for example, in criminal and divorce cases) are warranted? Why, or why not?

3. Do you believe the ethics rules should require all fee agreements to be in writing? Why, or why not?

4. Should the percentage of attorney's fees in contingency cases be limited by statute or ethical codes? Why, or why not? What do you think is the reason for limiting the amount of contingency fees in medical malpractice cases?

5. Do you think the trend to use alternative methods of fee structures—for instance, task-based, value or premium billing—in lieu of traditional hourly rates is a good one? Why, or why not?

6. What would you do if you became aware of several associates padding their hours?

7. What would you do if your firm expected you to bill 1800 hours annually, and you knew by September of that year that your hours were going to fall short?

8. What would you do if your firm expected you to bill 1500 hours a year, but you were not being delegated enough work to keep you busy for that many hours?

9. What would you do if you discovered that you and an associate were doing the same work on a case, and the client was being billed for the duplicative work?

10. What would you do if the supervising attorney in a matter continually wrote off your time as excessive, diminishing your billable hours?

11. What would you do if a client called and wanted to know the firm's hourly rates to handle certain kinds of legal work?
12. What would you do if a prospective personal injury client with a good case came into the office seeking representation, and the attorney was out of town for two weeks?
13. What would you do if an attorney was inflating the costs on clients' bills?
14. You are flying across country for client X and en route do some work for client Y. How do you bill your time?
15. Do you think the United States should have the kind of two-way fee-shifting that England and Canada have? Why or why not?
16. Outline the arguments in the *Missouri v. Jenkins* majority opinion and dissent on the award of paralegal's fees in attorney's fees awards. Which side do you find more convincing, and why? Outline the arguments for charging paralegal's fees at market rate as opposed to cost. Which do you find more convincing, and why?
17. Were there cases on paralegal fees in your state and your federal circuit before *Missouri v. Jenkins?* Were these supportive of paralegal's fees awards or not? Have there been any cases on paralegal fees awards since *Missouri v. Jenkins?*
18. Are there any statutes or court rules in your jurisdiction that provide for paralegal fees awards as part of attorney's fees awards?

D. Fee-Splitting, Referral Fees, and Partnerships between Nonlawyers and Lawyers

Ethics rules in every state carefully control the way in which lawyers and nonlawyers are compensated from fees that are collected by attorneys. These rules are designed with a number of important policies in mind: to prevent the unauthorized practice of law; to guard against interference with the lawyer's independent professional judgment; and to discourage unethical direct solicitation of clients by agents of the lawyer.

Ethics codes have long limited the splitting of fees between or among lawyers who are not members of the same firm. The ABA Model Code DR 2-107 allows fee-splitting among attorneys only with client consent after full disclosure, if the division is proportionate to the services, and the total fee is reasonable. The ABA Model Rules are somewhat more flexible. Model Rule 1.5(e) permits a division of fees if (1) the division is in proportion to services or the client agrees in writing and the attorneys assume joint responsibility; (2) the client is advised and does not object; and (3) the fee is reasonable.

The ABA Model Code provision has been interpreted to mean that an attorney may not pay a referral fee or a portion of a client's fee to another attorney simply for referring a case. Referral fees in either of these forms have long been thought to be unprofessional and to increase the cost to the client. However, a growing number of states (California, Connecticut, Kansas, Massachusetts, Pennsylvania, and Texas, for example) have recently revised rules to permit "forwarding fees" or to exclude the requirement that the fee division be proportionate to services, thereby effectively allowing referral fees. Proponents of referral fees say that they serve the client's interests by encouraging a thoughtful referral to a competent attorney and point out that clients are protected by the part of the rule that requires the fee to be reasonable.

Fee-splitting with nonlawyers, including legal assistants, is more strictly regulated because of the additional concerns of unauthorized practice, interference with the lawyer's independent professional judgment, and direct solicitation. The ABA Model Code DR 3-102 prohibits fee-splitting with nonlawyers, except when a lawyer dies and fees are paid to his or her estate or to compensate nonlawyer employees, "even though the plan is based in whole or in part on a profit-sharing arrangement." ABA Model Rule 5.4 is similar, specifically prohibiting sharing of fees in section (a), partnerships between lawyers and nonlawyers in (b) and (d), and referral fees in (c). Added is a new section that allows a lawyer to pay for the purchase of the practice of a deceased, disabled, or disappeared lawyer under Rule 1.17.

Most important for legal assistants is the provision that allows nonlawyer employees to be included in compensation and retirement plans based in whole or in part on profit sharing.

The ABA Model Guidelines follow the standard prohibitions against fee-splitting with nonlawyers in Guideline 9. As noted in the comment to that guideline, virtually all states that have adopted guidelines on legal assistants have noted the usual restriction on fee-splitting. Several examples of state guidelines are included in the footnote to this comment. Most state guidelines prohibit fee-splitting but emphasize that retirement plans and bonuses based in part on a firm's overall profitability are acceptable. Some states also specifically prohibit referral fees and compensation based in any way on referrals. Neither NALA nor NFPA has a specific prohibition against fee-splitting or referral fees in its code of ethics.

An early ABA ethics opinion endorsed the inclusion of nonlawyers in profit-based compensation and retirement plans (ABA Informal Opinion 1440 (1979)). There are a few local ethics opinions concerning compensation plans that are tied to profitability. For example, Mississippi Ethics Opinion 154 (1989) endorsed a bonus plan that compensated legal assistants and associates whose billable hours exceeded a set minimum. Iowa Ethics Opinion 90-9 (1990) allows firms to pay legal assistants a percentage of total firm income as an incentive. Virginia Ethics Opinion 885 (1987) allowed a collection attorney to have compensation plans for a legal assistant based on a percentage of profits from collections plus a base salary. Virginia Ethics Opinion 806 (1986) endorsed secretarial bonuses based on annual firm profits. Oregon Ethics Opinion 505 (1985) and Maryland Ethics Opinion 84-103 (1984) advise that lawyers may not compensate legal assistants on a contingent basis or only when fees are collected from a client. See also Philadelphia Ethics Opinion 80-14 (1980) and Virginia Ethics Opinion 767 (1986).

A few local bars also have ethics opinions relating to referral fees. Maryland Ethics Opinion 86-57 (1986) prohibits bonuses based on referrals. And Maryland Ethics Opinion 84-103 (1984) prohibits compensation calculated on a percentage of the recovery in a case. New York's Nassau County Ethics Opinion 87-38 (1987) states that a lawyer may not split fees with a paralegal who brings in clients, interviews them, and prepares legal documents under attorney supervision. The Oregon State Bar Legal Ethics Committee states that compensation may not be calculated on a contingency basis or paid only when fees are recovered (Oregon Ethics Opinion 505 (1985)).

The ethics rules and the opinions interpreting them make it clear that it is not acceptable for an attorney to pay a legal assistant for referring a case, by means of a direct bonus, increase in compensation, or payment of a portion of a fee received from the client. They also make it clear that an attorney may not pay a legal assistant, under any circumstances, a percentage of a fee from a specific client or case. See *In re Hessinger* at the end of this chapter at page 282 and *Florida Bar v. Beach* at page 101 in Chapter 3 for examples of unethical fee arrangements. Hence, a "bonus" tied to a particular client or case is not acceptable. However, it is appropriate for a firm to increase compensation, to pay bonuses, and to establish a retirement or other deferred compensation plan based on the firm's overall profitability. This kind of arrangement breaks the direct link between a legal assistant's action and a specific client, eliminating concerns about unauthorized practice and incentives to solicit clients by unethical or overly aggressive methods. And such bonus plans are commonly used by firms who want to reward legal assistants for their contribution to making the firm profitable. A few states, however, prohibit compensation to nonlawyer employees based on overall firm profitability. See, for example, Indiana Guideline 9.8.

A few exceptions to the prohibition against fee-splitting with non-lawyers do exist. As mentioned above, fees may be paid to the estate of a deceased lawyer. A lawyer may pay a fee to an approved lawyer referral service. Lawyer referral services are regulated by ethics rules and usually must be approved by the state bar or some other entity. Many are run by local bar associations. Lawyer referral services charge either a flat fee or a percentage of fees. Another exception is the prepaid legal plan, under which a member pays a fee for entitlement to a range of services, and the fee is divided between the lawyer and the plan sponsor. All jurisdictions permit such fee-splitting when the plan is nonprofit; some specifically prohibit lawyer participation in profit-making prepaid legal services plans.

The same theories underlying the prohibitions on fee-splitting with nonlawyers form the basis for rules prohibiting lawyers from entering into partnership with nonlawyers. ABA Model Code DR 3-103 and ABA Model Rule 5.4(b) prohibit a lawyer from forming a partnership with a nonlawyer "if any of the activities of the partnership consist of the practice of law." This rule is sometimes implicated when lawyers are disciplined for aiding in the unauthorized practice of law, fee-splitting, and unlawful solicitation if the arrangement with the nonlawyers looks like a partnership or business venture where the nonlawyer has an equal or greater voice in the operation of the firm. See, for example, *In re Hessinger*, at the end of this chapter at page 282.

All jurisdictions except the District of Columbia have such a rule, and most states that have guidelines for the utilization of legal assistants reiterate this rule as it applies to legal assistants. See Illinois Guideline (D), Kansas Guideline VII, Kentucky Supreme Court Rule 3.700 Sub-Rule 5, Michigan Guideline III(3), Missouri Guideline II(b), New Hampshire Supreme Court Rule 35 Sub-Rule 5, New Mexico Guideline V, North Carolina Guideline 8, and Rhode Island Guideline VIII.

Because of the changing nature of law practice and the desire of law firms, especially large law firms, to be full-service providers for their large corporate clients, a movement to modify this prohibition was launched in the 1980s. It has been successful to date only in the District of Columbia, which in 1990 adopted its own Rule 5.4, which provides that "[A] lawyer may practice law in a partnership or other form of organization in which a financial interest is held or managerial authority is exercised by an individual nonlawyer who performs professional services which assist the organization in providing legal services to clients. . . ." The rule continues with specified limitations and the comment makes it clear that legal assistants are not eligible to become partners. The comment differentiates between nonlawyer "assistants" and nonlawyer "professionals," specifically naming economists, psychologists or psychiatric social workers, lobbyists, certified public accountants, and professional managers and executive directors as examples of acceptable participants under the rule.

It should be noted that each jurisdiction's authority to establish rules prohibiting lawyers from having nonlawyer partners was upheld by the seventh circuit in the 1993 case of *Lawline v. American Bar Association,* 956 F.2d 1378 (7th Cir. 1993), which was let stand when the United States Supreme Court refused to take the case on appeal.

E. Client Funds

The mishandling of client funds is probably the leading cause of disciplinary sanctions imposed on attorneys. A typical scenario is a sole practitioner with cash-flow problems who "borrows" funds from a client trust account to tide him or her over. Often a shortfall in a client trust account is because of sloppy bookkeeping and management practices. In either case, the attorney will sooner or later find that a client's money just isn't there and the client will report this to the state or local bar and possibly to the local prosecutor's office.

The most important ethics rule related to client funds is the requirement to keep the client's money separate from the attorney's, in other words, not to commingle client and law firm funds. The rule against commingling also applies to funds from third parties held by the lawyer. This means that lawyers must have a separate bank account that contains only clients funds. Some clients may warrant having their own individual client trust account if the lawyer handles large amounts of funds or transactions for them. ABA Model Code 9-102(A) and ABA Model Rule 1.15(a) both require separate client trust accounts. The ABA Model Code specifies that the account or accounts must be in the state where the lawyer is situated. The ABA Model Rule allows another location with client consent.

Lawyers might hold client funds for many reasons; most typically funds in client trust accounts are estate or trust distributions, funds to be distributed at a real estate closing or on settlement of a matter, advanced fees, and awards of which the attorney is owed a portion under a contingency fee agreement. See the *Barrett* case at the end of this chapter for an example of the consequences of mishandling of client funds.

In the case of funds that are to be divided between the client and the attorney, the funds must remain in the client trust account until they are earned by the lawyer and she or he prepares an accounting for the client, indicating how the funds are to be divided under the fee agreement. In the event a dispute over the fee arises, the amount in dispute must be kept in the client trust account until the dispute is resolved. See ABA Model Code DR 9-102(A)(2); ABA Model Rule 1.15(c). A minority of jurisdictions allow advanced fees to be deposited into a lawyer's operating account. Remember that advances should be distinguished from retainers, which are nonrefundable and paid directly to the lawyer.

All jurisdictions in the United States except the state of Indiana have a program under which the interest on certain client trust accounts is used to fund the bar disciplinary system, client security fund, or legal services for the poor, specified by the state's bar, legislature, or supreme court. About $100 million a year is raised annually through these programs, known as IOLTA (Interest on Lawyers' Trust Accounts). They can be mandatory, voluntary, or "opt-out." A voluntary program means that a lawyer must affirmatively decide to participate; an opt-out program means that all lawyers participate unless they affirmatively declare *not* to. The plans ordinarily cover only client funds that are too small in amount or are to be held for too brief a period to earn interest for the client. Florida adopted the first IOLTA plan in 1981. The majority of jurisdictions have voluntary or opt-out plans, or some hybrid of the two, although a growing number of plans are being converted to mandatory status.

The funds collected by the states from IOLTA plans are substantial. Each state has its own rules about how these funds are expended. For example, Minnesota's plan allocates the funds to "the poor, law-related education and projects to improve the administration of justice." North Carolina designates its funds for lawyer referral services, attorney grievance and discipline, and a client security fund to reimburse clients for losses caused by the dishonest conduct of attorneys when no other recourse is available.

IOLTA plans are different from client security funds, which reimburse clients who have lost money or property as a result of lawyer misconduct. Forty-seven states and the District of Columbia have some kind of client security funds. (The three states who do not have plans had them in the past.) Funding of these plans usually comes from bonding insurance or, in a few states. IOLTAs.

The constitutionality of IOLTA programs has been challenged in the courts on the grounds that clients have property rights in the interest generated in these accounts, which rights are violated when the funds, however small, are not paid to the clients. In June 1998, the U.S. Supreme Court decided the case of *Phillips v. Washington Legal Foundation* (U.S. Supreme Court Docket No. 96-1578, affirming the Fifth Circuit in 94 F.3d 1996), concerning the Texas IOLTA plan. In a 5-4 ruling, the Court affirmed the holding that the interest on client trust accounts held in IOLTA accounts is the private property of the clients. The Court did not decide the issue of the constitutionality of the "taking" of these funds but remanded the case to the lower court. Most bar leaders contend that IOLTA accounts are constitutional and, until this issue is fully addressed by the courts, IOLTA programs will continue to operate as they have in the past.

Commingling of funds is a separate grounds for disciplinary action than is conversion of funds, a much more serious breach. Commingling refers only to mixing client funds with those of the attorney and does not require any intent to harm the client or actual harm to the client. Conversion is the misappropriation of the client's funds for the attorney's or firm's use. Conversion may take place when the attorney draws funds from the client trust account for personal use, for payment of firm expenses, or—more rarely—to cover another client's shortfall.

Disciplinary bodies are not sympathetic to most defenses that an attorney might use in such cases, including the intention to return the funds or the actual restoration of the funds. An attorney's personal or financial problems or the mismanagement of the firm are also not excuses; in fact, they may be considered aggravating circumstances as they may lead to repeated incidents.

The lawyer also has a duty to protect client property other than money. This duty to safeguard usually requires the lawyer to place the property in a safe deposit box. Property covered by these rules typically includes titles to real estate or valuable personal property, jewelry, and securities. If a safe deposit box is shared with other clients, the items must be identified and labeled. See ABA Model Code DR 9-102(B)(2); ABA Model Rule 1.15(a).

Lawyers have a duty to keep accurate and complete records of client funds and property. ABA Model Code DR 9-102(B)(3) and ABA Model Rule 1.15(a) both require this, with the Model Rule additionally providing for a specific number of years (five) that records must be kept. Several states have different periods (usually six or seven years) and more specific provisions on recordkeeping. A few jurisdictions' rules provide for random audits of client trust accounts and some for annual certification or verification of compliance with recordkeeping rules. Many states provide for audits in conjunction with disciplinary actions.

The kinds of bookkeeping mechanisms that a firm uses to comply with ethics recordkeeping rules vary from firm to firm. Several state bars have adopted model guidelines or standards, that usually require cash receipts journals for each account, disbursement journals for each account (with separate ledgers for each client showing monthly trial balances), monthly reconciliations of balances, bank statements, and cancelled checks, and records of other client property received and distributed.

Other duties specified in the ethics rules are the duty to notify the client on the receipt of funds or property, to deliver client funds or property promptly, and to provide a full accounting to the client on request. ABA Model Code DR 9-102(B); ABA Model Rule 1.15(b). The duties to notify, to deliver, and to account for client funds are most often breached because of lax office procedures, but sometimes are a result of a more egregious violation like conversion of client funds. Sometimes a third party will have a claim against the client funds; in this situation the lawyer may have a duty not to turn over the funds to the client until the various parties' rights are clarified. The notion of what is "prompt" delivery is sometimes an issue in disciplinary actions. The best practice certainly requires action within the month in which funds are received, if not more quickly. And finally, although neither the ABA Model Code nor the Model Rules require them, regular periodic accountings to clients (monthly or quarterly) are advisable rather than accountings only on client request.

All jurisdictions also have some special rules that require attorneys to turn over papers, funds, money, and unearned advanced fees on termination of representation. ABA Model Code DR 2-110(A) and ABA Model Rule 1.16(d) so provide, emphasizing the lawyer's obligation to protect the client's interest, with the extension of the lawyer's duty after representation ends.

One final matter in this area is the handling of a client file after work on the matter is completed. Firms should have policies on retention of files, turning files over to clients, destroying files, and security for files maintained in off-site storage. Since the client file is the property of the client, the attorney cannot destroy old files without first informing the client and getting permission and/or giving the client the chance to keep the file. Care should always be taken to retain important papers, such as wills, deeds, securities, and tax returns. It is good practice to include a provision about the handling of client files in the agreement for representation.

The rules governing the handling of client funds and property are especially important to legal assistants because legal assistants often must implement attorneys' instructions relating to client funds and may be delegated substantial responsibility for handling these matters. Checks or property are likely to come directly to the attorney who will instruct the legal assistant how to proceed. In small firms, a legal assistant may

258

perform some of the bookkeeping and recordkeeping functions. The legal assistant must know the rules well enough to identify improprieties and either to rectify them or to inform the supervising attorney. Legal assistants may not serve as signator on client trust accounts. It is not unusual for an attorney in trouble to blame the nonlawyer employee for poor office practice that has resulted in disciplinary action against the attorney, or worse. While such excuses do not mitigate against the attorney's misconduct, they can harm the legal assistant's reputation. While NALA's Code does not address this area directly, NFPA's ethics rules calls on paralegals to be "scrupulously thorough and honest" in handling client assets. NFPA Model Code of Ethics Professional Responsibility, EC-2.4.

REVIEW QUESTIONS

1. What are the rules about referral fees? What is the basis for these rules? Do the same rules apply to lawyers and legal assistants?
2. What are the rules about fee-splitting? Give several examples of payments to legal assistants that violate these rules.
3. What kinds of retirement, bonus, and profit-sharing plans are permitted under the ethics rules?
4. Why do the ethics rules prohibit lawyers from being partners with nonlawyers in a law practice?
5. What is the basis for the District of Columbia rules permitting nonlawyer partners? May legal assistants become partners under this rule?
6. What are the duties of lawyers regarding client funds?
7. What is IOLTA? How many states have one? What is a client security fund? How many states have one? How are the funds from these programs used?
8. Describe the difference between the commingling and the conversion of funds. Which is more serious?
9. Is mishandling of client funds common? Why?
10. How might a legal assistant violate ethics in the handling of client funds?
11. When a lawyer receives a check for a judgment or settlement and the case was taken on contingency, what should he or she do with the check?
12. Do the facts that an attorney is very busy, has high staff turnover, and has not had a bookkeeper in months mitigate against charges of commingling of funds?

13. What are the lawyer's duties with regard to client property held for client?
14. What are the lawyer's duties pertaining to client funds, files, and property when representation ceases?

DISCUSSION QUESTIONS

1. Do you think the rules prohibiting fee-splitting are well founded? Why, or why not? Do you think the rules should be different for lawyers and nonlawyers?
2. Do you think the rules prohibiting referral fees are well founded? Why, or why not? Does your jurisdiction allow attorneys to pay or receive referral fees? Is it common practice?
3. Can a personal injury firm pay a $500 bonus for every case you bring in? Can you be paid one-third of the fee when the case settled?
4. Call five local law firms and find out if they have pension or profit-sharing plans for their legal assistants or pay their legal assistants bonuses. Ask them how the amount of bonus is determined.
5. Do you think the rule prohibiting legal assistants from becoming partners in law firms is well founded? Why, or why not? Do you think this rule should be changed? Ask some lawyers and practicing legal assistants what they think. Has your jurisdiction considered adopting a rule like the District of Columbia's?
6. What would you do if an attorney handed you a settlement check in a contingency case and asked you to deposit it in the firm's operating account?
7. Is it ethical or acceptable for an attorney to keep the deed of trust to a client's real estate in his or her desk? In the client file? Under the floor board in his or her attic? Why, or why not? What if the property were a valuable diamond ring? Stock certificates?
8. What would you do if you found out your firm was having temporary cash-flow problems because of uncollected receivables and had borrowed from client trust accounts to make the payroll?
9. What is wrong with an attorney putting client funds in the firm's account if he or she plans to replace them in two days? Would it make any difference if the period were two weeks? If the client owed fees to the attorney? If the attorney were doing this for the benefit of another client and did not benefit himself or herself in any way?
10. What kind of IOLTA does your state have—voluntary, opt-out, or mandatory? How do attorneys pay the fund? What are the funds used for? How much money is currently in the fund?

11. Find out how the case concerning the constitutionality of IOLTA plans turned out. Read and brief the case for the class.
12. Does your state have a client security fund? How is it funded? How much money is in the fund? What kinds of payments have been made from the fund?
13. What would you do if your attorney-employer were very careful about handling client funds but kept no records other than bank reports and withdrawal slips?
14. What would you do if you discovered that a settlement check had come in and been deposited six months ago, and the client had never been notified?
15. What would you do if you found several month-old checks from clients, insurance companies, and others in the bottom of a desk drawer?
16. Draft a provision on handling of client files after the matter is closed.
17. Does your state or local bar have an opinion on how long lawyers should retain client files?

CASES FOR ANALYSIS

In the following landmark case, the U.S. Supreme Court held that attorney fees awards under the Civil Rights Act may include paralegal fees at market rates. Pay close attention to both issues—the payment of fees for paralegal time and the basis on which the fee should be calculated.

Missouri v. Jenkins
491 U.S. 274 (1989)

Justice BRENNAN delivered the opinion of the Court.

This is the attorney's-fee aftermath of major school desegregation litigation in Kansas City, Missouri. We granted certiorari, 488 U.S.—, 109 S. Ct. 218, 102 L. Ed. 2d 209 (1988), to resolve two questions relating to fees litigation under 42 U.S.C. §1988. First, does the Eleventh Amendment prohibit enhancement of a fee award against a State to compensate for delay in payment? Second, should the fee award compensate the work of paralegals and law clerks by applying the market rate for their work?

I

This litigation began in 1977 as a suit by the Kansas City Missouri School District (KCMSD), the School Board, and the children of two

School Board members, against the State of Missouri and other defendants. The plaintiffs alleged that the State, surrounding school districts, and various federal agencies had caused and perpetuated a system of racial segregation in the schools of the Kansas City metropolitan area. They sought various desegregation remedies. KCMSD was subsequently realigned as a nominal defendant, and a class of present and future KCMSD students was certified as plaintiffs. After lengthy proceedings, including a trial that lasted 7½ months during 1983 and 1984, the District Court found the State of Missouri and KCMSD liable, while dismissing the suburban school districts and the federal defendants. It ordered various intradistrict remedies, to be paid for by the State and KCMSD, including $260 million in capital improvements and a magnet-school plan costing over $200 million.

The plaintiff class has been represented, since 1979, by Kansas City lawyer Arthur Benson and, since 1982, by the NAACP Legal Defense and Educational Fund, Inc. (LDF). Benson and the LDF requested attorney's fees under the Civil Rights Attorney's Fees Awards Act of 1976, 42 U.S.C. §1988.[1] Benson and his associates had devoted 10,875 attorney hours to the litigation, as well as 8,108 hours of paralegal and law clerk time. For the LDF the corresponding figures were 10,854 hours for attorneys and 15,517 hours for paralegals and law clerks. Their fee applications deleted from these totals 3,628 attorney hours and 7,046 paralegal hours allocable to unsuccessful claims against the suburban school districts. With additions for post-judgment monitoring and for preparation of the fee application, the District Court awarded Benson a total of approximately $1.7 million and the LDF $2.3 million.

In calculating the hourly rate for Benson's fees the court noted that the market rate in Kansas City for attorneys of Benson's qualifications was in the range of $125 to $175 per hour, and found that "Mr. Benson's rate would fall at the higher end of this range based upon his expertise in the area of civil rights." It calculated his fees on the basis of an even higher hourly rate of $200, however, because of three additional factors: the preclusion of other employment, the undesirability of the case, and the delay in payment for Benson's services. The court also took account of the delay in payment in setting the rates for several of Benson's associates by using current market rates rather than those applicable at

---

1. Section 1988 provides in relevant part:

In any action or proceeding to enforce a provision of sections 1981, 1982, 1983, 1985, and 1986 of this title, title IX of Public Law 92-318 [20 U.S.C. 1681 et seq.], or title VI of the Civil Rights Act of 1964 [42 U.S.C. 2000d et seq.], the court, in its discretion, may allow the prevailing party, other than the United States, a reasonable attorney's fee as part of the costs.

the time the services were rendered. For the same reason, it calculated the fees for the LDF attorneys at current market rates.

Both Benson and the LDF employed numerous paralegals, law clerks (generally law students working part-time), and recent law graduates in this litigation. The court awarded fees for their work based on Kansas City market rates for those categories. As in the case of the attorneys, it used current rather than historic market rates in order to compensate for the delay in payment. It therefore awarded fees based on hourly rates of $35 for law clerks, $40 for paralegals, and $50 for recent law graduates. The Court of Appeals affirmed in all respects.

II

Our grant of certiorari extends to two issues raised by the State of Missouri. Missouri first contends that a State cannot, consistent with the principle of sovereign immunity this Court has found embodied in the Eleventh Amendment, be compelled to pay an attorney's fee enhanced to compensate for delay in payment. . . .

To summarize: We reaffirm our holding . . . that the Eleventh Amendment has no application to an award of attorney's fees, ancillary to a grant of prospective relief, against a State. It follows that the same is true for the calculation of the *amount* of the fee. An adjustment for delay in payment is, we hold, an appropriate factor in the determination of what constitutes a reasonable attorney's fee under §1988. An award against a State of a fee that includes such an enhancement for delay is not, therefore, barred by the Eleventh Amendment.

III

Missouri's second contention is that the District Court erred in compensating the work of law clerks and paralegals (hereinafter collectively "paralegals") at the market rates for their services, rather than at their cost to the attorney. While Missouri agrees that compensation for the cost of these personnel should be included in the fee award, it suggests that an hourly rate of $15—which it argued below corresponded to their salaries, benefits, and overhead—would be appropriate, rather than the market rates of $35 to $50. According to Missouri. §1988 does not authorize billing paralegals' hours at market rates, and doing so produces a "windfall" for the attorney.[7]

---

7. The Courts of Appeals have taken a variety of positions on this issue. Most permit separate billing of paralegal time. Some courts, on the other hand, have considered paralegal work "out-of-pocket expense," recoverable only at cost to the attorney. At least one Court of Appeals has refused to permit any recovery of paralegal expense apart from the attorney's hourly fee. *Abrams v. Baylor College of Medicine,* 805 F.2d 528, 535 (CA 1986).

We begin with the statutory language, which provides simply for "a reasonable attorney's fee as part of the costs." 42 U.S.C. §1988. Clearly, a "reasonable attorney's fee" cannot have been meant to compensate only work performed personally by members of the bar. Rather, the term must refer to a reasonable fee for the work product of an attorney. Thus, the fee must take into account the work not only of attorneys, but also of secretaries, messengers, librarians, janitors, and others whose labor contributes to the work product for which an attorney bills her client; and it must also take account of other expenses and profit. The parties have suggested no reason why the work of paralegals should not be similarly compensated, nor can we think of any. We thus take as our starting point the self-evident proposition that the "reasonable attorney's fee" provided for by statute should compensate the work of paralegals, as well as that of attorneys. The more difficult question is how the work of paralegals is to be valued in calculating the overall attorney's fee.

The statute specifies a "reasonable" fee for the attorney's work product. In determining how other elements of the attorney's fee are to be calculated, we have consistently looked to the marketplace as our guide to what is "reasonable." . . . A reasonable attorney's fee under §1988 is one calculated on the basis of rates and practices prevailing in the relevant market, i.e., "in line with those [rates] prevailing in the community for similar services by lawyers of reasonably comparable skill, experience, and reputation," and one that grants the successful civil rights plaintiff a "fully compensatory fee," comparable to what "is traditional with attorneys compensated by a fee-paying client."

If an attorney's fee awarded under §1988 is to yield the same level of compensation that would be available from the market, the "increasingly widespread custom of separately billing for the services of paralegals and law students who serve as clerks" must be taken into account. All else being equal, the hourly fee charged by an attorney whose rates include paralegal work in her hourly fee, or who bills separately for the work of paralegals at cost, will be higher than the hourly fee charged by an attorney competing in the same market who bills separately for the work of paralegals at "market rates." In other words, the prevailing "market rate" for attorney time is not independent of the manner in which paralegal time is accounted for.[8] Thus, if the prevailing practice in a given community were to bill paralegal time

---

8. The attorney who bills separately for paralegal time is merely distributing her costs and profit margin among the hourly fees of other members of her staff, rather than concentrating them in the fee she sets for her own time.

separately at market rates, fees awarded the attorney at market rates for attorney time would not be fully compensatory if the court refused to compensate hours billed by paralegals or did so only at "cost." Similarly, the fee awarded would be too high if the court accepted separate billing for paralegal hours in a market where that was not the custom.

We reject the argument that compensation for paralegals at rates above "cost" would yield a "windfall" for the prevailing attorney. Neither petitioners nor anyone else, to our knowledge, have ever suggested that the hourly rate applied to the work of an associate attorney in a law firm creates a windfall for the firm's partners or is otherwise improper under §1988, merely because it exceeds the cost of the attorney's services. If the fees are consistent with market rates and practices, the "windfall" argument has no more force with regard to paralegals than it does for associates. And it would hardly accord with Congress' intent to provide a "fully compensatory fee" if the prevailing plaintiff's attorney in a civil rights lawsuit were not permitted to bill separately for paralegals, while the defense attorney in the same litigation was able to take advantage of the prevailing practice and obtain market rates for such work. Yet that is precisely the result sought in this case by the State of Missouri, which appears to have paid its own outside counsel for the work of paralegals at the hourly rate of $35.[9]

Nothing in §1988 requires that the work of paralegals invariably be billed separately. If it is the practice in the relevant market not to do so, or to bill the work of paralegals only at cost, that is all that §1988 requires. Where, however, the prevailing practice is to bill paralegal work at market rates, treating civil rights lawyers' fee requests in the same way is not only permitted by §1988, but also makes economic sense. By encouraging the use of lower-cost paralegals rather than attorneys wherever possible, permitting market-rate billing of paralegal hours "encourages cost-effective delivery of legal services and, by reducing the spiraling cost of civil rights litigation, furthers the policies underlying civil rights statutes."[10]

---

9. A variant of Missouri's "windfall" argument is the following: "If paralegal expense is reimbursed at a rate many times the actual cost, will attorneys next try to bill separately—and at a profit—for such items as secretarial time, paper clips, electricity, and other expenses?" The answer to this question is, of course, that attorneys seeking fees under §1988 would have no basis for requesting separate compensation of such expenses unless this were the prevailing practice in the local community. The safeguard against the billing at a profit of secretarial services and paper clips is the discipline of the market.

10. It has frequently been recognized in the lower courts that paralegals are capable of carrying out many tasks, under the supervision of an attorney, that might otherwise be performed by a lawyer and billed at a higher rate. Such work might include, for example, factual investigation, including locating and interviewing witnesses; assistance with depositions, interrogatories, and document production; compilation of statistical and financial data; check-

Such separate billing appears to be the practice in most communities today.[11] In the present case, Missouri concedes that "the local market typically bills separately for paralegal services," and the District Court found that the requested hourly rates of $35 for law clerks, $40 for paralegals, and $50 for recent law graduates were the prevailing rates for such services in the Kansas City area. Under these circumstances, the court's decision to award separate compensation at these rates was fully in accord with §1988.

IV

The courts below correctly granted a fee enhancement to compensate for delay in payment and approved compensation of paralegals and law clerks at market rates. The judgment of the Court of Appeals is therefore
Affirmed.
Justice MARSHALL took no part in the consideration or decision of this case.

Justice O'CONNOR, with whom Justice SCALIA joins, and with whom THE CHIEF JUSTICE joins in part, concurring in part and dissenting in part.
I agree with the Court that 42 U.S.C. §1988 allows compensation for the work of paralegals and law clerks at market rates, and therefore join Parts I and III of its opinion. I do not join Part II, however, for in my view the Eleventh Amendment does not permit enhancement of attorney's fees assessed against a State as compensation for delay in payment. . . .

---

ing legal citations; and drafting correspondence. Much such work lies in a gray area of tasks that might appropriately be performed either by an attorney or a paralegal. To the extent that fee applicants under §1988 are not permitted to bill for the work of paralegals at market rates, it would not be surprising to see a greater amount of such work performed by attorneys themselves, thus increasing the overall cost of litigation.

Of course, purely clerical or secretarial tasks should not be billed at a paralegal rate, regardless of who performs them. What the court in *Johnson v. Georgia Highway Express, Inc.,* 488 F.2d 714, 717 (CA5 1974), said in regard to the work of attorneys is applicable by analogy to paralegals:

It is appropriate to distinguish between legal work, in the strict sense, and investigation, clerical work, compilation of facts and statistics and other work which can often be accomplished by non-lawyers but which a lawyer may do because he has no other help available. Such non-legal work may command a lesser rate. Its dollar value is not enhanced just because a lawyer does it.

11. *Amicus* National Association of Legal Assistants reports that 77 percent of 1,800 legal assistants responding to a survey of the association's membership stated that their law firms charged clients for paralegal work on an hourly billing basis. Brief for National Association of Legal Assistants as *Amicus Curiae* 11.

Chief Justice REHNQUIST, dissenting.

I agree with Justice O'CONNOR that the Eleventh Amendment does not permit an award of attorney's fees against a State which includes compensation for delay in payment. Unlike Justice O'CONNOR, however, I do not agree with the Court's approval of the award of law clerk and paralegal fees made here.

Section 1988 gives the district courts discretion to allow the prevailing party in an action under §1988 "a reasonable attorney's fee as part of the costs." 42 U.S.C. §1988. The Court reads this language as authorizing recovery of "a 'reasonable' fee for the attorney's work product," which, the Court concludes, may include separate compensation for the services of law clerks and paralegals. But the statute itself simply uses the very familiar term "a reasonable attorney's fee," which to those untutored in the Court's linguistic juggling means a fee charged for services rendered by an individual who has been licensed to practice law. Because law clerks and paralegals have not been licensed to practice law in Missouri, it is difficult to see how charges for their services may be separately billed as part of "attorney's fees." And since a prudent attorney customarily includes compensation for the cost of law clerk and paralegal services, like any other sort of office overhead—from secretarial staff, janitors, and librarians, to telephone service, stationery, and paper clips—in his own hourly billing rate, allowing the prevailing party to recover separate compensation for law clerk and paralegal services may result in "double recovery."

The Court finds justification for its ruling in the fact that the prevailing practice among attorneys in Kansas City is to bill clients separately for the services of law clerks and paralegals. But I do not think Congress intended the meaning of the statutory term "attorney's fee" to expand and contract with each and every vagary of local billing practice. Under the Court's logic, prevailing parties could recover at market rates for the cost of secretaries, private investigators, and other types of lay personnel who assist the attorney in preparing his case, so long as they could show that the prevailing practice in the local market was to bill separately for these services. Such a result would be a sufficiently drastic departure from the traditional concept of "attorney's fees" that I believe new statutory authorization should be required for it. That permitting separate billing of law clerk and paralegal hours at market rates might " 'reduc[e] the spiraling cost of civil rights litigation' " by encouraging attorneys to delegate to these individuals tasks which they would otherwise perform themselves at higher cost may be a persuasive reason for Congress to enact such additional legislation. It is not, however, a persuasive reason for us to rewrite the legislation which Congress has in fact enacted.

I also disagree with the State's suggestion that law clerk and paralegal expenses incurred by a prevailing party, if not recoverable at market rates as "attorney's fees" under §1988, are nonetheless recoverable at actual cost under that statute. The language of §1988 expands the traditional definition of "costs" to include "a reasonable attorney's fee," but it cannot fairly be read to authorize the recovery of all other out-of-pocket expenses actually incurred by the prevailing party in the course of litigation. Absent specific statutory authorization for the recovery of such expenses, the prevailing party remains subject to the limitations on cost recovery imposed by Federal Rule of Civil Procedure 54(d) and 28 U.S.C. §1920, which govern the taxation of costs in federal litigation where a cost shifting statute is not applicable. Section 1920 gives the district court discretion to tax certain types of costs against the losing party in any federal litigation. The statute specifically enumerates six categories of expenses which may be taxed as costs: fees of the court clerk and marshal; fees of the court reporter; printing fees and witness fees; copying fees; certain docket fees; and fees of court-appointed experts and interpreters. We have held that this list is exclusive. Since none of these categories can possibly be construed to include the fees of law clerks and paralegals. I would also hold that reimbursement for these expenses may not be separately awarded at actual cost.

I would therefore reverse the award of reimbursement for law clerk and paralegal expenses.

Questions about the Case

1. Do you agree that the language of the statute "[c]learly . . . cannot have been meant to compensate only work performed by members of the bar"? Is the Court's reasoning on this point persuasive?
2. Why does the Court hold that attorney fees generally should be calculated according to prevailing market rates?
3. Do you agree with the Court that attorneys should be able to make a profit off their paralegals in cases like this? Why, or why not?
4. Do you agree with the Court's comment in footnote 9 about the "discipline of the market"? Why, or why not?
5. What is the most convincing argument that the Court makes for using market rates to calculate paralegal fees awards?
6. What does the Court say about the nature of paralegal work that can be compensated in fee awards? Do you think that time spent numbering documents should be compensated as paralegal time? What about organizing documents? Summarizing depositions? Inputting data into a computer?
7. Summarize the points made by the dissent. Do you think any of them are valid?

In this case, the Supreme Court of Oklahoma determines that attorney's fees may also include paralegal work and addresses the issues of the proper rate for paralegal time and of the nature of the work that is compensable.

Taylor v. Chubb
874 P.2d 806 (Okla. 1994)

The United States District Court for the Northern District of Oklahoma certified questions of state law to this Court under the Oklahoma Uniform Certification of Questions of Law Act, 20 O.S. 1991 §§1601, et seq. The federal court asks two interrelated questions:

(1) Whether the phrase "attorneys fees," when used in Oklahoma statutory or case law providing for the award of costs to a prevailing party, should be interpreted to encompass all work product of an attorney, including fees for services performed by legal assistants or paralegals?
(2) If the preceding question is answered in the affirmative, whether the decision of the Oklahoma Supreme Court should be applied retroactively to provide for the award of fees in the present litigation?

. . . The Taylors' attorney fee application included time charges for services performed by a legal assistant, who was designated by the National Association of Legal Assistants as a Certified Legal Assistant and Civil Litigation Specialist. The legal assistant's services were performed under the supervision of counsel, were non-clerical in nature, and provided meaningful support to counsel in his handling of the case. The Taylors' lawyers practice in Tulsa, where the prevailing community practice is for lawyers to bill legal assistant's time to clients.

I.

We first consider whether charges for legal assistants' time are included in the term "attorney fees," as that term is used in 36 O.S. 1991 §3629.B.[2] This is a question of first impression. . . .

2. The implications of our inquiry are much broader than §3629.B. The Oklahoma Statutes fairly bristle with provisions calling for the award of attorney fees by trial courts to prevailing parties in various sorts of actions. *See,* for example, 12 O.S. 1991 §936 (notes, contracts for goods or services, etc.), 12 O.S. 1991 §937 (checks), 12 O.S. 1991 §938 (public utilities), 12 O.S. 1991 §939 (breach of express warranties under the Uniform Commercial

The parties have stipulated that the legal assistant's services were valuable to the Taylors during the litigation. They have also stipulated that the "prevailing practice in the community is for attorneys to bill legal assistant or paralegal time to clients." Under these circumstances we see no reason to ignore such charges. We believe the legislature would have said so had it intended the term "attorney fees" to except charges for the time of legal assistants in communities where the "prevailing practice" is to charge for such time.

The United States Supreme Court considered this issue in *Missouri v. Jenkins*, 491 U.S. 274, 109 S. Ct. 2463, 105 L. Ed. 2d 229 (1989). Seven of the eight justices participating agreed that hourly charges for paralegals and law clerks must be considered in setting an attorney's fee under federal civil rights statutes. . . .

Separately charging for the time of legal assistants has grown in larger communities in response to clients' desire to keep the average hourly rate as low as possible, consistent with competent handling of cases. The U.S. Supreme Court said that to the extent fee applicants for statutory attorney's fees "are not permitted to bill for the work of paralegals at market rates, it would not be surprising to see a greater amount of such work performed by attorneys themselves, thus increasing the overall cost of litigation." Missouri v. Jenkins, 491 U.S. at 288. . . .

There is no reason to exclude charges for the time of legal assistants in computing statutorily mandated attorney fees where such charges are customarily made to clients and the legal assistant's services are useful to the client. A contrary holding would require us to assume that the legislature intended the term "attorney fee" to mean something different from the meaning that the stipulation of the parties shows attorneys and clients give it. This we decline to do.

Our holding today, that the time of paralegals is properly includable as a component to be considered in the trial court's assessment of the total value of services rendered, is limited to charges for work performed, *which otherwise would have had to have been performed*

Code), 12 O.S. 1991 §940 (negligent or wilful injury to property), 18 O.S. 1991 §955.A (farm land unlawfully owned by a corporation), 63 O.S. Supp. 1992 §11818.B (polluters), 12A O.S. 1991 §2A-106 (unconscionability of a lease), 62 O.S. 1991 §206 (constitutionality or legality of fees or taxes), 79 O.S. 1991 §102 (statutory prohibition of pooling by bridge or other contractors), 42 O.S. 1991 §176 (lien foreclosures), 71 O.S. 1991 §824 (rescission of unlawful business opportunity sales), 10 O.S. 1991 §89.3 (paternity suits), 68 O.S. 1991 §343 (unfair tobacco product sales), 45 O.S. 1991 §774.D (mining law violations), 12 O.S. 1991 §3237 (failure to make discovery or to comply with various discovery requirements), 40 O.S. 1991 §197.9 (minimum wage law violations), 15 O.S. 1991 §761.1 (consumer protection act violations), 27 O.S. 1991 §11.3 (condemnation actions), 12 O.S. 1991 §1148.9 (forcible entry and detainer), 12 O.S. Supp. 1992 §1190 (garnishment), 47 O.S. 1991 §169.6 (motor carrier loss and damage claims).

by a licensed attorney at a higher rate. There are several charges in the Taylors' attorneys' billings, however, that apparently fail to satisfy this requirement. The billings reflect a charge for the legal assistants' time in court at the same rate, $150.00 per hour, as the licensed attorney charged for his own time. Charges were made for time spent in copying documents and in doing other secretarial tasks, rather than substantive legal work. Such charges are *not* includable in attorneys fees awarded under §3629.B. The only charges for nonlawyers' time that properly fall within the definition of "attorney fees," under §3629.B are those that are clearly shown to have been made (1) for the delegated performance of substantive legal work, that (2) would otherwise have to be performed by a lawyer, (3) at a rate higher than that charged for the nonlawyers' time. . . .

As its pattern of proof, a party seeking attorney fees must plead and prove that the charges made for non-lawyer's time covered work that a lawyer would have had to perform but for the performance of such services by a legal assistant. In addition, the total charges made for the legal assistant's services must be less than the total charges would have been, had a lawyer performed the services.

Among other tasks, a legal assistant may:

- interview clients
- draft pleadings and other documents
- carry on legal research, both conventional and computer aided
- research public records
- prepare discovery requests and responses
- schedule depositions and prepare notices and subpoenas
- summarize depositions and other discovery responses
- coordinate and manage document production
- locate and interview witnesses
- organize pleadings, trial exhibits, and other documents
- prepare witness and exhibit lists
- prepare trial notebooks
- prepare for the attendance of witnesses at trial
- assist lawyers at trials

II.

. . . Here, our conclusion that the term "attorney fees" includes time charges for legal assistants represents only a clarification of the law, not a change. Our holding is supported by the overwhelming weight of authority. Thus, today's pronouncement changes no preexisting rule of Oklahoma law. We see no reason to apply it prospectively only. We therefore answer yes to Certified Question number (2).

CERTIFIED QUESTIONS ANSWERED.

Questions about the Case

1. What were the credentials of the legal assistant whose time was at issue in this case?
2. What is the prevailing practice of attorneys in Oklahoma concerning billing of paralegal time?
3. Does this court limit its decision to the particular fee award statute in this case? What other kinds of statutes have such provisions?
4. What limitations are placed by the court on compensation for paralegal time?
5. What are some of the tasks that the court acknowledges that legal assistants perform?
6. What should paralegal rates be relative to attorney rates?
7. Does the court find this decision to be a "change" in the law? How does the court describe the ruling?

In upholding an attorney's fee award that included fees for paralegal time, the Washington Appeals Court sets forth a good set of criteria that courts should look to in evaluating whether the paralegal time is compensable.

Absher Construction Co. v. Kent School District

79 Wash.App. 841, 917 P.2d 1086 (Wash. App. Div. 1 1995)

. . . The appellants sued Kent for amounts they claimed were owing under a public works contract, approximately $205,000. Kent won on summary judgment and was awarded $34,648.86 in fees and costs. Kent also prevailed on appeal and now seeks an additional $36,911.54 in fees and costs. The basis for the award is RCW 39.04.240.

The fee request includes time for the following individuals:

(1) A partner in practice for 20 years billed 104.2 hours at $225.00 per hour ($23,445);

(2) A fourth-year associate billed 53.1 hours at $130.00 per hour ($6,903);

(3) A sixth-year associate billed 4.5 hours at $155.00 per hour ($697.50);

(4) A legal assistant billed 39.5 hours at $67.00 per hour ($2,646.50);

(5) A legal editor billed 4 hours at $62.00 per hour ($248); and

(6) A legal clerk billed 8.5 hours at $35.00 per hour ($297.50).

The latter three are not attorneys.

No case in Washington specifically addresses whether the time of non-lawyer personnel may be included in an attorney fee award.

We find persuasive the reasoning of the Arizona court in *Continental Townhouses East Unit One Ass'n v. Brockbank,* 152 Ariz. 537, 733 P.2d 1120, 73 A.L.R. 4th 921 (1986). Properly employed and supervised non-lawyer personnel can decrease litigation expense. Lawyers should not be forced to perform legal tasks solely so that their time may be compensable in an attorney fee award.

The question then becomes what sort of work performed by non-lawyer personnel is compensable. Regardless of the name given to the category of person who performs the work, we believe, as did the Arizona court, that the definition of legal assistant formulated by the American Bar Association Standing Committee on Legal Assistants provides appropriate guidance. . . .

The following criteria will be relevant in determining whether such services should be compensated: (1) the services performed by the non-lawyer personnel must be legal in nature; (2) the performance of these services must be supervised by an attorney; (3) the qualifications of the person performing the services must be specified in the request for fees in sufficient detail to demonstrate that the person is qualified by virtue of education, training, or work experience to perform substantive legal work; (4) the nature of the services performed must be specified in the request for fees in order to allow the reviewing court to determine that the services performed were legal rather than clerical; (5) as with attorney time, the amount of time expended must be set forth and must be reasonable; and (6) the amount charged must reflect reasonable community standards for charges by that category of personnel. . . .

Employing these criteria, we allow only part of the fees requested for the legal assistant's services. He has requested compensation for preparing pleadings for duplication, preparing and delivering copies, requesting copies, and obtaining and delivering a docket sheet. We do not view this time as work which falls within these guidelines. We do allow an award for time spent preparing the briefs and related work. In computing the time we allow for him, we will assume, absent any other evidence in the record, that the hourly rate of $67.00 is reasonable for this type of work. We allow an award of $2,110.50 for 31.5 hours. We allow the recovery of fees for the time claimed by the legal editor for verifying citations and quotations. We disallow the time claimed for the legal clerk, which appears to consist primarily of obtaining copies of pleadings and organizing working copies of the pleadings. . . .

In sum, we conclude that the fees of nonlawyer personnel may be properly requested as part of an attorney fee award. In this case, applying the factors and considerations listed above, we award $23,055.50 plus $1,633.74 as a reasonable attorney fee on appeal, together with $134.65 costs on appeal.

Questions about the Case

1. What were the titles, duties, and rates of the persons for whom this law firm sought compensation in this case? Which were lawyers and which were nonlawyers?
2. On what reasoning does the court rely in interpreting the statute to include paralegal time in attorney fee awards?
3. What are the criteria that a court should use in determining if the award should cover the paralegal time? Are these criteria the same as those noted in other cases in this chapter?
4. What paralegal time is allowed and disallowed in this case and why?
5. Is the time of the "legal editor" compensated and why?
6. What does the court decide about the time of the "legal clerk"?
7. Do the job titles of the nonlawyers in this case reflect accurately what these persons do? Are these common job titles in your community?

———

The Michigan appeals court in this case calls for the legislature to amend the statute at issue to include compensation for paralegal work. Note how the court deals with the contrary precedent on this issue.

Joerger v. Gordon Food Service, Inc.
224 Mich.App. 167, 568 N.W.2d 365
(Mich.App. 1997)

. . . Plaintiffs sued defendant, alleging breach of the oral contract, innocent misrepresentation, and promissory estoppel. The trial court granted defendant's motion for summary disposition with respect to plaintiffs' innocent misrepresentation claim, and directed a verdict against plaintiffs with respect to their breach of the oral contract claim. No appeal has been taken from these rulings. Following trial, the jury returned a verdict for plaintiffs, but made no damage award. The trial court denied plaintiffs' motion for additur or, in the alternative, for a new trial with respect to damages, finding that the verdict was justified. The trial court also granted defendant's motion for mediation sanctions of $131,540 in attorney fees and $7,348.95 in costs.

. . . Plaintiffs also challenge the billings attributable to two individuals identified only by the initials "NAS" and "LAD." Plaintiffs argue that the individuals were not identified and no billing rate was provided for these individuals. Contrary to plaintiffs' assertions, the record reveals that these individuals were identified, by name, as two paralegals employed by defense counsel. Defendant also informed plaintiffs and the court that their hourly rate was $75. Accordingly, these arguments are without merit.

We do find merit, however, in plaintiffs' argument that the independent expenses attributable to the use of paralegals is not recoverable as costs. For purposes of mediation sanctions, "actual costs" include "those costs taxable in any civil action." MCR 2.403(O)(6). Chapter 24 of the Revised Judicature Act, M.C.L. §600.2401 *et seq.;* M.S.A. §27A.2401 *et seq.,* governs costs. *Taylor v. Anesthesia Associates of Muskegon, PC,* 179 Mich.App. 384, 387, 445 N.W.2d 525 (1989). M.C.L. §600.2405; M.S.A. §27A.2405 provides that the following items may be taxed and awarded unless otherwise directed:

(1) Any of the fees of officers, witnesses, or other persons mentioned in this chapter or [M.C.L. §600.2501 *et seq.;* M.S.A. §27A.2501 *et seq.*] unless a contrary intention is stated.
(2) Matters specially made taxable elsewhere in the statutes or rules.
(3) The legal fees for any newspaper publication required by law.
(4) The reasonable expense of printing any required brief and appendix in the supreme court, including any brief on motion for leave to appeal.
(5) The reasonable costs of any bond required by law, including any stay of proceeding or appeal bond.
(6) Any attorney fees authorized by statute or by court rule.

Our review of the provisions of the statute indicates nothing supporting an award of costs for expenses generated by paralegals. In the absence of statutory authorization, costs may not be awarded to recompense for a claimed litigation expense. *Taylor, supra* at 387-388, 445 N.W.2d 525. . . .

Clearly, attorney fees are not meant to compensate only work performed personally by members of the bar. Rather, the term must refer to a reasonable fee for the work product of an attorney that necessarily includes support staff. The rule allowing an award of attorney fees has traditionally anticipated the allowance of a fee sufficient to cover the office overhead of an attorney together with a reasonable profit. The inclusion of factor 5, *the expenses incurred,* reflects the traditional understanding that attorney fees should be sufficient to recoup at least a portion of overhead costs. (Citations omitted.) Fixed overhead costs include such items as employee wages, rent, equipment rental, and so forth. Thus, until a statute or a court rule specifies otherwise, the attorney fees must take into account the work not only of attorneys, but also of secretaries, messengers, *paralegals,* and others whose labor contributes to the work product for which an attorney bills a client, and it must also take account of other expenses and profit. We therefore must rule, albeit reluctantly, that the reasonable "attorney fees" should already include the work of paralegals, as well as that of attorneys and other factors underlying the fee. Accordingly, we remand in order for the trial court to reduce the award of attorney fees by the amount attributable to the independent paralegal billings.

We, however, find it noteworthy that a growing number of our sister states have allowed an independent recovery of paralegal or legal assistant time in attorney fee awards under statute, rules of court, or decisional law authorizing awards of attorney fees. In most cases, with respect to paralegals and legal assistants, recovery is available "if a legal assistant performs work that has traditionally been done by any attorney." See, e.g., *Gill Savings Ass'n v. Int'l Supply Co. Inc.,* 759 S.W.2d 697, 702 (Tex.App., 1988). To qualify for such recovery, the evidence must establish: (1) that the legal assistant is qualified through education, training, or work experience to perform substantive legal work; (2) that substantive legal work was performed under the direction and supervision of an attorney; (3) the nature of the legal work that was performed; (4) the hourly rate being charged for the legal assistant; and (5) the number of hours expended by the legal assistant. *Id.*

We find that the increasing practice of allowing an independent recovery of paralegal or legal assistant time in attorney's fee awards has merit. We recognize that the day-to-day duties of a legal assistant will vary from law firm to law firm. If, however, the paralegal performs work that has traditionally been done by an attorney, we believe that it follows that a separate expense should be allowable. Neither statute nor court rule, however, currently allow such expenses as separate billable items. It is not our task to rewrite statutes. We therefore encourage the Legislature to change the statute or the Supreme Court to change the court rule to provide for appropriate billing for paralegal fees.

Affirmed in part, reversed in part, and remanded. . . .

Questions about the Case

1. What kind of an attorney fee statute or rule is at issue here? Does this make a difference in the way this court handles the issue?
2. Why are the paralegal fees listed as "costs" instead of part of the "reasonable attorney fees"? If the firm had listed the paralegal time as part of attorney fees, would the court have decided differently?
3. What does the court say about recovery of paralegal costs as mediation sanctions?
4. Does this court believe that only attorney time should be included in a fee award? Where does the court think that the paralegal time should be factored into the fee?
5. What does the court say about the contradictory decisions of other jurisdictions?
6. Does the court acknowledge that paralegal time is typically billed separately by firms and not included in overhead? What does the court say should be done to rectify this disparity between the ruling in this case and the prevailing practice?

In the following case, defendants seek a reduction of an attorney fee award based on several grounds pertinent to legal assistants, including what is the proper rate, whether or not the work is professional work that should be compensated, and whether the work is duplicative.

New Mexico Citizens for Clean Air and Water v. Espanola Mercantile Co.
72 F.3d 830 (10th Cir. 1996)

. . .

This is an action to enforce the Clean Water Act against defendant for unpermitted discharges and other violations at the Espanola Transit Mix Facility in Espanola, New Mexico. Plaintiff New Mexico Citizens for Clean Air and Water is an environmental group and plaintiff Pueblo of San Juan is an Indian tribe that owns the affected land. . . .

The consent decree further provided in pertinent part: "Defendant stipulates that it is not entitled to an award of attorneys fees. Plaintiffs shall submit their petition for attorneys fees within twenty (20) days after entry of this Consent Decree. Defendant agrees to pay attorney fees awarded to Plaintiffs by the Court."

After both plaintiffs submitted requests, the district court awarded $46,003.69 in fees and costs. Defendant appeals the award.

. . .

The Defendant's first challenge to the amount of fees awarded concerns the district court's failure to consider whether any modification of the lodestar figure should be made based on Citizens' limited success in the action. In the district court, defendant argued that plaintiffs were not as successful as they had portrayed themselves to be in their fee petition.

"When an adjustment is requested on the basis of either the exceptional or limited nature of the relief obtained by the plaintiff, the district court should make clear that it has considered the relationship between the amount of the fee awarded and the results obtained." *Hensley,* 461 U.S. at 437, 103 S. Ct. at 1941. In the absence of such finding in the record here, we must remand for the district court to consider to what extent the fee award should be adjusted based on Citizens' degree of success.

Defendant raises numerous other challenges to the amount of fees awarded, some of which were not specifically raised in the district court. Only three of these other objections merit consideration by the district court on remand.

The first is the defendant's contention that attorney Eric Ames improperly billed attorney rates for tasks that either could have been performed by someone other than an attorney or that are not properly compensable at any rate. Specifically, defendant objects to paying attorney rates for time spent investigating the factual basis for Citizens' claims and time spent performing what defendant characterizes as secretarial duties, e.g., copying documents, faxing documents, and filing documents.

"[W]hen a lawyer spends time on tasks that are easily delegable to non-professional assistance, legal service rates are not applicable." *Halderman ex rel. Halderman v. Pennhurst State Sch. & Hosp.,* 49 F.3d 939, 942 (3d Cir. 1995); *see also Ursic v. Bethlehem Mines,* 719 F.2d 670, 677 (3d Cir. 1983) ("Nor do we approve the wasteful use of highly skilled and highly priced talent for matters easily delegable to non-professionals or less experienced associates. . . . A Michelangelo should not charge Sistine Chapel rates for painting a farmer's barn."); *Mares,* 801 F.2d at 1204 (criticizing fees for messenger services).

Although commenting that Ames was not entitled to compensation for at least one secretarial task—organizing files—the district court's opinion does not reflect whether it carefully scrutinized some of the other seemingly secretarial work Ames performed. Further, the opinion does not reflect consideration of the defendant's argument that a paralegal or investigator could have performed much, if not all, of the factual investigation of Citizens' claims. We express no opinion as to whether any of the challenged time is properly compensable at attorney rates, but commend the matter to the district court's attention on remand.

The second matter the district court should consider is the potential duplication of effort. Defendant contends that the attendance of two attorneys for Citizens at various meetings was not necessary, and that only one attorney's time should be billed. While we have "decline[d] to require an automatic reduction of reported hours to adjust for multiple representation," we have advised district courts to "give particular attention to the possibility of duplication." *Ramos,* 713 F.2d at 554.

Here, the district court did consider whether the two attorneys properly billed for conferences with each other, but the opinion does not disclose whether the judge also considered potential duplication of effort by the attorneys when meeting with others, such as the plaintiffs, defense counsel, or the court. On remand, the district court should give attention to the possibility of duplication in these meetings as well.

Finally, defendant contends, and Citizens concedes, that the district court failed to eliminate all the time billed by counsel for communications with the press. The district court stated its intention to eliminate all time spent on press-related matters, except time spent in preparing a post-settlement press release, but the court overlooked some press-related billing entries in its reduction of counsel's fees. *See Halderman,* 49 F.3d at 942 ("[T]he proper forum for litigation is the courtroom, not the media."). On remand, the court should reduce the fee award accordingly.

The judgment of the United States District Court for the District of New Mexico is REVERSED, and the matter is REMANDED. . . .

Questions about the Case

1. What federal statute authorized the attorney fee award in this case?
2. What does the court say about lowering the fee because the plaintiffs were not completely successful?
3. Is it proper to charge attorney rates for copying, filing, and faxing? What did the trial court decide?
4. Should a fee award include compensation for all the persons attending meetings?
5. Should a fee award cover the time spent communicating with the press?

6. What does the case tell you about how to prepare or dispute a fee petition?

In this bankruptcy matter, the court lowers the rate of compensation to match the work that was performed, providing an incentive to firms to utilize the services of legal assistants to do work that does not require the application of an attorney's knowledge, skill, and judgment.

In re Music Merchants, Inc.
208 B.R. 944 (9th Cir. BAP 1997)

. . .

In July, 1987, Music Merchants, Inc. filed bankruptcy under chapter 11. In April, 1988, the U.S. Trustee appointed a creditors' committee, and a few weeks later, appellant T. Edward Malpass ("Malpass") was appointed its counsel. . . .

Following the hearing, by memorandum opinion entered on February 12, 1996, the trial court granted the motion for reconsideration and allowed Malpass approximately $13,000 in additional fees from the second interim and final fee applications but again denied enhancement of the award to compensate for delay in payment. . . .

Malpass timely filed a motion for alteration of the court's order, asserting that the court erred when it disallowed certain fees and refused to enhance the award to compensate for delays caused in part by Malpass's appeal of the court's erroneous ruling. The court denied this request on March 29, 1996 and Malpass filed this timely appeal. . . .

Although Malpass cites several alleged errors on the part of the trial court, he principally argues that "reasonable compensation must contain an enhancement to compensate for unreasonable delays in payment." Malpass states that "case law, including Ninth Circuit decisions . . . makes it clear that a reasonable attorney's fee is obtained only when payment is received within the time payment is normally received by similarly skilled professionals practicing in other areas of the law" and, therefore, calculation of Malpass's fee "must take into account whether payment has been delayed such that enhancement is necessary." . . .

None of the cases cited by Malpass supports his argument that enhancement is required by law. . . .

Malpass argues that the trial court erred when it deducted fees based upon Malpass's failure "to properly utilize junior associates or paralegals for less sophisticated legal tasks." Malpass claims that his firm's paralegals were not sophisticated litigation paralegals and were unable

280

to perform the services he performed. Malpass argued below that he should not be penalized because he is a sole practitioner. Malpass also states that the trial court did not point to a specific instance in which a paralegal was available to perform particular services.

Malpass misperceives the trial court's ruling. Although the trial court reasoned that certain tasks could have been performed by a paralegal, it also stated: "Even if he did not have any other staff members capable of performing less sophisticated legal tasks, Malpass is still not entitled to bill at a partner's rate for such work." The court, therefore, reduced Malpass's hourly rate from $195 to $125 for specific tasks "which could have been performed by a paralegal or a junior associate." Although the court did not state that a paralegal could have performed the specified tasks, the court listed the amount by which it would reduce the fee request. Malpass does not argue that the court is prohibited from reducing the fee award for work that could have been performed by a lower paid professional. Therefore, Malpass has not shown that the trial court abused its discretion on this issue. . . .

Malpass has litigated for the fees requested for more than eight years. Malpass acknowledges that "the amounts involved are relatively small," but he claims that "resolution [of the appeal] involves several important issues which are apparently open in the Ninth Circuit." However, Malpass has not shown that the trial court abused its discretion when it refused to enhance Malpass's fee for delay in payment or when it denied certain requested fees. Therefore, the trial court is AFFIRMED.

Questions about the Case

1. Under what kind of statute did the court award attorney's fees in this case?
2. Does this court believe that an "enhancement" of the fee is called for? Why or why not?
3. On what ground had the lower court deducted fees? What does this court decide about that matter?
4. Does this court require lawyers to employ legal assistants?
5. How could an attorney who does not use the services of legal assistants prevent a reduction in fees such as the one in this case?

The bankruptcy business in this case engaged in practices that violated several rules covered in this chapter, including the prohibitions on partnerships between lawyers and nonlawyers, fee-splitting, and excessive fees.

In re Hessinger & Associates
171 B.R. 366 (Bkrtcy.N.D.Calif. 1994)

. . .

Hessinger & Associates started out as Varbel & Associates, run by Earl Cook and Duane Varbel, an Arizona lawyer. The firm started in Arizona, and then expanded into southern and northern California as well as other areas. Its mode of operation was to advertise very heavily, with high-profile radio and television advertising as well as late-night "infomercials" touting the instant relief from debt problems and how bankruptcy was a "constitutional right" which every citizen should use to get out of debt. The advertising made heavy use of actors portraying harassed and troubled debtors.

Varbel & Associates hired a few young and inexperienced lawyers, but most of its work was performed by "paralegals" with little or no formal training. Within the firm, they were called "credit specialists." Their job was to lure the debtor into their offices, get them to sign a contract promising to pay the fee, then preparing and filing the bankruptcy papers. In the majority of cases, the debtor had no contact with a lawyer at all until the 341 meeting, when a Hessinger lawyer they had never met was present.

Varbel's main selling point, as well as its means of funneling funds to its nonlawyer principals, was to offer its services for no money down. The debtor was asked to sign a promissory note for the fees, to be paid after bankruptcy. The fees were typically set at three times the amount normally charged by lawyers for doing those types of consumer cases.

After bankruptcy, the notes were transferred to numerous "finance companies" set up by Cook. Some of these companies were owned by Cook himself, or by his relatives, some by Varbel, and at least one by Hessinger. These finance companies collected the fees from the debtors. If the debtors did not pay, they were dunned and sued by the finance companies.

In early 1993, Varbel was disbarred and, in his own words, Hessinger "took over" the practice. In reality, he became the figurehead for the firm, which continued doing business in the same way as before. The firm continued to be run overall by Cook and locally by Hansen, who made all the hiring and firing decisions and exercised complete control over the day-to-day operations of the business, including the conduct of the few lawyers employed by the firm.

Hessinger first came to the attention of this court when the U.S. Trustee objected to his fees in two Chapter 7 cases, which were two or three times as high as other attorneys were charging. Further investigation revealed that all of the work in the cases had been done by nonlawyers and without supervision, and that Hessinger was selling the fee contracts to finance companies for enforcement after bankruptcy even though the promissory notes were executed before bankruptcy and clearly had been discharged. It became clear to the court that more was involved here than simple overcharging, and that ethical issues must be addressed. . . .

Hessinger & Associates is nothing more than a get-rich-quick scheme of Earl Cook. Aided by a venal and morally bankrupt lawyer, Duane Varbel, Cook set up a business to sell bankruptcies to the public and reap the rewards. Upon Varbel's disbarment, Hessinger stepped in to become the front man for the enterprise.

Hessinger maintained that he was in charge of the firm, but the evidence is absolutely overwhelming that he exercised no actual control whatsoever and that all decisions regarding all phases of the operation are made by nonlawyers.

The court was very strongly affected by the testimony of Stephanie Morris, a young lawyer in need of a job who worked for Hessinger & Associates for several months. She was hired by Cook and met Hessinger only once, at a dinner party. She was expressly told by Cook that she was to take directions from only him and his local managers, Turan Kahraman in southern California and Gary Hansen in northern California, neither of whom were lawyers. She was directly and expressly told by Cook that she was not to contact Hessinger for any reason.

Morris was under the direct supervision of Kahraman and Hansen. On several occasions she had arguments with them over her conduct as a lawyer. They complained to her that her "sales" were considerably less than those of the paralegals who were performing the same duties as her. When she explained that she could not ethically file a bankruptcy for someone who did not need it, they told her that the firm's policy was to sign up every person who came in for an interview. They expected her to use the standard interview, called the "six-minute sell," whereby every debtor who came in was expected to be talked into signing the Hessinger fee agreement within six minutes of walking in the door.

Morris also was subject to rebuke by Kahraman and Hansen for refusing to quote every debtor a fee of $1,500.00. They told her that it was the firm's policy to charge every debtor this amount. Morris refused, on grounds that in many cases this amount was unconscionable.

The declaration of Jody L. Downey tells an almost identical story. . . .

Another former Hessinger lawyer, Rebekah M. Sutin, reported the same practices in family law cases. . . .

Jennifer Kung was a Hessinger lawyer from March to May, 1994, when she quit because of Hessinger's practices. In her declaration, she reported experiences identical to the other former Hessinger lawyers. . . .

Despite Hessinger's lame representation that all the decisions were his, it is clear that all of the decisions were made by Cook and his nonlawyer deputies. All of the attorneys . . . state that they were hired by Cook or Hansen or Kahraman without ever having seen Hessinger.

When [one attorney at the firm] wanted a raise in pay, he asked Cook, not Hessinger. In a declaration filed to discredit [an attorney employee, a firm paralegal] noted that he was fired by "our Administrator," not Hessinger. Morris' termination was the same. Hessinger presides over a "law firm" in which all the hiring, firing, and supervision of lawyers is done by nonlawyers who also set the fees.

No lawyer may ethically practice law under the direction of a nonlawyer. To do so violates Rule 1-600 of the California Rules of Professional Conduct, which forbids a lawyer to participate in any organization which allows any third person to interfere with the lawyer's independence or professional judgment or allows an unlicensed person to practice law. The reason for such a rule is to "prevent business relationships with non-lawyers from compromising a lawyer's independence of thought and action." G. Hazard, 2 *The Law of Lawyering* (2d Ed. 1990), 5.4:502.

By lending his name and license to an organization run by a layman, Hessinger has committed the grossest of ethical violations. He has allowed Cook to set up a system whereby nonlawyers supervise and direct lawyers and coerce them to do something not in their clients' best interests. This conduct is reprehensible beyond words. To anyone who has any degree of love for the law, it is physically revolting. . . .

The accounting of how much Cook is reaping from this operation is beyond the court's ability to investigate. However, the mechanics of it are fairly clear. First, Cook is paid a salary of $4,000.00 per month. Second, Cook is the owner of the advertising company which produces Hessinger's commercials. Third, Cook owns part or all of several of the finance companies to whom notes from clients are assigned for collection. Between all of these sources of revenue, Cook's income from Hessinger operations far outstrips that of Hessinger.

Rule 1-320 of the California Rules of Professional Conduct provides that a lawyer or law firm may not directly or indirectly share legal fees with a person who is not a lawyer. Rule 1-600 contains a similar ban. Hessinger's financial arrangements with Cook are clearly intended to circumvent these rules, and are not in any way legitimate exceptions to the rules. There is no legitimate employer-employee relationship between Hessinger and Cook. It is that latter who is the employee. The court accordingly finds a gross violation of Rule 1-320 and Rule 1-600. . . .

Rule 3-110(A) of the California Rules of Professional Conduct provides that a member shall not intentionally, recklessly, or repeatedly fail to perform legal services with competence. Hessinger has violated this rule in hundreds of cases, if not thousands.

First and foremost, the policies set by Cook and enforced by [non-lawyer administrators] were designed to maximize their income, not properly counsel clients as to whether or not they should file a bankruptcy petition. Within Hessinger, petition filings are referred to as "sales." All Hessinger employees who interviewed clients, whether attorneys or nonlawyer "credit specialists," were given specific and repeated directives to sign to a fee contract every person who came in the door within six minutes. Called the "six-minute sell," it was the official policy of Hessinger to sell every person who responded to one of their ads on filing a bankruptcy within six minutes of the start of the interview. Those attorneys who knew better and balked were criticized and let go. Nonlawyers, in addition to not having the training needed to evaluate if a bankruptcy was appropriate, had no ethical considerations to worry about.

Additionally, Hessinger regularly offered special bonuses, in the form of cash or trips, to attorneys or credit specialists who filed the most bankruptcy petitions. Hessinger's argument that these were only to "reduce the backlog" is nonsense; the bonuses were simply to encourage Hessinger employees to talk every single person whom they interviewed into filing a bankruptcy petition. The former Hessinger attorneys who have come forth have confirmed that this was the official policy of the firm.

Counseling is the fundamental function performed by consumer lawyers. By placing its interest in revenue ahead of its obligation to counsel its clients, Hessinger & Associates has acted recklessly and incompetently and has violated Rule 3-110(A). By failing to stop the practice and insure that each and every person who came into one of his offices received proper counseling, Joseph Hessinger has personally violated the rule.

Additionally, Hessinger has violated the rule by allowing nonlawyer employees, many with little or no legal training, to interview clients and prepare their bankruptcy papers without any significant (and in hundreds of cases not even insignificant) supervision by a lawyer. . . .

The way Cook has structured the Hessinger procedures, potential clients are directed to one person who interviews them, gets them to sign the fee agreement, and prepares the bankruptcy papers. Although a small number of young and inexperienced lawyers are used (mainly to sign the petitions and Rule 2016 statements), most of the cases are handled by nonlawyer "credit specialists" who are not under the supervision of a lawyer, are given bonuses based on the number of cases they file, and are directed as to policy by Cook and as to day-to-day activities by [nonlawyer administrators]. . . .

The incidental availability of a lawyer does not make the practice legal where the attorney exercised no actual and significant supervision over the nonlawyer. See *Glad,* supra; *In re Stone,* 166 B.R. 269 (Bkrtcy. W.D. Pa.1994). In *Stone,* the court held that a paralegal had been engaged in the unauthorized practice of law when he prepared bankruptcy petitions even though he had a lawyer check his paperwork for mistakes because the lawyer had no way of knowing what legal advice the paralegal had given or whether the advice was proper. 166 B.R. at 275. Here, the record shows that it was Hessinger's practice to present petitions prepared by nonlawyer "credit specialists" in large quantities for the few lawyers to sign, without even checking for obvious errors. Even if the Hessinger lawyers reviewed the credit specialists' work, Hessinger would still be guilty of aiding in the unauthorized practice of law. The fact that most of such petitions are signed without any review at all makes the offense particularly egregious. . . .

As noted above, at least two Hessinger attorneys pointed out to Cook that to charge a four-figure fee in every case is unconscionable and a violation of Rule 4-200(A) of the California Rules of Professional Conduct. Cook's response was to get rid of these lawyers. Hessinger apparently has no such qualms, and has accordingly violated this rule in hundreds or thousands of cases.

In one case now before this court, *In re Eleccion,* No. 94-10095, the debtor had only $2300 in assets including a $1300 rental security deposit. He had no secured debt, and $14,113.00 in unsecured debt. The case was as simple as they come, at least from the information Hessinger's "credit specialist" was able to garner. Even a seasoned bankruptcy lawyer would charge no more than $500 or $600 for such a bankruptcy, after first counseling the debtor as to other alternatives because of the small total debt. Many attorneys of lesser experience would charge around $300. Hessinger's fee in the case was $1,000. . . .

From the overwhelming record supplied by the U.S. Trustee, the court has no difficulty in finding that in the vast majority of Hessinger's cases the fees are unconscionable. The fees are set by nonlawyers, with no regard for the simplicity of the case. The cases are prepared either by nonlawyers or very inexperienced and unqualified lawyers. The individuals receive no counseling, and in fact are looked upon as customers to be bilked and milked rather than clients. The court finds that by charging fees in excess of those charged by experienced practitioners and delivering services of the lowest order Hessinger has violated Rule 4-200(A). . . .

Conclusion

Although the court has found hundreds or thousands of serious violations of the California Rules of Professional Conduct, it is important to note that even one single use of the "six minute sell" to one single client is enough justification for revoking an attorney's license to practice. Hessinger's violations of ethics are rampant and outrageous, and demand the strongest possible sanction. Accordingly, the court will order as follows:

1. Pursuant to Local Rule 110-6, an order to show cause will be issued requiring Hessinger to show cause to the district court, if any he has, why he should not be disbarred from practice in this district for the conduct set forth in this memorandum.
2. Pursuant to Local Rule 110-7, the court assesses a fine against Hessinger in the amount of $100,000.00, to be paid to the clerk of the court. Until the fine is paid in full, Hessinger and his firm will not be permitted to practice bankruptcy law in this district, nor charge any person any fee whatsoever for any bankruptcy-related service in this district. Provided, however, that any other judge in this district may modify this order as to cases pending before him or her as he or she sees fit.

Questions about the Case

1. Were the "legal assistants" in this firm properly trained and educated for their work?
2. What does the court say about who controlled the law firm operation? Which ethical rule or rules did this particular conduct breach?
3. How was the nonlawyer Cook paid? Who decided his compensation? Is this unethical fee-splitting? Why or why not?
4. Did the lawyer Hessinger perform legal services competently? Did clients get good legal advice and representation?
5. On what basis were bonuses paid to employees? Did this plan violate any ethical rules?
6. Did Hessinger supervise the "paralegals" properly? Were the paralegals doing any work that falls within the definition of unauthorized practice of law?

7. How did the firm determine how much a client would be charged for its services? Were the rates more or less than market rates? Was this method of setting fees proper?
8. Is the advertising in which this firm engaged permissible under the standards described in Chapter 6?

The *Barrett* case in an example of an attorney being disciplined for mishandling of funds. Pay special attention to the facts of the cases and the defenses asserted by Barrett.

State of Kansas v. Barrett
207 Kan. 178, 483 P.2d 1106 (1971)

This is an original proceeding in discipline against the respondent, Richard L. Barrett, of Pratt, Kansas, in which the State Board of Law Examiners has recommended disbarment. . . .

The respondent was admitted to practice law in the year 1950 and has continued to practice at Pratt, Kansas, since that date. . . .

The complaint in this proceeding involves two separate business transactions which respondent undertook for clients.

The first arose from a sale of $20,000 worth of real estate. Respondent drew a contract of sale dated October 7, 1968, which provided for the escrow of title documents and for payment of the purchase price. The purchase price was to be remitted promptly by respondent to the sellers when received. Respondent was designated as escrow agent in the contract and as such received two payments on the sale price. The first payment of $4,000 was received on October 17, 1968. This check was either cashed or deposited at the Greensburg State Bank on October 18, 1968, after being endorsed by respondent. On December 30, 1968, respondent received a second check as escrow agent in the amount of $5,157.50. On this same date respondent issued a check to the seller of the real estate covering only the $4,000 payment less sale expenses. Payment was refused on this check because of insufficient funds in the account.

. . . The $5,157.50 check received by respondent was not deposited for some time. It was held by him for two months until February 27, 1969, at which time it was deposited in this trust account.

On March 4, 1969, the Peoples Bank of Pratt refused payment of an unrelated check drawn by respondent on this trust account in the sum of $14,743.50 and payable to a bank in St. Louis, Missouri. The trust account had insufficient funds to cover the check. The check had been given to satisfy an unconnected escrow obligation of the respondent. Two days later the respondent deposited $9,085.78 in the trust account and re-issued the $14,743.50 check to the St. Louis bank. The $9,085.78 deposit was made up of $2,000 in currency, $4,500 which was transferred from the Barrett and Barrett, Attorneys, account in the Greensburg State Bank and a check for $2,585.78 received from another client. When the second check to the St. Louis bank was paid the trust account was reduced to a balance of $726.10.

Thereafter respondent issued a check for $5,157.50 payable to the seller named in the escrow agreement. On April 8, 1969, in response to a demand by the seller's attorney in Arkansas for payment of the $4,000 item, respondent took $5,000 in currency from his office safe and drove to Arkansas. He paid his obligation under the $4,000 payment in currency and returned to Pratt. Shortly thereafter demand was made upon him for the $5,157.50 payment. No payment was forthcoming and a suit was filed May 16, 1969, to recover this amount and to terminate his duties as escrow agent under the contract.

On July 3, 1969, a formal complaint was filed with the Kansas State Board of Law Examiners based upon his handling of the funds arising from the escrow agreement and upon his failure to carry out other duties as executor of an estate in the Probate Court of Pratt County, Kansas.

The suit against respondent to recover the $5,157.50 was settled on July 25, 1969, with funds obtained from a real estate loan on his personal real estate. He was relieved of all further duties as escrow agent under the contract.

The second matter called to the attention of the board arose from respondent's handling of the assets of what we will refer to as the Samples estate. He was appointed executor of the Samples will without bond on November 30, 1962. The estate consisted of roughly $71,000 in liquid assets such as cash in banks, savings and loan shares, mutual funds, Kansas Power and Light Company stock and real estate which was sold and payment received in full on or before March 18, 1966. At this time the estate was ready to close.

After many letters and calls from the heirs to respondent and after an informal complaint was made to the Kansas Bar Association, a decree of final settlement was obtained in the probate court. On April 12, 1967, respondent was directed to pay over the assets of the estate, file his receipts and receive his final discharge. No settlement with the beneficiaries of the will was forthcoming for more than two years thereafter.

On May 20, 1969, a suit was filed to remove respondent as executor of this estate and require him to turn over the assets of the estate. Respondent appeared in probate court in response to a petition for removal and sought additional time to respond to the petition. . . .

He thereafter failed to appear on the date set for hearing and a judgment was rendered removing him as executor on June 27, 1969. . . .

When respondent appeared before the State Board of Law Examiners he admitted that he was short $15,734.10 in assets belonging to the Samples estate. On July 18, 1969, he borrowed $21,000 on his home and real estate in order to raise the $15,734.10 which was then paid through the probate court. The balance of the loan was used by him to settle the suit over the escrow agreement as previously mentioned. . . .

All funds of clients paid to a lawyer or law firm, other than advances for costs and expenses, should be deposited in one or more identifiable bank accounts maintained in the state in which the law office is situated. A lawyer should promptly notify a client of the receipt of his funds, securities, or other property. A lawyer should maintain complete records of all funds, securities, and other properties of a client coming into the possession of the lawyer and render appropriate accounts to his client regarding them. In addition it is the duty of the lawyer to promptly pay or deliver to the client the funds, securities, or other properties in the possession of the lawyer which the client is entitled to receive.

Commingling is committed when a client's money is intermingled with that of his attorney and its separate identity lost so that it may be used for the attorney's personal or business expenses or subjected to claims of his creditors. The rule against commingling was adopted to provide against the probability in some cases, the possibility in many cases, and the danger in all cases that such commingling will result in the loss of the client's money. A trustee or attorney handling funds of a client cannot escape responsibility for a trust account by the simple act of not keeping any record or data from which an accounting might be made. . . .

Respondent states that possibly he erred somewhere along the line, and undoubtedly was negligent in the way this matter was handled but that he had no intention of defrauding anyone of any monies, and that all such monies were paid back. He concludes that his actions do not merit the discipline of disbarment.

The actions of respondent, the commingling of funds and the failure to fulfill trust obligations occurred over a period of several years. Insufficient fund checks were issued by him to cover his trust obligations when he either knew or should have known there was no money in the checking account to pay the same. K.S.A. 21-555b provides the issuance of an insufficient fund check shall be prima facie evidence of intent to defraud if payment is not made to the holder within seven days after receiving notice that such check has not been paid by the bank. His restoration of funds lost through commingling with his own came only after suits had been filed against him and after a formal complaint had been filed with the board. . . .

It is intimated by respondent that some of the shortcomings set forth in the record may have occurred by reason of the action of his secretaries and other lay persons in the office.

A lawyer often delegates tasks to clerks, secretaries and other lay persons in his office. Such delegation is proper if the lawyer maintains a direct relationship with his client, supervises the delegated work, and has complete professional responsibility for the work product.

The work done by secretaries and other lay persons is done as agents of the lawyer employing them. The lawyer must supervise their work and be responsible for their work product or the lack of it. . . .

On the basis of the record before us we have concluded that respondent has been guilty of flagrant disregard of the duties of honesty, fidelity, candor and fairness which he owed to clients and to the courts. The record demonstrates that he is an unsafe person to manage the legal business of others and justifies the ultimate discipline of disbarment.

Disbarment of Richard L. Barrett is decreed and the clerk of this court is directed to remove his name from the roll of attorneys.

Questions about the Case

1. What ethical violations did attorney Barrett commit regarding the escrow funds, and how?
2. What ethics violations did attorney Barrett commit regarding the Samples estate, and how?
3. How does the court define "commingling"?
4. What defense did attorney Barrett offer? Did the court find it convincing? Why, or why not?
5. Do you agree with the discipline imposed by the court?

Competence

This chapter addresses the issue of competence, understood to be one of the essential elements of every profession. Legal incompetence, not always easy to define, is grounds for both legal and disciplinary remedies. Chapter 8 covers:

- definitions of lawyer and paralegal competence
- the key components of competence for legal assistants, including

  - knowledge
  - skills
  - thoroughness and preparation
  - diligence and promptness
  - communication with clients

- sanctions for incompetence, including disciplinary actions and malpractice suits
- trends in malpractice, including the growth in claims and in third-party actions against lawyers
- common dilemmas confronting legal assistants in the area of competence, including those related to delegation, supervision, and attorney review of work
- factors in the work environment that affect competence

A. Introduction

Lawyers are bound to represent clients competently by both ethics codes and the common law rules of tort liability for professional negligence. A lawyer's duty to represent a client competently also makes him or her responsible for the work of legal assistants and others in the law firm; the ultimate responsibility for the competent handling of a client matter rests with the lawyer.

However, legal assistants must consider their own work competence one of their highest duties, both because they desire professional status and treatment and because they share with the lawyer the moral and ethical responsibility for providing quality legal services. As discussed in Section B of Chapter 2, legal assistants should also be mindful of their own personal tort liability in the event a malpractice case is brought by a client.

Since competence cannot be defined quantitatively and the range of incompetent acts is virtually limitless, competence seems like an amorphous notion. Most definitions of competence begin with the requisite legal knowledge and skill.

B. Legal Education

Legal knowledge for lawyer competence generally means, at a minimum, a law school education of three or four years followed by a bar examination, which primarily tests substantive legal knowledge and judgmental-analytical ability. There has been extensive discussion in legal education in the last two decades over the extent to which legal education and the bar exam should be more practical. Clinical programs, lawyering skills, and trial techniques courses have been added to the traditional law school curriculum in many law schools. Internship and externship programs, many for course credit, have been established. Programs to test more practical job-related skills on the bar exam have been established (for example, the performance portion of the bar exam now found on many states' exams). Finally, periodic calls are heard for mandatory apprenticeships as a prerequisite to bar admission.

In addition to a formal legal education, even if it does include a clinical component, legal knowledge and skills also encompass many things not covered in school. Lawyers learn on the job from more experienced lawyers in the firms that hire them. Some of this training is informal: learning by example, by models available in the firm, or by trial and error. Some is more formal: by means of in-house training programs, or by a more experienced attorney's mentoring of a new attorney.

A lawyer must continue to develop legal knowledge and skills throughout his or her career. Formal continuing education programs are an important aspect of this; 39 states now have mandatory continuing legal education. However, simply taking courses to gain new skills, or to refine old ones, is not alone sufficient for competence. Ideally, attorneys are committed to keeping abreast with changes in the law and to developing their talents to the fullest. Such is the aspiration of the professional: It is not predicated on mandates from the state but is a matter of commitment and integrity, driven by the sense of personal satisfaction derived from doing one's job well.

C. Paralegal Education

Legal assistants share a lawyer's commitment to education and skill development. Because legal assistants are not forced to comply with educational standards by state regulation, the responsibility for achieving and maintaining competence through education and skill development rests firmly with paralegals and the lawyers who employ them.

Paralegal education programs are as new as the profession itself—a little less than 30 years old. The first programs were established around 1970, an estimated half dozen scattered across the country. There are now at least 500 paralegal programs situated in a wide variety of institutions, including two- and four-year colleges (both public and private), multidisciplinary and freestanding proprietary institutions (some of which are vocationally oriented), even correspondence schools and most recently institutions offering programs exclusively by distance education. Unlike the law school curriculum, the paralegal curriculum is not standardized, and offerings vary widely in length, content, format, level of sophistication, and degree of specialization. Good programs teach an appropriate balance of substantive law and practical job skills.

More than two hundred of these paralegal programs are approved by the American Bar Association (ABA), having met guidelines on curriculum, admissions, faculty, administration, staff, facilities, finances, library, and support services, such as counseling and placement. ABA approval, first granted in 1975, is the only kind of specialized recognition of paralegal educational programs available; it is purely voluntary and is not formally recognized by the federal government. The ABA has never sought such recognition. In addition to the standards for paralegal education set in the American Bar Association Guidelines for the Approval of Legal Assistant Education Programs, the American Association of Paralegal Education has adopted a Statement of Quality in Paralegal Education that also establishes standards for the content and operation of formal educational programs for legal assistants.

A paralegal education is gradually becoming a minimum to enter the paralegal career, although firm hiring standards vary throughout the country. Many firms do not require a formal paralegal education but favor candidates who have formal training over those who do not. In some cities, a baccalaureate degree alone is the hiring standard in large law firms. Smaller firms often require previous legal work experience rather than formal education.

Guideline 1 of the ABA Model Guidelines for the Utilization of Legal Assistant Services (ABA Model Guidelines), in stating the lawyer's responsibility for the actions of legal assistants, emphasizes the importance of paralegal education to competence. The comment states that "[a]n attorney who utilizes a legal assistant's services is responsible for determining that the legal assistant is competent to perform the tasks assigned, based on the legal assistant's education, training and experience." This guideline follows ABA Model Rule 5.3. which requires lawyers to make reasonable efforts to ensure that the conduct of nonlawyer employees is compatible with the lawyer's professional obligations. This rule and the common law rules of tort liability are discussed in Chapter 2.

Whether or not employers require it, legal assistants should acquire appropriate formal education to meet their professional obligation of competence. This education should include not only a basic paralegal program but also regular and frequent continuing education that covers new practice areas, updates the legal assistant in his or her area of practice, and enhances paralegal skills. Continuing education is available to legal assistants in many forms, especially since legal assistants may take courses that are designed for lawyers as well as courses offered specifically to legal assistants. Continuing education for lawyers is readily available through state and local bar associations and independent providers. Courses for legal assistants are provided by paralegal programs; local, regional and national paralegal associations; and a few independent organizations.

Both national organizations, the National Association of Legal Assistants (NALA) and the National Federation of Paralegal Associations (NFPA), promote competence and education to their members. The NALA's Code of Ethics Canon 6 requires legal assistants to maintain a high degree of competency in the legal profession. The NALA has translated this ideal into action by offering its Certified Legal Assistant examination, discussed in Chapter 2. Educational or experience requirements must be met to sit for the C.L.A. exam, and Certified Legal Assistants must also meet continuing education requirements to maintain their certified status. The NFPA Model Code contains a strong statement concerning competence and education in Canon 1. This statement tells legal assistants that it is their professional responsibility to maintain competence through education, training, and work experience. NFPA also requires PACE certified paralegals to participate in continuing education. Both NALA and NFPA have annual national educational seminars and encourage their local chapters to provide frequent continuing education courses.

D. A Definition of Competency

Competence cannot be defined solely in terms of formal education and professional skill; these are essential preconditions to competence. Competence itself only has full meaning when it is applied to the tasks at hand, to the specific legal work to be done. At this point, factors other than knowledge and skill determine whether work will be carried out competently. The ABA Model Code does not define competence very completely. DR 6-101 only requires lawyers not to accept cases that they are not competent to handle without associating with a competent lawyer; not to handle cases without adequate preparation; and not to neglect a matter. The ABA Model Rules attempt to define competence in a more exacting way. Model Rule 1.1 defines competent representation as requiring "the legal knowledge, skill, thoroughness and preparation reasonably necessary for the representation." Model Rule 1.3 adds two more elements by requiring lawyers to "act with reasonable diligence and promptness." Finally, Rule 1.4 on communication adds that lawyers must keep clients "reasonably informed," must "comply with reasonable requests for information," and must explain matters to permit clients "to make informed decisions regarding the representation."

These ethics rules and cases interpreting them can be synthesized into a list of qualities that comprise competence for lawyers and legal assistants alike.

1. Knowledge. Both lawyers and legal assistants must have appropriate formal education, both legal and general, that enables them to communicate well, in oral and written form; that provides them with

297

knowledge of substantive law and procedure; that has developed their analytical and judgmental abilities; and that has provided them with the information and skills needed to resolve legal issues.

The bodies of knowledge needed by the lawyer and the legal assistant naturally differ because the lawyer makes substantive legal decisions about how to proceed, while the legal assistant participates in the practical steps both preliminary to these decisions (for example, interviewing clients, conducting legal and factual research) and later to implement these decisions (for example, drafting a document).

Increasingly, the legal knowledge needed to be competent is highly specialized. The law has become ever more complex, and most practitioners emphasize no more than a few areas of practice. This trend away from general practice is also evidenced by the growing number of states that have specialized certification programs for lawyers, by the departmentalization of large firms, and by the proliferation of "boutique" firms that devote themselves to one or two highly specialized areas of law. As a result of specialization, a lawyer has a duty to refer highly complex, specialized cases to an attorney with appropriate expertise if he or she doesn't have that expertise. Legal assistants also, especially in urban areas where highly specialized legal services are needed by clients, must be specialists in order to act competently. Most paralegal curricula, unlike those of law schools, include required specialty courses, and most paralegal continuing education programs are devoted to specialized or advanced coursework.

Orientation and formal on-the-job training have become important elements of legal training. During the 1980s, many large law firms developed formal in-house training programs for lawyers and legal assistants, which not only oriented them to the firm's "way of doing things" but covered substantive knowledge and skills as well. Many firms have courses for lawyers on advocacy skills and trial techniques; courses have been developed for legal assistants on topics such as research, deposition summarizing, and document productions.

Keeping abreast with changes in law and practice is critical in the application of technology. There are ample opportunities for errors to be made on documents by anyone who is not careful while working on a computer. For example, key documents or entries can be lost; errors can be made by selecting the wrong form, using the wrong paragraphs, or changing some but not all names, numbers, or provisions. It has been suggested that competence standards will soon require attorneys to perform computerized legal research that is more thorough, up-to-date, and complete than manual research.

2. Skills. Skills are acquired through formal education and through training and experience on the job. The term "skills" refers primarily to proficiency in the execution of tasks and the implementation of legal decisions into action, as opposed to the mastery of a body of substantive information. Lawyers and legal assistants both must have the ability to apply their skills to the resolution of legal problems in carrying out their respective roles. Skills needed most by legal assistants include drafting documents, analyzing documents, summarizing information, handling procedural matters, gathering information, and conducting legal research. Lawyers need different skills, such as trial advocacy and negotiating. Most studies show that lawyers continue to retain the most complex and sophisticated tasks and to delegate to legal assistants duties that require organizational and oral and written communication skills.

3. Thoroughness and Preparation.

In applying knowledge and skills to any legal problem, both lawyers and legal assistants must be careful and complete in their information gathering, analysis, application of judgment, and actions. Neglecting to learn all the facts, to fill out forms properly, or to be meticulous about every detail can have devastating consequences for the client. Because legal assistants are especially valued for their knowledge of the facts in the cases they work on and for their attention to detail, thoroughness is one of the most critical aspects of paralegal competence.

Related is preparation. Most successful lawyers credit a large part of their success to their careful and thorough preparation. Legal assistants play an important part in this preparation since they are often delegated considerable responsibility for preparation, for example, by organizing documents and other information before trial or by drafting and organizing documents for a real estate closing. The paralegal and attorney must work together as a team in preparation. The attorney relies on the preparation done by the legal assistant while readying for his or her distinct role (representing the client in court, for instance).

4. Diligence and Promptness.

Legal knowledge and skills are worthless unless applied to a client's case in a timely and attentive manner. Diligence in this context means the persistent attention to the legal matter to ensure it is resolved with the best possible outcome for the client. A lack of diligence or promptness is evidenced by delays that may cause harm to a client's case or cause the client unnecessary anxiety. Examples of failure to act diligently and promptly include missing court dates or appointments, frequently needing continuances, missing a statute of limitations, not pursuing discovery, or taking an unnecessarily long time to act. Implied in the duty of diligence is the necessity for firm organization and management that ensure against the missing of critical deadlines, scheduling of conflicting court dates, and so forth. Often these important organizational tasks are delegated to a legal assistant.

5. Communication with Clients. The importance of clear and complete communication with clients cannot be underestimated. The good work of a competent lawyer and legal assistant will not be recognized if the client is not fully informed about the status of a case at each step of the process. It may not matter how successfully the client's case is resolved if the firm never returns the client's phone calls. Most ethics experts say that the best advice to an attorney is to return clients' phone calls promptly. Ongoing communication with clients is an important and potentially large role for legal assistants. Attorneys, especially trial attorneys, often are too busy to return clients' calls promptly or to make regular calls or written reports on how matters are proceeding. A legal assistant is ideally situated to handle this task and usually very effective in keeping the client satisfied that the lines of communication are open.

E. Sanctions for Incompetence

Incompetence can be fatal to a client's rights and to a lawyer's or a legal assistant's career. Incompetence in the handling of a case is the most common basis for malpractice actions against attorneys. Incompetence in the malpractice context is defined as the failure to exercise the level of care commonly observed in other professionals. The remedy is compensation for the loss of the client's legal rights, in other words, damages for losing a case in which the client would have prevailed if the lawyer had acted competently. Some cases also permit recovery to third persons who are damaged by an attorney's failure to act competently (discussed in more detail in the next section).

As discussed in Chapter 2, legal assistants also may be named in malpractice actions including independent contractors working under the direction of a lawyer. Most lawyers carry malpractice insurance that covers the actions of their employees including legal assistants; such insurance is mandatory in some states. Legal assistants should be certain their firm has adequate malpractice coverage that also covers them.

Incompetence is also grounds for disciplinary action against an attorney, although normally the incompetence must be severe or repeated before sanctions are imposed. Recent studies by malpractice insurance providers have shown that the most common bases for claims are

1) substantive incompetence, 2) management incompetence, 3) poor communication skills and practices, 4) fee misunderstandings, and 5) substance abuse and stress. Frequently the incompetence is coupled with other ethical violations such as commingling or conversion of client trust account funds or failure to turn over client papers after representation is terminated. The incidents of discipline for competence-related violations have increased significantly in recent years, including cases in which attorneys were found incompetent for failing to supervise legal assistants properly and for aiding in the unauthorized practice of law by allowing legal assistants to give legal advice and prepare legal documents without supervision or review.

In recent years, some former clients have successfully used violations of ethics rules as a basis for malpractice suits. Since legal assistants are not subject to discipline by the bar and not usually named in malpractice suits, the most likely sanction against an incompetent legal assistant is losing his or her position and perhaps employability.

Many malpractice and disciplinary cases involving competence relate to procrastination or to a lack of promptness, thoroughness, or communication. Typical scenarios include missing statutes of limitations, failing to proceed on a client's case after agreeing to representation, and not returning phone calls for an extended period, usually because the lawyer has not taken proper actions in a matter. These allegations are sometimes tied to financial improprieties as well, such as not returning advanced fees, not turning over a settlement check or client's file promptly, or "borrowing" from a client trust account. Some cases of this type are the result of mismanaged law offices; some, troubled attorneys. Personal problems—such as financial, marital, or health problems—often interfere with an attorney's ability to function competently. A significant number of attorneys with disciplinary records have alcohol or drug dependency problems or emotional and personal problems that prevent them from operating in an ethical and effective manner. Many state bars now have programs to help attorneys with these problems, either voluntarily before they begin to affect the lawyer's professional actions or involuntarily as part of the sanctions imposed on lawyers who have been disciplined.

For examples of malpractice cases in which nonlawyers were implicated, see *Busch v. Flangas* and *Webb v. Pomeroy* at the end of this chapter. While these cases have quite different scenarios and results, they are useful in analyzing how courts might decide the liability of legal assistants. Also see *Musselman v. Willoughby Corp.* in Chapter 2 and *In re Hessinger* in Chapter 7 both of which present fact patterns where the lawyer has failed to exercise adequate oversight of legal assistants who have made substantive errors that damaged clients. Finally, see *In re Gillaspy* at the

301

end of this chapter for a disciplinary action against a lawyer who was sanctioned for incompetence and other related violations when he abdicated authority to legal assistants who made the legal decisions and gave the legal advice in cases.

F. Trends in Legal Malpractice

The late 1980s and early 1990s saw a tremendous increase in the number and size of malpractice claims made against attorneys. Much of this increase can be attributed to third-party claims by non-clients who were harmed by the actions of clients from whom they could no longer recover. Corporate securities work carries a high risk of third-party malpractice actions because of the additional duties to the purchasers of securities imposed by federal law. Under the securities laws, attorneys may be liable under some circumstances when material false or misleading statements are included in offerings. The result is the imposition upon counsel of additional duties of due diligence and fact checking. Private investors who lose see attorneys who represented promoters as possible defendants when promoters have misled investors.

The principles underlying third-party liability in securities cases were broadly applied during the savings and loan crisis in lawsuits by the federal government against firms who represented failed thrift institutions. Most suits claimed that firms failed to advise their clients properly; in many cases, firms relied on information provided by clients. In many suits, the lawyers also served on the savings and loan's boards, exacerbating the malpractice issue because of the possible conflict of interest and exposure to details of many questionable transactions. Most of the cases were settled out of court. Serious unresolved issues still exist about the extent of an attorney's duty to disclose information to the government or the public, and the impact of this duty on the attorney-client privilege.

Another area where third-party plaintiffs are becoming common is in estate planning work. When a gift to an intended beneficiary fails because of an attorney's negligence, the intended beneficiary may seek damages from the attorney, even though the attorney represented the testator, not the beneficiary. Similar cases have held attorneys who represented sellers in real estate transactions liable to buyers for making misleading statements that the buyer relied on in making the purchase. (See the *Biakanja* case at the end of this chapter for an example.)

As plaintiffs look for a "deep pocket," attorneys with malpractice insurance coverage make attractive defendants. Further extensions of third-party liability promise to be in the future, especially in areas heavily regulated by the government, such as environmental law. Another area of increased activity is civil lawsuits by insurance companies against the lawyers who represented their insureds and lost. The jurisdictions are split on whether such actions are permitted. In addition, there are more and more cases in which former clients sue on the basis of conflict of interest. Some cases have revolved around a firm's representation of two clients who ultimately became adversaries. Some have concerned conflicts that arose when an attorney did business with clients or served on a corporate client's board of directors.

The growth in lawsuits against lawyers has resulted in major increases in the cost of malpractice insurance and in a flood of literature and continuing education programs designed to warn how to avoid malpractice suits. The advice given in these programs is as valuable to legal assistants as it is to lawyers. A summary of the typical advice follows:

1. Lawyers should use carefully drafted **letters of engagement** as well as **letters terminating or declining representation**. These documents must spell out and limit the extent and nature of the representation and the expectations and responsibilities of the law firm and the client and should clearly indicate that the lawyer is not guaranteeing a particular outcome.
2. **Clients should be selected carefully.** Difficult personalities and questionable cases should not be accepted.
3. Lawyers and clients should enter into complete and well-drafted **fee agreements** for each representation that cover all the terms noted in Chapter 7. Fee agreements should be entered into as soon as possible in the representation and should be followed meticulously.
4. Clients should be charged **reasonable fees** that are in accord with the fee agreements. Bills should be detailed and should be reviewed before being sent. Excessive, duplicative, or inappropriate charges should be removed before sending bills. Billing should be done regularly and timely.
5. Clients' **phone calls and e-mails should be returned promptly**, preferably the same day. The attorney and paralegal should take the time to educate the client about the law and legal process involved and show that they care about clients' concerns. Clients should be sent copies of documents and work product. Correspondence and other materials from clients should be promptly acknowledged.
6. Lawyers and legal assistants should **listen to clients** carefully and try to understand their goals and expectations. Unrealistic expectations should be addressed immediately and thoughtfully.

7. Lawyers should exercise **independent judgment** on clients' behalf and should **respect clients' decisions**.
8. Law firms should have **good management systems** and well-trained personnel in place, especially concerning the following matters:
   - conflicts checks and screens
   - protection of client confidentiality
   - calendaring deadlines, court dates, and the like
   - billing and time keeping
   - handling client property
   - client trust accounts.
9. Lawyers and legal assistants should be scrupulous in the handling of **clients' funds** in keeping with the rules set forth in Chapter 7. Client trust accounts and related records must be perfectly maintained with no commingling or other irregularities. Client files must be turned over promptly upon termination and settlements must be paid promptly after receipt.
10. Lawyers and legal assistants should know the **limits of their competence** and should seek guidance and consultation when in doubt about how to proceed on a matter.

Paralegals play a major role in following this good advice. Communication with clients is greatly improved when an attorney delegates to a legal assistant responsibility for keeping clients informed, in writing and by phone. When clients call and the lawyer is unavailable, the legal assistant can take or return the call. Legal assistants can keep the lawyer informed of client concerns and keep clients informed of progress in the handling of the matter. Keeping accurate and detailed time records and alerting the lawyer to potential problems in time and billing are valuable roles of the paralegal. Legal assistants often have responsibility for monitoring deadlines and handling client funds, especially in small law firms.

G. Factors Affecting Paralegal Competence

Legal assistants need to be cognizant of not only the meaning of competence and how it is embodied in their work, but the factors that may either enhance their competence or detract from it. Since legal assistants work under the direction and supervision of lawyers, they are not the ones who establish the quality standards for the firm or set the professional tone that determines the attitude that employees at all levels take toward their work. Legal assistants, especially those in small firms, do have influence over firm standards and culture, but in most cases, they are subject to the environment established by the lawyers. Given that legal assistants are not in a position to set firm standards and attitudes, they must seek out firms that have high standards of quality and encourage competence and professionalism in their lawyers and legal assistants. It is unlikely that a legal assistant will be able to function in a competent fashion in a firm that does not demand competence of its professional and nonprofessional staff.

There are several common competence-related problems with which legal assistants are frequently confronted. Perhaps the most common is being asked to perform a task that the legal assistant does not have the requisite knowledge or skill to perform. This presents an especially difficult dilemma for legal assistants who want to do challenging, interesting work and who know their value is in relieving the attorney from tasks that he or she would otherwise have to perform. A conflict thus may arise between the legal assistant's desire to take the assignment and his or her ability to handle the assignment competently. A new legal assistant, like a lawyer just out of law school, must learn on the job. With a strong education, good research and drafting skills, and self-confidence and motivation, a legal assistant can learn how to perform the assigned task on his or her own by conducting research, finding a model in firm files, and so forth. The legal assistant may ask for some guidance from the attorney who assigned the task, or seek out assistance from another lawyer or a more experienced legal assistant. Paralegal colleagues in other firms may be able to guide the legal assistant to the necessary sources. In any event, the supervising lawyer should be made aware that the legal assistant has not previously undertaken such a task, so that the legal assistant's work is evaluated fairly and reviewed carefully.

A related concern is the proper delegation, supervision, and review of paralegal work by attorneys. The ethics and agency rules discussed above and in Chapter 2 make it clear that the lawyer is ultimately responsible for the work of the legal assistant. This responsibility is described in the ABA Model Guidelines in Guideline 1 and its comment and in ABA Model Rule 5.3. For a variety of reasons, attorneys do not always carry out their supervisory responsibilities as well as they should. Many lawyers are not skilled delegators; they often do not give adequate information and instructions when assigning work to legal assistants and others. Many lawyers are overloaded and simply don't take the time to delegate and review thoroughly. Proper

305

delegation requires selecting the appropriately skilled person for the task and giving sufficient direction to see that the finished product meets expectations. The information that must be given to the one performing the task includes background on the matter or reference to appropriate files that contain relevant information; an exact description of the end product desired; references to sources that may be of assistance; deadline dates; and, if possible, an estimate of the time the task should take. If a legal assistant is assigned a task without all this information, he or she runs the the risk that too much time will be spent, the end product will not be what was desired, or the project will be turned in later than needed, all of which reflect on the legal assistant's competence. The legal assistant who works for a poor delegator must take the responsibility for getting the information and instructions necessary to complete the project correctly and on time by asking the appropriate questions, repeating back instructions to make sure that they have been understood, and reducing oral instructions to writing, usually in a short confirming memorandum sent back to the attorney.

Legal assistants also find that attorney review of their work is not always as thorough as it should be, especially when the legal assistant is a long-term, trusted employee whose competence has been proven. Even if the legal assistant is confident in his or her work product, the lawyer must review it. If a legal assistant is aware that the lawyer is not reviewing adequately, the legal assistant has an obligation to discuss the matter with the lawyer to encourage more careful review. The problem of inadequate review is exacerbated when a legal assistant is working for an inexperienced attorney or one who does not have expertise in the area of law in which he or she is working. If the legal assistant is very experienced, the lawyer may rely too heavily or even completely on the legal assistant's expertise. Legal assistants in this situation should take measures to see that proper review is conducted by an attorney with sufficient knowledge of the area. For an example of a nonlawyer employee not being properly supervised, read *De Vaux v. American Home Assurance Co.* at the end of this chapter.

A heavy workload often interferes with the performance of lawyers, legal assistants, and other law firm employees. Many factors can make for an unreasonably heavy workload, including taking on too many cases, being poorly organized or managed, or not having adequate staff. Sometimes, especially in litigation, temporary crisis periods emerge before and during trial that require everyone involved in a case to work long and hard hours. Also, legal assistants are sometimes not assertive enough in their dealings with lawyers and take on more work than they can competently handle. There is no doubt that too heavy a workload causes a decline in productivity and quality and increases the likelihood of shortcuts being taken and mistakes being made. A firm that continually operates in this crisis mode is not a good place to work—the work will not be done competently, the stress will be unhealthy, and the staff will not feel personally or professionally satisfied. Legal assistants should avoid working for law firms characterized by such constant pressure caused by excessive workloads. They also should be aware of the potential problems created by a temporary heavy workload. When a project or group of projects require long hours and create high pressure over an extended period, the legal assistant should talk to the appropriate person to see what measures can be taken to remedy the situation. Additional support staff and temporary legal assistants to do the most routine paralegal and clerical work may relieve the situation, making it possible for everyone to function more effectively.

Legal assistants should have a thorough understanding of their own level of competence and, while striving to learn and develop, should not get so far ahead of their knowledge and skills that they are no longer acting competently. This is where continuing education, in-house training programs, and mentoring can come into play. Good legal assistants who want long and satisfying careers are, in essence, always "in school."

An honest self-assessment will help legal assistants identify those personal characteristics that may affect their competence. Well-qualified legal assistants know what particular talents and qualities they do or do not possess and they maximize strong points and minimize deficiencies accordingly. This means working to improve in deficient areas, to strengthen and emphasize natural abilities, and to seek work that matches one's attributes. A legal assistant who is not a good writer should strive to improve those skills but should also avoid positions that require a lot of sophisticated writing. A legal assistant who works well with people should seek a position that will make use of that ability, such as one that involves supervision of others or frequent client contact.

Legal assistants who are having personal, health, or family problems must consider how these problems will impact their work. No one functions as effectively when he or she is troubled, worried, or distracted. A legal assistant who is experiencing difficulties outside the office must be alert to the potential for a decline in productivity and accuracy. He or she should take steps to ensure that quality is maintained. If the problems are serious or ongoing, the legal assistant may want to discuss them with a supervisor to get both the emotional and the practical support needed to carry on competently, and to make sure that the legal assistant's behavior is not misinterpreted. Legal assistants who have alcohol and drug dependency problems should seek professional help, and colleagues and friends in the workplace should encourage them to do so.

REVIEW QUESTIONS

1. What are the elements of competence?
2. Are lawyers responsible for the conduct of their legal assistants? Cite the relevant ABA Model Rule and the relevant section of the ABA Model Guidelines.
3. If lawyers are responsible for the professional actions of their legal assistants, why should legal assistants be concerned about competence? Name as many reasons as you can.
4. Describe and compare legal and paralegal education.
5. What education do lawyers and legal assistants need in addition to their formal professional education?
6. What are three good sources of continuing education programs for legal assistants?
7. What do the NALA and NFPA ethics guidelines say about competence?
8. How does the ABA Model Code define competence? How do the Model Rules define competence?
9. Do lawyers and legal assistants need to have the same knowledge and skills to be competent? How do they differ? What skills might they need in common?
10. How does the trend toward increasing legal specialization affect competence?
11. What role do law firms' in-house training and orientation programs play in developing competence?
12. How does a legal assistant demonstrate competence in preparing a case?
13. What does diligence mean? What is the legal assistant's role in ensuring diligence?
14. Give three examples of common problems associated with a lack of diligence or promptness.
15. Why is communication with clients included in the definition of competence? What role can a legal assistant play in this area?
16. What are three possible consequences of a lawyer's incompetence? What are the possible consequences of a legal assistant's incompetence?
17. Give five examples of common grounds for malpractice claims.

18. What is third-party liability? How is it affecting lawyers who work in governmentally regulated areas of practice?
19. What other kinds of cases might give rise to third-party malpractice claims?
20. Name five steps that a firm can take to prevent malpractice claims.
21. How should a legal assistant respond if he or she is asked to perform a function in which he or she has no expertise?
22. What steps should a legal assistant take if his or her supervising attorney gives incomplete instructions on a project?
23. What should a legal assistant do if the supervising attorney is not carefully reviewing his or her work?
24. What should a legal assistant do if his or her workload is too heavy and cannot be handled in a timely, competent manner?
25. How should a legal assistant react upon learning that another legal assistant has a substance abuse problem that is affecting work?

DISCUSSION QUESTIONS

1. Check the local ethics code in your jurisdiction to see what provisions it contains on competence.
2. Get a listing and description of the disciplinary actions recently taken against attorneys in your state or county. (This information may be published in the local legal newspaper or state bar magazine.) What kinds of ethics violations appear? To what extent do these relate to competence?
3. Do you think states should set minimum levels of education for legal assistants? Why, or why not?
4. What would your model of paralegal education be if you were required to set minimum standards? Consider how much college education and paralegal education should be included. How would your model look if it were an ideal, rather than a minimum?
5. Do you think legal assistants should have to take a licensing exam to demonstrate their competence? Why, or why not?
6. Call five local law firms and find out:

   a. their hiring standards for legal assistants;
   b. whether or not they have in-house orientation or training programs for legal assistants;
   c. whether or not they have a mentoring program for legal assistants; and
   d. whether they pay the cost for their legal assistants to take continuing education or other job-relevant courses.

7. Call your local paralegal association and get a listing of its continuing education programs for the upcoming year.
8. Obtain the current informational materials on NALA's Certified Legal Assistant program and NFPA's PACE program. What are the requirements to take these exams? What is tested on these exams? What percentage of the legal assistants in your area are certified by one of those organizations? Ask ten paralegals who are certified why they took the exam and how it has affected their careers.
9. Are there any other elements you would like to add to the definition of competence given in the ABA Model Rules 1.1, 1.3, and 1.4?
10. To what extent is legal specialization important in your area? Does your jurisdiction have a certified specialist program for attorneys? In what areas of law? How many lawyers are certified? Do most legal assistants "specialize"?
11. Interview five legal assistants who work in five different areas of law, asking them to list the functions that they perform and the functions that their attorney-supervisors perform. Compare the lists and look for functions in common. Is there a difference in the competence needed by lawyers and legal assistants? What generalities can you draw about the differences and commonalities?
12. How can you tell whether or not a law firm encourages competence and quality?
13. What would you do if on your first day on the job, right out of paralegal school, an attorney asked you to draft an antitrust complaint for filing the next day in federal court? Assume that your specialties in school were probate and real estate.
14. What would you do if you were an independent probate paralegal and were asked to do work for an attorney who admittedly knew nothing about probate?
15. What would you do if an attorney passed you in the hall, handed you a phone message, and told you to call the client back and draft whatever documents the client asked for?
16. Describe to what extent an attorney should review the following work:

    a. form complaint;
    b. articles of incorporation;
    c. a trial notebook;
    d. answers to interrogatories;
    e. deposition summaries;
    f. abstracts of documents in a computerized retrieval system.

17. What would you do if you worked for a firm that was always in an overworked, crisis mode?
18. What would you do if you knew that attorneys in your firm frequently took short cuts, such as not gathering facts carefully or not researching legal issues thoroughly?
19. Name three of your personal strengths that may help you in your career as a legal assistant. Name three weaknesses that might interfere with your competence or success. Considering these, what should you do to maximize your strengths and minimize your weaknesses? What kind of work is best suited to you? What kind of work environment?
20. What would you do if your best paralegal friend at work was having a personal problem and asked you to cover for his or her tardiness, long personal phone calls, and so forth? What if you could see that this friend was making a lot of mistakes at work? Would it make any difference if the friend were an attorney? Your supervising attorney?
21. Look for articles in the local legal newspaper and bar journals about malpractice cases and bring them to class to discuss.

CASES FOR ANALYSIS

In this disciplinary matter, a lawyer was sanctioned for incompetence and violations arising out of the same relationship with nonlawyers.

In re Gillaspy
640 N.E.2d 1054 (Ind. 1994)

Respondent Joseph M. Gillaspy was charged by Verified Complaint for Disciplinary Action with numerous violations of the *Rules of Professional Conduct for Attorneys at Law.* . . . Rothfuss referred Hamilton and Hamilton's wife to James Wilson ("Wilson") of JNW Management Corporation for the purpose of filing a petition for bankruptcy, pursuant to Chapter 13 of the United States Bankruptcy Code. Like Rothfuss, Wilson was not a lawyer. On August 1, 1991, a voluntary petition for bankruptcy was filed in United States Bankruptcy Court, Southern Division, Indianapolis, on behalf of Hamilton and his wife. The petition listed Respondent as the attorney of record, even though Wilson had prepared the paperwork relative to the petition. On November 7, 1991,

Hamilton and his wife attended the first meeting of creditors, pursuant to Section 341 of the bankruptcy code. At this meeting, Hamilton met Respondent for the first time.

Hamilton did not pay Respondent for the legal services. Respondent received a check for $300.00 from Benefit Planners as payment for the legal services he rendered on behalf of Hamilton. Rothfuss, as president of Benefit Planners, signed the check. Respondent undertook to represent other individuals in bankruptcy matters under circumstances similar to those in the Hamilton bankruptcy.

The agreed facts clearly and convincingly establish that Respondent violated Ind. Professional Conduct Rule 1.4(b) since, having never even met Hamilton or his wife prior to the filing of the bankruptcy petition, Respondent did not explain matters to them to the extent reasonably necessary to permit them to make informed decisions regarding the representation. Because he abdicated the factual and legal analysis of this matter to non-lawyers Rothfuss and Wilson, Respondent failed to provide competent representation and therefore violated Prof.Cond.R. 1.1. Respondent violated Prof.Cond.R. 1.8(f) by accepting compensation from Rothfuss for representing Hamilton, while non-lawyers Rothfuss and Wilson exercised what should have been Respondent's independent professional judgment and confidential lawyer-client relationship between Respondent and the Hamiltons. By sharing fees with Rothfuss and Wilson, allowing them to direct and regulate his professional judgment in rendering legal services, and by assisting Rothfuss and Wilson in activity which constituted the unauthorized practice of law, Respondent violated Prof.Cond.R. 5.4(a), 5.4(c), and 5.5(b). . . .

We are inclined to accept the agreed sanction, noting that Respondent's fee-sharing arrangement with non-lawyers clearly threatened Respondent's independent professional judgment and competence. However, we are also cognizant of the fact that none of the bankruptcy petitioners filed grievances relating to any unprofessional or incompetent representation by Respondent; that Respondent ceased his affiliation with Benefit Planners immediately upon learning that there were ethical problems with the arrangement; and that Respondent was completely cooperative and truthful during the Commission's investigation of this matter. The Commission and Respondent characterize Respondent's dealings with Benefit Planners as resulting from professional naivete, rather than from a willful scheme to take advantage of clients. . . .

It is, therefore, ordered that Respondent, Joseph M. Gillaspy, is suspended from the practice of law for a period of not less than ninety (90) days, beginning November 14, 1994, with automatic reinstatement to occur immediately after the conclusion of the suspension period. . . .

Questions about the Case

1. Who prepared and filed the bankruptcy? Who appeared at the hearing?
2. What functions did the lawyer Gillaspy and the nonlawyer involved perform in this legal matter? Which constituted the practice of law?
3. Why did the representation here amount to "incompetence"?
4. Who did the clients pay? How was Gillaspy paid?
5. What were the mitigating factors in setting the sanction? What was the sanction? Do you believe that it was an appropriate sanction?

A case of a missed statute of limitations illustrates how an attorney is held responsible for the acts of his or her employees in a malpractice case. As you read, consider how a legal assistant might get into a situation like this.

De Vaux v. American Home Assurance Co.
387 Mass. 814, 444 N.E.2d 355 (1983)

. . . We summarize the facts found by the master. On July 17, 1971, the plaintiff fell as she entered a Curtis Compact Store in Hanover. The plaintiff claims that she suffered a serious back injury as a result of this fall. On May 11, 1973, the plaintiff was admitted to South Shore Hospital for removal of a spinal disc.

A few days after her fall, the plaintiff called the defendant attorney's office seeking legal advice. That day a secretary in the attorney's office returned the plaintiff's call and advised her to write a letter to the store stating that she had fallen in the store and received an injury. The secretary also arranged a medical examination for the plaintiff with the store's insurance company. Finally, the secretary instructed the plaintiff to write a letter to the defendant attorney requesting legal assistance.

Following that instruction, the plaintiff personally delivered a letter to the attorney's secretary. In this letter, the plaintiff described her fall. The letter ended with the question. "Would you kindly advise me legally?" The secretary misfiled this letter. The defendant did not discover the letter until June, 1974, after the statute of limitations on the plaintiff's tort claim had run.

313

From the date she delivered the letter in 1971 until June, 1974, the plaintiff did not visit the defendant attorney's office or speak with him. In the interim, the plaintiff called the attorney's office a number of times. Each time, the plaintiff was told that her calls would be returned. But the attorney never returned any of her calls.

In February, 1978, the plaintiff filed a complaint in the Superior Court alleging that she retained the attorney to represent her concerning the fall at the store. In his answer, the defendant attorney denied that he was ever retained to represent the plaintiff in regard to the fall. . . . "It is the general rule that an attorney's liability for malpractice is limited to some duty owed to a client. . . . Where there is no attorney/client relationship there is no breach or dereliction of duty and therefore no liability."

On appeal, the plaintiff advances two theories in support of her claim that there was an attorney-client relationship between the plaintiff and the attorney. First, the plaintiff argues that the secretary had actual authority to take the actions that she did. Therefore, the secretary's knowledge of the plaintiff's request for legal assistance can be imputed to the attorney. When an agent acquires knowledge in the scope of her employment, the principal, here the attorney, is held to have constructive knowledge of that information. There is a question for the jury whether the secretary's actions concerning the plaintiff's request for the attorney's services were within the scope of her employment. The plaintiff argues that, because the attorney had constructive knowledge of her problem, she reasonably relied on him to provide her with legal assistance. The plaintiff asserts that, therefore, her reliance established an attorney-client relationship.

The plaintiff also contends that the secretary had apparent authority to establish an attorney-client relationship on behalf of the defendant. Apparent authority "results from conduct by the principal which causes a third person reasonably to believe that a particular person . . . has authority to enter into negotiations or to make representations as his agent." Applying the doctrine of apparent authority to this case, the plaintiff claims that the attorney placed his secretary in a position where prospective clients might reasonably believe that she had the authority to establish an attorney-client relationship. There is a question of fact for the jury whether the attorney permitted his secretary to act as she did, thereby creating the appearance of authority. . . .

We find support for both of the plaintiff's theories in the Massachusetts Canons of Ethics and Disciplinary Rules . . . particularly Canon 3, a structure against the unauthorized practice of law. The Canons can be interpreted using the Ethical Considerations of the American Bar

Association, Code of Professional Responsibility and Canons of Judicial Ethics (1970). Ethical Consideration 3-6 states:

> A lawyer often delegates tasks to clerks, secretaries, and other lay persons. Such delegation is proper if the lawyer maintains a direct relationship with his client, supervises the delegated work, and has complete professional responsibility for the work product. This delegation enables a lawyer to render legal service more economically and efficiently.

The supervised use of lay persons in a legal office is intended to permit their involvement in most matters, but not in the direct practice of law. See ABA Comm. on Professional Ethics, Formal Op. 316 (1967).

Therefore an attorney should not permit lay persons even to appear to form the attorney-client relationship with a prospective client, because that is part of the practice of law. See ABA Comm. on Ethics and Professional Responsibility, Informal Op. 998 (1967) (advising against a lay employee conducting the initial interview of a client if the client does not confer with the attorney soon afterwards). It is a question for the jury whether the attorney allowed his secretary to act as she did, and whether he knew what she was doing. We believe that an attorney who places his lay employees in a position which may deceive prospective clients as to the attorney's willingness or ability to represent them may be liable for malpractice for the negligence of those employees.

Therefore, there are factual issues for the jury whether the attorney in this case put himself in a position in which he should be liable to the plaintiff. We reverse the judgment of dismissal and remand the case to the Superior Court for trial.

So ordered.

Questions about the Case

1. Why do you think the secretary acted as she did in this case? What ethics rules did she break? Were her functions akin to those of a legal assistant?
2. Explain the two arguments of the plaintiff about actual authority and apparent authority. What does the court decide about these theories, and why?
3. What rule covered in Chapter 3 on unauthorized practice was violated by the secretary's actions in this case?
4. How does the court dispose of this case?

In the following malpractice case, a former client sought recovery from the law clerk who mishandled the transaction.

Busch v. Flangas
837 P.2d 438 (Nev. 1992)

Appellant Mary Busch is the former owner of the Busch Bavarian Pastry Shop. In 1984, Busch agreed to sell the shop. A customer suggested that Busch contact respondent Delwin Potter, who worked for respondent Peter Flangas, to help draw up documents pertaining to the sale of the bakery. Believing Potter to be a lawyer, Busch contacted Flangas' law office and made an appointment with Potter. Potter was in fact a law clerk employed by Flangas. The necessary documents for the sale of the bakery were prepared, but a UCC-1 financing statement necessary to the perfecting of Busch's security interest in the bakery equipment pending final payment was never filed. The buyers failed to satisfy their financial obligation to Busch and eventually filed bankruptcy. Busch, as an unsecured creditor, lost her interest in the bakery equipment.

Busch instituted a malpractice action against Potter and Flangas, alleging that Potter's negligence caused her to lose her security interest in the bakery equipment. Busch claimed that Flangas was also liable for his employee's negligence. Potter and Flangas claimed that another attorney had supervised Potter's work, thus relieving both of them of any liability. The district court granted summary judgment in favor of Potter and Flangas, and Busch appealed. . . .

Busch presented substantial evidence indicating that the transaction required a UCC-1 financing statement, which Potter failed to file, to secure her interest in the bakery equipment. Although Potter is not an attorney, he can be subject to a legal malpractice claim if he attempts to provide legal services. (Citation omitted.) Therefore, summary judgment was improperly granted as to Potter.

Flangas contends that he cannot be liable for malpractice because he never met Busch nor attempted to provide legal services for her. Clearly, this contention is without merit. Busch's claim against Flangas states a cause of action on a *respondeat superior* theory. Thus, Flangas may be liable for Potter's negligence if Potter was acting within the scope of his employment when he performed services for Busch. (Citation omitted.)

Respondents concede that Potter was employed by Flangas, but claim that on this occasion Potter was supervised by another attorney[1] who maintains a separate practice, but who nevertheless occasionally utilized the services of Potter or Flangas' secretaries.

Busch claims that Flangas was responsible for supervising Potter's work, and attached to her opposition to the motions for summary judgment copies of Potter's paychecks from Flangas covering the period of time when Potter performed services for Busch. At a minimum, Busch raised a genuine issue below as to Flangas' liability. Therefore, summary judgment was improperly granted as to Flangas. (Citation omitted.)

After careful consideration, we have determined that the other issues raised by the parties are without merit. The summary judgment in favor of respondents is reversed, and the case is remanded to the district court for a trial on the merits.

SPRINGER, Justice, with whom LEAVITT, District Judge, agrees, dissenting:

I conclude that the trial court was correct in granting summary judgment; therefore, I respectfully dissent.

The Flangas Judgment

The case against Flangas is based on actual negligence on his part and not on vicarious liability. An employer is liable for an employee's acts which the employer authorized or ratified, upon familiar principles of negligence and agency. Vicarious liability, on the other hand, is based on conduct which is not the conduct of the employer but which extends to any and all *tortious* conduct which an agent performs within the "scope of employment." Busch does not plead a case for vicarious liability nor does she aver that all of Potter's tortious acts were done in the scope of his employment for Flangas.

Rather than trying to impute Potter's negligence to Flangas under the doctrine of *respondeat superior,* Busch's complaint charges specific and independent negligence on the part of Flangas. According to the complaint, "Flangas knew that Defendant Potter was representing himself as an attorney and performing legal services on behalf of Defendant Flangas." In other words, Flangas knowingly let a non-lawyer work in his office *as* a lawyer. There is no evidence that this charge is true.

Busch argues in her "Opposition to Motion for Summary Judgment" that Potter is guilty of "malpractice per se." This may be true, but absent an allegation that such untoward and outrageous action by

1. The statute of limitations has run against this other attorney, precluding a claim against him.

Potter was done in the scope and power of his employment by Flangas, no vicarious liability can exist.

Because there is no claim for vicarious liability and because there is no evidence to support actual negligence on the part of Flangas, I would affirm the trial court's summary judgment in his favor.

The Potter Judgment

The gist of Busch's claim against Potter is that Potter "represented himself to Plaintiff as an attorney and further represented that he was competent and able to prepare all documents . . . and . . . to protect the Plaintiff's [legal] interests," and that Potter was then guilty of legal malpractice when he "negligently failed and omitted to cause the UCC-1 Financing Statement to be filed with the appropriate agency."

If, as is clearly the case, Potter had not "represented himself to Plaintiff as an attorney," he could not, of course, have undertaken the duty "to prepare all documents" nor "to fully protect the Plaintiff's [legal] interests." By Busch's own testimony, neither Flangas nor Potter ever represented that Potter was a lawyer. Busch "assumed" that Potter was a lawyer because one of her customers at the bakery told her so. There is no evidence that Potter was either acting as a lawyer or representing himself to be a lawyer. According to Potter's affidavit, he prepared the documents in question at the behest of and *under* the supervision of another attorney, John Stone. I believe that the trial court was correct in concluding that there was no evidence to support the allegation that Potter "represented himself to Plaintiff as an attorney" or that as a non-attorney working for attorney Stone, Potter owed a duty to Busch relative to the preparation and filing of the UCC documents. I would affirm the trial court's summary judgment in favor of Potter.

Questions about the Case

1. What was the error that constituted incompetence in this case?
2. What functions did the law clerk perform in the rendering of legal services in this transaction?
3. What attorneys were named? What was their defense?
4. Who is the lawyer who is not named in the complaint but was involved? Why wasn't this attorney named?
5. What are the possible results at the trial court?
6. What two major points did the dissent make?
7. Do you agree with the majority opinion or the dissent? Why?

The court in this malpractice case holds a nonlawyer who provided legal services to the same standard as a lawyer.

Webb v. Pomeroy
8 Kan. App. 2d 246, 655 P.2d 465 (1983)

The plaintiffs directly appeal from a directed verdict at the conclusion of the evidence entered in favor of each defendant during a jury trial. In chronological order, the issues involved in this appeal are:

1. A claim of legal malpractice against Charles Pomeroy, who is not an attorney, in representing plaintiffs in a real estate transaction.
2. A claim of fraudulent misrepresentation and concealment by Charles Pomeroy as to the effectiveness of the services he undertook for the plaintiffs.
3. A claim of legal malpractice against Charles' brother, Emerson Pomeroy (hereafter E. Pomeroy), who is an attorney, in representing plaintiffs in a lawsuit he filed which purported to establish the validity of the services his brother performed for the plaintiffs.

As will be detailed, in 1971 the plaintiffs transferred their interest in 56 acres of land and their home to Mr. and Mrs. Earnest Emerson in order to prevent foreclosure and cancellation of their contract of sale. Charles handled the transaction and, according to plaintiff, continually promised to secure repurchase rights from the Emersons and repeatedly indicated that he had done so. When the Emersons indicated the property was theirs some years later, the plaintiffs, as suggested by Charles, employed Emerson Pomeroy to represent them in a lawsuit. He appeared in court in their 1975 suit against the Emersons to quiet plaintiffs' title to the land. That suit resulted in title being found to be in the Emersons, notwithstanding Charles' work and his assurances. That suit will be referred to as "the underlying suit."

Within seven months after the decision in the underlying suit, this suit was brought claiming malpractice by both Charles and E. Pomeroy. . . .

Charles advised them he could handle everything except appearing in court. He prepared a deed from them to the Emersons, a repurchase contract from the Emersons to the Webbs, with many conditions left blank, and a deed from the Emersons to the Webbs. Charles handled the paper work for "the closing" at a savings association which loaned the money to the Emersons. The deed to the Emersons was delivered to them. Although he did sign the deed back to plaintiffs, Earnest Emerson later refused to sign the repurchase contract. When advised of this, Charles said he would take care of it and assured the Webbs then, and periodically through the years from 1971 until 1975, that they had an enforceable agreement.

The Webbs continued to live on the property, made some improvements, and until 1975 made most of the monthly payments due the savings company on Emersons' loan plus several $1,000 per year payments to the Emersons which they claimed was in accordance with their agreement as reimbursement for the $5,900 advanced by the Emersons. The Emersons regarded this as rent.

In 1975 the Webbs learned that the Emersons were considering selling the farm. They contacted Charles and he indicated he would file a quiet title suit on their behalf. This underlying suit was filed in July and E. Pomeroy appeared for plaintiffs in that proceeding. At E. Pomeroy's direction, they thereafter made payments under the alleged repurchase agreement into Topeka Escrow Service. . . .

Directed Verdict as to Emerson Pomeroy

The Webbs recognize that in order to recover against E. Pomeroy they are subject to the "but for" rule: But for the negligence of our attorney we would have had a successful result in the (underlying) lawsuit. To satisfy this rule, it was necessary that the Webbs successfully retry the underlying lawsuit in this suit. . . .

For a number of reasons, the Webbs in this suit failed to prove their underlying suit, *i.e.,* that they had a valid enforceable contract with the Emersons. Of controlling significance is their failure to show a meeting of the minds on interest. . . .

We hold that the directed verdict in favor of E. Pomeroy was proper. His request for costs and attorney fees, however, is denied.

Directed Verdict as to Charles Pomeroy

The validity of the trial court's judgment in favor of C. Pomeroy is not so readily resolved. The petition alleges breach of contract and tort. We believe it sounds basically in tort and address that only. The trial court found it was barred by the two-year statute of limitations, measured from the commission of the tort in 1971. . . .

Before discussing our position as to . . . determining when the statute of limitations began to run, it is necessary to consider what was the legal relationship between Charles and the plaintiffs, and what was his resulting duty. We hold he was in the same position as a regularly admitted practicing attorney and bound to the same degree of knowledge, skill, dedication, and ethical conduct as the average member of the bar.

In *Ford v. Guarantee Abstract & Title Co.,* 220 Kan. 244, 553 P.2d 254 (1976), a nonlawyer corporation undertook the handling of legal papers relative to the purchase of a house. Upon its mishandling the matter, it was found to have "assumed to discharge the same duties as an individual conveyancer or attorney." Having done so, it was "governed by the principles applicable to attorney and client." The court also noted that "the relationship of an attorney to his client is fiduciary in character, binding the attorney to the highest degree of fidelity and good faith to his client." 220 Kan. at 261, 553 P.2d 254.

To apply these rules to Charles, he is held to have known, whether he really did or not, that there was no binding oral reconveyance contract. His conduct in adding the phrase to the signed copy of the first contract, his assurance that he would get Mr. Emerson's signature to the reconveyance contract, and his handling of the reconveyance deed would suggest he did know.

This brings us to his assurances that the Webbs had a valid repurchase agreement. It is not consistent with "the highest degree of fidelity and good faith" to a client, as expressed in *Ford* to knowingly misrepresent. Rather, the lawyer's duty is to fully disclose. A client is entitled to rely on that duty. In our view, these reassurances constituted fraudulent concealment. . . .

It therefore follows that Charles seeks to take advantage of his wrongful conduct when he claims the plaintiffs should have sought a lawyer. He suggested this to support his claim that their injury was "reasonably ascertainable" as soon as Mr. Emerson refused to sign the repurchase agreement. . . .

The directed verdict is affirmed as to Emerson Pomeroy and reversed and remanded for a new trial as to Charles Pomeroy.

Questions about the Case

1. What legal work was performed by the lawyer and the nonlawyer in this case?
2. Did the nonlawyer hold himself out to be a lawyer? Did he purport to have the authority and knowledge needed to effectuate the clients' wishes?
3. What mistake was made that caused the clients to lose their rights? Who made this mistake?
4. What did the court decide about the lawyer's liability? Why?

321

5. What did the court decide about the nonlawyer's liability? Why?
6. Does the court's reasoning apply to legal assistants?

In the following case, a nonlawyer makes a serious error in preparing a legal document for a client. The plaintiff, a third party, is damaged and sues the nonlawyer for the amount of damages. Think about how this case might be used in situations in which a "legal technician" acts incompetently.

Biakanja v. Irving
49 Cal.2d 647, 320 P.2d 16 (1958)

Plaintiff's brother, John Maroevich, died, leaving a will which devised and bequeathed all of his property to plaintiff. The will, which was prepared by defendant, a notary public, was denied probate for lack of sufficient attestation. Plaintiff, by intestate succession, received only one-eighth of the estate, and she recovered a judgment against defendant for the difference between the amount which she would have received had the will been valid and the amount distributed to her.

Defendant, who is not an attorney, had for several years written letters and prepared income tax returns for Maroevich. The will was typed in defendant's office and "subscribed and sworn to" by Maroevich in the presence of defendant, who affixed his signature and notarial seal to the instrument. Sometime later Maroevich obtained the signatures of two witnesses to the will, neither of whom was present when Maroevich signed it. These witnesses did not sign in the presence of each other, and Maroevich did not acknowledge his signature in their presence.

An attorney who represented Maroevich's stepson in the probate proceedings testified that he had a telephone conversation with defendant shortly after Maroevich's death, in which defendant said he prepared the will and notarized it. According to the attorney, defendant, in discussing how the will was witnessed, "admonished me to the effect that I was a young lawyer, I'd better go back and study my law books some more, that anybody knew a will which bore a notarial seal was a valid will, didn't have to be witnessed by any witnesses."

The court found that defendant agreed and undertook to prepare a valid will and that it was invalid because defendant negligently failed to have it properly attested. The findings are supported by the evidence.

The principal question is whether defendant was under a duty to exercise due care to protect plaintiff from injury and was liable for damage caused plaintiff by his negligence even though they were not in privity of contract. In *Buckley v. Gray* (1895), 110 Cal. 339 142 P. 900, 52 Am. St. Rep. 88, 31 A.L.R. 862, it was held that a person who was named as a beneficiary under a will could not recover damages from an attorney who negligently drafted and directed the execution of the will with the result that the intended beneficiary was deprived of substantial benefits. The court based its decision on the ground that the attorney owed no duty to the beneficiary because there was no privity of contract between them. *Mickel v. Murphy*, 147 Cal. App. 2d 718 [305 P.2d 993], relying on *Buckley v. Gray*, supra, held that a notary public who prepared a will was not liable to the beneficiary for failing to have it properly executed. When *Buckley v. Gray*, supra, was decided in 1895, it was generally accepted that, with the few exceptions noted in the opinion in that case, there was no liability for negligence committed in the performance of a contract in the absence of privity. Since that time the rule has been greatly liberalized, and the courts have permitted a plaintiff not in privity to recover damages in many situations for the negligent performance of a contract. . . .

The determination whether in a specific case the defendant will be held liable to a third person not in privity is a matter of policy and involves the balancing of various factors, among which are the extent to which the transaction was intended to affect the plaintiff, the foresee-ability of harm to him, the degree of certainty that the plaintiff suffered injury, the closeness of the connection between the defendant's conduct and the injury suffered, the moral blame attached to the defendant's conduct, and the policy of preventing future harm. Here, the "end and aim" of the transaction was to provide for the passing of Maroevich's estate to plaintiff. Defendant must have been aware from the terms of the will itself that, if faulty solemnization caused the will to be invalid, plaintiff would suffer the very loss which occurred. As Maroevich died without revoking his will, plaintiff, but for defendant's negligence, would have received all of the Maroevich estate, and the fact that she received only one-eighth of the estate was directly caused by defendant's conduct.

Defendant undertook to provide for the formal disposition of Maroevich's estate by drafting and supervising the execution of a will. This was an important transaction requiring specialized skill, and defen-dant clearly was not qualified to undertake it. His conduct was not only negligent but was also highly improper. He engaged in the unauthorized practice of the law, which is a misdemeanor in violation of section 6126 of the Business and Professions Code. Such conduct should be discouraged and not protected by immunity from civil liability, as would be the case if plaintiff, the only person who suffered a loss, were denied a right of action.

We have concluded that plaintiff should be allowed recovery despite the absence of privity, and the cases of *Buckley v. Gray* and *Mickel v. Murphy,* are disapproved insofar as they are in conflict with this decision.

The judgment is affirmed.

Questions about the Case

1. Why do you think the defendant prepared the will? What was the mistake in preparing the will that caused it to be invalid?
2. Explain who the plaintiff is in this case. What is privity of contract? How does it apply here?
3. What was the rule on third-party recovery in such cases prior to this decision?
4. What factors will the court consider in future cases to determine whether to allow third-party liability?
5. How is this ruling relevant to the increase in malpractice claims by nonclients?

Special Issues
in Advocacy

This chapter describes the most critical of the many dilemmas that confront litigation paralegals during the adversarial process. It also explores the ethics principles that govern advocacy for both attorneys and legal assistants. Chapter 9 covers:

- the role of the attorney and legal assistant in litigation and their duty to represent clients zealously
- ethics rules and statutes that prohibit unmeritorious claims, delay, and abuse of discovery
- disruptive courtroom tactics and sanctions for those actions
- sanctions for disobeying court orders
- the court's contempt power and its use
- duties of candor and honesty in areas involving legal assistants
- prohibited relationships and communications with judges
- prohibited contact with jurors
- restrictions on contact with represented parties and unrepresented persons
- contact with witnesses
- rules on trial publicity and how these affect legal assistants
- special rules for prosecutors and their legal assistants

A. Introduction

The practice of law has changed over the past 50 years in response to the proliferation of laws, their increased complexity, and their now-pervasive impact on so many areas of modern life and business. One aspect of this change is that most lawyers no longer go to court regularly. The majority of lawyers in this country do not litigate matters, either civil or criminal, and many lawyers never go to court. The areas of law in which these lawyers practice are many, including corporate, tax, business transactions, real estate, estate planning, probate, environmental law, trademark, and copyright and patent.

At the same time, there has been considerable debate over whether society is too litigious, as people look to the courts to handle all kinds of disputes not necessarily suited for judicial resolution. Some commentators believe that there is a litigation explosion; others argue that this claim is not borne out by empirical research. Politicians blame the rising cost of medical services and insurance on the growth in litigation against doctors and hospitals. Punitive damage awards have been vigorously attacked. From within the bench and bar, there has been considerable discussion about, and some progress toward, streamlining the litigation process by encouraging alternate dispute resolution, limiting discovery, and instituting more effective trial procedures. This environment dictates that litigation paralegals must not only be diligent in their efforts to meet high standards of competence and ethics but that they keep up with the ever-changing ethics rules and court decisions that govern conduct in litigation.

Unlike lawyers, the majority of legal assistants work in litigation. And, contrary to the commonly held perception of litigation, most of the work is done out of court, before trial. The role for the legal assistant in litigation is expansive, including fact gathering, interviewing clients and witnesses, drafting pleadings and motions, conducting legal research, drafting discovery requests and motions and responding to discovery, preparing for trial by summarizing and indexing documents and depositions, locating and preparing expert witnesses, and preparing demonstrative evidence. Many litigation paralegals accompany their attorney-employers to court and assist in court by taking notes, making observations about jurors' reactions to the proceedings, handling logistics and emergencies, and doing last-minute research. As the discovery experts in a case, legal assistants frequently have a mastery of the facts and evidence that is of tremendous help to the attorney, who must concentrate his or her attention on presenting the case, examining and cross-examining witnesses, and making objections.

326

Because legal assistants play such a major role in litigation, they need a strong understanding of the ethics rules governing advocacy. Violations of these rules are often not committed by an attorney acting alone; the attorney may act through an agent or may involve an unwitting legal assistant.

All attorneys have an ethical duty to represent clients zealously. ABA Model Code of Professional Responsibility, Canon 7, DR 7-101, EC 7-1; ABA Model Rules of Professional Conduct 1.3 and comment. Zealous representation entails exercising one's best efforts on the client's behalf within the boundaries of law and ethics. The duty to represent clients zealously has special meaning in the context of the lawyer's role as an advocate. It sometimes clashes with other legal-ethical duties or moral imperatives, such as the lawyer's duty of candor to the court and the proper administration of justice, the rules of client confidentiality, and the search for the truth that forms the basis of the adversary system. The following sections will cover some of these conflicts and the ethics rules on advocacy that affect legal assistants most directly.

B. Unmeritorious Claims, Delay, and Discovery Abuse

Both the ABA Model Code and ABA Model Rules have provisions that prohibit lawyers from bringing *unmeritorious claims* or *defenses*. DR 7-102 identies two specific kinds of positions that fall into this category. DR 7-102(A)(1) prohibits any action that would only serve to harass or to injure another maliciously, and (A)(2) forbids advancing a claim or defense that is unwarranted under existing law unless the lawyer has a good faith argument to change the law. ABA Model Rule 3.1 contains comparable provisions, using the term "frivolous" for unmeritorious claims made for whatever purpose.

Violations of this rule most commonly occur when an attorney brings an unwarranted action to gain some advantage over the opposition, to force a party to expend funds to defend the action, or simply to earn fees. Sometimes a lawyer will bring an action based on inaccurate information supplied by the client, without conducting any investigation of his or her own. If the action is in fact unmeritorious, the attorney may be found to have violated ethics rules, court rules, or statutes for failing to investigate. Many courts have held the attorney to a duty to make a reasonable inquiry unless immediate

327

action is necessary to protect the client's interests; others have found that the attorney may proceed in reliance on the truth of a client's story. An example of an unmeritorious claim is a plaintiff who sues his competitor without proper grounds under the law merely for the purpose of driving him or her out of business. The ethics rules on unmeritorious claims do provide an important exception: if there is a good faith argument for changing the existing law. The rule also acknowledges the criminal defense lawyer's right to require that all elements of a crime be proven.

Related to unmeritorious claims are *abuses of the discovery process.* Conducting excessive or unnecessary discovery has been employed as a strategy to delay litigation, to burden the opposing counsel, to raise the cost to the opposition and, generally, to wear down the opposing party and counsel. Manipulation of discovery rules to gain tactical advantage has become quite common, but it causes judicial ire and increases the public's disdain for lawyers. Most states have attempted to address the problems of discovery abuse by adopting statutes and/or court rules to streamline discovery, to expedite the pre-trial stage and to discourage excessive and unnecessarily lengthy discovery. Such rules set limits on the number of interrogatories that can be served on others, establish strict deadlines for completion of discovery, and mandate alternative dispute resolution and pre-trial settlement procedures.

The ABA Model Code DR 7-102(A) brings discovery abuse within its range, but the ABA Model Rules were expanded to contain more specific provisions about discovery. Rule 3.4(d) specifically forbids making frivolous pretrial discovery requests and failing to comply with proper discovery requests. Violations of this rule occur, for example, when an attorney requests discovery that is beyond the scope of the case, for example, flooding the opposition with irrelevant interrogatories; giving incomplete answers to interrogatories; requesting discovery of confidential, sensitive, or embarrassing information; or making unfounded objections to discovery. Or, an attorney may respond to discovery such as a document production by providing much more than what was requested, perhaps "hiding" a relevant document in the volumes of paper.

DR 7-102(A)(1) prohibits a lawyer from delaying a trial solely to harass another. ABA Model Rule 3.2 is more specific and directive in its language about delay, requiring lawyers to make reasonable efforts to expedite litigation consistent with clients' interests. The comment to this rule uses strong language, citing as improper causes for delay a lawyer's convenience, a deliberate frustration of the opposition's legitimate goals, and financial gain. Some real-life examples of unethical delays for which attorneys have been sanctioned are refusing to respond to communications of opposing counsel; repeated failure to appear at hearings, settlement conferences, or depositions; unnecessary delays in filing motions to disqualify counsel; failing to complete discovery in accordance with court rules, court orders, or statutes.

Violations of this rule may also cross over with incompetence as timeliness in handling client matters is an element of competence. But often intentional delays are created to gain a tactical advantage over the opposition. Discipline for bringing unmeritorious claims or defenses, abusing discovery, or causing unnecessary delays is relatively rare. When it does occur, it is usually in a particularly egregious case, such as a multiplicity of frivolous lawsuits, or when coupled with other violations like incompetence or failure to obey a court order.

One important remedy available to the victims of such conduct is a civil suit against the client, the lawyer, or both for *malicious prosecution or abuse of process*. Grounds for malicious prosecution exist when a civil lawsuit or criminal prosecution has been brought, without probable cause and with malice, after the defendant prevails in the action. Limited immunity for attorneys exists in some states if it is shown that the lawyer acted in good faith. An abuse of process action may be brought when the legal process is misused to achieve other than legitimate legal purposes, such as filing a criminal complaint to force the defendant to pay a debt.

Another more frequently employed remedy is the imposition of sanctions under the contempt power of the court, which is usually used when a lawyer disobeys a court order or acts in a manner that is extremely disruptive to the proceedings. Contempt is covered in more detail under Section C below.

A related court-imposed remedy that has become quite effective is the use of *monetary sanctions*. Under federal statutes and procedural rules, and under court rules or statutes, in most states and the District of Columbia, courts are granted authority to impose sanctions against lawyers, clients, or both for actions that are unwarranted, delaying, or harassing. The most frequently used rule in federal court is Federal Rule of Civil Procedure 11 which provides for appropriate sanctions against attorneys, clients, or both for filing unwarranted or other objectionable pleadings and papers. Rule 11 is supplemented by Federal Rule of Civil Procedure 37, which provides for sanctions for failure to make or cooperate in discovery. Rule 11 specifically requires that documents be "well grounded in fact" and "warranted by existing law or a good faith argument for the extension, modification or reversal of existing law"; that documents not be filed for "any improper purpose, such as to harass or to cause unnecessary delay or needless increase in the cost of litigation." Sanctions may include payment of expenses and attorney's fees to the opposing party or parties. Some courts have also ordered attorneys, clients, or both to pay fines to the court. A judge may also dismiss a complaint with prejudice under Rule 11.

Rule 11 was adopted to help alleviate unnecessary delays and paperwork in federal court, and has been widely used by federal judges. The amount of sanction awards is sometimes quite substantial. Examples of some kinds of cases in which sanctions have been awarded under Rule 11 are using abusive language in a motion, filing an action unwarranted by law for purely political reasons, asking for an inflated amount of damages, and filing a motion to disqualify counsel purely to delay the proceedings.

Amendments to Rule 11 adopted recently attempted to make the application of sanctions more uniform and fair. These changes are: (1) make the imposition of sanctions discretionary instead of mandatory; (2) allow time for a party to remedy conduct after mandatory notification that sanctions will be sought; (3) allow attorneys to file pleadings based on information and belief, after a reasonable inquiry; (4) favor nonmonetary sanctions that will deter the wrongful conduct; and (5) make law firms, not just individual attorneys, responsible for violations.

Rule 11 applies only to pleadings, motions, and other documents filed with the court. Other federal statutes, however, provide for sanctions for abuses that do not fit into this category of actions. The U.S. Code authorizes federal judges to impose sanctions against an attorney who "multiplies the proceedings in any case unreasonably and vexatiously." 28 U.S.C. §1927. Section 1928 and Federal Rule of Appellate Procedure 38 provide for damages awarded to the prevailing party for delays caused by frivolous appeals.

While most states also have specific rules or statutes authorizing sanctions, some cases recognize the inherent authority of a court over its proceedings as the basis for imposing sanctions. See the *Chira v. Lockheed* case at end of this chapter for an example of sanctions being imposed by a trial judge for delays and abuse of discovery.

C. Disruption in the Courtroom and Disobeying Court Orders

Trial lawyers are bound by ethics rules to conduct themselves in a dignified and courteous manner in court (ABA Model Code DR 7-106(C)(6)) and not to disrupt proceedings (ABA Model Rule 3.5(c)).

Most interpretations of these two rules have found that the Model Rule requires an intent to disrupt whereas the Model Code does not.

Frequently, conduct that judges may consider disruptive is the result of a lawyer's efforts to represent his or her client zealously. Sometimes a lawyer's zeal is transformed into an enthusiasm that oversteps the bounds of courtesy. Sometimes unacceptable conduct in court is designed to influence the jury or to throw the opposing counsel off-track.

Some examples of *disruptive conduct* or dirty tricks in the courtroom are raising an unfounded objection to break opposing counsel's train of thought; making faces or gestures to the judge or the jury; asking a question that alludes to evidence known to be inadmissible; insulting the judge or opposing counsel, for example, by calling them names or accusing them of collusion, racism, incompetence, or bias; referring to the proceedings in an insulting or rude manner; making unsupportable, inflammatory, or prejudicial side remarks to the jury. Disobeying a court order is categorized as disruptive conduct because it interferes with the smooth administration of proceedings and demonstrates disrespect for the tribunal. ABA Model Code DR 7-106(A); ABA Model Rule 3.4(c).

While acts reflecting a lack of respect for the court may subject an attorney to disciplinary action, they are more likely to elicit an immediate response from the judge. Judges may hold an attorney in *contempt* for offensive courtroom conduct or disobeying a court order. Their contempt power is reserved for situations in which the administration of justice and orderly proceedings are immediately and substantially threatened. Generally, the court will warn a lawyer repeatedly before holding him or her in contempt. Contempt is punishable by jail time and may give rise to disciplinary proceedings.

Judges have imposed the contempt sanction on attorneys for a wide variety of disruptive conduct, including continued argument of a point on which the court has ruled; continued mention of inadmissible evidence or prohibited arguments; absence from or tardiness for scheduled court dates; presentation of false evidence; the use of abusive, vulgar, and obscene language; disrespectful, irrelevant, or unjustified criticism of the court. Insults, sarcasm, and the like are not punishable by contempt unless they also obstruct the proceedings.

While most legal assistants are not often in a situation in which they would have the opportunity to engage in this kind of conduct, they should honor this important prohibition. Many legal assistants working in civil litigation and criminal law attend court proceedings and must be aware of and abide by these rules governing conduct in court. NFPA Model Code EC-3.1 calls on paralegals to refrain from "conduct that offends the dignity and decorum" of courts.

D. Candor and Honesty

Both the ABA Model Code and ABA Model Rules contain several provisions calling for lawyers to be *honest* in their representation of clients. Lawyers are not obligated to disclose evidence that is prejudicial to their client unless such information is not privileged and is requested through proper discovery or the lawyer is obligated by some special rule of law. See ABA Model Code DR 7-102(A)(3). But lawyers must otherwise be honest in their presentation of the law and the facts.

The ethics rules specifically prohibit a lawyer from making a false statement of law or fact, ABA Model Code DR 7-102(A)(5) and ABA Model Rule 3.3(a)(1); offering false evidence, DR 7-102(A)(4) and Rule 3.3(a)(4); and not disclosing adverse controlling authority when opposing counsel fails to do so, DR 7-106(B)(1) and Rule 3.3(a)(3). Both the Model Code and Model Rules further require an attorney who later discovers that false evidence has been submitted to correct the fraud on the court. Model Code DR 7-102(B) requires the lawyer to call on the client to rectify the fraud or to reveal the fraud to the court unless the information is privileged. A nonclient's fraud on the court must be promptly revealed to the court. Model Rule 3.3(b) requires disclosure even if the information is protected by confidentiality. Model Rule 3.4 further prohibits lawyers from obstructing access to evidence; altering, destroying, or concealing evidence; and falsifying or allowing others to falsify evidence. (See the section below on witnesses for more on false testimony by witnesses.) Also see Model Code DR 7-109.

Some examples may be instructive. In a disciplinary case, an attorney was censured for failing to disclose to arbitrators that a doctor had changed his diagnosis of the condition of the client. In another case, a court ordered a default judgment against a defendant whose attorney refused to produce a witness that had avoided service. In another, a federal court ordered a default in a race discrimination case against a corporate defendant for altering and destroying key documents, leaving critical information out of affidavits, blocking access in court to relevant information, and intimidating a witness. Other cases have involved a lawyer requesting that his client be released from custody to attend his mother's funeral after it had been held; an attorney providing false information on the value of a client's property; and a lawyer conveying property with the intent to defraud a creditor.

Client perjury has been a difficult legal and ethical dilemma for lawyers. The courts have not been uniform in their handling of this area, and ethics rules and their interpretations also vary from one jurisdiction to the next. As a general rule in a civil case, the lawyer who knows that his or her client intends to commit perjury should not call the client to testify. Most courts recommend or mandate withdrawal from representation or disclosure to the court if the client testifies dishonestly.

Criminal cases present even more difficult problems because of the client's right to testify and to be represented by competent counsel. The U.S. Supreme Court has held that withdrawal is the appropriate action, *Nix v. Whiteside*, 475 U.S. 157 (1986). However, withdrawal may not be allowed by the court at the time of trial, and authorities are split on whether the lawyer should then disclose the intended perjury. Some courts endorse the attorney allowing the defendant to testify in narrative form without the attorney's help. After the perjury has occurred, most courts require the lawyer to seek withdrawal. If withdrawal is not granted, some then require disclosure of the perjury.

Many lawyers believe that client and witness perjury is widespread and on the rise. Recent cases in which judges referred conduct to prosecutors for investigation for perjury have involved relatives (usually mothers) testifying falsely as alibi witnesses for their children; spouses hiding assets in marital dissolution cases; and police lying under oath about the circumstances of an arrest, a search and seizure, or an informant. Some commentators believe that this dishonesty is a natural consequence of the adversarial system. Judges and most lawyers lament this situation but believe that it is unlikely to stop because perjury is so hard to prove and is rarely prosecuted.

The aspect of the *duty of candor* that most often confronts legal assistants is the requirement that adverse authority be disclosed to the court. A legal assistant who finds adverse authority while conducting legal research must report the authority to the attorney, who should include it in appropriate motions or briefs. Generally, the authority must be revealed if it is controlling in the jurisdiction. Because one should assume that the opposing counsel will also find the authority, the best practice is always to cite it and either criticize it or distinguish it legally or factually from the client's case. The *Massey* Case on page 350 illustrates one possible result of controlling adverse authority not being cited. In many other cases, sanctions were imposed directly on the lawyers who were also reported to disciplinary authorities.

Remedies for destroying, altering, or suppressing evidence imposed by disciplinary bodies and the courts are supplemented by obstruction of justice statutes, at both state and federal levels. In addition to criminal charges being brought against the attorney, client, or both, these statutes often provide for sanctions in the pending case, such as default, fines, dismissal, legal fees and costs, and civil causes of action by the injured party. Destruction of evidence also gives rise in some jurisdictions to a civil cause of action for spoliation in which the injured party can collect damages for substantial interference with the ability to prove a claim or defense because the evidence is no longer available. And in some states, courts allow an adverse inference to be drawn from a party's failure to produce the evidence.

REVIEW QUESTIONS

1. Why do legal assistants have to know about the rules governing advocacy?
2. What is zealous representation, and what other ethics rules does it sometimes conflict with?
3. Define two kinds of unmeritorious claims, and give an example of each.
4. When can a lawyer make a claim that is not warranted under existing law?
5. Does a lawyer have a duty to investigate a client's story before filing an action?
6. Give three examples of abuses of the discovery process. How do the ABA Model Code and ABA Model Rules treat such abuses?
7. Give an example of an unethical delay. How do the ABA Model Code and ABA Model Rules treat such delays? What other ethics violations might be involved in an unnecessary delay?
8. Name four kinds of remedies or sanctions that might result from bringing unmeritorious claims, abusing discovery, or causing unnecessary delays.
9. Under what circumstances may an action for malicious prosecution be brought? Abuse of process?
10. What kinds of sanctions may a court impose for unwarranted, delaying, or harassing actions? On whom are they imposed?
11. Give three examples of actions by lawyers that would be disruptive in the courtroom. What do the ethics rules prohibiting such disruptions say? For what reasons might a lawyer be disruptive?
12. What is the most immediate remedy for disruptive conduct in the courtroom or disobedience of a court order?
13. What kinds of actions are prohibited by a lawyer's duty of candor?
14. What must a lawyer do if he or she discovers that false testimony has been given by a nonclient witness? What if the false testimony is given by a client in a civil case? In a criminal case?
15. What should a legal assistant do if he or she discovers adverse controlling authority in the course of research?

16. What are three things that might happen if a lawyer presents false evidence or permits false testimony in court?

DISCUSSION QUESTIONS

1. Why are there proportionately more litigation paralegals than trial lawyers?
2. Are you surprised that lawyers have duties that temper their duty to represent clients zealously? Did you know that a lawyer's highest duty is not just to win?
3. What would you do if you interviewed a client who told you a story that you did not fully believe, and on telling your supervising attorney, he or she told you to draft a complaint on the client's behalf based solely on the client's story?
4. How would you respond if your supervising attorney asked you to prepare an involuntary bankruptcy petition that you knew was unwarranted and designed solely to stop a foreclosure proceeding against your client?
5. What would you do if a supervising attorney asked you to prepare requests for continuances in virtually every case he or she handled? What if you knew it was because the attorney was unprepared and behind in his or her work? What if you knew it was because your client was ill and the attorney was trying to avoid going to trial before the client's death?
6. How would you handle it if the supervising attorney asked you to prepare 300 interrogatories in a case that you knew only warranted 50?
7. What would you do if the supervising attorney asked you to give nonresponsive or incomplete answers to interrogatories? Asked you not to produce certain documents that you believe were requested in a proper document production?
8. How would you react if you were asked to draft interrogatories about the opposition's personal affairs that had no relationship to the case? Interrogatories requesting what you knew was privileged information?
9. Why are court-imposed sanctions such a powerful remedy for abuses in pleading and discovery?
10. Does your jurisdiction have rules or statutes comparable to the federal rules cited in this chapter?
11. Suppose you are responsible for handling the discovery in a case, and the supervising lawyer tells you to disregard a court order to complete discovery. What do you do?

12. Suppose you are a litigation paralegal who is accompanying a lawyer to court for an important trial. What would you do if the supervising lawyer kept whispering to you during opposing counsel's examination of witnesses? What if you knew he or she was doing this to distract the jury?

13. How would you respond if the supervising lawyer asked you to shred documents that you knew were discoverable?

14. What would you do if you found adverse authority in researching a case but did not believe the authority was controlling?

15. What steps would you take if you knew that a client was planning to lie during testimony? What if you knew a nonclient witness was planning to lie? Would your answer depend on whether or not the supervising attorney knew too?

16. Do you believe that the adversary system encourages perjury? Contact the local federal and or state prosecutors and interview several lawyers for their opinions on the matter and ask them how many prosecutions for perjury have been brought in recent years.

E. Relationships and Communications with Judges

As mentioned in Section C above, inappropriate criticism of judges in court may give rise to disciplinary action, although it is not ordinarily grounds for contempt proceedings because of free speech considerations. Ethics rules also prohibit lawyers from making false accusations against a judge. ABA Model Code DR 8-102(A); ABA Model Rule 8.2(a). In most jurisdictions, the courts have held that the First Amendment does not protect lawyers who criticize judges inappropriately because of the strong state interest in protecting public officials and in maintaining respect for the courts. However, in a minority of jurisdictions, particularly California and Texas, discipline of lawyers who criticized judges has been struck down on appeal. In one such case, the lawyer called a judge an anti-Semite and a drunk. In the other, the lawyer called a local judge "a midget among giants" in a letter to the newspaper.

Ethics rules prohibit lawyers from attempting to influence judges and from implying that they can influence a judge. Model Code DR 7-110(A) prohibits a lawyer from giving or lending anything of value to a judge, except a campaign contribution. Model Rule 3.5(a) is more generally worded, prohibiting a lawyer from seeking to influence a judge by any illegal means, for example, bribery. Bribery, of course, is a crime punishable under state law. Rule 8.4(f) also prohibits knowingly assisting a judge in violating the law or the judicial canons. Implying or stating that one can influence a judge (or other public official) is forbidden by DR 9-101(C) and Model Rule 8.4(e). It should be noted that judges are bound by their own ethical canons and rules of conduct in every jurisdiction and that these rules parallel those stated above.

Most likely to come up for legal assistants working in litigation are prohibitions on *ex parte communications* with judges. To ensure fairness in the adversary process, lawyers are prohibited from having contact with the judge in a case without the presence of the opposing counsel. Such secret communications might give the communicating party an unfair advantage or give an appearance of influence or favoritism. The ethics rules that prohibit ex parte communications with judges are set forth in DR 7-110(B) and Model Rule 3.5(b). Exceptions to these rules are made for special ex parte proceedings that legally do not require opposing counsel's presence, such as petitions for a temporary restraining order. The newly revised NFPA Model Code calls attention to the rules regarding ex parte communications in EC-2.1.

F. Contact with Jurors

Ex parte communications with jurors and prospective jurors, before and during trial, are expressly prohibited by ethics rules to prevent influence and bribery. ABA Model Code DR 7-108(A), (B); ABA Model Rule 3.5(a), (b). Lawyers are prohibited from such communications even if they are not involved in the case. A lawyer may not circumvent these rules by using an agent, such as the client or a legal assistant. And legal assistants should honor these rules with great care.

In addition to disciplinary action for such conduct, a *mistrial* is likely to be declared if ex parte communications with jurors come to light. The lawyer's intent or lack of intent to influence the juror or jurors is not relevant in such cases. A lawyer's research on prospective jurors by using an investigator to contact them and ask them questions from a standard questionnaire has been held to be impermissible and led to the criminal conviction and disbarment of the lawyer in one case. Even simple socializing during a break has been held to be grounds to declare a mistrial. See the *Omaha Bank* case on page 359 for an illustration of what can happen when a lawyer has contact with a juror outside the courtroom. Some courts have also disqualified counsel for such improprieties.

Jury tampering is, of course, a crime in every jurisdiction and under federal laws. For example, 18 U.S.C. §§1503 and 1504 make it a crime to attempt to influence a juror.

Communicating with jurors after the conclusion of a trial is forbidden in some states. Other states do not prohibit post-trial communications, which attorneys may desire to help them evaluate their presentation, to find out what influenced the jurors, and to ascertain whether or not the jury deliberated appropriately. The ABA Model Code allows post-trial communications with the limitations that communications may not be made merely "to harass or embarrass the juror or to influence his actions in future jury service." DR 7-108(D). The ABA Model Rules' general provisions on ex parte communications allow post-trial communications if permitted by law, including a court order. Harassment of jurors is prohibited under ABA Model Rules 3.5(b) and 4.4.

Finally, a lawyer is obligated to reveal improper conduct toward or among jurors to the court under ABA Model Code DR 7-108(G). No comparable provision exists under the Model Rules.

G. Contact with Parties and Unrepresented Persons

Attorneys are prohibited from communicating with parties who are represented by counsel and must communicate directly with the person's counsel. ABA Model Code DR 7-104(A)(1); ABA Model Rule 4.2. This rule is based primarily on concerns about overreaching conduct designed to gain advantage over an opponent by disrupting the trust between the attorney and client or influencing the client when he or she is vulnerable because counsel is not present. Unethical solicitation is also a concern. Both the ABA Model Code and ABA Model Rules create two exceptions to the general prohibition against such communications: prior consent of the party's lawyer and when authorized by law.

Rules that limit communication with represented parties have been held not to apply when the represented party is not truly adverse, is seeking a second opinion or new counsel, or is disgruntled with his or her lawyer over the representation or fee and is considering taking action against the lawyer. It should be noted that this prohibition does not restrict the actions of the parties who are free to speak to each other, although most lawyers warn their clients not to do so because of the potential for such conversations interfering with the representation and strategy in the case. The *Crane* case at the end of this chapter illustrates how a lawyer might break this rule and what consequences might follow. Remedies during proceedings may include suppression of evidence and disqualification of counsel. Ethical sanctions would likely follow, especially if the conduct involved blatant dishonesty.

An important debate about the rules prohibiting attorneys from contacting represented persons has been taking place for the last decade in the arena of federal criminal law. In 1989, the United States Attorney General issued a memorandum to prosecutors in the Department of Justice informing them that they were not subject to state ethical codes prohibiting such contacts based on the exception that such acts are "authorized by law." In 1994, the substance of this memorandum was codified in regulations authorizing Department of Justice lawyers to make unconsented ex parte contacts with represented parties and persons during investigations. 28 C.F.R. 77 (1994). The American Bar Association and most other professional associations of lawyers have objected vigorously to this assault on state ethics rules.

The issue may be resolved when a decision is reached in a case on appeal before the Eighth Circuit Court of Appeals. The trial court in that case held that since the legislation authorizing the justice department appropriations requires lawyers to be licensed by a state, Congress must have intended the lawyers to be subject to the ethics rules of the states where they are licensed. *United States v. McDonnell Douglas Corp.*, 961 F. Supp. 1288 (E.D. Mo. 1997). All 50 state supreme court justices have joined in an amicus brief in support of holding federal prosecutors to state ethics rules. The decision has important ramifications beyond the rule on prohibited contact with represented persons since the Department of Justice in at least five states is seeking exemptions from other state ethical constraints.

Ethics rules also restrict the communications a lawyer may have with a party not represented by counsel. Under the ABA Model Code, a lawyer is prohibited from giving advice to such a person if there is a possibility that his or her interests may conflict with a client's. DR 7-104(B). ABA Model Rule 4.3 focuses not on the potential conflict, which would be covered by other rules, but on concern that the party might misunderstand the role of the lawyer. The rule prohibits the lawyer from misrepresenting his or her interest in the matter and requires the lawyer to clarify any misunderstanding about his or her role.

Determining who a lawyer may speak to in a corporate environment is sometimes difficult. Most cases hold that a lawyer may speak to unrepresented former employees of a corporation on the opposing side of litigation unless the employees were privy to privileged information. Current employees may be represented "persons" if the corporation provides counsel to them. Members of a class in a class action are also considered to be represented parties.

Since a lawyer may not circumvent these rules by using an agent, a legal assistant should not engage in improper ex parte communications as part of his or her role in litigation. Legal assistants frequently have contact with clients, opposing counsel, and witnesses. They must refrain from communicating with persons represented by counsel and from misleading persons not represented by counsel about their interest in a matter. Relevant to legal assistants is a recent ABA Formal Ethics Opinion in which it was concluded that a lawyer is responsible for the improper ex parte contacts of an investigator under his or her supervision if the lawyer did not try to prevent the improper contacts, told the investigator to make them, or failed to tell him or her not to make them once the contact came to light. ABA Formal Opinion 95-396 (1995).

H. Contact with Witnesses

A few special rules govern lawyers' contact with witnesses. Like most other rules related to advocacy, these provisions are intended to protect the integrity of the adversary system.

The first category of witness-related rules concerns the communication between the attorney and the witness. A lawyer is forbidden from advising or causing a witness to flee the jurisdiction or to hide to avoid testifying. ABA Model Code DR 7-109(B); ABA Model Rule 3.4(a), (f). In addition to violating ethics rules, such conduct constitutes obstruction of justice and violates statutes that make it a crime to tamper with a witness or to delay, hinder, or prevent a witness from testifying. See, e.g., 18 U.S.C. §1512.

An attorney may not advise a witness to testify falsely. ABA Model Code DR 7-109(A); ABA Model Rule 3.4(b). Giving false testimony under oath constitutes perjury, and counseling a witness to do so constitutes the crime of subornation of perjury.

Lawyers and their employees can and do interview witnesses in depth to ascertain as exactly as possible the content of the witnesses' testimony, their credibility, and their consistency. Witnesses sometimes change their stories, providing the opposing counsel with a chance to impeach the credibility of the witness.

Ethics rules do not prohibit lawyers from preparing witnesses, including clients, to testify effectively. A witness who is familiar with courtroom procedure and who knows the kinds of questions that counsel and opposing counsel will ask is more likely to be consistent and clear, and less likely to be confused by opposing counsel. Lawyers and legal assistants who handle witness preparation must be careful not to encourage witnesses to give false testimony or to overcoach witnesses so that their testimony seems "prepared" and they lose credibility.

A few high-profile incidents of coaching of witnesses have recently focused attention on this important ethical concern. In the sexual harassment case brought by Paula Jones against President Bill Clinton, there have been allegations that the President's advisers attempted to tell witnesses what to say in their depositions. In a large asbestos case, the plaintiffs' lawyers prepared a detailed memorandum to their clients telling them how to testify, including what to say about their injuries. When the defense counsel was inadvertently given a copy of this memorandum, the firm stopped sending it to the plaintiffs and blamed an overzealous paralegal for writing it. The judge reported the matter to the state bar but no action was taken against the lawyers involved.

The line between preparing witnesses to give their testimony effectively and encouraging them to testify untruthfully must not be crossed and legal assistants who play a part in preparing witnesses must be careful not to cross it. As noted, perjury is rarely prosecuted and hard to prove. Perjury is even harder to prove when the witness is also a client since communications between the lawyer and legal assistant and the client are protected by the privilege. But a judge or jury who perceives the deception, as they often do, will find the witness lacking in credibility to the detriment of the case.

General rules about the treatment of third persons serve to prohibit lawyers from harassing witnesses, both inside and outside the courtroom. ABA Model Rule 4.4 prohibits lawyers from engaging in any conduct the only purpose of which is to "embarrass, delay, or burden a third person." The ABA Model Code provides that a lawyer should not ask questions intended to degrade a witness, DR 7-106(C)(2), or to take any action that would merely harass another, DR 7-102(A)(1).

Related to these ethics prohibitions are statutes that prohibit the tape recording of a person without his or her permission. For example, a federal statute provides criminal and civil remedies for interception and disclosure of wire, oral, or electronic communications, 18 U.S.C. §2511, and prohibits the use of such communications as evidence in any court, 18 U.S.C. §2515. Not all jurisdictions prohibit secret tape recording of conversations, and some states have endorsed the practice. See, for example, *Mississippi Bar v. Attorney ST*, 621 So. 2d 229 (Miss. 1993). However, an ABA advisory opinion recommends against it on ethical grounds (ABA Formal Opinion 331 (1974)). Attorneys and legal assistants must consult state statutes and rules before engaging in such conduct.

Lawyers may pay witnesses for expenses related to their testifying. The usual and permissible expenses are travel and lost wages. Expert witnesses may also be paid a reasonable fee for their professional services. No witness may be paid a fee or bonus that is contingent on the outcome of a case, as this would obviously provide an incentive for false testimony. ABA Model Code DR 7-109(C) contains these restrictions in detail; ABA Model Rule 3.4(b) prohibits attorneys from offering an illegal "inducement" to a witness.

As discussed in Section D above, with regard to client perjury, a lawyer has special duties to prevent the introduction of false testimony and to take corrective measures if false testimony is given by a witness. The ethical dilemma presented by a witness's false testimony is not difficult to resolve when the witness is not a client. The lawyer has no ethical duties to a witness that conflict with the lawyer's duty of candor to the court. A lawyer who knows a witness intends to testify falsely should advise the witness not to do so and should refuse to call the witness if he or she persists in intending to commit perjury. Once false testimony is given by a witness, the lawyer must inform the court. See ABA Model Code DR 7-102(A)(4); ABA Model Rule 3.3(c).

I. Trial Publicity

Balancing the right of free expression and the right to a fair trial is a precarious and constant struggle. The public interest in both criminal and civil cases and the pervasiveness of the modern media have frequently clashed with the smooth administration of the court system and assurance of a fair trial, especially in criminal cases and those in which a jury is involved. This conflict has most visibly presented itself in sensational cases, especially those in which the press sought a presence by camera in the courtroom or in which a judge issued a gag order, or when attorneys have sought to "try a case in the press."

The ABA Model Code provisions have been attacked in court as unconstitutional. At least three appellate courts have found that they interfere with free speech, although the U.S. Supreme Court has not decided the matter. Because of the questionable constitutionality of the provision, the Model Rule, adopted in 1983, was structured differently, containing a general admonition against extrajudicial statements likely to be publicly disseminated "if the lawyer knows or reasonably should know that it will have a substantial likelihood of materially prejudicing an adjudicative proceeding." This version of the rule lists the kinds of information that presumably would and would not be prejudicial. Many states (about 30) adopted some version of this rule. Then, in 1990, the Supreme Court rendered a decision that raised questions about the constitutionality of one of the new rule's provisions, namely the section that allowed an attorney to explain the "general nature" of a client's defense "without elaboration." This so-called safe harbor provision was deemed by a 5 to 4 majority of the Court to be constitutionally vague. *Gentile v. Nevada State Bar,* 501 U.S. 1030 (1990).

The ABA revised Model Rule 3.6 in response, moving the list of information likely to be prejudicial to the comment section and revising it, and revising the safe harbor provision by deleting the objectionable language cited by the Court. The revisions also make it clear that all lawyers in a firm involved in the case are covered but others are not. These changes, along with comparable changes to Model Rule 3.8 governing prosecutors, were adopted by the ABA House of Delegates in August 1994. The amendments also included a provision that permits lawyers to make statements to protect their clients in response to publicity not generated by the lawyer or the client.

California was the last state to adopt an ethics rule on trial publicity when it adopted a variation of Model Rule 3.6 under a legislative mandate passed in the heat of the O. J. Simpson trial. Some states have retained the rule from the old Model Code but most have adopted some version of Model Rule 3.6. A few, namely Colorado and Illinois, have established a more permissive standard, prohibiting only statements that create a danger of "imminent and substantial harm" of prejudicing the adjudicative proceeding. While disciplinary actions against lawyers for violations of these provisions are relatively rare, they do occur, usually in sensational cases that are closely covered by the media. For example, the lawyer representing criminal underworld figure John Gotti was held in contempt for statements made in his media campaign, particularly for statements intended for potential jurors. The defense lawyers in the O. J. Simpson case were investigated for statements made to the media about a frame and cover-up of a frame of their client, but no charges were brought. A few courts have imposed gag orders to prevent lawyers from making any statements but when challenged these gag orders are usually struck down as unconstitutional prior restraints on speech.

The debate over lawyer conduct in high-profile cases continues to be heated. Discussions cover not only the ethics rules on trial publicity, but on the impact of such lawyers' conduct on public opinion of lawyers. In a 1997 Harris poll, 55 percent of the group polled viewed lawyers more negatively because of their high profile in the media. Ninety-one percent indicated that they believe lawyers use the media to influence public opinion about their cases although 58 percent believe this conduct is inappropriate. There is also ample evidence that jurors are not influenced by the parallel "trial in the press" that often takes place. This is especially true when the jury is sequestered and does not have access to the daily barrage of statements by lawyers and lawyer-commentators. Among the initiatives proposed to address some of these concerns is a set of standards for lawyers who serve as news commentators on cases.

ABA Model Code DR 7-108 contains a provision of special interest to legal assistants that is absent in the comparable ABA Model Rule. Section (J) of this disciplinary rule requires lawyers to exercise reasonable care to prevent employees and associates from making statements prohibited by the rule. The general provision in the ABA Model Rules covering a lawyer's responsibility for acts of employees would have the same effect. See ABA Model Rule 5.3.

J. Special Rules for Prosecutors

As representatives of the government and "the people," prosecutors have a special duty of truth and fairness in the administration of justice. Prosecutors must not seek only to convict but must also seek justice and ensure that all citizens are afforded their rights. Separate rules included in the ABA Model Code and ABA Model Rules set forth these obligations, and local laws frequently impose additional obligations.

One critical duty of the prosecutor is not to institute unsupported criminal charges or to continue to pursue an unsupported action. Probable cause is required. ABA Model Code DR 7-103(A); ABA Model Rule 3.8(a). This limitation also prevents prosecutors from abusing their discretion in prosecuting cases by singling someone out for prosecution on a discriminatory basis. Prosecutors are also required to disclose information that tends to negate or mitigate guilt or to reduce punishment. ABA Model Code DR 7-103(B); ABA Model Rule 3.8(d).

The ABA Model Rules contain additional provisions that require prosecutors to make reasonable efforts to see that the accused knows of his or her right to counsel and has had an opportunity to secure counsel, ABA Model Rule 3.8(b); not to obtain a waiver of rights from an unrepresented accused, ABA Model Rule 3.8(c); and to exercise reasonable care to prevent employees and others involved with the prosecution from making prohibited extrajudicial statements, ABA Model Rule 3.8(e). Finally, ABA Model Rule 3.8(f), added in 1990, limits a prosecutor's right to subpoena a lawyer to testify about a client or former client. A prosecutor may subpoena a lawyer only if the information sought is not privileged, is essential to the case and not otherwise available, and the prosecutor has prior judicial approval. For additional guidance on ethical issues in the criminal area, see the ABA Standards for Criminal Justice, which include separate sections on the prosecutorial and defense functions.

In addition to disciplinary sanctions for violations of these rules, courts may impose remedies in a pending case if the defendant's constitutional rights have been violated. For example, a court may reverse a conviction, suppress evidence, dismiss charges, or order a new trial. In one recent case, a murder conviction was reversed on appeal when the appellate court found extensive prosecutorial misconduct, including misrepresenting the law and the facts and intimidating witnesses. The prosecutor was reassigned to a desk job.

REVIEW QUESTIONS

1. What are the three main ethics rules governing lawyers' relationships with judges?
2. How do the ABA Model Code and ABA Model Rules differ in their handling of lawyers' influencing of judges? What crime might occur when a lawyer tries to influence a judge?
3. Can a lawyer give a judge a gift? What if they are good friends?
4. Why are lawyers and their employees prohibited from having ex parte communications with judges?
5. What kinds of contact with jurors are prohibited by the ethics rules and why? What crime might be involved when a lawyer or legal assistant tries to influence a juror?
6. What are the general rules about lawyers and their agents having contact with persons who already have a lawyer? Why? What are the exceptions?
7. What is the general rule about contact with persons who are not represented by counsel?
8. Describe the rules that the U.S. Attorney General's office has issued on contact with unrepresented and represented persons.
9. What is prohibited by the ethics rules in lawyers' contact with witnesses? What crimes might such actions constitute?
10. What contact can lawyers have with witnesses?
11. What actions might constitute harassing a witness? What crime (or crimes) might be committed in addition to violations of ethics rules?

345

12. May a lawyer pay a witness to testify? What are the applicable restrictions?

13. May a lawyer pay an expert witness? May the amount be based on the outcome in the case?

14. What two important constitutional interests are being balanced in the ethics rules on trial publicity?

15. What kinds of extrajudicial statements are generally permitted by ethics rules? Prohibited?

16. May a lawyer have a legal assistant speak to the press and reveal information about a pending case that the lawyer could not under the ethics rules? Why, or why not?

17. Why are prosecutors bound by additional ethics rules? Name four ethical duties that prosecutors have that other lawyers do not have.

18. What sanctions and remedies may be imposed for prosecutorial misconduct?

DISCUSSION QUESTIONS

1. What would you do if your attorney-employer asked you to invite a judge who was serving in one of your cases to a social event you were planning? If your attorney-employer asked you to try to find out what a judge who was a friend of yours was thinking about a pending case?

2. Do you think lawyers and their employees should be prohibited from giving campaign contributions to judges?

3. What would you do if your supervisor asked you to give a sealed note to a juror during a recess?

4. Does your state have ethics rules that govern communication with jurors after trial? Do you think lawyers should be able to interview jurors after a trial is over? Why, or why not?

5. Why are lawyers not involved in a case prohibited from talking to jurors about the case?

6. Suppose you work for the U.S. Attorney General's office. You are asked to call a person who is being investigated in a major organized crime case. You know that the person is likely to be indicted and is already represented by counsel. What do you do? Do you think that federal prosecutors should be exempt from state ethics rules? Why, or why not?

7. What would you do if the supervising attorney asked you to contact the opposing party in a divorce case to see if the spouses could meet without the lawyers present to work out an amiable settlement?

8. What would you do if a co-plaintiff who was not represented by

your firm contacted you to discuss changing lawyers? What if the party wanted to discuss the merits of the case? The performance of his or her lawyer?

9. What would you do if you were interviewing a potential witness who did not have an attorney, and you suddenly realized that he seemed to believe that you and your firm were representing him?

10. Suppose that one of your duties as a litigation paralegal is to prepare witnesses for trial. What would you do if you were preparing a witness and his or her story kept changing? What if the witness seemed to be changing his or her version of the facts to be more favorable to you? Suppose the witness, although generally favorable to your client, has some information that is adverse to your client. What do you tell the witness about how to handle this information while he or she is on the stand?

11. What would you do if you discovered that a client was sending anonymous threatening letters to a witness who planned to testify against her? Would it make any difference if you knew the witness's testimony would be false?

12. Does your jurisdiction have a statute that prohibits or limits the tape recording of conversations? What does it say about permission from the party or parties? About the admissibility of illegally tape-recorded conversations?

13. What would you do if your firm paid a witness, who was not an expert, a witness fee that was three times his normal salary?

14. Review the rules governing a lawyer's handling of client perjury. Do you think a lawyer should be bound to tell the court if her client commits perjury? Would you answer differently in criminal and civil cases? What does your jurisdiction's ethics rule say? Are there any cases on the issue in your jurisdiction?

15. What does your jurisdiction's ethics code say about extrajudicial statements or trial publicity? Do you think the rule strikes the right balance between free speech and fair trial? Have any lawyers in your jurisdiction been disciplined under the Rule?

16. What would you do if your attorney-employer asked you to leak information to the press that you know is prohibited by ethics rules? Would it make any difference if you were certain that without press coverage of this information your client would be unfairly convicted of a serious crime?

17. Suppose you work for the local prosecuting attorney. What would you do if you uncovered information that proved a criminal defendant in a case was innocent? What if you went to the supervising attorney and he refused to drop the charges or to turn over the exculpatory evidence to the defendant's counsel?

18. What would you do if your supervisor, the prosecuting attorney, asked you to obtain a statement from a recently arrested person, and in doing so you discovered that the person had not been advised of her right to counsel? What if the accused had been advised of her right to counsel but had not yet been able to reach an attorney?
19. Obtain a copy of your state judicial canons and compare the relevant provisions to those for lawyers covered in this chapter.

CASES FOR ANALYSIS

In the following case, the court dismisses the complaint of a "languid litigant" who fails to move forward with this case. As you read, consider what conduct by a litigant might warrant this harsh sanction.

Chira v. Lockheed
634 F.2d 664 (2d Cir. 1980)

. . . On July 18, 1978, Richard Chira, by his attorney, Martin Paul Solomon, sued Lockheed Aircraft Corp. for various claims arising out of Lockheed's termination of Chira's employment in July 1977. Chira, a lawyer, had worked in the general counsel's office of a Lockheed subsidiary in California since 1974, and Lockheed discharged him after Chira took an allegedly unauthorized leave of absence. Chira sued for, inter alia, fraud, breach of contract, wrongful discharge, tortious interference with career opportunities, defamation of his professional reputation, harassment, intentional infliction of emotional distress, and job discrimination on the basis of age (Chira was 45), marital status (he is single), ethnic background (he is of Arab descent), and medical condition. Chira claimed damages of $96 million.

Lockheed moved quickly to transfer the suit to the Central District of California. Judge Knapp denied the motion with leave to make it again at a later date, and filed, on December 20, 1978, the following order: "We further direct that plaintiff's discovery be completed within six months, at which time plaintiff is directed to file a statement showing exactly what he proposes to prove, what witnesses he plans to call and giving a brief resume of the testimony expected from each witness."

After the order, Lockheed tried to depose Chira. Chira failed to appear for his first scheduled deposition, and filed a motion to disqualify Lockheed's counsel, Rogers & Wells. Judge Knapp found the motion frivolous and denied it. The deposition was eventually held on four days in early April 1979; Lockheed asked Chira questions concerning, inter alia, his medical complaints, his past employment record, and his current professional reputation. After consulting with Chira, Solomon directed Chira not to answer 120 of the questions, most frequently on the ground of relevance. Lockheed requested documents from Chira on the same topics; Chira produced some of them, and refused to produce others on the same ground asserted at the deposition. Lockheed objected strenuously, but did not secure an order from Judge Knapp directing Chira to answer or produce.

While Chira and Solomon were thus encumbering Lockheed's efforts to discern the basis of the complaint, the time was running on Judge Knapp's six-month deadline. By the end of the six-month period on June 20, 1979, Chira had not filed the required list of witnesses, nor had he completed his discovery. Our independent examination of the record, confirmed by Chira's counsel on appeal, reveals that during the six-month period, Chira and Solomon did absolutely nothing at all to move their case to trial.

Lockheed finally moved for an order compelling discovery after Chira's period for compliance had expired. It also renewed its motion to transfer, and moved in the alternative to dismiss the suit under Rule 41(b), for failure to prosecute or to comply with an order of the court. The district court granted the motion to dismiss. 85 F.R.D. 93 (S.D.N.Y.). Chira, represented by new counsel, appeals. . . .

Chira does not contend that he complied with the terms of Judge Knapp's order. Instead he argues that, even assuming his tardiness, dismissal was too harsh a remedy. Had Chira complied in part, or been frustrated in good faith efforts to comply, the argument might be colorable, but given his complete intransigence in the face of a clear court order, we reject it. . . .

Conceding the total failure to comply, Chira offers as an excuse his "right to counsel," i.e., his right to rely on Solomon. However, absent a truly extraordinary situation, e.g., *United States v. Cirami*, 563 F.2d 26, 35 (2d Cir. 1977), the client is not excused from the consequences of his attorney's nonfeasance. . . .

Chira's effort to excuse himself from the consequences of Solomon's nonfeasance is especially weak, because Chira is an attorney. . . .

The language of Rule 41 makes Chira's failure to comply with Judge Knapp's order a clear basis on which to affirm the dismissal. Chira's indolence, however, runs deeper, for beyond his failure to comply with the district court's specific directions for the prosecution of his suit, Chira failed to take any other action to move his case to trial. Completely aside from his failure to comply with the order, a dismissal is justified for Chira's failure to prosecute at all. . . .

Only on rare occasions should a district judge deprive the languid litigant of his right to a trial on the merits. It is with reluctance that an appellate court will approve a dismissal with prejudice. But fairness to other litigants, whether in the same case or merely in the same court (as competitors for scarce judicial resources), requires us to affirm and endorse the district court's action here. Burgeoning filings and crowded calendars have shorn courts of the luxury of tolerating procrastination.

Delays have dangerous ends, and unless district judges use the clear power to impose the ultimate sanction when appropriate, exhortations of diligence are impotent. While we agree that "a court must not let its zeal for a tidy calendar overcome its duty to do justice," that same goal of justice, here in the guise of judicial administration, mandates our affirmance of the order of dismissal.

Questions about the Case

1. List the things that the plaintiff Chira and his attorney Solomon did that violate the rules described in this chapter. Why do you think the plaintiff and his lawyer conducted the case this way?
2. Could the court have imposed sanctions without the court order of December 20, 1978? What would the one or more sanctions probably have been?
3. What do you think of attorney Solomon's advice to Chira not to answer the questions at his deposition regarding his medical complaints, employment record, and professional reputation?
4. Do you agree or disagree that the sanction of dismissal is appropriate in this case?
5. What factors does Chira say mitigate against dismissal? How does the court treat these?
6. Under what circumstances is the remedy of dismissal appropriate? Write a general rule covering this.

In the following case, the lawyers on both sides missed the controlling legal authority at the trial court and the matter had to be corrected after an incorrect ruling was made.

Massey v. Prince George's County
907 F.Supp. 138 (D. Md. 1995)

. . . Plaintiff Willie Massey alleges that in the early morning hours of November 4, 1992 he was sleeping in a vacant or abandoned building in Cheverly, Maryland. He contends that all of a sudden he was awakened by Prince George's County police officers who, without warning, set their police dog upon him. Massey says that although he offered no resistance, the animal proceeded to bite him and inflict painful and permanent injury all over his body. In his Third Amended Complaint before the Court, Massey has sued the individual officers for assault and battery under Maryland law and for deprivation of his Fourth Amendment rights, i.e. for use of excessive force, under 42 U.S.C. §1983. The officers have denied liability, claiming that Massey was warned about the dog in a loud voice and that he resisted their efforts to arrest him.

Earlier in these proceedings, Defendants filed a fifteen page Motion for Summary Judgment to which excerpts from depositions of Plaintiff and various officers were appended. With regard to the Section 1983 claims, Defendants argued that their seizure of Plaintiff and the force used by them were reasonable as a matter of law. After citing general Supreme Court law regarding such claims, defense counsel invited the Court's attention to the case of *Robinette v. Barnes,* 854 F.2d 909 (6th Cir. 1988), in which the U.S. Court of Appeals for the Sixth Circuit concluded that the use of a trained police dog in circumstances comparable to those in the case at bar was reasonable as a matter of law. . . .

In the present case, Plaintiff's Response to Defendants' Motion for Summary Judgment consisted of a single page, his Statement of Material Facts in Dispute barely more than two. In these, Plaintiff's counsel cited one case and one alone, namely the *Robinette* case already cited by defense counsel, which Plaintiff's counsel did no more than attempt to distinguish on its facts.

When the matter came on for oral argument, defense counsel again argued the applicability of *Robinette* to the present case, while Plaintiff's counsel again tried to distinguish *Robinette* on its facts, offering no further citation to authority.

At the conclusion of oral argument, largely on the strength of *Robinette,* the Court announced its decision to dismiss the two counts of excessive force, finding the officers' actions reasonable as a matter of law. What remained open, however, was the issue of whether Plaintiff's state law cause of action for assault and battery could survive in the face of the Court's ruling with regard to the two federal constitutional torts. . . .

Defense counsel has now submitted a one-page letter brief in conformity with the Court's request. Plaintiff's counsel has submitted a six-page letter which, while it comports with the Court's directive in part, in effect invites the Court to reconsider its dismissal of the two federal constitutional counts. Plaintiff seems to understand that his request for reconsideration is out of order at this time, but there is a feature of counsel's letter that

351

cannot go unremarked even now. The critical feature is that for the first time Plaintiff's counsel cites legal authority directly on point to the case at bar. The case, *Kopf v. Wing,* 942 F.2d 265 (4th Cir. 1991), is not only an excessive force case involving a police dog, but is the controlling law in this Circuit. As the Court will discuss presently, that case clearly mandates denial of Defendants' Motion for Summary Judgment, which is to say reinstatement of the excessive force claims the Court recently dismissed. But the fact that *Kopf* has been cited for the first time by Plaintiff's counsel in a supplemental letter—well after the filing of his threadbare initial response to Defendants' Motion for Summary Judgment and his equally scant oral argument on the motion—is a cause for considerable concern. At the same time, the fact that this case has never been cited by defense counsel in his initial pleadings, in oral argument or indeed to this day, gives cause for even greater concern. . . .

The parallels between *Kopf* and the case at bar are striking and need little elaboration. The Court accepts without question that, on the authority of *Kopf,* Plaintiff ought to have prevailed as against Defendants' Motion for Summary Judgment. Notwithstanding this, neither Plaintiff's nor Defendants' counsel brought the case to the Court's attention even through oral argument. Thereafter, only Plaintiff's counsel, never defense counsel, cited the case, and then only because the Court had directed briefing on another point of law. . . .

One must assume that had Plaintiff's counsel, in preparing his initial Opposition to the Motion for Summary Judgment, exhibited the same degree of diligence that ultimately permitted him to locate the case in untimely fashion, he could have located the case in timely fashion. Instead, counsel offered only the sketchiest statement of grounds, reflecting a bare minimum of legal research, showing every sign of having been dictated on the run. The net effect of this truncated effort was to consume valuable court time in oral argument and the preparation of supplemental briefs (not to mention preparation of the present Opinion), all of which could have been avoided by earlier diligence on counsel's part. Counsel appears to have forgotten two of the most fundamental rules of professional conduct. First, Rule of Professional Conduct 1.1 provides that:

> [a] lawyer shall provide competent representation to a client. Competent representation requires the legal knowledge, skill, thoroughness and preparation reasonably necessary for the representation.

. . .

The other Rule of Professional Conduct counsel has apparently misplaced is Rule 1.3 which holds that "[a] lawyer shall act with reasonable diligence and promptness in representing a client." Failure to pursue applicable legal authority in timely fashion may well constitute a violation of this rule.

The action of defense counsel in this case raises a far more serious concern. It is possible that defense counsel also overlooked the *Kopf* precedent, but if he did, the oversight was glaring and extremely troublesome. *Kopf* not only deals with a claim of excessive force against police where a police dog was involved; individual Prince George's County police officers and the County itself were defendants in that case. Indeed, at least one attorney for Prince George's County in *Kopf*, as shown in the reported case, was an individual, whom the Court judicially notices, was still in the County Attorney's office at the time of the filing of the present Motion for Summary Judgment.

The regrettable inference is that defense counsel in the instant case may in fact have deliberately failed to disclose to the Court directly controlling authority from this Circuit. If so, the action would constitute a clear violation of the Rules of Professional Conduct.

Thus, Rule 3.3(a)(3) provides that "a lawyer shall not knowingly . . . fail to disclose to the tribunal legal authority in the controlling jurisdiction known to the lawyer to be directly adverse to the position of the client and not disclosed by opposing counsel." In federal court, the "controlling jurisdiction" is the circuit in which the district court sits. *Hazard & Hodes, op. cit.* §3.3.207. Particularly disturbing is the type of case encountered here—a litigant who was an unsuccessful party to a directly relevant adverse precedent who has failed to cite that precedent to the court. (Citations omitted.) . . .

Under the circumstances, the Court will direct defense counsel to show cause to the Court in writing within thirty (30) days why citation to the *Kopf* case was omitted from his Motion for Summary Judgment, oral argument, and indeed from any pleading or communication to date.

The Court also recollects that in the last several months counsel for Prince George's County was before the Court in at least one other police dog excessive force case in which a Motion for Summary Judgment in favor of the County was granted. It may be that *Kopf* was omitted from the pleading in that proceeding as well. Accordingly, the Court directs defense counsel and the Office of the Prince George's County attorney, within sixty (60) days to disclose to the Court the status of that case and any and all police dog excessive force cases involving Prince George's County that were pending as of August 9, 1991, the date *Kopf* was decided by the Fourth Circuit, or that have been filed from that date to the present. The Court's Show-Cause Order, entered simultaneously with this Opinion, spells out the information that is to be provided. Any further sanctions that may be imposed by the Court will depend on the County's showing of cause pursuant to this directive.

Enough has been said for now. No formal Motion for Reconsideration need be filed by Plaintiff's counsel since, as indicated, *Kopf* clearly dictates reinstatement of the excessive force claims. In consequence, the state court claim for assault and battery also remains in the case. . . .

Questions about the Case

1. What was the disposition of the case at the hearing on the summary judgment? On what case did the court rely and what did it hold?
2. What was the correct statement of the law? What happened to the case as a result of this ruling?
3. Why does it appear that the plaintiff's counsel did not cite the case? Why did the defense not cite the case?
4. What are the possible ethical violations of both the lawyers involved? Which is most egregious?
5. What remedy is the court likely to impose on the lawyers if they cannot justify their actions?
6. What disciplinary sanction do you think might be appropriate?
7. Why do courts disapprove of this particular ethical violation so strongly?

In the following case, sanctions were imposed on attorneys who knowingly failed to cite adverse controlling authority. Consider why the attorneys might have done this and how the trial judge reacted when he discovered the omitted cases.

Jorgenson v. County of Volusia
846 F.2d 1350 (11th Cir. 1988)

PER CURIAM:

The appellants, attorneys Eric Latinsky and Fred Fendt, were sanctioned by the district court pursuant to Fed. R. Civ. P. 11 for failing to cite adverse, controlling precedent in a memorandum filed in support of an application for a temporary restraining order and a preliminary injunction. In the appellants initial appeal to this court, the case was remanded to the district court because the court had failed to notify the attorneys in advance that it was considering sanctions, and did not give them an opportunity to respond. *Jorgenson v. County of Volusia,* 824 F.2d 973 (11th Cir. 1987) (unpublished opinion). On remand, the district court reaffirmed the imposition of sanctions, and the attorneys appeal. . . .

Appellants filed an application in the district court for a temporary restraining order and a preliminary injunction on behalf of their clients, who own and operate a lounge known as "Porky's." In support of the application, appellants filed a memorandum of law which challenged the validity of a Volusia County ordinance prohibiting nude or semi-nude entertainment in commercial establishments at which alcoholic beverages are offered for sale or consumption. The memorandum failed to discuss or cite two clearly relevant cases: *City of Daytona Beach v. Del Percio,* 476 So. 2d 197 (Fla. 1985) and *New York State Liquor Authority v. Bellanca,* 452 U.S. 714, 101 S. Ct. 2599, 69 L. Ed. 2d 357 (1981). We find that this failure supports the imposition of Rule 11 sanctions in the circumstances of this case.

The field of law concerning the regulation of the sale and consumption of alcohol in connection with nude entertainment is a narrow and somewhat specialized field. Prior to the opinion of the Supreme Court of Florida in *Del Percio,* the critical question of whether the state of Florida had delegated its powers under the Twenty-First Amendment to counties and municipalities had gone unanswered. In some circles, that decision was long-awaited. If the state had delegated the authority, local ordinances regulating the sale or consumption of alcohol would be entitled to a presumption in favor of their validity which is conferred by the Twenty-First Amendment. *See Bellanca,* 452 U.S. at 718, 101 S. Ct. at 2601. If the state had not delegated the authority, the ordinances would be subject to the stricter review applicable to exercises of the general police power. See *Krueger v. City of Pensacola,* 759 F.2d 851, 852 (11th Cir. 1985).

The question regarding Florida's delegation of its powers under the Twenty-First Amendment was answered by the Supreme Court of Florida in *Del Percio,* a case in which one of the appellants, Latinsky, participated. The court held that the powers had been delegated. Less than one year later, on or about January 13, 1986, Latinsky and an associate brought the instant suit seeking a declaration that a similar ordinance was unconstitutional and requesting a temporary restraining order and a preliminary injunction. In their presentation to the court, the appellants cited a number of cases describing the limits on the exercise of the general police power. However, they did not advise the court in any way that *Del Percio* had been decided, despite the fact that *Del Percio* required that the validity of the ordinance be judged in light of powers retained under the Twenty-First Amendment rather than the general police power.

The appellants purported to describe the law to the district court in the hope that the description would guide and inform the court's decision. With apparently studied care, however, they withheld the fact that the long-awaited decision by the Supreme Court of Florida had been handed down. This will not do. The appellants are not redeemed by the fact that opposing counsel *subsequently* cited the controlling precedent. The appellants had a duty to refrain from affirmatively misleading the court as to the state of the law. They were not relieved of this duty by the possibility that opposing counsel might find and cite the controlling precedent, particularly where as here, a temporary restraining order might have been issued ex parte.

In this court, appellants argue that the cases were not cited because they are not controlling. We certainly acknowledge that attorneys are legitimately entitled to press their own interpretations of precedent, including interpretations which render particular cases inapplicable. It is clear, however, that appellants' attempts to show that *Del Percio* and *Bellanca* are not controlling are simply post hoc efforts to evade the imposition of sanctions. Neither the original complaint nor the memorandum of law filed by appellants in the district court reflect or support the arguments they now raise. Indeed, it is likely that the arguments were not raised previously because they are completely without merit. In the circumstances of this case, the imposition of Rule 11 sanctions by the district court was warranted. The judgment of the district court is affirmed.

Questions about the Case

1. What ethics rules did the attorneys violate in this case?
2. What cases should the attorneys have cited, and why?
3. Is it possible that the attorneys did not know about these cases?
4. What were the attorneys intending to do by not citing these cases?
5. Did the opposing attorneys cite the cases in question? Why did the court say that it made no difference whether the opposing attorneys did or didn't cite the cases?
6. Are the cases in question controlling? How does the court treat this matter?
7. On whom was the sanction imposed in this case? Should it also have been imposed on the client? Why, or why not?
8. Under what rule was the sanction imposed? Might the attorneys also be disciplined for an ethics violation? Under what rule?
9. Why does the court react so strongly to having the law misrepresented? What if the court wrote a decision based on an inaccurate statement of the law?

The following case illustrates how the advocacy rules may apply even when there is no lawsuit pending. The attorney who is being disciplined in this case engages in more than one kind of the prohibited conduct discussed in this chapter. He claims that nonlawyers in his office were partly responsible.

Crane v. State Bar of California
30 Cal. 3d 117, 635 P.2d 163, 177 Cal.Rptr. 670
(1981)

. . . 1. *The Mercury Case*

Representing the sellers of a residence, in April 1978 petitioner sought and obtained from Mercury Savings and Loan Association (Mercury), the beneficiary under a first trust deed, a beneficiary statement describing the status and indebtedness of the underlying loan. Without either the consent or knowledge of Mercury, he then "crossed out" certain printed material included in the statement by Mercury. The deleted language gave notice that Mercury intended to enforce an acceleration clause in the note and deed of trust unless it received an assumption agreement executed by any purchaser of the premises. Petitioner subsequently forwarded the altered statement to the escrow company handling the sale, describing it as "the Beneficiary Statement from the . . . lender on your escrow," and without notifying that company that the deletions were made by him and were wholly unauthorized.

The State Bar Court found petitioner's conduct in this regard to be wilful, improper and a dishonest act under the statute.

2. *The Robinson Case*

In December 1978 petitioner communicated with counsel for Mr. and Mrs. Robinson both by telephone and by mail in connection with the unrecorded claim of petitioner's client to real property which was subject to a trust deed then being foreclosed by the Robinsons. Both orally and in writing, the Robinsons' attorney specifically advised petitioner that he represented the Robinsons. Thereafter, petitioner's office sent two letters directly to the Robinsons without notifying their lawyer. The first—which apparently was a "follow-up" to a still earlier letter sent to the Robinsons before petitioner had been contacted by their lawyer—repeated a request for a beneficiary statement on their trust deed and offered to "waive" the $100 statutory penalty if it was received promptly. The second, sent seven days later, demanded that the Robinsons forward "forthwith" the $100 and the beneficiary statement. It stated further that if the statement was not received within five days, an action would be commenced against the Robinsons to recover both damages and the forfeiture, and that "the Department of Savings and Loan and the Attorney General's office will be requested to assist us in solution." A notation on the last letter indicated that copies were being sent to a named commissioner of the Department of Savings and Loan and to a named deputy attorney general. The letters were on petitioner's legal stationery and purported to be signed by him.

The State Bar Court found that petitioner's direct communication with the Robinsons despite his knowledge that they were represented by a lawyer was a clear violation of rule 7-103 of the Rules of Professional Conduct, and that his final letter to them constituted an impermissible threat in violation of rule 7-104.

Discussion

With respect to the Mercury matter, petitioner admits both his unauthorized alteration of the beneficiary statement and his failure to advise the escrow company that the deletion was his, and not that of the beneficiary or trustee under the trust deed. He denies, however, that he was "dishonest," arguing that he had no intent to deceive the escrow company, but merely sought to prevent Mercury from improperly interfering with the prospective sale by asserting demands which Mercury had no right to make in the beneficiary statement.

We reject petitioner's disavowal of any dishonest intent. Even if we assume for purposes of argument that Mercury endangered the successful closing of escrow by asserting a right which it did not have, any such risk could be removed or minimized *only* if the reader of the statement believed the acceleration language was deleted by Mercury itself. The circumstances of petitioner's unauthorized unilateral alteration were deceptive and known by him to be so. . . .

In the Robinson matter, petitioner also admitted in a stipulation of facts filed with the State Bar Court his "technical violation" of rule 7-103 of the Rules of Professional Conduct by communicating directly with the Robinsons despite his awareness that they were represented by counsel. He now contends, however, that the letters to the Robinsons requesting, and then demanding, the beneficiary statement and statutory penalty, and threatening suit and action by state officials, were not "upon a subject of controversy" and that his client and the Robinsons were not "adverse parties" within the meaning of that rule.

There was substantial evidence to the contrary, however, including testimony of the Robinsons' lawyer that he had discussed with petitioner the adverse interest of the parties in connection with the foreclosure of the trust deed, and beyond that evidence, the contents of the letters themselves belie petitioner's claims.

We similarly reject petitioner's asserted excuse that any violation of rule 7-103 was inadvertent and precipitated by members of his staff. Acknowledging negligence in failing properly to prevent direct contact with represented parties by correspondence on his letterhead and over his purported signature, petitioner contends that the discipline proposed for that negligence is unduly severe. Petitioner's attempt to avoid the blame for his violation of the Rules of Professional Conduct is unconvincing. An attorney is responsible for the work product of his employees which is performed pursuant to his direction and authority. The legal onus for the violation of rule 7-103 rests upon petitioner alone. . . .

Accordingly, it is ordered that Fred R. Crane be suspended from the practice of law in this state for a period of one year. . . .

Questions about the Case

1. Describe the acts that constituted breaches of ethics in the *Mercury* and *Robinson* cases. What ethical principles presented in this chapter do these acts offend?
2. What was attorney Crane's defense in the *Mercury* matter? How did the court handle this defense?
3. What were Crane's defenses in the *Robinson* case? How did the court handle them?
4. Was Crane aware of the correspondence with the Robinsons? Would it have made any difference whether he knew it or not?
5. What sanction was imposed? Do you think it was appropriate?

In the *Omaha Bank* case that follows, an appellate court examines the decision of a lower court that refused to replace a juror after the juror had contact with the defendant's attorneys outside the courtroom. As you read, consider whether this incident might also give rise to a disciplinary action.

Omaha Bank v. Siouxland Cattle Cooperative
305 N.W.2d 458 (Iowa 1981)

Siouxland Cattle Cooperative (Siouxland) appeals from an adverse judgment on its damage claim in a law action for fraud against Omaha

Bank for Cooperatives (Omaha Bank) and Robert Zuber, a bank officer, and from the trial court's order for a sheriff's deed to the bank in a foreclosure action. Siouxland claims that the trial court erred in failing to replace a juror with an alternate, in its instructions to the jury, and in ruling that Siouxland has lost a right of redemption from the foreclosure sale. . . .

. . . After a day at trial on March 3, 1980, Omaha Bank's lawyers, Robert J. Banta and Gerald P. Laughlin, stopped for dinner in Merrill, Iowa. After finishing dinner, they entered the bar portion of the restaurant to pay their bill. Juror Adamson was seated at the bar. He offered to buy the lawyers a drink and they declined. Adamson was insistent and offered again. The lawyers then sat at a booth near the bar and received a drink, courtesy of Adamson. Adamson introduced the lawyers to other patrons and they all conversed about various subjects. There is no evidence that the pending trial was discussed.

On March 6 attorney Laughlin informed the court, in the presence of lawyers for other parties, of the contact with juror Adamson. We do not have a transcript of the meeting but apparently the trial court concluded that nothing improper had occurred.

On March 11 Siouxland's attorney, Steven A. Carter, reported to the court that he had advised his client to move for a mistrial because of the misconduct. Carter also stated that Siouxland did not want a mistrial and wanted to proceed with the jury. Because Siouxland would not follow Carter's advice to move for a mistrial, Carter requested the court, before the case was submitted to the jury, to remove Adamson and replace him with an alternate juror under Iowa R. Civ. P. 189, as then in effect. The trial court denied the request, stating, "I said at the time there was nothing wrong with it and found that, and I do now." The court also indicated that a motion for a mistrial was the only proper procedure to follow.

After the jury returned a verdict for the bank and Zuber, Siouxland moved for a new trial because of misconduct by juror Adamson, who had become foreman of the jury. Iowa R. Civ. P. 244(b). The trial court overruled the motion primarily because Siouxland had not moved for a mistrial during trial.

The juror's offer of drinks and the lawyers' acceptance was clearly misconduct by all of them. Adamson, in speaking to the lawyers and offering and buying them drinks, violated the standard admonition given by the court to refrain from contact with the lawyers involved in the case. The bank's lawyers violated their ethical obligation prohibiting communication with a juror during trial unless it is in the course of official proceedings. Iowa Code of Professional Responsibility DR 7-108(B) and (C).

Omaha Bank and Zuber apparently concede that the contact was misconduct but argue that Siouxland has waived any claim for a new trial. The waiver argument is based on Siouxland's refusal to move for a mistrial after discovering the misconduct. A party learning during trial of misconduct by a juror must complain to the trial court rather than wait for the outcome and then move for a new trial after losing.

Siouxland declined to move for a mistrial during trial. The record does not indicate, however, that Siouxland elected to wait until the adverse verdict before complaining to the court about the misconduct. Rather, before the case was submitted for jury decision, Siouxland requested the court to replace Adamson with an available alternate. Iowa R. Civ. P. 189, The Code 1979. We conclude that Siouxland adequately made its record to the court by requesting that an alternate replace the offending juror. . . .

In this case, we conclude that the trial court abused its discretion because there is not substantial evidence to support a finding that the contact was not prejudicial to Siouxland. Adamson and the lawyers did not merely meet and exchange greetings, but rather had an extended conversation. (Citations omitted.) The lawyers accepted a drink and participated with the juror in the gathering in the bar. The circumstances surrounding the contact are the only bases upon which to determine whether the contact may have influenced the juror or the jury.

In addition, we conclude that the fraud claim must be retried to "zealously [guard] the utter independence of jurors." *State v. Carey,* 165 N.W.2d 27, 29 (Iowa 1969). We simply cannot allow a foreman of a jury to purchase drinks during trial for lawyers representing a party. In cases of such gross impropriety, even if the meeting were unintentional, we are not only concerned with injustice to particular litigants but also with the appearance of impropriety that casts doubt on our jury system. Attempts to ingratiate one side to a juror by extended conversation and acceptance of drinks must be condemned. . . .

Questions about the Case

1. What ethics rule did the attorneys violate in this case? Could their acts have been grounds for discipline?
2. Exactly what contact did the bank's attorneys have with the juror Adamson? Who instigated the contact? Did they discuss the case? Does it matter? Why, or why not?
3. Why wasn't a mistrial declared when the trial judge discovered the

contact? Why wasn't the juror replaced? When was the trial judge informed of this conduct?

4. Since the juror and attorneys did not discuss the case, what is the potential prejudice to the other party?

5. What reasons does the court give for reversing the decision of the lower court? With which court do you agree? Why?

10

Professionalism

This chapter gives an overview of the current state of professionalism, one of the most talked about issues in the legal field today. It then goes on to outline the major challenges confronting lawyers and legal assistants. Chapter 10 covers:

- a discussion of the unique place of legal assistants in the legal profession
- definitions of professionalism for legal assistants
- a discussion of the elements of professionalism
- issues in professionalism facing legal assistants, including

  - regulation of legal assistants
  - paralegal education
  - full utilization of legal assistants
  - overtime compensation for legal assistants
  - gender and bias issues

- the importance and value of paralegal participation in pro bono activities

A. The State of Professionalism in the Legal Field

A poor public image has plagued the legal profession for the last 20 years—ever since the dishonest and manipulative conduct of White House lawyers was revealed in the Watergate scandal. The notion that lawyers could engage in such unscrupulous behavior was not counteracted during the succeeding years but exacerbated by media attention focusing on a wide variety of problems within the profession.

Society has become more litigious. Lawyers—what many people consider an oversupply of them—have been blamed for the tremendous increase in litigation during the past two decades. The public looks to the law to solve many of its problems, sometimes social and personal ones, which prior to the 1960s would have been dealt with in other ways. Public opinion polls show that lawyers rate well below most other occupations in the areas of honesty and integrity. Many clients polled believe that lawyers are greedy, unethical, hard to communicate with, and lacking in compassion and respect for others' rights. The high salaries paid to lawyers—especially new lawyers right out of law school—have shocked and dismayed many Americans, who cannot hope to achieve such salaries in a lifetime of work. The high legal fees generated in major litigation have likewise added to the perception of lawyers as overpaid and greedy.

Related is the public perception that lawyers manipulate the legal process, finding clever ways to circumvent the law in order to prevail. This goal of winning at all costs has made many lawyers seem like contentious and overzealous abusers of the system. Lawyers' involvement in highly publicized criminal cases and business-related scandals have validated public opinion that lawyers' knowledge and skills are for sale to the highest bidder and that lawyers will not hesitate to use their talents to line their client's or their own pockets, whatever the cost to the public. Despite the poor regard in which lawyers are held, many clients look for and expect "attack dog" behavior when they need legal representation, further exacerbating this dilemma. A related client complaint is that lawyers are too chummy with one another; some clients complain when their lawyers extend professional courtesies such as extensions to opposing counsel.

Within the legal profession, lawyers in leadership positions recognize the poor image of lawyers and acknowledge additional problems that trouble lawyers and law practice. Some studies estimate that at least half the lawyers disciplined for misconduct are "impaired," usually by some type of substance abuse. Law firms have become very "bottomline-oriented," building in size and salary at astronomical rates, and sometimes placing horrendous pressure on lawyers to bill an unrealistically high number of hours. This pressure leads many lawyers to inflate or pad bills, especially bills of wealthy clients. It also drives clients away, creating a cycle of competitiveness and higher billable hours. This, in turn, undermines loyalty within the law firm, which once held most lawyers to one firm for their entire career. Lawyers now commonly move three or four times before they stick with a firm. Even big-name senior partners have abdicated from their firms for "better" ones. The overwhelming sense of law practice as a business first, a profession second, has caused great turnover and instability in firms, which themselves dissolve and merge frequently.

Finally, the competitiveness and zeal of lawyers has led to abuses of the system, such as those described in Chapter 9 on trial advocacy. Many lawyers view the litigation process as a game where tactics and strategy are more important than merit and substance. Bringing frivolous cases and motions, flooding an opponent with irrelevant and unwarranted discovery, behaving discourteously and disrespectfully to other lawyers and even to judges have become the daily method of operation for some lawyers.

Historically, there have been relatively few instances where lawyers openly reported misconduct within their law firms despite the "snitch rules" that are contained in most states' ethics rules. Firms have usually handled these matters internally and as privately as possible. But this silence has been broken by billing and related kinds of scandals in recent years. Most courts that have addressed the matter hold that attorneys who report violations as required by the codes cannot be fired for these actions. A few states also have whistleblower statutes that protect employees from being discharged in retaliation for reporting violations. It should be noted that the NFPA Model Code requires legal assistants to report ethical and legal violations.

For the past decade, the organized bar has developed initiatives relating to *professionalism.* Disciplinary systems have been found lacking and are being revamped throughout the country. Bar-sponsored programs for impaired lawyers are found in almost every state. Recently enacted court rules and statutes limit discovery and provide for severe sanctions against lawyers for abuse. Bar associations have launched public relations campaigns to improve their image. They have encouraged lawyers to engage in pro bono work and to support local charities and community activities. More than one hundred state and local bar associations, and some courts, have adopted codes of professional courtesy and civility or litigation guidelines, which advise lawyers how to conduct themselves.

The general courtesy or professionalism guidelines typically cover client relations (including communicating frequently, advising mediation, resolving matters expeditiously, not overcharging); relations with other lawyers and parties (including acting courteously, not engaging in delay or unmeritorious tactics, cooperating in scheduling and resolving disputes, not disparaging other lawyers, not harassing the opposition); relations with courts (including advocating vigorously but with civility, being punctual, being honest with the court); and duty to the public and the profession (including keeping current in practice areas, supporting the profession, upholding the profession's image). Litigation guidelines usually contain rules covering continuances, extensions, service of process, communication with adversaries, discovery, and motions. They specify conduct that is courteous, honest, and not designed to harass or unduly burden opponents.

Among the other recommendations to address these professional concerns coming from the organized bar are improvements in undergraduate education in ethics, teaching ethics and professionalism across the curriculum in law school, more aggressive judicial intervention in litigation, more pro bono and public interest work. Some local bars offer client relations programs that attempt to alter lawyers' attitudes toward and treatment of clients. Increasingly the conversation about these issues turns to the matter of morality and ethics in law practice. Many ethicists and bar leaders have called upon lawyers to examine the ethical and moral content of their actions and to avoid separating their values and beliefs as persons from their conduct as lawyers.

Many lawyers have left the profession because of the problems that characterize law practice today. Some surveys show that as many as half the lawyers in practice would not become lawyers if they had it to do all over again. Some firms have started to deal with quality of life issues by creating counseling programs for troubled lawyers, providing part-time and flexible scheduling options, encouraging sabbaticals, increasing pro bono work, and establishing a firm culture that places more value on collegiality and gives staff more time for their lives outside law practice. Firms have also designated an in-house ethics guru or committee to help lawyers with ethical dilemmas and have established one-on-one or small group mentoring for new lawyers to mitigate the negative effects of working in isolation and to build collegiality and trust.

Many studies have shown that lawyers are much more likely than persons in other occupations to be alcoholics or chemically dependent. There is also a strong correlation between disciplinary actions and substance abuse or emotional problems. In the last decade, many bar associations have been proactive in developing programs to identify and help lawyers who are impaired before the impairment leads to unethical and destructive conduct.

Burnout and stress have also been recognized as factors in conduct that leads to discipline. The pressures of the billable hours, the competitive environment of the legal world, the lack of loyalty among clients and law firms, the constant work of meeting other peoples' needs, the feeling of not having any control all contribute to burnout, detachment from relationships with others, loss of job satisfaction, and even to chronic anger and anxiety.

This troubled milieu is the one in which legal assistants find themselves working. These concerns, voiced both by the public and within the profession, affect the way in which legal assistants are viewed and view themselves. A legal assistant can be part of the problem—working for a firm that utilizes legal assistants' talents principally to abuse the legal process and to accumulate wealth—or part of the solution—working for a firm that utilizes legal assistants' talents to improve efficiency, to perform work competently and ethically, and to lower the cost of legal services to its clients. In the coming years, as the problems plaguing the profession and the proposals to solve them begin to shape a new image for law practice, legal assistants can help determine what they will look like in that picture.

B. Professionalism and the Legal Assistant

Legal assistants are in a sometimes difficult and ambiguous position in the legal profession. Because they are not lawyers, they may not legally engage in certain activities carved out exclusively for the lawyer. But they do engage in substantive legal work that otherwise would have to be done by lawyers and that is paid for by the client. The line between permissible and impermissible conduct is not always clear. Although legal assistants are part of the professional staff engaging in legal work, not part of the support staff, they can never be full and equal members of the professional team as partners in the firm. And, as a relatively new occupation, the parameters of paralegal job responsibilities remain unclear, evolving over time and changing with every new supervisor. Also, because of the relative youth of the occupation, the legal assistant's role is not well understood either by those in the legal profession or by the general public. Legal assistants frequently must explain what they do to lay persons while developing their own job descriptions and defining their role in the law firm hierarchy.

The dilemma posed by this ambiguity has many ramifications for the daily work lives of legal assistants. But the overriding question is how legal assistants can forge a role for themselves—a professional role that holds them to high standards of ethics and performance while affording them the opportunity for long, satisfying, and challenging careers. Defining professionalism is an essential first step in this process.

Most dictionaries define "profession" as an occupation that involves a special education and requires mental rather than manual labor. Most sociologists define the term as an occupation whose members have the exclusive right to engage in certain activities that are intellectual in nature and require special education; professions are bound by codes of ethics and are generally self-regulating. Philosophers tend to define a profession as a calling that requires a special commitment to public service.

Legal assistants usually are classified as *paraprofessionals,* performing legal work under the supervision of a lawyer, but having special education and sharing in the societal prestige of the lawyer. Analogous to the legal assistant are the many paraprofessionals in the allied health fields, for example, physical therapists and dental assistants.

Some research has been done on the paralegal occupation. In their excellent book, Paralegals: Progress and Prospects of a Satellite Occupation, Quintin Johnstone and Martin Wenglinsky analyze how the paralegal occupation fits the sociologist's definition of a profession, emphasizing three main characteristics—*collegiality, occupational prestige,* and *overtraining.* They find many inconsistencies, reinforcing the ambiguity that legal assistants frequently feel about their own role. For example, many law firms do not require formal paralegal training, creating nonuniform and sometimes low hiring standards in the field. On the other hand, legal assistants who have a formal education, frequently a baccalaureate degree and postgraduate certificate, find themselves "overtrained" for many of the tasks that they perform. Prestige for legal assistants is found mainly in the reflected prestige of the lawyers for whom legal assistants work. This status may be enhanced by the law firm's treatment of legal assistants, affording them a meaningful career path and appropriate perquisites, or undermined by treating them as support staff.

Collegiality also presents dichotomies. Legal assistants often do not feel a common bond with and loyalty to their paralegal colleagues, not having had a shared educational experience and not possessing a common exclusive grant to engage in certain work. Aggravating this lack of bond is the fact that many legal assistants view themselves as competitors within the firm for the most interesting work and highest pay. Thus, they often express their primary loyalty to the firm or to their supervising attorney, not to their occupation. Many legal assistants work in small or mid-sized firms where they may be the only legal assistant, lending to their feelings of isolation from others. On the other hand, paralegal associations have been quite successful in building a strong sense of camaraderie and shared interests and responsibilities among their members. See Q. Johnstone & M. Wenglinsky, Paralegals: Progress and Prospects of a Satellite Occupation, pp. 183 et seq. (1985).

Another interesting analysis of the paralegal occupation traces its evolution from an occupation to a profession, as defined by sociologists who study occupations. Green, Snell, Corgiat, and Paramanith, *The Professionalization of the Legal Assistant: Identity, Maturation States and Goal Attainment,* 7 J. Para. Ed. & Prac. 35 (1990). This article cites five stages in the development of a profession: diffusion, education, associations, agitation and self-regulation, and formulation of a professional code. The authors find the paralegal field advancing, although not smoothly, in the second stage (education) and recommend a strengthened and standardized paralegal curriculum. It is also notable that legal assistants have made considerable efforts—if not strides—simultaneously in the last three stages.

In the past five years, considerable progress has been made in the "professionalization" of the paralegal occupation. Levels of education, both general and specialized paralegal education, are rising according to NALA, surveys conducted by LAMA, NFPA, and others. The duties legal assistants are performing have greatly broadened, and include more client contact and more sophisticated work. Billing rates and salaries are up. Both national associations are now promoting voluntary certification, and budding statewide certification programs exist in four states.

Professionalism has been a topic of much discussion in the ranks of legal assistants, within their professional associations and workplaces and in their literature. Discussion of the quest for professionalism has taken the form of magazine articles, studies, and advice that ranges the full gamut from "dressing as a professional" to conducting oneself ethically.

Taking all these views into account, professionalism as applied to legal assistants might require the following elements:

1. Commitment to Public Service. Legal assistants should always remember that their highest goal is to assist in the delivery of legal services to the public, legal services that are delivered ethically, competently, and efficiently. In addition to being reflected in their daily work lives, this commitment also requires legal assistants to engage in

369

activities that improve the system of delivery of legal services overall, such as pro bono programs. See Section D below.

2. *Commitment to Education.* Fulfilling this commitment includes participating in formal education, continuing education, and on-the-job learning that enhance knowledge and skills and continually develop the legal assistant's potential. Education heightens the legal assistant's ability to deliver quality legal services and enriches long-term career satisfaction.

3. *Commitment to the Highest Standards of Ethical Conduct.* Legal assistants must know the rules of ethics that bind lawyers and understand how these rules apply to them. Legal assistants also must develop their own personal standards of ethics and morality that reach beyond the minimums imposed by law. Legal assistants must be scrupulously honest in their relations with clients, courts, attorneys, and co-workers.

4. *Commitment to Excellence.* Paralegals must set high standards of performance for themselves and seek to meet those standards in all the work they undertake. They should approach each task with an attitude of seriousness and apply all their knowledge, skill, and talent to accomplish their work.

5. *Commitment to the Paralegal Profession.* Legal assistants must view themselves as part of a common occupation, with interests and goals that are shared by other legal assistants. They must support joint paralegal activities organized through professional associations, bar associations, and alumni associations. Legal assistants must also engender collegiality among the legal assistants with whom they work, mentoring new legal assistants when appropriate and acting as a role model and source of information for those who aspire to the paralegal profession.

6. *Commitment to a Strong Work Ethic.* Legal assistants must strive to do their best on every task and to serve the clients of their firms diligently. They should be meticulous and thorough, organized in their work process, prompt in meeting deadlines, and always do more than the minimum. They should take pride in their work and always do work that merits that pride.

7. *Commitment to Acting with Integrity and Honor.* Legal assistants must be courteous, respectful, and fair in their dealings with lawyers, other legal assistants, support staff, clients, and others both within and outside their firm. They must demonstrate maturity, patience, and thoughtfulness in their actions, avoiding gossip, undue criticism of others, prejudice, and favoritism. This commitment also requires legal assistants to show sensitivity to the needs and talents of others, appreciation for the differences in people's backgrounds, tolerance, helpfulness, and a sense of recognition for others' achievements.

8. Commitment to the Development of the Whole Person. Legal assistants must not become so consumed by their work that they neglect the other aspects of their life, like family, friends, health, and personal interests and activities. They should seek to be well-rounded persons, with a variety of interests. Commitment to a profession need not prevent a person from leading a full life; in fact, a person who narrows his or her interests only to work will not be as effective in relations with others and will not possess the sense of proportion and balance needed to fulfill his or her commitments as a professional.

9. Commitment to Exercising Good Judgment, Common Sense, and Communication Skills. Legal assistants must use their understanding of human nature as a guide in their relations with others. They must listen to others carefully and communicate, both orally and in writing, clearly and persuasively.

C. Current Issues in Professionalism

A number of important issues now face the paralegal profession that the legal assistants of today will be instrumental in resolving. Many of these have ramifications for the ethics and professionalism of legal assistants.

One issue that has always been central to the debate about the evolution of the paralegal field is regulation. Discussed in Chapter 2, regulation is a complex question that will not be resolved without a good deal of stress on legal assistants and the organizations that represent them. The debate has raised many difficult questions:

- Is there a need for regulation?
- Who should be regulated?
- Who should do the regulating?

- Should regulation be mandatory?
- What level of regulation is appropriate?
- What educational requirements should be established?
- What kind of examination, if any, should be required?
- What, if any, tasks should legal assistants be authorized to perform only if they are regulated?

The resolution of the regulation issue will determine the future of the career, the extent to which it becomes an independent "profession," and the nature and character of legal assistants and their work.

As the debate on regulation continues, NALA promotes voluntary regulation through its CLA program and encourages states to adopt its exam for use in their own certification programs. NFPA has endorsed a two-tier regulatory scheme with general and specialized certification and has started to offer its PACE examination in Tier One. Every year, a few jurisdictions explore the idea of regulating attorney-supervised legal assistants.

Education is another important issue for legal assistants. The lack of consistency in hiring standards and in uniformity in the paralegal curriculum prevent legal assistants from having a shared body of knowledge and a shared educational experience, two important characteristics that distinguish occupations from professions. The lack of common educational experience also inhibits the development of collegiality among paralegals. However, the diversity within paralegal education and the variety of ways used to enter the field have allowed the paralegal profession to flourish and to move in directions many thought impossible. Legal assistants have a continuously expanding bank of job responsibilities, unhindered by a standardized, limiting education that trains everyone to perform the same tasks. The diverse work and life experiences that are brought to the profession by the wide variety of people who become legal assistants have enriched both the career possibilities and legal profession itself.

As indicated earlier, educational achievement among legal assistants is rising. While the ABA and the American Association for Paralegal Education endorse two years of college as a minimum for entry into the paralegal field, the Legal Assistant Management Association, representing corporate counsel offices and large law firms, favors a four-year degree and the National Federation of Paralegal Associations has set the baccalaureate degree as a minimum to take the PACE examination after a brief "grand-parenting" period. And the paralegal educators, ABA, and paralegal associations continue to discuss appropriate minimal and aspirational levels of education for legal assistants as well as what competencies should be required of legal assistants.

The ambiguity that accompanies the growth of any new profession has also created problems for legal assistants. Even now, more than 20 years after the advent of the modern American legal assistant, many lawyers still resist using legal assistants' services. Others are unclear on how to utilize their talents and skills or reluctant to delegate anything more than routine or repetitive work to them. While all large law firms and many mid-sized ones employ legal assistants, sole practitioners and small firms continue not to use the services in large numbers. Some lawyers and law firms treat their legal assistants poorly—by not compensating them fairly, not providing appropriate working conditions and clerical support, or not giving them recognition when deserved—but still expect professional work and attitudes. This treatment has resulted in high turnover within those firms and relatively high turnover in the occupation as a whole as legal assistants leave the profession, dissatisfied with their treatment, compensation, and the nature of their work.

Related is the question of whether legal assistants should be classified as exempt or nonexempt employees. If nonexempt, they are entitled to overtime compensation under the Fair Labor Standards Act and similar state laws. Under U.S. Department of Labor Letter Rulings issued between 1977 and 1995, legal assistants as a group may not be classified as exempt because they are not required to have advanced professional knowledge acquired through prolonged, specialized instruction and study, and are not generally involved in the performance of duties that require the exercise of discretion and independent judgment. (Employees must meet definitions for Executive, Professional, or Administrative status in order to be classified exempt. See 29 C.F.R. §541.) In the 1980s and early 1990s the Department of Labor charged some firms with unfair labor practices for not paying overtime to legal assistants. As a result, the number of firms paying overtime increased. Most surveys now show that at least 50 percent of legal assistants are categorized by their employers as nonexempt.

Legal assistants, including those who are members of the two leading paralegal associations, are divided on the issue, many believing that their classification as nonexempt is degrading and does not accurately reflect their professional work and status. Others believe that they will not be fairly compensated for their long hours of work unless they get overtime pay and that overtime pay does not lower their status or prestige in the law firm.

And while more firms are paying overtime now than a decade ago, not all firms have changed their policies or pay all their legal assistants in the same way. For example, many law firms that have career paths for legal assistants classify the lower rungs of the ladder as nonexempt and the top level or levels as exempt, based on the nature and complexity of the specific responsibilities and the degree of independence exercised by the legal assistant at each level.

Finally, the paralegal career is a female-dominated occupation that serves a still male-dominated profession. Other traditionally female-dominated professions like nursing and teaching have struggled very hard—not always successfully—to achieve status and recognition, fair treatment, good working conditions, and compensation that is based on the value, nature, and difficulty of their work.

Gender-related issues have come to the forefront in recent years in discussions about law practice. Ethics rules barring attorneys from having sexual relations with clients have been adopted in several states. A 1992 ABA Formal Ethics Opinion (92-364) advises attorneys against sexual relations with clients because of the inherent dangers of "unfair exploitation" and the threat to the lawyer's independent judgment. Most experts believe attorneys are subject to discipline for such conduct without a specific ethics rule. Some jurisdictions have experienced a rise in lawsuits against attorneys who have had sexual relations with clients, and in some cases substantial judgments have been awarded.

High-profile sexual harassment and sex discrimination cases have been brought and won against several prominent law firms. Some suits have been brought by women lawyers and some by support staff. Surveys show that 50 percent of the women lawyers in the United States believe they have been harassed. Most women do not report such incidents out of fear of retaliation and marginalization. Many firms have instituted sexual harassment policies that define prohibited conduct, establish procedures and sanctions, and include sensitivity training.

Bias against lawyers on the basis of race, sex, or sexual orientation has been documented in many studies that show women and minority lawyers make less money, are less likely to make partner, and are excluded from key firm committees and prestigious practice areas. About 20 jurisdictions have adopted antibias rules that make it an ethical violation to discriminate in the operation of a practice and/or to disparage or humiliate someone on the basis of race, national origin, sex, sexual orientation, religion, age, or disability. For example, see California Rules of Professional Conduct 2-400 and Florida Rule 4-8.4. And the Americans with Disabilities Act has added new protection for disabled employees and other persons in their interactions with law firms.

These issues must be addressed by legal assistants, who have the biggest stake in determining their outcome. Legal assistants must be aware of the many dilemmas with which the profession is confronted and take an active part—on the job and through their professional associations—to build a solid future for the profession.

374

D. Pro Bono Work

The fact that the legal needs of the vast majority of Americans are going unmet is undisputed. Study after study has proven that most Americans—including poor and middle-income persons—do not have access to a lawyer when they need one. Most Americans cannot afford a lawyer; many who actually can afford one perceive that they cannot. Most would not know how to go about finding a lawyer.

To cope with this problem, the organized bar has encouraged individual lawyers to engage in pro bono work and has sponsored a wide variety of pro bono programs to which lawyers can contribute their time and expertise. Most states that have addressed this issue have adopted voluntary aspirational guidelines for lawyers, usually for 50 hours of pro bono work a year. Only a few have mandatory rules, which can fulfilled by making a donation in lieu of doing the work. Some law schools have a requirement for public service or pro bono work, and many law firms have policies that encourage their attorneys to engage in such activities.

During the past few years, there has been an increase in voluntary pro bono work being done by lawyers and law firms. The need for legal services is still unmet, however, and legal assistants have an opportunity to help fill this need. Participating in pro bono activities as part of one's professional commitment not only produces psychic rewards but increases career satisfaction and self-esteem.

Guideline 10 to the ABA Model Guidelines for the Utilization of Legal Assistant Services (ABA Model Guidelines) encourages lawyers to facilitate paralegal participation in pro bono activities. Many state guidelines on legal assistants follow suit. See, for example, Indiana Guideline 9.9 and Michigan Guideline 8. Lawyers have a duty to provide pro bono services under ABA Model Rule 6.1 and Canon 2 of the ABA Model Code and the ABA has called on lawyers to fulfill this duty by aspiring to do 50 hours of pro bono work annually.

Many law firms that do pro bono work include legal assistants in these activities. Legal assistants who do not have an opportunity to become involved in pro bono work through their jobs should seek out activities on their own. Local bar associations and paralegal associations usually have several kinds of pro bono projects on which legal assistants can work. Legal aid organizations and law clinics are always in need of volunteers.

Pro bono programs have been established in many specialized areas of law, affording legal assistants a chance either to exercise their expertise or to learn a new area. Examples of what areas some of the programs

375

cover are: court-appointed special advocates in juvenile and family law, consumer disputes, landlord-tenant matters, major public interest litigation (for example, housing or employment discrimination or children's rights), immigration, indigent taxpayers, elder law, bankruptcy, family law, mental health advocacy, domestic violence counseling, AIDS, and homeless projects.

Legal assistants who do pro bono work often find themselves working more independently than they do in their law firms, engaged in challenging tasks that they would not be delegated on their jobs. Legal assistants in legal aid settings very often have extensive client contact, handling intake interviews and helping clients directly with matters not requiring a lawyer. Legal assistants are often called on in these settings to advocate for clients before administrative agencies, to conduct in-depth research, and to draft documents and memoranda.

Besides skill development and growth, legal assistants who do pro bono work derive the ultimate satisfaction of helping someone who needs help and who might not otherwise have gotten that help. Usually the assistance needed and provided is of the most critical kind—for instance, keeping someone from losing a home or welfare benefits—and is a matter of survival to the clients.

Excellent materials on paralegal involvement in pro bono activities are available through local bar associations, the National Federation of Paralegal Associations, and the National Association of Legal Assistants, and their local chapters and affiliates.

REVIEW QUESTIONS

1. Give five reasons why the public image of lawyers is so poor.
2. What are lawyers doing to improve their public image?
3. What is a code of professional courtesy? What kinds of conduct does it require?
4. How can a legal assistant make a difference in improving the professionalism and public image of the legal field?
5. Why are legal assistants in an ambiguous position in the legal environment? Give at least three reasons.
6. How is "profession" defined?
7. What is a paraprofessional?
8. What is collegiality? Why is collegiality difficult for legal assistants to have?
9. To what extent are legal assistants overtrained?

10. Describe the nine professional commitments that legal assistants should make.
11. Name and discuss three issues facing today's legal assistants.
12. What is the basis for classifying a legal assistant as an exempt or nonexempt employee? What is the law currently?
13. Does the fact that legal assistants are predominately female affect the career? How?
14. What is the current state of legal services for poor and middle-income Americans?
15. Have pro bono activities increased or decreased in the last decade?
16. What kinds of pro bono activities do lawyers and legal assistants engage in?
17. What are the benefits to a legal assistant of doing pro bono work?
18. How can a legal assistant get involved in pro bono work?
19. What are some of the gender-related issues that law firms face?

DISCUSSION QUESTIONS

1. Do you think the legal profession deserves its poor public image? Why, or why not?
2. Read the newspaper every day for a month and clip out all the articles that mention lawyers. How many are favorable? What image do they present?
3. How can the legal profession overcome its poor image?
4. Do you think lawyers' salaries are disproportionately high? Why, or why not?
5. Do you think lawyers' increased mobility is a good or bad thing? Why?
6. Does your local bar association or court have a code of professional courtesy? Do you think a nonbinding code such as this is appropriate for a court or bar association to have? Why, or why not? Should such a code be binding? Why, or why not? Do such codes derogate the lawyer's duty of zealousness? Do they contribute to lawyers' "clubbiness"? Do they work?
7. Contact your local paralegal association and get salary surveys that ask about job satisfaction, career paths, pro bono work, exempt/nonexempt status.
8. Contact five legal assistants at local law firms and ask them:

   a. if they regard their paralegal career as a profession;
   b. if they are treated as professionals by their employers;

377

    c. if they plan to continue as a legal assistant indefinitely, and if not;

- what they plan to do;
- why they are leaving the career;

    d. if they are members of the local paralegal association;
    e. if their firm does pro bono work;
    f. if they do pro bono work;
    g. if their education and training are well utilized;
    h. if they are paid overtime;
    i. if they have experienced gender-related discrimination.

9. Do you think legal assistants are professionals or paraprofessionals? Is this distinction important to you? Why?

10. Do you think Johnstone and Wenglinsky's three characteristics (collegiality, overtraining, and prestige) are instructive in evaluating the paralegal occupation as a profession? Why, or why not?

11. Do you think standardization in paralegal education would be good or bad for the career? Why?

12. How can legal assistants build collegiality? Why is it important?

13. Do you think voluntary certification is good for paralegals? Why, or why not? What about mandatory regulation? Why, or why not?

14. Looking at the five stages toward professionalization presented by the Green article, where do you think the paralegal occupation fits?

15. Do you agree with the nine professional commitments for legal assistants? Why, or why not? How would you prioritize their relative importance? What would you add or delete?

16. Do you think regulation of legal assistants would enhance their professional status? Why, or why not?

17. How can legal assistants help overcome lawyers' reluctance to utilize their services? How can legal assistants encourage lawyers to utilize their services more effectively and fully?

18. Contact the local bar and paralegal associations and find out what kinds of pro bono opportunities are available to legal assistants in your area.

ABA Model Guidelines for the Utilization of Legal Assistant Services

Preamble

State courts, bar associations, or bar committees in at least seventeen states have prepared recommendations[1] for the utilization of legal assistant services.[2] While their content varies, their purpose appears uniform: to provide lawyers with a reliable basis for delegating responsibility for performing a portion of the lawyer's tasks to legal assistants. The purpose of preparing model guidelines is not to contradict the guidelines already adopted or to suggest that other guidelines may be more appropriate in a particular jurisdiction. It is the view of the Standing Committee on Legal Assistants of the American Bar Association, however, that a model set of guidelines for the utilization of legal assistant services may assist many states in adopting or revising such guidelines. The Standing Com-

1. An appendix identifies the guidelines, court rules, and recommendations that were reviewed in drafting these Model Guidelines.
2. On February 6, 1986, the ABA Board of Governors approved the following definition of the term "legal assistant":

> A legal assistant is a person, qualified through education, training, or work experience, who is employed or retained by a lawyer, law office, governmental agency, or other entity in a capacity or function which involves the performance, under the ultimate direction and supervision of an attorney, of specifically delegated substantive legal work, which work, for the most part, requires a sufficient knowledge of legal concepts that, absent such assistant, the attorney would perform the task.

In some contexts, the term "paralegal" is used interchangeably with the term legal assistant.

mittee is of the view that guidelines will encourage lawyers to utilize legal assistant services effectively and promote the growth of the legal assistant profession.[3] In undertaking this project, the Standing Committee has attempted to state guidelines that conform with the American Bar Association's Model Rules of Professional Conduct, decided authority, and contemporary practice. Lawyers, of course, are to be first directed by Rule 5.3 of the Model Rules in the utilization of legal assistant services, and nothing contained in these guidelines is intended to be inconsistent with that rule. Specific ethical considerations in particular states, however, may require modification of these guidelines before their adoption. In the commentary after each guideline, we have attempted to identify the basis for the guideline and any issues of which we are aware that the guideline may present; those drafting such guidelines may wish to take them into account.

Guideline 1: **A lawyer is responsible for all of the professional actions of a legal assistant performing legal assistant services at the lawyer's direction and should take reasonable measures to ensure that the legal assistant's conduct is consistent with the lawyer's obligations under the ABA Model Rules of Professional Conduct.**

Comment to Guideline 1

An attorney who utilizes a legal assistant's services is responsible for determining that the legal assistant is competent to perform the tasks assigned, based on the legal assistant's education, training, and experience, and for ensuring that the legal assistant is familiar with the responsibilities of attorneys and legal assistants under the applicable rules governing professional conduct.[4]

Under principles of agency law and rules governing the conduct of attorneys, lawyers are responsible for the actions and the work product

---

3. While necessarily mentioning legal assistant conduct, lawyers are the intended audience of these Guidelines. The Guidelines, therefore, are addressed to lawyer conduct and not directly to the conduct of the legal assistant. Both the National Association of Legal Assistants (NALA) and the National Federation of Paralegal Associations (NFPA) have adopted guidelines of conduct that are directed to legal assistants. See NALA, "Code of Ethics and Professional Responsibility of the National Association of Legal Assistants, Inc." (adopted May 1975, revised November 1979 and September 1988); NFPA, "Affirmation of Responsibility" (adopted 1977, revised 1981).

4. Attorneys, of course, are not liable for violations of the ABA Model Rules of Professional Conduct ("Model Rules") unless the Model Rules have been adopted as the code of professional conduct in a jurisdiction in which the lawyer practices. They are referenced in this model guideline for illustrative purposes; if the guideline is to be adopted, the reference should be modified to the jurisdiction's rules of professional conduct.

of the non-lawyers they employ. Rule 5.3 of the Model Rules[5] requires that partners and supervising attorneys ensure that the conduct of nonlawyer assistants is compatible with the lawyer's professional obligations. Several state guidelines have adopted this language. E.g., Commentary to Illinois Recommendation (A), Kansas Guideline III(a), New Hampshire Rule 35, Sub-Rule 9, and North Carolina Guideline 4. Ethical Consideration 3-6 of the Model Code encouraged lawyers to delegate tasks to legal assistants provided the lawyer maintained a direct relationship with the client, supervised appropriately, and had complete responsibility for the work product. The adoption of Rule 5.3, which incorporates these principles, implicitly reaffirms this encouragement.

Several states have addressed the issue of the lawyer's ultimate responsibility for work performed by subordinates. For example, Colorado Guideline 1.c, Kentucky Supreme Court Rule 3.700, Sub-Rule 2.C, and Michigan Guideline I provide: "The lawyer remains responsible for the actions of the legal assistant to the same extent as if such representation had been furnished entirely by the lawyer and such actions were those of the lawyer." New Mexico Guideline X states "[the] lawyer maintains ultimate responsibility for and has an ongoing duty to actively supervise the legal assistant's work performance, conduct and product." Connecticut Recommendation 2 and Rhode Island Guideline III state specifically that lawyers are liable for malpractice for the mistakes and omissions of their legal assistants.

Finally, the lawyer should ensure that legal assistants supervised by the lawyer are familiar with the rules governing attorney conduct and that they follow those rules. See Comment to Model Rule 5.3; Illinois Recommendation (A)(5), New Hampshire Supreme Court Rule 35, Sub-Rule 9, and New Mexico, Statement of Purpose; see also NALA's Model Standards and Guidelines for the Utilization of Legal Assistants, guildeines IV, V, and VIII (1985, revised 1990) (hereafter "NALA Guidelines").

The Standing Committee and several of those who have commented upon these Guidelines regard Guideline I as a comprehensive statement of general principle governing lawyers who utilize legal assistant services in the practice of law. As such it, in effect, is a part of each of the remaining Guidelines.

---

5. The Model Rules were first adopted by the ABA House of Delegates in August of 1983. Since that time many states have adopted the Model Rules to govern the professional conduct of lawyers licensed in those states. Since a number of states still utilize a version of the Model Code of Professional Responsibility ("Model Code"), which was adopted by the House of Delegates in August of 1969, however, these comments will refer to both the Model Rules and the predecessor Model Code (and to the Ethical Considerations and Disciplinary Rules found under the canons in the Model Codes).

Guideline 2:   **Provided the lawyer maintains responsibility for the work product, a lawyer may delegate to a legal assistant any task normally performed by the lawyer except those tasks proscribed to one not licensed as a lawyer by statute, court rule, administrative rule or regulation, controlling authority, the ABA Model Rules of Professional Conduct, or these Guidelines.**

Comment to Guideline 2

The essence of the definition of the term legal assistant adopted by the ABA Board of Governors in 1986 is that, so long as appropriate supervision is maintained, many tasks normally performed by lawyers may be delegated to legal assistants. Of course, Rule 5.5 of the Model Rules, DR 3-101 of the Model Code, and most states specifically prohibit lawyers from assisting or aiding a non-lawyer in the unauthorized practice of law. Thus, while appropriate delegation of tasks to legal assistants is encouraged, the lawyer may not permit the legal assistant to engage in the "practice of law." Neither the Model Rules nor the Model Code define the "practice of law." EC 3-5 under the Model Code gave some guidance by equating the practice of law to the application of the professional judgment of the lawyer in solving clients' legal problems. Further, ABA Opinion 316 (1967) states: "A lawyer can employ lay secretaries, lay investigators, lay detectives, lay researchers, accountants, lay scriveners, nonlawyer draftsmen or nonlawyer researchers. In fact, he may employ nonlawyers to do any task for him except counsel clients about law matters, engage directly in the practice of law, appear in court or appear in formal proceedings as part of the judicial process, so long as it is he who takes the work and vouches for it to the client and becomes responsible for it to the client."

Most state guidelines specify that legal assistants may not appear before courts, administrative tribunals, or other adjudicatory bodies unless their rules authorize such appearances; may not conduct depositions; and may not give legal advice to clients. E.g., Connecticut Recommendation 4; Florida EC 3-6 (327 So. 2d at 16); and Michigan Guideline II. Also see NALA Guidelines IV and VI. But it is also important to note that, as some guidelines have recognized, pursuant to federal or state statute legal assistants are permitted to provide direct client representation in certain administrative proceedings. E.g., South Carolina Guideline II. While this does not obviate the attorney's responsibility for the legal assistant's work, it does change the nature of the attorney supervision of the legal assistant. The opportunity to use such legal assistant services has particular benefits to legal services programs and does not violate

Guideline 2. See generally ABA Standards for Providers of Civil Legal Services to the Poor, Std. 6.3, at 6.17–6.18 (1986).

The Model Rules emphasize the importance of appropriate delegation. The key to appropriate delegation is proper supervision, which includes adequate instruction when assigning projects, monitoring of the project, and review of the completed project. The Supreme Court of Virginia upheld a malpractice verdict against a lawyer based in part on negligent actions of a legal assistant in performing tasks that evidently were properly delegable. *Musselman v. Willoughby Corp.*, 230 Va. 337, 337 S.E.2d 724 (1985). See also C. Wolfram, Modern Legal Ethics (1986), at 236, 896. All state guidelines refer to the requirement that the lawyer "supervise" legal assistants in the performance of their duties. Lawyers should also take care in hiring and choosing a legal assistant to work on a specific project to ensure that the legal assistant has the education, knowledge, and ability necessary to perform the delegated tasks competently. See Connecticut Recommendation 14, Kansas Standards I, II, and III, and New Mexico Guideline VIII. Finally, some states describe appropriate delegation and review in terms of the delegated work losing its identity and becoming "merged" into the work product of the attorney. See Florida EC 3-6 (327 So. 2d at 16).

Legal assistants often play an important role in improving communication between the attorney and the client. EC 3-6 under the Model Code mentioned three specific kinds of tasks that legal assistants may perform under appropriate lawyer supervision: factual investigation and research, legal research, and the preparation of legal documents. Some states delineate more specific tasks in their guidelines, such as attending client conferences, corresponding with and obtaining information from clients, handling witness execution of documents, preparing transmittal letters, maintaining estate/guardianship trust accounts, etc. See, e.g., Colorado (lists of specialized functions in several areas follow guidelines); Michigan, Comment to Definition of Legal Assistant; New York, Specialized Skills of Legal Assistants; Rhode Island Guideline II; and NALA Guideline IX. The two-volume Working with Legal Assistants, published by the Standing Committee in 1982, attempted to provide a general description of the types of tasks that may be delegated to legal assistants in various practice areas.

There are tasks that have been specifically prohibited in some states, but that may be delegated in others. For example, legal assistants may not supervise will executions or represent clients at real estate closings in some jurisdictions, but may in others. Compare Connecticut Recommendation 7 and Illinois State Bar Association Position Paper on Use of Attorney Assistants in Real Estate Transactions (May 16, 1984), which proscribe legal assistants conducting real estate closings, with Georgia "real estate job description," Florida Professional Ethics Committee Advisory Opinion 89-5 (1989), and Missouri, Comment to Guideline I, which permit legal assistants to conduct real estate closings. Also compare Connecticut Recommendation 8 (prohibiting attorneys from authorizing legal assistants to supervise will executions) with Colorado "estate planning job description," Georgia "estate, trusts, and wills job description," Missouri, Comment to Guideline I, and Rhode Island Guideline II (suggesting that legal assistants may supervise the execution of wills, trusts, and other documents).

> *Guideline 3:* **A lawyer may not delegate to a legal assistant:**
>
> **(a) Responsibility for establishing an attorney–client relationship.**
> **(b) Responsibility for establishing the amount of a fee to be charged for a legal service.**
> **(c) Responsibility for a legal opinion rendered to a client.**

Comment to Guideline 3

The Model Rules and most state codes require that lawyers communicate with their clients in order for clients to make well-informed decisions about their representation and resolution of legal issues. Model Rule 1.4, Ethical Consideration 3-6 under the Model Code emphasized that "delegation [of legal tasks to nonlawyers] is proper if the lawyer *maintains a direct relationship with his client,* supervises the delegated work and has complete professional responsibility for the work product." (Emphasis added.) Accordingly, most state guidelines also stress the importance of a direct attorney-client relationship. See Colorado Guideline 1, Florida EC 3-6, Illinois Recommendation (A)(1), Iowa EC 3-6(2), and New Mexico Guideline IV. The direct personal relationship between client and lawyer is necessary to the exercise of the lawyer's trained professional judgment.

An essential aspect of the lawyer-client relationship is the agreement to undertake representation and the related fee arrangement. The Model Rules and most states require that fee arrangements be agreed upon early on and be communicated to the client by the lawyer, in some circumstances in writing. Model Rule 1.5 and Comments. Many state guidelines prohibit legal assistants from "setting fees" or "accepting cases." See, e.g., Colorado Guideline 1 and NALA Guideline VI. Connecticut recommends that legal assistants be prohibited from accepting or rejecting cases or setting fees "if these tasks entail any discretion on the part of the paralegals." Connecticut Recommendation 9.

EC 3-5 states: "[T]he essence of the professional judgment of the lawyer is his educated ability to relate the general body and philosophy of law to a specific legal problem of a client; and thus, the public interest will be better served if only lawyers are permitted to act in matters involving professional judgment." Clients are entitled to their lawyers' professional judgment and opinion. Legal assistants may, however, be authorized to communicate legal advice so long as they do not interpret or expand on that advice. Typically, state guidelines phrase this prohibition in terms of legal assistants being forbidden from "giving legal advice" or "counseling clients about legal matters." See, e.g., Colorado Guideline 2, Connecticut Recommendation 6, Florida DR 3-104, Iowa EC 3-6(3), Kansas Guideline I, Kentucky Sub-Rule 2, New Hampshire Rule 35, Sub-Rule 1, Texas Guideline I, and NALA Guideline VI. Some states have more expansive wording that prohibits legal assistants from engaging in any activity that would require the exercise of independent legal judgment. Nevertheless, it is clear that all states, as well as the Model Rules, encourage direct communication between clients and a legal assistant insofar as the legal assistant is performing a task properly delegated by a lawyer. It should be noted that a lawyer who permits a legal assistant to assist in establishing the attorney-client relationship, communicating a fee, or preparing a legal opinion is not delegating responsibility for those matters and, therefore, may be complying with this guideline.

Guideline 4: **It is the lawyer's responsibility to take reasonable measures to ensure that clients, courts, and other lawyers are aware that a legal assistant, whose services are utilized by the lawyer in performing legal services, is not licensed to practice law.**

Comment to Guideline 4

Since, in most instances, a legal assistant is not licensed as a lawyer, it is important that those with whom the legal assistant deals are aware of that fact. Several state guidelines impose on the lawyer responsibility for instructing a legal assistant whose services are utilized by the lawyer to disclose the legal assistant's status in any dealings with a third party. See, e.g., Michigan Guideline III, part 5, New Hampshire Rule 35, Sub-Rule 8, and NALA Guideline V. While requiring the legal assistant to make such disclosure is one way in which the attorney's responsibility to third parties may be discharged, the Standing Committee is of the view that it is desirable to emphasize the lawyer's responsibility for the disclosure and leave to the lawyer the discretion to decide whether the lawyer will discharge that responsibility by direct communication with the client, by requiring the legal assistant to make the disclosure, by a written memorandum, or by some other means. Although in most initial engagements by a client it may be prudent for the attorney to discharge this responsibility with a writing, the guideline requires only that the lawyer recognize the responsibility and ensure that it is discharged. Clearly, when a client has been adequately informed of the lawyer's utilization of legal assistant services, it is unnecessary to make additional formalistic disclosures as the client retains the lawyer for other services.

Most state guidelines specifically endorse legal assistants signing correspondence so long as their status as a legal assistant is indicated by an appropriate title. E.g., Colorado Guideline 2; Kansas, Comment to Guideline IX; and North Carolina Guideline 9; also see ABA Informal Opinion 1367 (1976). The comment to New Mexico Guideline XI warns against the use of the title "associate" since it may be construed to mean associate-attorney.

Guideline 5: A lawyer may identify legal assistants by name and title on the lawyer's letterhead and on business cards identifying the lawyer's firm.

Comment to Guideline 5

Under Guideline 4, above, an attorney who employs a legal assistant has an obligation to ensure that the status of the legal assistant as a non-lawyer is fully disclosed. The primary purpose of this disclosure is to avoid confusion that might lead someone to believe that the legal assistant is a lawyer. The identification suggested by this guideline is consistent with that objective, while also affording the legal assistant recognition as an important part of the legal services team.

Recent ABA Informal Opinion 1527 (1989) provides that non-lawyer support personnel, including legal assistants, may be listed on a law firm's letterhead and reiterates previous opinions that approve of legal assistants having business cards. See also ABA Informal Opinion 1185 (1971). The listing must not be false or misleading and "must make it clear that the support personnel who are listed are not lawyers."

Nearly all state guidelines approve of business cards for legal assistants, but some prescribe the contents and format of the card. E.g., Iowa Guideline 4 and Texas Guideline VIII. All agree the legal assistant's status must be clearly indicated and the card may not be used in a deceptive way. New Hampshire Supreme Court Rule 7 approves the use of business cards so long as the card is not used for unethical solicitation.

Some states do not permit attorneys to list legal assistants on their letterhead. E.g., Kansas Guideline VIII, Michigan Guideline III, New Hampshire Rule 35, Sub-Rule 7, New Mexico Guideline XI, and North Carolina Guideline 9. Several of these states rely on earlier ABA Informal Opinions 619 (1962), 845 (1965), and 1000 (1977), all of which were expressly withdrawn by ABA Informal Opinion 1527. These earlier opinions interpreted the predecessor Model Code and DR 2-102 (A), which, prior to *Bates v. State Bar of Arizona,* 433 U.S. 350 (1977), had strict limitations on the information that could be listed on letterheads. States which do permit attorneys to list names of legal assistants on their stationery, if the listing is not deceptive and the legal assistant's status is clearly identified, include: Arizona Committee on Rules of Professional Conduct Formal Opinion 3/90 (1990); Connecticut Recommendation 12; Florida Professional Ethics Committee Advisory Opinion 86-4 (1986); Hawaii, Formal Opinion 78-8-19 (1978, as revised 1984); Illinois State Bar Association Advisory Opinion 87-1 (1987); Kentucky Sub-Rule 6; Mississippi State Bar Ethics Committee Opinion No. 93 (1984); Missouri Guideline IV; New York State Bar Association Committee on Professional Ethics Opinion 500 (1978); Oregon, Ethical Opinion No. 349 (1977); and Texas, Ethics Committee Opinion 436 (1983). In light of the United States Supreme Court opinion in *Peel v. Attorney Registration and Disciplinary Commission of Illinois,* — U.S. —, 110 S. Ct. 2281 (1990), it may be that a restriction on letterhead identification of legal assistants that is not deceptive and clearly identifies the legal assistant's status violates the First Amendment rights of the lawyer.

Guideline 6: **It is the responsibility of a lawyer to take reasonable measures to ensure that all client confidences are preserved by a legal assistant.**

Comment to Guideline 6

A fundamental principle underlying the free exchange of information in a lawyer-client relationship is that the lawyer maintain the confidentiality of information relating to the representation. "It is a matter of common knowledge that the normal operation of a law office exposes confidential professional information to non-lawyer employees of the office. This obligates a lawyer to exercise care in selecting and training his employees so that the sanctity of all confidences and secrets of his clients may be preserved." EC 4-2, Model Code.

Rule 5.3 of the Model Rules requires "a lawyer who has direct supervisory authority over the nonlawyer [to] make reasonable efforts to ensure that the person's conduct is compatible with the professional obligations of the lawyer." The Comment to Rule 5.3 makes it clear that lawyers should give legal assistants "appropriate instruction and supervision concerning the ethical aspects of their employment, particularly regarding the obligation not to disclose information relating to the representation of the client." DR 4-101(D) under the Model Code provides that: "A lawyer shall exercise reasonable care to prevent his employees, associates and others whose services are utilized by him from discharging or using confidences or secrets of a client. . . ."

It is particularly important that the lawyer ensure that the legal assistant understands that *all* information concerning the client, even the mere fact that a person is a client of the firm, may be strictly confidential. Rule 1.6 of the Model Rules expanded the definition of confidential information ". . . not merely to matters communicated in confidence by the client but also to all information relating to the representation, whatever its source."[6] It is therefore the lawyer's obligation to instruct clearly and to take reasonable steps to ensure the legal assistant's preservation of client confidences. Nearly all states that have guidelines for the utilization of legal assistants require the lawyer "to instruct legal assistants concerning client confidences" and "to exercise care to ensure that legal assistants comply" with the Code in this regard. Even if the client consents to divulging information, this information must not be used to the disadvantage of the client. See, e.g., Connecticut Recommendation 3; New Hampshire Rule 35, Sub-Rule 4; NALA Guideline V.

Guideline 7: A lawyer should take reasonable measures to prevent conflicts of interest resulting from a legal assistant's other employment or interests insofar as such other employment or interests would present a conflict of interest if it were that of the lawyer.

Comment to Guideline 7

A lawyer must make "reasonable efforts to ensure that [a] legal assistant's conduct is compatible with the professional obligations of the lawyer." Model Rule 5.3. These professional obligations include the duty to exercise independent professional judgment on behalf of a client,

---

6. Rule 1.05 of the Texas Disciplinary Rules of Professional Conduct (1990) provides a different formulation, which is equally expansive:

"Confidential information" includes both "privileged information" and "unprivileged client information." "Privileged information" refers to the information of a client protected by the lawyer-client privilege of Rule 503 of the Texas Rules of Evidence or of Rule 503 of the Texas Rules of Criminal Evidence or by the principles of attorney-client privilege governed by Rule 501 of the Federal Rules of Evidence for United States Courts and Magistrates. "Unprivileged client information" means all information relating to a client or furnished by the client, other than privileged information, acquired by the lawyer during the course of or by reason of the representation of the client.

"free of compromising influences and loyalties." ABA Model Rules 1.7 through 1.13. Therefore, legal assistants should be instructed to inform the supervising attorney of any interest that could result in a conflict of interest or even give the appearance of a conflict. The guideline intentionally speaks to other employment rather than only past employment, since there are instances where legal assistants are employed by more than one law firm at the same time. The guideline's reference to "other interests" is intended to include personal relationships as well as instances where a legal assistant may have a financial interest (i.e., as stockholder, trust beneficiary or trustee, etc.) that would conflict with the client's in the matter in which the lawyer has been employed.

"Imputed Disqualification Arising from Change in Employment by Non-lawyer Employee," ABA Informal Opinion 1526 (1988), defines the duties of both the present and former employing lawyers and reasons that the restrictions on legal assistants' employment should be kept to "the minimum necessary to protect confidentiality" in order to prevent legal assistants from being forced to leave their careers, which "would disserve clients as well as the legal profession." The Opinion describes the attorney's obligations (1) to caution the legal assistant not to disclose any information and (2) to prevent the legal assistant from working on any matter on which the legal assistant worked for a prior employer or respecting which the employee has confidential information.

If a conflict is discovered, it may be possible to "wall" the legal assistant from the conflict area so that the entire firm need not be disqualified and the legal assistant is effectively screened from information concerning the matter. The American Bar Association has taken the position that what historically has been described as a "Chinese wall" will allow non-lawyer personnel (including legal assistants) who are in possession of confidential client information to accept employment with a law firm opposing the former client so long as the wall is observed and effectively screens the non-lawyer from confidential information. ABA Informal Opinion 1526 (1988). See also Tennessee Formal Ethics Opinion 89-F-118 (March 10, 1989). The implication of this Informal Opinion is that if a wall is not in place, the employer may be disqualified from representing either party to the controversy. One court has so held. *In re: Complex Asbestoses Litigation,* No. 828684 (San Francisco Superior Court, September 19, 1989).

It is not clear that a wall will prevent disqualification in the case of a lawyer employed to work for a law firm representing a client with an adverse interest to a client of the lawyer's former employer. Under Model Rule 1.10, when a lawyer moves to a firm that represents an adverse party in a matter in which the lawyer's former firm was involved, absent a waiver by the client, the new firm's representation may continue only if the newly employed lawyer acquired no protected information and did not work directly on the matter in the former employment. The new Rules of Professional Conduct in Kentucky and Texas (both effective on January 1, 1990) specifically provide for disqualification. Rule 1.10(b) in the District of Columbia, which became effective January 1, 1991, does so as well. The Sixth Circuit, however, has held that the wall will effectively insulate the new firm from disqualification if it prevents the new lawyer-employee from access to information concerning the client with the adverse interest. *Manning v. Waring, Cox, James, Sklar & Allen,* 849 F.2d 222 (6th Cir. 1988). [As a result of the Sixth Circuit opinion, Tennessee revised its formal ethics opinion, which is cited above, and now applies the same rule to lawyers, legal assistants, law clerks, and legal secretaries.] See generally NFPA, "The Chinese Wall—Its Application to Paralegals" (1990).

The states that have guidelines that address the legal assistant conflict of interest refer to the lawyer's responsibility to ensure against personal, business or social interests of the legal assistant that would conflict with the representation of the client or impinge on the services rendered to the client. E.g., Kansas Guideline X, New Mexico Guideline VI, and North Carolina Guideline 7. Florida Professional Ethics Opinion 86-5 (1986) discusses a legal assistant's move from one firm to another and the obligations of each not to disclose confidences. See also Vermont Ethics Opinion 85-8 (1985) (a legal assistant is not bound by the Code of Professional Responsibility and, absent an absolute waiver by the client, the new firm should not represent client if legal assistant possessed confidential information from old firm).

Guideline 8: A lawyer may include a charge for the work performed by a legal assistant in setting a charge for legal services.

Comment to Guideline 8

The U.S. Supreme Court in *Missouri v. Jenkins,* 491 U.S. 274 (1989), held that in setting a reasonable attorney's fee under 28 U.S.C. §1988, a legal fee may include a charge for legal assistant services at "market rates" rather than "actual cost" to the attorneys. This decision should resolve any question concerning the propriety of setting a charge for legal services based on work performed by a legal assistant. Its rationale favors setting a charge based on the "market" rate for such services, rather than their direct cost to the lawyer. This result was recognized by Connecticut Recommendation 11, Illinois Recommendation D, and Texas Guideline V prior to the Supreme Court decision. See also Fla. Stat. Ann. §57.104 (1991 Supp.) (adopted in 1987 and permitting consideration of legal assistant services in computing attorney's fees) and Fla. Stat. Ann. §744.108 (1991 Supp.) (adopted in 1989 and permitting recovery of "customary and reasonable charges for work performed by legal assistants" as fees for legal services in guardianship matters).

It is important to note, however, that *Missouri v. Jenkins* does not abrogate the attorney's responsibilities under Model Rule 1.5 to set a reasonable fee for legal services and it follows that those considerations apply to a fee that includes a fee for legal assistant services. Accordingly, the effect of combining a market rate charge for the services of lawyers and legal assistants should, in most instances, result in a lower total cost for the legal service than if the lawyer had performed the service alone.

Guideline 9: A lawyer may not split legal fees with a legal assistant nor pay a legal assistant for the referral of legal business. A lawyer may compensate a legal assistant based on the quantity and quality of the legal assistant's work and the value of that work to a law practice, but the legal assistant's compensation may not be contingent, by advance agreement, upon the profitability of the lawyer's practice.

Comment to Guideline 9

Model Rule 5.4 and DR 3-102(A) and 3-103(A) under the Model Code clearly prohibit fee "splitting" with legal assistants, whether characterized as splitting of contingent fees, "forwarding" fees, or other sharing of legal fees. Virtually all guidelines adopted by state bar associations have continued this prohibition in one form or another.[7] It appears clear that a legal assistant may not be compensated on a contingent basis for a particular case or paid for "signing up" clients for a legal practice.

Having stated this prohibition, however, the guideline attempts to deal with the practical consideration of how a legal assistant properly may be compensated by an attorney or law firm. The linchpin of the prohibition seems to be the advance agreement of the lawyer to "split" a fee based on a pre-existing contingent arrangement.[8] There is no

7. Connecticut Recommendation 10; Illinois Recommendation D, Kansas Guideline VI; Kentucky Supreme Court Rule 3.700, sub-rule 5; Michigan Guideline III, part 2; Missouri Guideline II; New Hampshire Rule 35, Sub-Rules 5 and 6; New Mexico Guideline IX; Rhode Island Guideline VIII and IX; South Carolina Guideline V; Texas Guideline V.

8. In its Rule 5.4, which will become effective on January 1, 1991, the District of Columbia will permit lawyers to form legal service partnerships that include non-lawyer participants. Comments 5 and 6 to that rule, however, state that the term "nonlawyer participants" should not be confused with the term "nonlawyer assistants" and that "[n]onlawyer assistants under Rule 5.3 do not have managerial authority or financial interests in the organization."

general prohibition against a lawyer who enjoys a particularly profitable period recognizing the contribution of the legal assistant to that profitability with a discretionary bonus. Likewise, a lawyer engaged in a particularly profitable specialty of legal practice is not prohibited from compensating the legal assistant who aids materially in that practice more handsomely than the compensation generally awarded to legal assistants in that geographic area who work in law practices that are less lucrative. Indeed, any effort to fix a compensation level for legal assistants and prohibit greater compensation would appear to violate the federal antitrust laws. See, e.g., *Goldfarb v. Virginia State Bar,* 421 U.S. 773 (1975).

Guideline 10: **A lawyer who employs a legal assistant should facilitate the legal assistant's participation in appropriate continuing education and pro bono publico activities.**

Comment to Guideline 10

While Guideline 10 does not appear to have been adopted in the guidelines of any state bar association, the Standing Committee on Legal Assistants believes that its adoption would be appropriate.[9] For many years the Standing Committee on Legal Assistants has advocated that the improvement of formal legal assistant education will generally improve the legal services rendered by lawyers employing legal assistants and provide a more satisfying professional atmosphere in which legal assistants may work. See, e.g., ABA, Board of Governors, Policy on Legal Assistant Licensure and/or Certification, Statement 4 (February 6, 1986); ABA, Standing Committee on Legal Assistants, "Position Paper on the Question of Legal Assistant Licensure or Certification" (December 10, 1985), at 6 and Conclusion 3. Recognition of the employing lawyer's obligation to facilitate the legal assistant's continuing professional education is, therefore, appropriate because of the benefits to both the law practice and the legal assistants and is consistent with the lawyer's own responsibility to maintain professional competence under Model Rule 1.1. See also EC 6-2 of the Model Code.

The Standing Committee is of the view that similar benefits will accrue to the lawyer and legal assistant if the legal assistant is included

9. While no state has apparently adopted a guideline similar to Model Guideline 10, parts 4 and 5 of NALA Guideline VIII suggest similar requirements. Sections III and V of NFPA's "Affirmation of Professional Responsibility" recognize a legal assistant's obligations to "maintain a high level of competence" which "is achieved through continuing education, . . ." and to "serve the public interest." NFPA has also published a guide to assist legal assistant groups in developing public service projects. See NFPA "Pro Bono Publico (For the Good of the People)" (1987).

in the pro bono publico legal services that a lawyer has a clear obligation to provide under Model Rule 6.1 and, where appropriate, the legal assistant is encouraged to provide such services independently. The ability of a law firm to provide more pro bono publico services will be enhanced if legal assistants are included. Recognition of the legal assistant's role in such services is consistent with the role of the legal assistant in the contemporary delivery of legal services generally and is consistent with the lawyer's duty to the legal profession under Canon 2 of the Model Code.

THE STANDING COMMITTEE ON
LEGAL ASSISTANTS OF THE
AMERICAN BAR ASSOCIATION

May 1991

ADOPTED BY
ABA HOUSE OF DELEGATES

August 1991

B

NALA Model Standards and Guidelines for Utilization of Legal Assistants

Introduction

The purpose of this annotated version of the National Association of Legal Assistants, Inc. Model Standards and Guidelines for the Utilization of Legal Assistants (the "Model," "Standards" and/or the "Guidelines") is to provide references to the existing case law and other authorities where the underlying issues have been considered. The authorities cited will serve as a basis upon which conduct of a legal assistant may be analyzed as proper or improper.

The Guidelines represent a statement of how the legal assistant may function. The Guidelines are not intended to be a comprehensive or exhaustive list of the proper duties of a legal assistant. Rather, they are designed as guides to what may or may not be proper conduct for the legal assistant. In formulating the Guidelines, the reasoning and rules of law in many reported decisions of disciplinary cases and unauthorized practice of law cases have been analyzed and considered. In addition, the provisions of the American Bar Association's Model Rules of Professional Conduct, as well as the ethical promulgations of various state courts and bar associations have been considered in the development of the Guidelines.

These Guidelines form a sound basis for the legal assistant and the supervising attorney to follow. This Model will serve as a comprehensive resource document and as a definitive, well reasoned guide to those considering voluntary standards and guidelines for legal assistants.

I. Preamble

Proper utilization of the services of legal assistants contributes to the delivery of cost-effective, high-quality legal services. Legal assistants and the legal profession should be assured that measures exist for identifying legal assistants and their role in assisting attorneys in the delivery of legal services. Therefore, the National Association of Legal Assistants, Inc., hereby adopts these Standards and Guidelines as an educational document for the benefit of legal assistants and the legal profession.

Comment

The three most frequently raised questions concerning legal assistants are (1) How do you define a legal assistant; (2) Who is qualified to be identified as a legal assistant; and (3) What duties may a legal assistant perform? The definition adopted in 1984 by the National Association of Legal Assistants answers the first question. The Model sets forth minimum education, training and experience through standards which will assure that an individual utilizing the title "legal assistant" has the qualifications to be held out to the legal community and the public in that capacity. The Guidelines identify those acts which the reported cases hold to be proscribed and give examples of services which the legal assistant may perform under the supervision of a licensed attorney.

These Guidelines constitute a statement relating to services performed by legal assistants, as defined herein, as approved by court decisions and other sources of authority. The purpose of the Guidelines is not to place limitations or restrictions on the legal assistant profession. Rather, the Guidelines are intended to outline for the legal profession an acceptable course of conduct. Voluntary recognition and utilization of the Standards and Guidelines will benefit the entire legal profession and the public it serves.

II. Definition

The National Association of Legal Assistants adopted the following definition in 1984:

> Legal assistants, also known as paralegals, are a distinguishable group of persons who assist attorneys in the delivery of legal services. Through formal education, training, and experience, legal assistants have knowledge and expertise regarding the legal system and substantive and procedural law which qualify them to do work of a legal nature under the supervision of an attorney.

Comment

This definition emphasizes the knowledge and expertise of legal assistants in substantive and procedural law obtained through education and work experience. It further defines the legal assistant or paralegal as a professional working under the supervision of an attorney as distinguished from a non-lawyer who delivers services directly to the public without any intervention or review of work product by an attorney. Statutes, court rules, case law and bar associations are additional sources for legal assistant or paralegal definitions. In applying the Standards and Guidelines, it is important to remember that they were developed to apply to the legal assistant as defined herein.

Lawyers should refrain from labeling those who do not meet the criteria set forth in this definition, such as secretaries and other administrative staff, as legal assistants.

For billing purposes, the services of a legal secretary are considered part of overhead costs and are not recoverable in fee awards. However, the courts have held that fees for paralegal services are recoverable as long as they are not clerical functions, such as organizing files, copying documents, checking docket, updating files, checking court dates and delivering papers. As established in *Missouri v. Jenkins,* 491 U.S. 274, 109 S. Ct. 2463, 2471, n.10 (1989) tasks performed by legal assistants must be substantive in nature which, absent the legal assistant, the attorney would perform.

There are also case law and Supreme Court Rules addressing the issue of a disbarred attorney serving in the capacity of a legal assistant.

III. Standards

A legal assistant should meet certain minimum qualifications. The following standards may be used to determine an individual's qualifications as a legal assistant:

1. Successful completion of the Certified Legal Assistant ("CLA") certifying examination of the National Association of Legal Assistants, Inc.;
2. Graduation from an ABA approved program of study for legal assistants;
3. Graduation from a course of study for legal assistants which is institutionally accredited but not ABA approved, and which requires not less than the equivalent of 60 semester hours of classroom study;
4. Graduation from a course of study for legal assistants, other than those set forth in (2) and (3) above, plus not less than six months of in-house training as a legal assistant;
5. A baccalaureate degree in any field, plus not less than six months in-house training as a legal assistant;
6. A minimum of three years of law-related experience under the supervision of an attorney, including at least six months of in-house training as a legal assistant; or
7. Two years of in-house training as a legal assistant.

For purposes of these Standards, "in-house training as a legal assistant" means attorney education of the employee concerning legal assistant duties and these Guidelines. In addition to review and analysis of assignments, the legal assistant should receive a reasonable amount of instruction directly related to the duties and obligations of the legal assistant.

Comment

The Standards set forth suggest minimum qualifications for a legal assistant. These minimum qualifications, as adopted, recognize legal related work backgrounds and formal education backgrounds, both of which provide the legal assistant with a broad base in exposure to and knowledge of the legal profession. This background is necessary to assure the public and the legal profession that the employee identified as a legal assistant is qualified.

The Certified Legal Assistant ("CLA") examination established by NALA in 1976 is a voluntary nationwide certification program for legal assistants. The CLA designation is a statement to the legal profession and the public that the legal assistant has met the high levels of knowledge and professionalism required by NALA's certification program. Continuing education requirements, which all certified legal assistants must meet, assure that high standards are maintained. The CLA designation has been recognized as a means of establishing the qualifications of a legal assistant in supreme court rules, state court and bar association standards and utilization guidelines.

Certification through NALA is available to all legal assistants meeting the educational and experience requirements. Certified Legal Assistants may also pursue advanced specialty certification ("CLAS") in the areas of bankruptcy, civil litigation, probate and estate planning, corporate and business law, criminal law and procedure, real estate, intellectual property, and may also pursue state certification based on state laws and procedures in California, Florida, Louisiana and Texas.[1]

IV. Guidelines

These Guidelines relating to standards of performance and professional responsibility are intended to aid legal assistants and attorneys. The ultimate responsibility rests with an attorney who employs legal assistants to educate them with respect to the duties they are assigned and to supervise the manner in which such duties are accomplished.

Comment

In general, a legal assistant is allowed to perform any task which is properly delegated and supervised by an attorney, as long as the attorney is ultimately responsible to the client and assumes complete professional responsibility for the work product.

ABA Model Rules of Professional Conduct, Rule 5.3 provides:

> With respect to a non-lawyer employed or retained by or associated with a lawyer:
> (a) a partner in a law firm shall make reasonable efforts to ensure that the firm has in effect measures giving reasonable assurance that

---

1. The United States Supreme Court has addressed the issue concerning the utilization of professional credentials awarded by private organizations. In *Peel v. Attorney Registration and Disciplinary Committee of Illinois*, 496 U.S. 91, 110 S. Ct. 2281 (1990), the Court suggested that a claim of certification is truthful and not misleading if:

   1) the claim itself is true;
   2) the bases on which certification was awarded are factual and verifiable;
   3) the certification in question is available to all professionals in the field who meet relevant, objective and consistently applied standards; and
   4) the certification claim does not suggest any greater degree of professional qualification than reasonably may be inferred from an evaluation of the certification program's requirements.

Further, the Court advised that there must be a qualified organization to stand behind the certification process. For a detailed discussion of the *Peel* decision and the Certified Legal Assistant program, see "The Certified Legal Assistant Credential and Guidelines of the United States Supreme Court," 1996, National Association of Legal Assistants, 1516 S. Boston, #200, Tulsa, OK 74119 or http://www.nala.org.

the person's conduct is compatible with the professional obligations of the lawyer;

(b) a lawyer having direct supervisory authority over the non-lawyer shall make reasonable efforts to ensure that the person's conduct is compatible with the professional obligations of the lawyer, and

(c) a lawyer shall be responsible for conduct of such a person that would be a violation of the rules of professional conduct if engaged in by a lawyer if:

(1) the lawyer orders or, with the knowledge of the specific conduct ratifies the conduct involved; or

(2) the lawyer is a partner in the law firm in which the person is employed, or has direct supervisory authority over the person, and knows of the conduct at a time when its consequences can be avoided or mitigated but fails to take remedial action.

There are many interesting and complex issues involving the use of legal assistants. In any discussion of the proper role of a legal assistant, attention must be directed to what constitutes the practice of law. Proper delegation to legal assistants is further complicated and confused by the lack of an adequate definition of the practice of law.

Kentucky became the first state to adopt a Paralegal Code by Supreme Court Rule. This Code sets forth certain exclusions to the unauthorized practice of law:

> For purposes of this rule, the unauthorized practice of law shall not include any service rendered involving legal knowledge or advice, whether representation, counsel or advocacy, in or out of court, rendered in respect to the acts, duties, obligations, liabilities or business relations of the one requiring services where:
>
> A. The client understands that the paralegal is not a lawyer;
> B. The lawyer supervises the paralegal in the performance of his or her duties; and
> C. The lawyer remains fully responsible for such representation including all actions taken or not taken in connection therewith by the paralegal to the same extent as if such representation had been furnished entirely by the lawyer and all such actions had been taken or not taken directly by the attorney.

Paralegal Code, Ky. S. Ct. R 3.700, Sub-Rule 2.

South Dakota Supreme Court Rule 97-25 Utilization Rule a(4) states:

> The attorney remains responsible for the services performed by the legal assistant to the same extent as though such services had been furnished entirely by the attorney and such actions were those of the attorney.

400

Guideline 1

Legal assistants should:

1. Disclose their status as legal assistants at the outset of any professional relationship with a client, other attorneys, a court or administrative agency or personnel thereof, or members of the general public;
2. Preserve the confidences and secrets of all clients; and
3. Understand the attorney's Rules of Professional Responsibility and these Guidelines in order to avoid any action which would involve the attorney in a violation of the Rules, or give the appearance of professional impropriety.

Comment

Routine early disclosure of the legal assistant's status when dealing with persons outside the attorney's office is necessary to assure that there will be no misunderstanding as to the responsibilities and role of the legal assistant. Disclosure may be made in any way that avoids confusion. If the person dealing with the legal assistant already knows of his/her status, further disclosure is unnecessary. If at any time in written or oral communication the legal assistant becomes aware that the other person may believe the legal assistant is an attorney, immediate disclosure should be made as to the legal assistant's status.

The attorney should exercise care that the legal assistant preserves and refrains from using any confidence or secrets of a client, and should instruct the legal assistant not to disclose or use any such confidences or secrets.

The legal assistant must take any and all steps necessary to prevent conflicts of interest and fully disclose such conflicts to the supervising attorney. Failure to do so may jeopardize both the attorney's representation of the client and the case itself.

Guidelines for the Utilization of Legal Assistant Services adopted December 3, 1994, by the Washington State Bar Association Board of Governors states:

Guideline 7: A lawyer shall take reasonable measures to prevent conflicts of interest resulting from a legal assistant's other employment or interest insofar as such other employment or interests would present a conflict of interest if it were that of the lawyer.

In Re Complex Asbestos Litigation, 232 Cal. App. 3d 572 (Cal. 1991), addresses the issue wherein a law firm was disqualified due to possession of attorney-client confidences by a legal assistant employee resulting from previous employment by opposing counsel.

The ultimate responsibility for compliance with approved standards of professional conduct rests with the supervising attorney. The burden rests upon the attorney who employs a legal assistant to educate the latter with respect to the duties which may be assigned and then to supervise the manner in which the legal assistant carries out such duties. However, this does not relieve the legal assistant from an independent obligation to refrain from illegal conduct. Additionally, and notwithstanding that the Rules are not binding upon non-lawyers, the very nature of a legal assistant's employment imposes an obligation not to engage in conduct which would involve the supervising attorney in a violation of the Rules.

The attorney must make sufficient background investigation of the prior activities and character and integrity of his or her legal assistants.

Further, the attorney must take all measures necessary to avoid and fully disclose conflicts of interest due to other employment or interests. Failure to do so may jeopardize both the attorney's representation of the client and the case itself.

Legal assistant associations strive to maintain the high level of integrity and competence expected of the legal profession and, further, strive to uphold the high standards of ethics.

NALA's Code of Ethics and Professional Responsibility states:

> A legal assistant's conduct is guided by bar associations' codes of professional responsibility and rules of professional conduct.

Guideline 2

Legal assistants should not:

1. Establish attorney-client relationships; set legal fees; give legal opinions or advice; or represent a client before a court, unless authorized to do so by said court; nor
2. Engage in, encourage, or contribute to any act which could constitute the unauthorized practice law.

Comment

Case law, court rules, codes of ethics and professional responsibilities, as well as bar ethics opinions now hold which acts can and cannot be performed by a legal assistant. Generally, the determination of what acts constitute the unauthorized practice of law is made by State Supreme Courts.

Numerous cases exist relating to the unauthorized practice of law. Courts have gone so far as to prohibit the legal assistant from preparation of divorce kits and assisting in preparation of bankruptcy forms and, more specifically, from providing basic information about procedures and requirements, deciding where information should be placed on forms, and responding to questions from debtors regarding the interpretation or definition of terms.

Cases have identified certain areas in which an attorney has a duty to act, but it is interesting to note that none of these cases state that it is improper for an attorney to have the initial work performed by the legal assistant. This again points out the importance of adequate supervision by the employing attorney.

An attorney can be found to have aided in the unauthorized practice of law when delegating acts which cannot be performed by a legal assistant.

Guideline 3

Legal assistants may perform services for an attorney in the representation of a client, provided:

1. The services performed by the legal assistant do not require the exercise of independent professional legal judgment;
2. The attorney maintains a direct relationship with the client and maintains control of all client matters;
3. The attorney supervises the legal assistant;
4. The attorney remains professionally responsible for all work on behalf of the client, including any actions taken or not taken by the legal assistant in connection therewith; and
5. The services performed supplement, merge with and become the attorney's work product.

Comment

Legal assistants, whether employees or independent contractors, perform services for the attorney in the representation of a client. Attorneys should delegate work to legal assistants commensurate with their knowledge and experience and provide appropriate instruction and supervision concerning the delegated work, as well as ethical acts of their employment. Ultimate responsibility for the work product of a legal assistant rests with the attorney. However, a legal assistant must use discretion and professional judgment and must not render independent legal judgment in place of an attorney.

The work product of a legal assistant is subject to civil rules governing discovery of materials prepared in anticipation of litigation, whether the legal assistant is viewed as an extension of the attorney or as another representative of the party itself. Fed. R.Civ.P. 26 (b)(2).

Guideline 4

In the supervision of a legal assistant, consideration should be given to:

1. Designating work assignments that correspond to the legal assistant's abilities, knowledge, training and experience;
2. Educating and training the legal assistant with respect to professional responsibility, local rules and practices, and firm policies;
3. Monitoring the work and professional conduct of the legal assistant to ensure that the work is substantively correct and timely performed;
4. Providing continuing education for the legal assistant in substantive matters through courses, institutes, workshops, seminars and in-house training; and
5. Encouraging and supporting membership and active participation in professional organizations.

Comment

Attorneys are responsible for the actions of their employees in both malpractice and disciplinary proceedings. In the vast majority of cases, the courts have not censured attorneys for a particular act delegated to the legal assistant, but rather, have been critical of and imposed sanctions against attorneys for failure to adequately supervise the legal assistant. The attorney's responsibility for supervision of his or her legal assistant must be more than a willingness to accept responsibility and liability for the legal assistant's work. Supervision of a legal assistant must be offered in both the procedural and substantive legal areas. The attorney must delegate work based upon the education, knowledge and abilities of the legal assistant and must monitor the work product and conduct of the legal assistant to insure that the work performed is substantively correct and competently performed in a professional manner.

Michigan State Board of Commissioners has adopted Guidelines for the Utilization of Legal Assistants (April 23, 1993). These guidelines, in part, encourage employers to support legal assistant participation in continuing education programs to ensure that the legal assistant remains competent in the fields of practice in which the legal assistant is assigned.

The working relationship between the lawyer and the legal assistant should extend to cooperative efforts on public service activities wherever possible. Participation in pro bono activities is encouraged in ABA Guideline 10.

Guideline 5

Except as otherwise provided by statute, court rule or decision, administrative rule or regulation, or the attorney's rules of professional responsibility, and within the preceding parameters and proscriptions, a legal assistant may perform any function delegated by an attorney, including, but not limited to the following:

1. Conduct client interviews and maintain general contact with the client after the establishment of the attorney-client relationship, so long as the client is aware of the status and function of the legal assistant, and the client contact is under the supervision of the attorney.
2. Locate and interview witnesses, so long as the witnesses are aware of the status and function of the legal assistant.
3. Conduct investigations and statistical and documentary research for review by the attorney.
4. Conduct legal research for review by the attorney.
5. Draft legal documents for review by the attorney.
6. Draft correspondence and pleadings for review by and signature of the attorney.
7. Summarize depositions, interrogatories and testimony for review by the attorney.
8. Attend executions of wills, real estate closings, depositions, court or administrative hearings and trials with the attorney.
9. Author and sign letters providing the legal assistant's status is clearly indicated and the correspondence does not contain independent legal opinions or legal advice.

Comment

The United States Supreme Court has recognized the variety of tasks being performed by legal assistants and has noted that use of legal assistants encourages cost-effective delivery of legal services, *Missouri v. Jenkins,* 491 U.S. 274, 109 S. Ct. 2463, 2471, n. 10 (1989). In *Jenkins,* the court further held that legal assistant time should be included in compensation for attorney fee awards at the rate in the relevant community to bill legal assistant time.

Courts have held that legal assistant fees are not a part of the overall overhead of a law firm. Legal assistant services are billed separately by attorneys, and decrease litigation expenses. Tasks performed by legal assistants must contain substantive legal work under the direction or supervision of an attorney, such that if the legal assistant were not present, the work would be performed by the attorney.

In *Taylor v. Chubb*, 874 P.2d 806 (Okla. 1994), the Court ruled that attorney fees awarded should include fees for services performed by legal assistants and, further, defined tasks which may be performed by the legal assistant under the supervision of an attorney including, among others: interview clients; draft pleadings and other documents; carry on legal research, both conventional and computer aided; research public records; prepare discovery requests and responses; schedule depositions and prepare notices and subpoenas; summarize depositions and other discovery responses; coordinate and manage document production; locate and interview witnesses; organize pleadings, trial exhibits and other documents; prepare witness and exhibit lists; prepare trial notebooks; prepare for the attendance of witnesses at trial; and assist lawyers at trials.

Except for the specific proscription contained in Guideline 1, the reported cases do not limit the duties which may be performed by a legal assistant under the supervision of the attorney.

An attorney may not split legal fees with a legal assistant, nor pay a legal assistant for the referral of legal business. An attorney may compensate a legal assistant based on the quantity and quality of the legal assistant's work and value of that work to a law practice.

Conclusion

These Standards and Guidelines were developed from generally accepted practices. Each supervising attorney must be aware of the specific rules, decisions and statutes applicable to legal assistants within his/her jurisdiction.

© Copyright, 1997; Adopted 1984; revised 1991, 1997.
National Association of Legal Assistants, Inc.
1516 Boston, Suite 200
Tulsa, OK 74119
http://www.nala.org

NALA Code of Ethics and Professional Responsibility

A legal assistant must adhere strictly to the accepted standards of legal ethics and to the general principles of proper conduct. The performance of the duties of the legal assistant shall be governed by specific canons as defined herein so that justice will be served and goals of the profession attained. (See Model Standards and Guidelines for Utilization of Legal Assistants, Section II.)

The canons of ethics set forth hereafter are adopted by the National Association of Legal Assistants, Inc. as a general guide intended to aid legal assistants and attorneys. The enumeration of these rules does not mean there are not others of equal importance although not specifically mentioned. Court rules, agency rules and statutes must be taken into consideration when interpreting the canons.

Definition: Legal assistants, also known as paralegals, are a distinguishable group of persons who assist attorneys in the delivery of legal services. Through formal education, training and experience, legal assistants have knowledge and expertise regarding the legal system and substantive and procedural law which qualify them to do work of a legal nature under the supervision of an attorney.

Canon 1.

A legal assistant must not perform any of the duties that attorneys only may perform nor take any actions that attorneys may not take.

Canon 2.

A legal assistant may perform any task which is properly delegated and supervised by an attorney, as long as the attorney is ultimately responsible to the client, maintains a direct relationship with the client, and assumes professional responsibility for the work product. (See NALA Model Standards and Guidelines for Utilization of Legal Assistants, Sections IV and VII.)

Canon 3.

A legal assistant must not: (a) engage in, encourage, or contribute to any act which could constitute the unauthorized practice of law; and (b) establish attorney-client relationships, set fees, give legal opinions or advice, or represent a client before a court or agency unless so authorized by that court or agency; and (c) engage in conduct or take any action which would assist or involve the attorney in a violation of professional ethics or give the appearance of professional impropriety. (See NALA Model Standards and Guidelines for Utilization of Legal Assistants, Section V.)

Canon 4.

A legal assistant must use discretion and professional judgment commensurate with knowledge and experience but must not render independent legal judgment in place of an attorney. The services of an attorney are essential in the public interest whenever such legal judgment is required. (See NALA Model Standards and Guidelines for Utilization of Legal Assistants, Section VII.)

Canon 5.

A legal assistant must disclose his or her status as a legal assistant at the outset of any professional relationship with a client, attorney, a court or administrative agency or personnel thereof, or a member of the general public. A legal assistant must act prudently in determining the extent to which a client may be assisted without the presence of an attorney. (See NALA Model Standards and Guidelines for Utilization of Legal Assistants, Section V.)

Canon 6.

A legal assistant must strive to maintain integrity and a high degree of competency through education and training with respect to professional responsibility, local rules and practice, and through continuing education in substantive areas of law to better assist the legal profession in fulfilling its duty to provide legal service.

Canon 7.

A legal assistant must protect the confidences of a client and must not violate any rule or statute now in effect or hereafter enacted controlling the doctrine of privileged communications between a client and an attorney. (See NALA Model Standards and Guidelines for Utilization of Legal Assistants, Section V.)

Canon 8.

A legal assistant must do all other things incidental, necessary, or expedient for the attainment of the ethics and responsibilities as defined by statute or rule of court.

Canon 9.

A legal assistant's conduct is guided by bar associations' codes of professional responsibility and rules of professional conduct.

Adopted: May 1, 1975
Revised, 1979, 1988 and 1995,
National Association of Legal Assistants

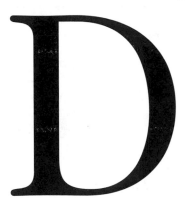

NFPA Model Code of Ethics and Professional Responsibility

Preamble

The National Federation of Paralegal Associations, Inc. ("NFPA") is a professional organization comprised of paralegal associations and individual paralegals throughout the United States. Members of NFPA have varying types of backgrounds, experience, education, and job responsibilities which reflect the diversity of the paralegal profession. NFPA promotes the growth, development and recognition of the paralegal profession as an integral partner in the delivery of legal services.

NFPA recognizes that the creation of guidelines and standards for professional conduct are important for the development and expansion of the paralegal profession. In May 1993, NFPA adopted this Model Code of Ethics and Professional Responsibility ("Model Code") to delineate the principles for ethics and conduct to which every paralegal should aspire. The Model Code expresses NFPA's commitment to increasing the quality and efficiency of legal services and recognizes the profession's responsibilities to the public, the legal community, and colleagues.

Paralegals perform many different functions, and these functions differ greatly among practice areas. In addition, each jurisdiction has its own unique legal authority and practices governing ethical conduct and professional responsibilities.

It is essential that each paralegal strive for personal and professional excellence and encourage the professional development of other parale-gals as well as those entering the profession. Participation in professional associations intended to advance the quality and standards of the legal profession is of particular importance. Paralegals should possess integrity, professional skill and dedication to the improvement of the legal system and should strive to expand the paralegal role in the delivery of legal services.

Canon 1.   A paralegal[1] shall achieve and maintain a high level of competence.

EC-1.1 A paralegal shall achieve competency through education, training, and work experience.

EC-1.2 A paralegal shall participate in continuing education to keep informed of current legal, technical and general developments.

EC-1.3 A paralegal shall perform all assignments promptly and efficiently.

Canon 2.   A paralegal shall maintain a high level of personal and professional integrity.

EC-2.1 A paralegal shall not engage in any ex parte[2] communica-tions involving the courts or any other adjudicatory body in an attempt to exert undue influence or to obtain advantage for the benefit of only one party.

EC-2.2 A paralegal shall not communicate, or cause another to communicate, with a party the paralegal knows to be represented by a lawyer in a pending matter without the prior consent of the lawyer representing such other party.

EC-2.3 A paralegal shall ensure that all timekeeping and billing records prepared by the paralegal are thorough, accurate, and honest.

EC-2.4 A paralegal shall be scrupulous, thorough and honest in the identification and maintenance of all funds, securities, and other assets of a client and shall provide accurate accountings as appropriate.

1. "Paralegal" is synonymous with "Legal Assistant" and is defined as a person qualified through education, training, or work experience to perform substantive legal work that requires knowledge of legal concepts and is customarily, but not exclusively performed by a lawyer. This person may be retained or employed by a lawyer, law office, governmental agency or other entity or may be authorized by administrative, statutory or court authority to perform this work.

2. "Ex parte" denotes actions or communications conducted at the instance and for the benefit of one party only, and without notice to, or contestation by, any person adversely interested.

EC-2.5 A paralegal shall advise the proper authority of any dishonest or fraudulent acts by any person pertaining to the handling of the funds, securities or other assets of a client.

Canon 3. A paralegal shall maintain a high standard of professional conduct.

EC-3.1 A paralegal shall refrain from engaging in any conduct that offends the dignity and decorum of proceedings before a court or other adjudicatory body and shall be respectful of all rules and procedures.

EC-3.2 A paralegal shall advise the proper authority of any action of another legal professional which clearly demonstrates fraud, deceit, dishonesty, or misrepresentation.

EC-3.3 A paralegal shall avoid impropriety and the appearance of impropriety.

Canon 4. A paralegal shall serve the public interest by contributing to the delivery of quality legal services and the improvement of the legal system.

EC-4.1 A paralegal shall be sensitive to the legal needs of the public and shall promote the development and implementation of programs that address those needs.

EC-4.2 A paralegal shall support bona fide efforts to meet the need for legal services by those unable to pay reasonable or customary fees; for example, participation in pro bono projects and volunteer work.

EC-4.3 A paralegal shall support efforts to improve the legal system and shall assist in making changes.

Canon 5. A paralegal shall preserve all confidential information[3] provided by the client or acquired from other sources before, during, and after the course of the professional relationship.

EC-5.1 A paralegal shall be aware of and abide by all legal authority governing confidential information.

EC-5.2 A paralegal shall not use confidential information to the disadvantage of the client.

---

3. "Confidential Information" denotes information relating to a client, whatever its source, which is not public knowledge nor available to the public. "Non-Confidential Information" would generally include the name of the client and the identity of the matter for which the paralegal provided services.

EC-5.3 A paralegal shall not use confidential information to the advantage of the paralegal or of a third person.

EC-5.4 A paralegal may reveal confidential information only after full disclosure and with the client's written consent; or, when required by law or court order; or, when necessary to prevent the client from committing an act which could result in death or serious bodily harm.

EC-5.5 A paralegal shall keep those individuals responsible for the legal representation of a client fully informed of any confidential information the paralegal may have pertaining to that client.

EC-5.6 A paralegal shall not engage in any indiscreet communications concerning clients.

Canon 6. A paralegal's title shall be fully disclosed.[4]

EC-6.1 A paralegal's title shall clearly indicate the individual's status and shall be disclosed in all business and professional communications to avoid misunderstandings and misconceptions about the paralegal's role and responsibilities.

EC-6.2 A paralegal's title shall be included if the paralegal's name appears on business cards, letterhead, brochures, directories, and advertisements.

Canon 7. A paralegal shall not engage in the unauthorized practice of law.

EC-7.1 A paralegal shall comply with the applicable legal authority governing the unauthorized practice of law.

Canon 8. A paralegal shall avoid conflicts of interest and shall disclose any possible conflict to the employer or client, as well as to the prospective employers or clients.

EC-8.1 A paralegal shall act within the bounds of the law, solely for the benefit of the client, and shall be free of compromising influences and loyalties. Neither the paralegal's personal or business interest, nor those of other clients or third persons, should compromise the paralegal's professional judgment and loyalty to the client.

EC-8.2 A paralegal shall avoid conflicts of interest which may arise from previous assignments whether for a present or past employer or client.

---

4. "Disclose" denotes communication of information reasonably sufficient to permit identification of the significance of the matter in question.

EC-8.3 A paralegal shall avoid conflicts of interest which may arise from family relationships and from personal and business interests.

EC-8.4 A paralegal shall create and maintain an effective record-keeping system that identifies clients, matters, and parties with which the paralegal has worked, to be able to determine whether an actual or potential conflict of interest exists.

EC-8.5 A paralegal shall reveal sufficient nonconfidential information about a client or former client to reasonably ascertain if an actual or potential conflict of interest exists.

EC-8.6 A paralegal shall not participate in or conduct work on any matter where a conflict of interest has been identified.

EC-8.7 In matters where a conflict of interest has been identified and the client consents to continued representation, a paralegal shall comply fully with the implementation and maintenance of an Ethical Wall.[5]

---

5. "Ethical Wall" refers to the screening method implemented in order to protect a client from a conflict of interest. An Ethical Wall generally includes, but is not limited to, the following elements; (1) prohibit the paralegal from having any connection with the matter; (2) ban discussions with or the transfer of documents to or from the paralegal; (3) restrict access to files; and (4) educate all members of the firm, corporation or entity as to the separation of the paralegal (both organizationally and physically) from the pending matter. For more information regarding the Ethical Wall, see the NFPA publication entitled "The Ethical Wall—Its Application to Paralegals."

Table of Cases

417

418

Index